'A timely a   itial reading on ma   – **Martin
Polley**, *Uni*

Sport has a h   ntemporary
Britain. This   tion of the
causes and c   n between
sport and the

   Kevin Jeff   he evolving
s
a
th
2(
sp
th
sh
de

Kevin Jefferys is Professor of Contemporary History at Plymouth University. His previous publications include works of political history such as *Retreat from New Jerusalem: British Politics, 1951–1964* (also in the British Studies series). He has published articles on sporting themes in the journals *Sport in History* and the *International Journal of the History of Sport*.

British Studies Series

General Editor JEREMY BLACK

Alan Booth **The British Economy in the Twentieth Century**
Glenn Burgess **British Political Thought, 1500–1600: The Politics of the Post-Reformation**
John Charmley **A History of Conservative Politics since 1830 (2nd edn)**
David Childs **Britain since 1939 (2nd edn)**
John Davis **A History of Britain, 1885–1939**
David Eastwood **Government and Community in the English Provinces, 1700–1870**
W. H. Fraser **A History of British Trade Unionism, 1700–1998**
Philip Edwards **The Making of the Modern English State, 1460–1660**
John Gerrard **Democratisation in Britain Elites, Civil Society and Reform since 1800**
Brian Hill **The Early Parties and Politics in Britain, 1688–1832**
Katrina Honeyman **Women, Gender and Industrialisation in England, 1700–1870**
Kevin Jefferys **Retreat from New Jerusalem: British Politics, 1951–1964**
Kevin Jefferys **Sport and Politics in Modern Britain: The Road to 2012**
T. A. Jenkins **The Liberal Ascendancy, 1830–1886**
David Loades **Power in Tudor England**
Ian Machin **The Rise of Democracy in Britain, 1830–1918**
Alan I. Macinnes **The British Revolution, 1629–1660**
Alexander Murdoch **British History, 1660–1832: National Identity And Local Culture**
Anthony Musson and W. M. Ormrod **The Evolution of English Justice: Law, Politics and Society in the Fourteenth Century**
Murray G. H. Pittock **Inventing and Resisting Britain: Cultural Identities in Britain and Ireland, 1685–1789**
Nick Smart **The National Government, 1931–40**
Howard Temperley **Britain and America since Independence**
Andrew Thorpe **A History of the British Labour Party (3rd edn)**
Michael J. Turner **Britain's International Role 1970–1991**

British Studies Series
Series Standing Order
ISBN 0–333–71691–4 hardcover
ISBN 0–333–69332–9 paperback
(*outside North America only*)

You can receive future titles in this series as they are published by placing a standing order. Please contact your bookseller or, in case of difficulty, write to us at the address below with your name and address, the title of the series and one of the ISBNs quoted above.

Customer Services Department, Macmillan Distribution Ltd
Houndmills, Basingstoke, Hampshire RG21 6XS, England

Sport and Politics in Modern Britain

The Road to 2012

Kevin Jefferys

First published 2012 by
PALGRAVE MACMILLAN

Palgrave Macmillan in the UK is an imprint of Macmillan Publishers Limited, registered in England, company number 785998, of Houndmills, Basingstoke, Hampshire RG21 6XS.

Palgrave Macmillan in the US is a division of St Martin's Press LLC, 175 Fifth Avenue, New York, NY 10010.

Palgrave Macmillan is the global academic imprint of the above companies and has companies and representatives throughout the world.

Palgrave® and Macmillan® are registered trademarks in the United States, the United Kingdom, Europe and other countries.

ISBN: 978–0–230–29186–7 hardback
ISBN: 978–0–230–29187–4 paperback

This book is printed on paper suitable for recycling and made from fully managed and sustained forest sources. Logging, pulping and manufacturing processes are expected to conform to the environmental regulations of the country of origin.

A catalogue record for this book is available from the British Library.

A catalog record for this book is available from the Library of Congress.

10 9 8 7 6 5 4 3 2 1
21 20 19 18 17 16 15 14 13 12

Printed in China

Contents

Acknowledgements vi

Abbreviations vii

Introduction 1
1 Sport and Politics in Austerity Britain, 1945–51 9
2 *Britain in the World of Sport*, 1951–59 31
3 The Impact of the Wolfenden Report, 1960–64 53
4 Creating and Running the Sports Council, 1964–67 77
5 'Ballyhoo' about Sport in the Late 1960s 101
6 Battling for 'Sport and Recreation' in the 1970s 124
7 The Olympics and International Sport 149
8 The 1980s: 'Years of Concern' 172
9 *Raising the Game*, 1990–97 195
10 Regions and Localities 214
11 New Labour and Sport, 1997–2010 233
Epilogue: Towards 2012 259

Chronology of Main Events 266

Notes 270

Select Bibliography 298

Index 307

Acknowledgements

For supporting this book from planning to publication, I am grateful to Professor Jeremy Black, editor of the British Studies series, and also to Sonya Barker, Senior Editor for History and Literature at Palgrave Macmillan. I would like to thank history and sport policy colleagues at Plymouth University and elsewhere who have made numerous pertinent comments and helpful suggestions on papers presented at research seminars and conferences in recent years, and a particular note of thanks to the MA students at Plymouth who stimulated much discussion and who tolerated listening to my thoughts on sport and politics at greater length than they might have wished. I would also like to express my gratitude to the archivists and librarians at various institutions (acknowledged more fully in the Notes) for facilitating access to important collections of sport-related primary sources. I would like to thank Edward Gosling for compiling the index. While grateful to many for advice and invaluable guidance, it should be added that responsibility for any errors or infelicitous judgements in what follows rests with me alone.

The author and publishers are grateful to the following for granting permission to quote from copyright material: Churchill Archives Centre, Cambridge (the papers of Baron Noel-Baker); the Bodleian Library, Oxford (Conservative Party archive); Special Collections, the University of Reading (Lord Wolfenden papers); and the University of East London (British Olympic Association archive).

Every effort has been made to trace the copyright holders but if any have been inadvertently overlooked, the publishers will be pleased to make the necessary arrangement at the first opportunity.

Abbreviations

AAA	Amateur Athletics Association
AAM	Anti-Apartheid Movement
BOA	British Olympic Association
BRSLC	Bristol Region Sports Liaison Council
CCPR	Central Council of Physical Recreation
CCT	Compulsory Competitive Tendering
CDS	Committee for the Development of Sport
CIPFA	Chartered Institute of Public Finance and Accounting
DCMS	Department of Culture, Media and Sport
DES	Department of Education and Science
DNH	Department of National Heritage
DoE	Department of the Environment
FA	Football Association
FCO	Foreign and Commonwealth Office
FO	Foreign Office
IMF	International Monetary Fund
IOC	International Olympic Committee
LEA	Local Education Authority
LTA	Lawn Tennis Association
MCC	Marylebone Cricket Club
MHLG	Ministry of Housing and Local Government
NGB	National Governing Body
NHS	National Health Service
NPFA	National Playing Fields Association
PE	Physical Education
PSC	Parliamentary Sports Committee
RAF	Royal Air Force
RCSR	Regional Councils for Sport and Recreation
RSC	Regional Sports Council
SARD	Sport and Recreation Division (of the civil service)

SDC Sports Development Council (advocated by 1960
Wolfenden Report)
TST Stop the Seventy Tour
UGC University Grants Committee

Introduction

In July 2005 the British Prime Minister, Tony Blair, flew to Singapore, where the International Olympic Committee (IOC) was meeting to decide the venue of the 2012 Olympics. Blair later wrote that there was a 'fierce debate' among his advisers about whether he should go in person to Singapore. Although recently returned to power, securing an unprecedented third successive Labour election victory in the spring of 2005, Blair's popularity had taken a battering because of Britain's involvement in the Iraq war. He also faced considerable behind-the-scenes pressure to step down and pave the way for his brooding heir apparent, the Chancellor of the Exchequer Gordon Brown, to assume the reins of power. The Prime Minister knew that to go to Singapore risked further damage to his authority and credibility. Informed observers believed that, although the organizers of London's bid had done everything in their power, Paris remained the front-runner in the race to host the 2012 Games; unlike the British capital, Paris had the advantage of a main Olympic stadium and many of the required facilities already in place. After much agonizing, Blair decided he would make the trip, primarily for political reasons: the danger of being humiliated was outweighed by his desire 'to avoid being criticised for not trying hard enough'.[1]

When the Prime Minister arrived at Singapore airport, he was met by the head of the London bid team, former Olympic athlete Sebastian Coe, who greeted Blair with the words that the IOC could still be swayed, but 'it's down to you'.[2] Without pausing for a break, the Prime Minister was whisked to a hotel, where he engaged in hours of back-to-back individual meetings with about 40 of the 115 IOC members who were due to vote. Exhausted from his endeavours, Blair left ahead of the IOC vote to prepare for a tricky summit of G8 world leaders due to meet in London, with personal calculations still prominent in his mind. 'I was more and more conscious of the double-whammy possibilities of failure', he

1

wrote in his memoirs: 'lose the Olympics, screw up the G8.'[3] The Prime Minister was back in Britain when the news came through on 6 July that his efforts had been worthwhile: London defeated Paris by the narrow margin of 54 votes to 50. As joyous celebrations got under way in Trafalgar Square, it was quickly agreed that Blair made a decisive contribution to the outcome. A former IOC Vice President, Dick Pound, was reported as saying that London owed its success to a great collective effort in which Coe had been a fine figurehead, straight from 'central casting', but it was the Prime Minister who 'made the difference', swinging just enough votes to tip the balance in London's favour.[4]

By taking the risk of high-profile intervention, Tony Blair scored a major political triumph, followed by some of the best newspaper coverage of his entire ten-year premiership. The victory for London announced in Singapore was widely treated as a marker of international prestige, giving Britain the right to stage the world's premier athletics festival for the first time in more than half a century. Under the watchful eye of a 'Minister for the Olympics', lengthy preparations were soon under way to ensure that London 2012 became the most spectacular Games in living memory, likely to be followed on television by over two-thirds of the world's population. Massive sums of public money, in excess of £9 billion, were committed to ensure the construction of a range of state-of-the-art sporting and media venues, improved transport links and purpose-built housing for competitors on the Olympic site in East London.

It had all seemed so different when London previously hosted the Games in 1948. At that time, Britain was still recovering from the ravages of the Second World War. Much of the capital continued to bear the hallmarks of Nazi bombing and the population remained in the grip of rationing and everyday shortages. There was no prospect of building a new Olympic site, and venues that had escaped war damage such as Wembley Stadium had to be hastily adapted. Accommodation arrangements for competitors were also improvised in a spirit of 'make do and mend'. While BBC radio coverage ensured an international audience for the Games, television was in its infancy; the number able to watch in Britain was put at about half a million, most of these living within a forty-mile radius of London. The idea of lavish government investment in 1948 was a non-starter; the Labour government of the day made it clear that Olympic organizers had to cover all costs from a modest budget. Not surprisingly, the 1948 Games are commonly remembered as 'the austerity Olympics'.[5]

There are some intriguing parallels between the Olympics of 1948 and 2012. Both have a common backdrop where the British government faced in 1948, and is facing now in 2012, crippling public debt at home and dangers aplenty overseas. But the contrasts are more striking than the similarities, not only in the scale and cost of the two events – one put together hastily at a time when much of world sport was unpaid and based on amateur principles and the other meticulously planned in an era of commercialization and professionalism – but also in the degree of involvement by political leaders. Before the post-1945 age of the welfare state, Britain was characterized by limited central government intervention in much of the nation's economic, social and cultural life. Sport was a largely voluntary enterprise, freely entered into by enthusiasts and overseen by individual national governing bodies (NGBs) responsible for running hundreds of separate sports. What happened on the athletics track, the tennis court or the football pitch was not considered to be the preserve of the state. Direct and sustained interest of the type shown by Tony Blair in the framing and winning of the 2012 Olympic bid was unimaginable in the era of his 1940s predecessor, Clement Attlee, although as we will see, Attlee's government provided important moral and practical backing to London's cause.

It would be misleading to suggest that sport and politics operated in entirely separate compartments before 1945. The machinery of the central state was not extensively deployed for economic and social ends, but at the same time Britain had a tradition, stretching back to the Victorian period, of local authorities providing (on an optional and so variable basis) parks and other recreational facilities such as swimming baths. And with the spread of international competition in the first half of the twentieth century, government ministers and Whitehall civil servants sometimes found themselves embroiled in unwelcome diplomatic disputes arising from sporting controversy. In the wake of the bitter dispute over the tactics of the English cricket team battling the Australians for the Ashes in 1933, J. H. Thomas, the Dominions Secretary, remarked: 'No politics ever introduced in the British Empire ever caused me so much trouble as this damn Bodyline bowling.' After

Hitler blatantly used the Berlin Olympics of 1936 to showcase Nazi ideology, the Conservative-dominated National administration in Britain responded with the first large-scale initiative in sport dictated by central government. Looking to improve standards of fitness as the prospect of war came closer, a Physical Training and Recreation Act was passed in 1937, prompting the unfolding of a 'National Fitness Campaign'. This went some way towards stimulating new local schemes, though critics felt it was half-hearted compared with Hitler's methods of training young people and in the words of the leading sports administrator Stanley Rous, the whole campaign faded away unlamented in 1939, an 'early casualty of the war'.[6]

The reality remained that, in an age when the role of the state was much less intrusive than today, it was commonplace to assume that sport and politics did not mix. Politicians might be unavoidably drawn in at times, but this was mostly as a result of one-off international crises, and sport was generally left to run its own affairs. The contrasts between then and now – epitomized by the sharp differences between the 1948 and 2012 Olympics – point us towards the main concern of this book, which is to examine the greatly increased interaction between sport and politics since the Second World War. This interaction can be gauged in various ways, among them the manner in which, by the end of the twentieth century, prime ministers were routinely expected to lend support to efforts to bring major sporting events to British shores. Tony Blair was not the first, or the last, national leader to put his reputation on the line in the interests of sport. His Conservative predecessor John Major pulled out all the stops in supporting an earlier Olympic bid made by Manchester, and in December 2010 Prime Minister David Cameron travelled to Zurich to personally lobby (alongside Prince William and David Beckham) on behalf of England's failed attempt to secure the right to host the 2018 football World Cup. Far from being dragged reluctantly into proceedings, as before 1939, the contemporary politician is often found showcasing the virtues of international sport.

Domestically, the relationship between sport and politics has also converged. One key illustration of this trend has been the development of administrative machinery, both local and central, devoted to sport and recreation: minimal in 1945, today leisure departments are commonplace in local government and sport features (as it has since 1997) in the title of a Whitehall department, the Department for Culture, Media and Sport (DCMS). There has also been a steady rise in central government funding for sport. This was almost non-existent at the end of the Second World War, whereas hundreds of millions of pounds are now channelled annually through the DCMS and distributed via several sports councils, established to drive forward improvements in sport from the grass roots to the elite level. Large sums are also provided by other Whitehall ministries, notably the Department for Education, which funds sport in state schools. The value placed on sport in political circles by the beginning of the twenty-first century was illustrated when, despite embarking on rigorous spending cuts to reduce Britain's bloated public debt, the coalition government elected in 2010 left untouched the multi-billion pound budget earmarked for the London Olympics. The starting point for this book is thus to pose some historical questions: in what ways and for what reasons has the relationship between sport and politics in Britain become closer since 1945? And what does the historical record tell us about the place of sport in contemporary British society and politics?

To an extent, these questions have already been addressed by scholars from a variety of academic disciplines. The lead has been taken by social and political scientists and sport policy experts, notably Lincoln Allison, John Hargreaves, Ian Henry and above all Barrie Houlihan, the last of whom has published a string of key works on the policy-making process in contemporary sport.[7] Among sport historians, there have been valuable contributions by the likes of Martin Polley, Richard Holt and Tony Mason and Jeffrey Hill.[8] Between them, these authors have illuminated the varying forms of state intervention in sport since 1945: legislative, administrative, regulatory and fiscal. They have also outlined many of the broad underlying causes of the growing association between sport and politics, including pressure on politicians applied by the media and sports lobby groups; political responses to the relentless rise of sport as a cultural and economic phenomenon; and the likelihood that political leaders were drawn towards sport 'not least' because of a perceived cross-party 'commitment towards developing and sustaining ... welfare state ideology'.[9] Some of the published research, however, has been broad brush in approach or strongly polemical in tone, as in the case of the quasi-Marxist account of sport as a vehicle for social control presented by Hargreaves. The main focus of the literature has also been 'present-centred' rather than historical, with a concentration on developments in the recent past and not the post-war period as a whole.

Despite the quality of much of what has been written (and this author's debt to existing scholarship is acknowledged in the Notes which follow the main text), it remains the case that until now there has been no systematic long-term historical study of the relationship between sport and politics in Britain from 1945 to the present day.[10] In particular what has been missing from earlier accounts is any detailed assessment of the motives and actions of British politicians, those serving as ministers in successive governments (supported by the civil service in Whitehall) and those found representing the major political parties in parliament at Westminster, both in the House of Commons and the House of Lords. Official attitudes to sport have usually been explored through the scrutiny of documents ranging from the influential 'Wolfenden Report' of 1960 to Sports Council publications and DCMS strategy papers. Important though these set-piece statements are, more can be done to place them within their prevailing socio-economic and political context, and efforts are also made in what follows to explore behind and beneath the surface of official reports by drawing on the evidence of government papers held at the National Archives (hitherto largely unused) as well as a range of other primary sources such as private papers, party records, election manifestos, newspapers, diaries and autobiographies. *Sport and Politics in Modern Britain* therefore aims to provide the fullest account yet of this important topic, balancing an appreciation of continuity and change on the road to 2012 and bringing sport more into focus as a contested domain with the mainstream of British politics.

In employing the historian's standard empirical methodology and attempting to capture development over time, the main chapters following this Introduction range chronologically from a consideration of sport under Labour's 1945 administration through the creation of an advisory Sports Council under Harold Wilson in the 1960s to John Major's direction of substantial National Lottery funds to sport in the 1990s and the importance attached to sport by 'New Labour' after 1997. Integrated within these chapters is consideration of the many suddenly occurring high-profile crises that brought sport to prominence in the nation's political consciousness, varying from football hooliganism and its links with working-class culture to the controversies generated by fox-hunting, traditionally associated with the most elite sections of British society. Discussion of sporting concerns at different spatial levels – local and regional, national and international – is weaved in at various points, though separate thematic chapters have also been included to provide fuller consideration of the evolving links between international sport and British diplomacy (a dimension traditionally dealt with by the Foreign Office) and the key role played by local authorities in the provision of parks, playing fields and swimming pools for everyday use.

A few caveats about the scope of the coverage might be noted at the outset. The first is that 'sport', which comes in an enormous number of guises, embracing the individual and the collective, the competitive and strenuous to the recreational and less physically exertive, can only be selectively assessed within the constraints of a single book. The spotlight throughout will be on those areas and issues that have most directly concerned politicians. Hence some popular sports that hardly ever surfaced in political debate barely feature (golf and cycling, for instance), whereas others are more prominent: notably athletics and other Olympic sports in the first decades after the war when amateurism still characterized much top-level sport, and football, which fully supplanted cricket as Britain's 'national game' in the ensuing era of rampant com-mercialization and globalization. In addition, much of the focus in what follows centres on Westminster as the executive heart of British politics; Scotland, Wales and Northern Ireland deserve and await fuller treatment in their own right. A further caveat is that while attention is given to sporting interest groups such as the British Olympic Association and to the various sports coun-cils created since the 1960s (the delivery agencies of government), these are looked at primarily in terms of how they interacted with ministers and party politicians. While these bodies drive much of the detailed, day-to-day development of sport, distributing grants for community projects or to elite athletes, the main stage here is occupied by the political classes, with the intention of showcas-ing extensively for the first time what contribution to sport has been made by prime ministers, cabinet ministers, MPs, peers of the realm and Whitehall civil servants.

The concern in the following pages with politicians and officials enables some of the prevailing assumptions about sport–state relationships to be elaborated upon, adapted or challenged. In looking at the nature of political involvement, for example, it becomes possible to provide a fuller assessment than hitherto of the shifting balance between reluctant activity (occasions when political leaders had no choice but to intervene in sport, as in the case of football hooliganism) and more creative efforts to shape and influence sporting development. In relation to timing, there has been a tendency to think in terms of a linear, steadily advancing closeness in the relationship between sport and politics. But this view needs to be amended in the light of the sporadic, uneven interest in sport by politicians from 1945 onwards; links between sport and politics were ruptured and regressed at times, rather than always proceeding smoothly to an agreed final destination. Above all, the contention that the growing entanglement of sport and politics reflected a cross-party consensus around 'welfare state ideology' requires revision. Sport did not somehow stand above and apart from party politics, and, as will be seen, while there were areas of agreement there were also some sharp differences between the main parties at Westminster over sport: a function of contrasting shades of ideological commitment as well as varying perceptions about the value of sport in political and electoral discourse. This book attempts to bring out the richness and complexity of the maturing bond between sport and politics, though it also cautions against exaggerating the extent to which the two have become natural bedfellows. In his recent book *Sport in History*, Jeffrey Hill discusses the many ways in which 'sport matters' in contemporary society.[11] As the extravaganza of London 2012 illustrates, sport is without question important to political leaders and parties today, but the approach of post-war politicians towards sport has also been characterized in places by prevarication, ambiguity and hostility. Sport matters, but in the light of fresh spending cutbacks projected beyond the 2012 Olympics the depth of the commitment of British politicians remains questionable.

1 Sport and Politics in Austerity Britain, 1945–51

Introduction

The second half of the 1940s was characterized by immense everyday hardships as the nation struggled to recover from six years of total war. But all was not gloom and doom in austerity Britain. As historian Paul Addison notes, the stock images of the immediate post-war period – in which the nation was always in the grip of hard winter snow, men were digging coal and women queuing for offal – should not overshadow the fact that 'there was plenty of fun to be had in the Attlee years'.[1] In reality, summers were generally long and hot, and the playing and watching of sport, regarded by foreign observers as a British obsession, resumed with a vengeance after the restrictions of the war years. The continuation of rationing made daily living conditions stressful, but high levels of employment gave the majority of families more disposable income than ever before, and while commodities for the home remained in short supply, leisure pursuits provided a valuable outlet. With television still in its infancy, long-established spectator sports quickly revived and reached new levels of popularity. Almost 100,000 people attended the first post-war Cup final at Wembley in April 1946, and the spring and summer witnessed the return of other traditional dates in the annual sporting calendar such as the Boat Race, the Grand National and Wimbledon. Of the nation's two favourite sports, first-class cricket pulled in some three million paying customers in the glorious summer of 1947 and aggregate levels of attendance for top-flight football – the preferred sport of the industrial masses – were higher in the late 1940s than either before or since. At the peak in 1948–49, forty-one million spectators attended league fixtures. Although the Soviet team Moscow Dynamo performed strongly when they toured in late 1945, the notion that Britain remained pre-eminent at football continued on the basis that neither England nor Scotland had hitherto been beaten on home soil by a foreign team. In May 1947 the 6–1 thrashing of a Rest of Europe team by Britain kept this complacent view of superiority intact, at least for the time being.[2]

What the writer Norman Baker describes as the desire for a 'return to normalcy' in sport appeared to have little to do with the government of the day. Elected with a landslide majority at the 1945 election, the Labour administration under Clement Attlee, the British prime minister, is mainly remembered for implementing a major programme of reforms in health, housing, social insurance and education, the key components of a newly forged 'welfare state'. But if the power of the Westminster government was considerably extended in many spheres, sport was not one of them. As far as the relationship between sport and politics was concerned, existing accounts of the post-war era generally agree that continuity rather than change was the order of the day. 'Until the 1960s', the sports administrator John Coghlan argues, 'central government played little or no part in sport'.[3] In his overview of twentieth-century developments, Jeffrey Hill refers to 'the low level of interest displayed in sport by the Labour governments of 1945–51'. For those keen on active recreation, Hill adds, the National Parks Act of 1949, protecting large areas of outstanding natural beauty such as Snowdonia and the Lake District from commercial or residential development, was a 'notable exception to the endeavours of a government which continued to believe that sport and leisure were matters for individuals to sort out for themselves'.[4] Some observers credit Labour with wider achievements, though still within narrow confines. In their jointly authored volume on post-war British sport Richard Holt and Tony Mason note that Attlee's administration played a 'crucial role' in the hosting of the 1948 London Olympics and intervened at other points when it was deemed in the national interest. Even so, they conclude: 'None of this could be remotely called a sports policy.'[5] And Peter Beck, in an important article on the 1948 London Olympics, while agreeing on Labour's contribution to the success of the Olympics, believes this episode did not mark the arrival of a defined, coherent government strategy towards international sport. In spite of its activist role, Beck argues, the 'government inclined towards traditional lines of policy based on pragmatic one-off responses to sporting questions'.[6]

There are some compelling factors that lend credence to the conventional view of the role of government in sport after 1945. The euphoria surrounding Labour's stunning election victory gradually dissipated when it became obvious that a huge task beckoned in rebuilding the nation's economic and social infrastructure. Victory over Nazism came at the cost of leaving Britain close to bankruptcy, facing what the economist John Maynard Keynes famously called a 'financial Dunkirk'. Sport, inevitably, struggled to find any place on a list of priorities that started with the need to revive industrial production, avoid a return to a 1930s-style mass unemployment and fulfil pledges for extensive welfare reform, the latter only made possible with the aid of an enormous loan from the United States. The terms of the US loan were so stringent that Labour's time in power was punctuated by recurrent economic crises, notably in 1947 and 1949. Aside from the government having more pressing concerns than the nation's sporting activities, it also mattered that sport valued its autonomy. Sport and recreation formed part of the wider tradition of voluntarism in which British people freely pursued a host of cultural, intellectual and social activities. Since the Victorian period sport had been largely controlled by a host of individual governing bodies, the likes of the Football Association (FA), the Amateur Athletics Association (AAA) and the Lawn Tennis Association (LTA). These bodies wrote their own rulebooks and arranged annual calendars of events and fixtures, and with the impediment of wartime disruption out of the way, they were keen to resume their established role without any expectation of state interference. With no strong impulse or desire from any quarter to depart from earlier traditions, it comes as no surprise that many of the existing accounts of the Attlee years cite a response to a parliamentary question in 1946 by the Prime Minister, using this to reinforce the point that the pre-war 'hands-off' government approach to sport continued undisturbed. When asked by the Labour MP and sports enthusiast Arthur Lewis if he might consider appointing a minister for sport and physical culture, Attlee gave a typically terse and emphatic reply: 'No, Sir.'[7]

This chapter, while accepting that the Attlee years did not mark a significant or lasting turning point in the relationship between sport and politics, will argue that the picture was not as straightforward as often portrayed. For one thing, Hill's reference to the 'low level of interest' displayed by the government runs counter to the degree of enthusiasm for sport found within the highest echelons of government. There was much greater personal interest in sport in the 1945 Cabinet than in many administrations both before and after. Unlike his Conservative successors Churchill, Eden and Macmillan, Attlee was an avid sports fan, a follower of cricket in particular and known to enjoy playing tennis.[8] The Home Secretary, James Chuter Ede, was an aficionado of horse racing and Chancellor of the Exchequer Hugh Dalton's passion for rambling was reflected in the terms and passage of the National Parks Act. Another key figure was Philip Noel-Baker, who held several ministerial posts under Attlee. Noel-Baker was an Olympic medallist in 1920 and captain of the British Olympic track team in 1920 and 1924. His Quaker upbringing helps to explain a lifelong commitment to the idea of sport as a solvent of international disputes. Noel-Baker, as will be seen, was to be at the forefront of moves to forge a closer relationship between sport and politics in the postwar era. As Peter Beck has acknowledged, while sport did not warrant a ministerial portfolio before the 1960s, 'in many respects Attlee treated Noel-Baker as his government's de facto minister of sport'.[9] This level of personal enthusiasm in the upper reaches of government may not have resulted in a permanent break from the pre-1939 tradition of limited state involvement with sport, but it did count for something. Attlee's administration did not have a 'sports policy', in the sense that it had a 'health policy' that hinged on creating the National Health Service (NHS), but more so than any previous government it brought a sympathetic approach to sport and recreation.

Sport as Crisis Management: The Midweek Fixture Ban, Gambling and Hunting

In certain respects, the 1945 government, like its pre-war predecessors, was drawn towards sport through crisis management, reluctantly responding to events when there was no choice. One notable illustration of how Labour's approach to sport was reactive as much as proactive came during the winter crisis of early 1947 when severe weather conditions brought much of Britain's coal-dependent industrial sector to a standstill and added to strains on the economy. Instances such as this demonstrated that, in the absence of a single figure with clearly defined responsibilities for sport, ministerial reaction had to be led by those whose remit was closest to the problem under discussion. Under pressure to show the government was not powerless in the face of the winter crisis, the Minister of Fuel and Power, Manny Shinwell ('Shiver with Shinwell', Tory opponents teased), called among other things for the restriction of sporting events to weekends only, claiming that industrial production was being lost by absenteeism among coal miners and assorted groups of workers at midweek football and other sporting fixtures.[10] Hasty Cabinet discussions ensued in which the Home Secretary, Chuter Ede, tasked with negotiating with individual governing bodies, cautioned against a blanket ban. The Jockey Club, he argued (possibly reflecting his personal interest), should be encouraged to arrange the best-attended horse racing events at weekends, but to abandon all midweek fixtures might undermine the valuable contribution the bloodstock industry was making to agriculture. Cricket, the Home Secretary believed (another of his personal passions), should also be exempt: 'Cricket does not normally attract anything like the same crowds as football or greyhound areas, nor is it played to any great extent in the mining areas of Tyneside, South Wales, or Scotland.'[11]

When Chuter Ede made a statement in the Commons to clarify the government's position in March 1947, restrictions on midweek sport were mainly confined to football league fixtures and greyhound racing. Although the new dispensation was agreed voluntarily with the governing bodies concerned, the restrictions added to a growing sense of public disillusionment with the government, whose lead in the opinion polls evaporated during the winter crisis for the first time since the 1945 election. The Home Secretary was given a rough ride in parliament. His opposite number in the Commons described the measures as 'necessary though most unpalatable', and called for the earliest possible end to the restrictions. Conservative-supporting newspapers were presented with an easy target, the *Daily Express* calling the announcement 'austerity for the sake of it'.[12] From his own side of the House, Ede was attacked for not having hard evidence of the scale of lost production occasioned by midweek sporting fixtures and for appearing to discriminate against the preferred sports of the working masses. Enthusiasm for cricket around the Cabinet table was not shared by all Labour backbenchers, some of whom questioned why it should be exempt when the county game was built around mid-week fixtures. To have taken this step, ministers knew, would have incurred the full wrath of Fleet Street. *The Times*, while accepting that curtailment of some sport was unavoidable, thundered that the threat to cricket must be fought at all costs: 'To restrict it is to kill it'. A *Times* editorial asserted: 'Cricket has a special place in the national ... tradition, and it is impossible to believe that a good case can be made on industrial grounds for its destruction.'[13]

In spite of the adverse publicity generated, ministers decided some months later that the restrictions should stay in force over the winter of 1947–48. Once again, no limitations were proposed on particular sports such as speedway (attended mainly, it was believed, by women and adolescents) or on summer sports like cricket and tennis; the Olympic Games were also treated on a separate basis, as an international event planned to take place over a short, concentrated period. Cabinet discussions indicated that several ministers felt any damage occasioned by upsetting some of the government's natural working-class supporters was outweighed by the need to prioritize industrial recovery at all costs. The Minister of Labour, George Isaacs, spoke of the importance of late shifts being worked in mining areas, making it impossible to contemplate evening midweek dog racing. Nye Bevan, the Minister of Health, said it was 'absurd' in the prevailing economic circumstances to contemplate a return of midweek sport. And Stafford Cripps, who replaced Dalton as Chancellor of the Exchequer in 1947, weighed in with a stern warning, as recorded in the Cabinet Secretary's note of the discussions: 'Mustn't give appearance of relaxing.'[14] Once again it was left to the Home Secretary to take the flak from anxious Labour backbenchers. When questioned, he conceded that there were no statistics as to the extent of improved production owing to the curtailment of midweek sport, but claimed information from across the country persuaded the government that to relax or discontinue the restrictions in force 'could not fail to have a harmful effect on production'.[15]

A second example of the government being drawn into sport through the scale of its economic difficulties came in the area of gambling. Britain had a long tradition of gambling, especially in sports such as horse racing, football and greyhound racing, and moral reformers had often complained of the sums of money lost to working-class families through indulgence in betting. In many

European nations state-controlled lotteries were in place, which allowed governments to devote proceeds to various worthy causes (including sport). By contrast British governments were generally reluctant to interfere with privately run enterprises, though the prohibition of off-course betting after 1906 was an attempt to restrict the practice to those who went to dog and race tracks in person. Against the backdrop of the economic crisis in 1947, ministers gave in to the temptation to regard gambling as a useful source of tax revenue. With attendance at sporting events reaching a peak in the aftermath of war, more than ever was being spent on gambling. Estimates of the total invested in bets in the 1930s were of the order of £300 to £500 million per year, and by the late 1940s the figure stood in excess of £700 million. The lion's share of the total was spent on horse racing, about twice that invested on dogs; at the same time about ten million people were thought to regularly fill in the football pools, hoping to win prizes by guessing the outcome of Saturday league fixtures. Although many who participated appeared to be indulging in what was known as 'a little flutter', and despite most bets being redistributed among the gambling fraternity (80% of money placed on the pools, for example, was returned to lucky winners), critics attacked some perennial problems: off-course betting, though illegal, was rumoured to be widespread, and a minority clearly engaged in high levels of gambling.[16]

In 1947 the government announced a tax of 10 per cent on the football pools and on greyhound racing. In the case of the pools, the ease of collecting the tax before prizes were distributed meant that within a couple of years the government decided to raise the levy to 30 per cent. As the economic historian Roger Munting notes, it was ironic that a left-wing administration should take a tough line on a largely working-class activity: 'The new betting taxes were not only regressive but socially discriminatory as well.'[17] When Cripps as Chancellor spoke in Cabinet, in 1948, of the need to amend the 'chaotic and illogical' gambling laws, he alluded to the criticism that ministers were – as over midweek sport – discriminating against Labour's natural supporters. Betting tax applied to football pools and greyhounds, but not horse racing, so giving an impression, Cripps noted, of 'favouritism to the wealthier man's sport'. This was an unsatisfactory position, the Chancellor felt, though he believed it was unavoidable while illegal street betting

remained widespread.[18] Rather than confront the complex issue
of gambling head on, in April 1949 the government established
a Royal Commission, chaired by the prominent Conservative
politician Sir Henry Willink. In taking evidence, the Commission
received a wide range of opinions, with church representatives in
particular arguing that gambling contributed to social evils such
as poverty, petty crime and absenteeism in the workplace. But the
Commission had little sympathy for calls to abolish the football
pools and curtail greyhound racing. Other witnesses, including
policemen and social workers, claimed that concerns about the
adverse effects of betting were exaggerated. In its report, published in 1951, the Commission criticized gambling as 'self-regard-
ing and essentially uncreative', but concluded that it was 'of little
significance' either to the running of the economy or as a cause of
crime and other social misdemeanours.[19] With wholesale changes
in the law deemed unnecessary, Labour made no attempt to act
on the recommendations of the Commission before it lost power
in 1951.

Restrictions on midweek fixtures and gambling thus cast the government's approach to sport in a defensive light. But perhaps the
major example in the Attlee years of the government responding
to events rather than leading from the front came in its handling
of the contentious issue of hunting. As well as seeing a resurgence
of games like football favoured by the working classes who made
up the bulk of the population, the post-war period witnessed a
revival of traditionally upper-class sporting activities. Although
not exclusively associated with landed elites, the local aristocracy
and landowners in rural areas were the driving force in a steady
increase in the number of fox-hunting packs with hounds, rising
from 170 in 1939 to 190 in 1953. At the same time, Labour's overwhelming election victory in 1945 gave encouragement to those
who opposed blood sports. Sharp divisions between the hunting
fraternity and anti-hunt protestors went back a long way, but had
hitherto rarely surfaced in the Westminster arena. Private members' bills were frequently drawn up with the aim of restricting
hunting, but most never got beyond a preliminary first reading in
the Commons. In early 1949, however, two such bills won a place
to go to second reading, which ensured a more extensive parliamentary airing. The first, in the name of Seymour Cocks, Labour
MP for Ashfield in Derbyshire, was directed mainly at banning

stag hunting, while the second had as its focus fox hunting. The stage was set for a major confrontation. Strong backing came as expected from anti-hunt groups outside parliament, and there was some press speculation that the government might back the case for changing the law.[20]

In practice, this was a fight ministers were anxious to avoid. Although the upper-class associations of hunting made it a target for criticism among many Labour members – with motions against blood sports nodded through at party conferences in the 1920s and 1930s – an outright ban was not welcomed by the strand of working-class opinion that indulged in and supported rabbit and hare coursing in particular. There were, in other words, divisions in Labour ranks which until this time had been concealed by the absence of full-scale parliamentary discussion. In addition, senior Labour figures were aware of their obligation to represent all parts of the community, including the countryside, not simply the urban areas in which the party garnered most of its electoral support. Labour performed surprisingly well in rural constituencies at the 1945 election, and in office developed a close relationship with the National Famers' Union. In 1947 legislation was passed to extend the wartime system of annual price reviews designed to address food shortages and reduce the nation's dependency on imports. From both electoral and economic perspectives, the government was reluctant to upset its good working ties with farmers, who were felt to be making a valuable contribution to the nation's recovery after the war.[21] Farmers' groups, inevitably, were prominently represented in the deluge of letters sent to ministers early in 1949 urging them not to consent to ill-thought out bans on hunting.[22]

Ministers therefore found themselves in an awkward position as the hunting debate gathered pace. While many Labour MPs were vociferously opposed to hunting, for the government to back the abolitionist case would damage its improving relationship with the rural community. In Cabinet on 10 February it was agreed that as this was an issue of conscience a free vote should be allowed, rather than insisting on a party line. The consensus around the Cabinet table, however, was that electoral considerations must be paramount. Although he was the mover of hostile resolutions at party conferences before the war, the Minister of Agriculture, Tom Williams, said that hunting was 'part of rural life'; the proposed changes would 'undo all the good we have done by our agricultural policy'. Among Cabinet heavyweights, the Lord President of the Council, Herbert Morrison, described hunting as now mostly 'a farmers' recreation – not aristocrats', and Hugh Dalton called it the 'height of political lunacy' to contemplate reform with a general election looming on the horizon. Even if the hurdle of the Commons was jumped, the Conservatives would engineer defeat in the House of Lords and so garner any electoral credit from the issue. Home Secretary Chuter Ede noted that many urban Labour supporters would back a ban, and probably the majority of party members also, but on the merits of the case he felt the threat to rural life was a serious one. The Cabinet's decision was that, while allowing a free vote, the government's view would be made clear in advance: it wished to see the Commons reject both measures.[23]

On 25 February Seymour Cocks, backed by Anthony Greenwood, Labour MP for Heywood and Radcliffe and later to be president of the National Society for the Abolition of Cruel Sports, confidently spoke of cross-party support in introducing his first bill. 'Compassion for suffering is not the prerogative of any political party', Cocks noted: 'Hatred of cruelty is common to every civilised, humane and adult mind.' But the Agriculture Minister Tom Williams, brushing aside charges of hypocrisy ('one should never be ashamed to own that sometimes one may have been wrong'), countered that the measure would not lessen cruelty and 'would alienate the support of the rural population to our food production programme, which is vital in the national interest'. Cocks' bill was heavily defeated by 214 votes to 101, with several Labour ministers in the majority.[24] In return for the reformers not pressing ahead with the second bill, the government appointed a committee of inquiry under John Scott Henderson, King's Counsel, to study all the issues associated with cruelty to wild animals. But when this committee reported in June 1951 it turned into a resounding defeat for the anti-hunting lobby. Dominated by pro-hunt sympathizers, the committee concluded that field sport, aside from being 'healthy recreation', was a less cruel method of pest control than other alternatives, and on this basis should not be banned. The cause of the anti-hunt protestors was set back a generation; there was no question that the Tory administrations which followed Labour in the 1950s would contemplate any form of anti-hunting legislation. On this divisive topic, Attlee's government clearly put electoral expediency above conscience. Labour's desire to hold on to rural constituencies meant it was, as historian Michael Tichelar notes, 'not prepared to confront countryside interests on a number of controversial policy issues ranging from land nationalisation to blood sports'.[25]

Sport as Internationalism: The 1948 London Olympics

The example of hunting, like those of midweek fixtures and gambling, highlighted a defensive strain in Labour's attitude towards sport. In these instances the pre-war pattern of ministers regarding sport as a by-product of other, more important concerns, such as industrial production and taxation levels, remained alive and well. But this was not the whole story. In one major case there was strong evidence both of forward planning and a desire to promote sporting ideals. This came with the government's firm support for hosting the Olympic Games, which remained – before the spread of television in the 1950s helped to make football's World Cup a significant rival – the pre-eminent sporting spectacle on the global stage. While Labour's backing for the London Olympics of 1948 has been acknowledged in many existing accounts, the vital part played by ministers at all stages of the process, pointing to a more creative side of the government's approach to sport, cannot be overestimated. Nowhere was this more evident than in allowing the Games to go ahead in London in the first place.

Decisions about where to host the Olympics were the preserve, in the first instance, of the world-controlling authority of the Games, the International Olympic Committee, an unelected body of patrician figures including princes, generals, aristocrats and businessmen. Key individuals such as the Swedish President of the International Olympic Committee (IOC) Sigfrid Edstrom and American businessman Avery Brundage, determined to revive the Olympics after the aborted Games of 1940 and 1944, met in London shortly after the end of the war to discuss possible venues. The British capital did not seem a logical or obvious choice in the aftermath of wartime bombing; it was still short of accommodation, food and adequate transport, though other possible locations also had shortcomings. The cost and difficulties of travel to the United States would limit the scale of the Games, and choosing a venue in a neutral wartime country such as Sweden or Switzerland would not be popular so soon after the ending of hostilities. Although far from ideal, London seemed better placed than much of war-ravaged Europe to host a major event, and so on this basis (and because London was the intended venue for 1944) the IOC decided to offer the 1948 Games to the British Olympic Association (BOA).[26] But it was one thing to make the offer and another to secure backing for the Olympics to take place.

The BOA was crucial to making the prospect of the London Games a reality. It was charged with responsibility for preparing a team to compete at the Olympics wherever they were held in the world. As a voluntary organization with no financial support from government, the BOA also raised funds to cover the travel and subsistence costs of the amateurs who competed in athletics and a range of other Olympic sports. Like the IOC, the BOA was dominated by men of independent means, often former athletes possessing a title or high military rank and invariably staunch advocates of the amateur principle that taking part was more important than winning. One man above all, David Cecil, Lord Burghley, played a central part in driving forward the 1948 Games. Burghley, a product of Eton and Cambridge, was an Olympic hurdles champion in 1928 and captain of the British team at the 1932 and 1936 events. During the 1930s he was a Conservative MP and later British governor in Bermuda, and as Chairman of the BOA since 1936 he was also renowned as a champion of sport as a palliative of international tension. A dynamic figure in his early forties at the end of the war, his importance has been noted in Janie Hampton's book *The Austerity Olympics*: 'Handsome and articulate, calm and genial, Burghley successfully torpedoed opposition to the Games with charm and persuasion.'[27]

Yet for all his influence, Burghley would not have got far without the endorsement of Labour ministers. Although technically the Olympiad was awarded to the BOA, if the government had been opposed to the idea the Games could not have gone ahead in London. In 1936, with the National government in power, lack of ministerial backing forced the BOA to withdraw from the contest to stage the (eventually abandoned) 1940 Olympics.[28] In the circumstances – faced with the enormous practical difficulties of hosting the Games in harsh economic times in a capital city still ravaged by war damage – it would have been easy for Attlee's administration to adopt a more non-committal approach. The willingness of senior ministers not to take the easy route, however, was a significant affirmation of the value they placed on sport; in the final reckoning, without this blessing the London Olympics would not have taken place.

Aside from Attlee, who consistently adopted a position of low-key but firm support, two ministers in particular were the lynch-pins of government backing for the Olympics. One was the Foreign Secretary, Ernest Bevin, who regarded the hosting of the Games as an opportunity not to be missed to assist economic recovery by boosting tourism and earning vital dollars to pay for imports. In January 1946, after a meeting with the BOA in which Burghley spoke of foreign visitors to the Games bringing in over one million pounds in hard currency, Bevin sought backing from the Chancellor of the Exchequer, Dalton, and by the spring he had prepared the ground sufficiently to seek Cabinet approval for the venture.[29] The Foreign Secretary told colleagues that aside from the honour of the invitation to host the Games, 'the occasion would provide an excellent opportunity for an organized drive to attract tourists to this country'. While responsibility for organizing the event rested in the hands of the BOA, which would bear the finan-cial responsibility, government machinery was needed to assist in providing facilities for competitors and visitors, and the Cabinet agreed with Bevin's proposal to set up a small executive agency, working under an interdepartmental committee, to liaise with the BOA.[30] After this crucial moment Bevin was not greatly involved in working out the practical details, though his sympathetic stance never wavered and his intervention proved decisive. Before the war, as Peter Beck notes, matters pertaining to international sport had been dealt with mostly by civil servants at the Foreign Office, 'and rarely referred to ministers, let alone the Cabinet'. Yet Bevin's forcefulness, as one of the most powerful personalities in the gov-ernment, meant he was prepared to defy past convention by bring-ing the matter to senior colleagues, even if this meant overriding the concern of some of his officials (with memories of the 1936 Berlin Games in mind) that the Olympics could be more trouble than they were worth.[31]

The second key figure in determining Labour's approach was Philip Noel-Baker, Minister of State at the Foreign Office from August 1945 until October 1946. As Bevin's deputy, he was well placed to press the case for the value of hosting the

Olympics. Having been a professor of international relations at London University before becoming a Labour MP, Noel-Baker had a reputation as an intellectual in politics. When he joined the Cabinet in late 1947 as Commonwealth Secretary Herbert Morrison was quoted as saying it would be important to 'keep Noel-Baker practical'.[32] Yet he was to be an astute advocate of the London Olympics from start to finish, and was given special responsibility by Attlee to liaise with the organizers and to chair or host numerous Olympic-related events; he later described himself as the 'Government Adviser' to the BOA in the organization and carrying through of the Games.[33] Noel-Baker knew the benefits sought by his boss Bevin would only be secured if the Games were well run and favourably reported around the world. 'The national reputation', he recognized, 'will be largely involved in this highly risky undertaking'.[34] Noel-Baker therefore threw himself energetically into ensuring the government gave 'all possible assistance', but he moved carefully in looking to keep Cabinet colleagues on board, stressing for the most part the economic case for hosting the Games. It was only rarely that his well-known Olympic idealism got the better of him, notably when the Chancellor Dalton warned him at one point: 'Don't overdo your pressure'.[35]

The winter crisis of 1947, with its attendant disruption to the economy, did cause a wobble in government circles about the wisdom of backing the Games. In March 1947 Noel-Baker asked the Cabinet for approval of plans to house thousands of competitors from overseas who would take part in the Olympics. With the construction of an Olympic village out of the question, agreement had been reached to use Royal Air Force (RAF) bases at West Drayton and Uxbridge, close to the main Wembley venue, and also a War Office Depot in Richmond Park. Building works and redecoration at the RAF bases, however, would require an upfront commitment of £700,000, to be later reclaimed from funds raised by the BOA.[36] The Cabinet Secretary's notes show that Noel-Baker's request caused some consternation. 'This comes at a v. unfortunate time', Attlee said, and the Home Secretary Ede agreed the request did not look good at a time when restrictions were being imposed on midweek sport. When one minister, George Isaacs, appeared to suggest that because of labour shortages in London the invitation to host the Games should be withdrawn, others rallied

behind Noel-Baker. The Cabinet agreed it would be 'most inex-
pedient' to withdraw from the commitments already made, and
that the Games would in due course assist with economic recovery. Eventually ministers settled on a compromise under which
the redecoration of premises but no new building was sanctioned.
Competitors would be spread around locations more widely than
initially planned, including alternative venues not previously considered, and the Ministry of Works was charged with providing the
labour and material necessary to complete all necessary changes
by June 1948.[37] The logic of the argument, as well as the momentum already generated in favour of going ahead, note Holt and
Mason, 'swayed what few Cabinet doubters there appear to have
been'.[38]

Confident of steadfast endorsement from his colleagues, Noel-
Baker was able to shrug off any remaining concerns in the year
before the start of the Games. The onset of the Cold War, as relations between the wartime allies in the west and the Soviet Union
deteriorated, added to the concern of critics that there were more
important concerns for Britain than hosting an Olympiad. The
Soviets decided not to participate, joining a list of nations who
would not attend that already included Germany and Japan (barred
by the IOC with wartime atrocities still fresh in the mind). Noel-
Baker nevertheless dismissed what he called a 'foolish' campaign
in the summer of 1947 by sections of the anti-Labour press. The
Evening Standard in particular called for the cancellation of the
Olympics: 'The average range of British enthusiasm for the Games
stretches from lukewarm to dislike. It is not too late for invitations
to be politely withdrawn.' Anti-government rhetoric was tinged
with a strong xenophobic element. In such straitened times, the
Standard argued, British people were not keen to see money spent
on preparing for 'an army of foreign athletes'.[39] Noel-Baker rallied
other sections of the press, who he noted 'were more than ready to
help'. He also looked to calm the nerves of the BOA, which feared
the whole project would be abandoned with the 'starting post' in
sight. Attlee provided reassurances that the government was still
fully committed to the cause.[40]

The organizers did face some further tricky issues. A key
aspect of the case for holding the event in London was the prospect of substantial revenue from overseas tourists, but if visitors
and competitors were accorded special treatment this was likely

to antagonize a British populace resentful of continuing hardships. On the other hand, to insist that all those visiting Britain
in 1948 should be exposed to the full rigours of rationing would
be to invite international ridicule. Seeking a middle course, the
President of the Board of Trade, Harold Wilson, announced that
special clothing coupons would be issued to overseas competitors,
officials, press reporters and their families. Competitors were also
granted the maximum food allowances, comparable to the highest scale for British workers in key industries, and in an effort to
maximize tourist income, customs regulations were eased to avoid
delays at airports and ports and generous petrol allowances were
granted for overseas visitors.[41]

With everything in place, the Games proceeded without significant controversy or rancour, despite the backdrop of a fast
deteriorating international situation. The Soviet Union closed
off access to Berlin in late June 1948, and the 'Berlin airlift' that
followed – with tons of food being flown into the city each day
by British and American transport planes – prompted large numbers of cancelled bookings for the Olympics, especially from the
United States. Any shortfall in ticket sales was taken up, though,
by British spectators, who ensured that Wembley was packed for a
successful opening ceremony on a gloriously sunny day on 29 July.
Attlee attended before leaving for a golfing holiday, and the slick
ceremony impressed some 2000 foreign correspondents in attendance. This set the tone for what followed. Although the weather
was variable as competition got underway and there were some
grumbling about the drabness of living conditions in London,
there was a general sense of relief that the Olympics were able
to resume after a twelve-year hiatus. As Bob Phillips notes in his
history of the Games: 'On the track, the pitches, river and sea,
and in the covered arenas, the competitors – of whom there would
actually be some 4,000 or so from 59 countries – would ensure
that there was nothing "austere" in their endeavours.'[42] In terms of
medals, although the IOC did not publish an official table, which
it regarded as unnecessarily nationalistic, it was clear the United
States was the world's predominant athletics nation. The performance of the British team was patchy, with three gold medals but
none in track and field: a tally that left Britain trailing behind
other European nations such as Sweden and France. Although
women constituted less than 10 per cent of all competitors, the

real star of the Games was the Dutch athlete Fanny Blankers-Koen, who won four gold medals.

As the participants prepared to leave British shores in August 1948, most contemporary observers were agreed that the Games had been a resounding success. Some of the most fulsome praise came from those who had been outspoken in attacking the idea that sport somehow acted as an agent of global cooperation. John Macadam of the *Daily Express* conceded: 'The success of the Games completely confounded those critics who had pessimistically forecast dire failure and international discord.'[43] Much of the comment praised the impeccable organization, as well as the way in which the friendly and relaxed atmosphere contrasted sharply with that of Berlin in 1936. *The Observer* felt the Games had been held 'with none of the nationalistic ostentation which travestied the Olympic spirit in Berlin'. Britain might not dominate world athletics as it once did, 'but we can feel modest pride that London Games have been one of the most successful of these festivals of sport and quite the most harmonious and sensible in temper'.[44] *The Economist* believed that bold claims about sport as a solvent of international disputes still sat uneasily with the reality offered by the Berlin crisis, especially as the Russians had not come to London.[45] But for Philip Noel-Baker, it was impossible to resist a note of triumphalism. 'The Olympic Games have gone *miraculously* well', he wrote to the Prime Minister, who asked Noel-Baker to script a radio broadcast reflecting on the value of the whole exercise. In spite of the 'havoc' of warfare in the modern era, the broadcast noted, 'the Olympic movement has come through unscathed', and stronger than ever in terms of numbers of nations and athletes taking part. More important, radio listeners were told, the Olympics answered 'something universal and eternal in the human heart... the flame is out but the Olympic spirit lingers and it leaves us with a vision and a hope'.[46]

Some historians offer less upbeat assessments of the Games. While recognizing the value of ministerial support, Peter Beck argues that poor performances in many events did little 'for the image of the British sporting model'. In addition the Games produced only a 'modest' profit of some £30,000, confounding promises of large tourist revenue and dollar earnings, and the Olympics did not inspire a new dawn in the relationship between politicians and sport: only a week before the Games began, the government rejected the need for a royal commission or select committee to investigate the organization and functioning of British sport.[47] But there are good reasons for regarding this as an unduly pessimistic summing up of the Olympics. In some of the unofficial rankings, Britain finished sixth: a reasonable outcome in the aftermath of a war that severely curtailed much of British sport. The profits made by the organizing committee were equivalent to millions of pounds today; it was to be over thirty years before another Olympiad (at Los Angeles, in 1984) secured such a profit margin. While precise figures on tourist revenue are not available, it was later estimated that 40 per cent more overseas visitors came to Britain in July 1948 than in the same month the previous year, and ministers claimed in parliament that such visitors – whether attending the Games or not – made a significant contribution to British foreign currency reserves and provided a key source of US dollars.[48] As for the rejection of the appointment of a royal commission, the eve of the start of the Olympics would have been a strange moment to have launched such an initiative. The government was satisfied that, despite acute economic difficulties, it had held its nerve in the face of critics who regarded the Olympics as an unwelcome irrelevance, proving that the Games could be utilized for purposes of sporting idealism as well as national prestige and financial well-being.

Sport as Administration:
The Role of the Ministry of Education

London 1948 constituted a high profile, one-off event in the history of political involvement with sport after the war. The prospect of hosting the world's leading sporting spectacle was not likely to recur for a generation or more, and if Labour's record was to be remembered for anything more than ad hoc intervention in this single case, it was important that the government could point to an enduring legacy in the more routine administration of domestic sport. Although, as we have seen, responsibility for dealing with sporting issues was spread across numerous Whitehall departments from the Foreign Office to the Ministry of Agriculture, giving the impression of fragmentation, one department – the Ministry of Education – did assume a more central role in the day-to-day oversight of sport and recreation on the home front in the immediate post-war years. There was, in other words, a tentative move away from the pre-1939 hands-off approach of government towards something more systematic, and the chief reason for this departure was Labour's determination to implement the provisions of a major piece of wartime legislation, the 1944 Education Act. This landmark measure paved the way for free secondary education for all children, superseding the old divide in the state system between elementary schools and largely fee-paying post-11 schooling for a minority. Outside the small, highly prized independent sector, most children before the war attended a single elementary school from the age of 5 until leaving at 14. As well as leading to the introduction of a three-tier system of state secondary schools – grammars, technical schools and secondary moderns – the 1944 Act proposed the raising of the leaving age to 15. In 1947 the government, despite the swirling sense of economic crisis, agreed to implement this part of the Act, requiring the provision of thousands of extra school places, new teachers and facilities.

While political attention centred on the structure and length of compulsory education, the 1944 Act also had some important implications for sport. In the first place, the curriculum of school sport was gradually transformed. Under earlier permissive legislation, local authorities in times of economic hardship cut back on physical education (mostly of a gym or drill variety) in elementary schools, leading to a patchwork of provision across the country. Many local authorities were also unwilling or unable to embark on capital projects to provide for facilities commonplace in private schools: gymnasia, swimming baths or playing fields.[49] But Section 53 of the 1944 Act put a specific duty on all Local Education Authorities (LEAs) to provide adequate facilities for recreation and physical training. By early 1947 all but 8 of over 150 LEAs had appointed organizers for physical education (PE), and the remainder reflected posts at that moment vacant rather than a lack of willingness to follow government guidelines.[50] Curriculum change emerged in the years that followed when it became widely agreed that older children in particular, those remaining up to age 15, required more varied types of physical activity than before. Within a generation PE programmes proliferated to include 30 or 40 different types of games and sports, and thousands of grammar and secondary modern schools became affiliated to the likes of the Schools Football Association and the Schools Athletics Association. Organized games, hitherto largely confined to the independent sector, were opened up to state school pupils, making for a type of provision of school-backed sport that was unusual in Europe and which widened the talent pool for elite performers in a range of sports.[51]

In addition to its key role in school sport, the Ministry of Education was also given powers to support the development of recreation in communities at large. In assuming responsibilities formerly held by the National Fitness Council under the 1937 Physical Training and Recreation Act, the Ministry became involved in a range of initiatives, for example funding 80 per cent of the salary of qualified national coaches in a range of sports. Before the war national coaches were a rarity, but after 1945 they came into fashion; many governing bodies of individual sports regarded them as useful in driving up standards and participation rates.[52] The organization of new coaching schemes was largely taken on by the Central Council of Physical Recreation (CCPR), which since its creation in the mid-1930s had been the major voluntary lobby group advocating the development of mass recreation. The CCPR had good links with the hundreds of governing bodies of individual sports, for whom it tried to provide a collective voice, and it worked closely with the Ministry (from which it received an annual grant) to implement some of the provisions of the 1944 Act. While specializing in coaching, it also regarded new facilities as imperative, and used some of its grant from government to help establish Britain's first national indoor centre for sport, at Bisham Abbey in 1946. Inevitably there was some frustration at the slow rate of progress. The CCPR's annual report in 1946 commented that in the aftermath of war many playing fields were still given over to cultivating food or were being used for urgent housing needs. Games equipment was scarce, and the claims of industry meant it unlikely for a while ahead that labour and materials would be diverted to the building of swimming baths, gyms and other 'desperately needed' recreational facilities. But the CCPR's determination that austerity should not dampen enthusiasm for sport was appreciated by the government, which increased its annual grant via the Ministry of Education budget from c.£54,000 in 1946–47 to £66,000 in 1950–51.[53]

Funding levels for sport across the board tended to fluctuate, in line with the state of the economy, across the Attlee years. In 1948 George Tomlinson, the education minister, reported in the House of Commons that the sum allocated in the ministry's budget for developing sport and allied activities under the Physical Training and Recreation Act was £350,000, more than double compared with the previous year. When combined with grants to the Youth Service, which also contributed to the recreational opportunities of those of post-school age, the funding level for sport – in the wake of a successful Olympics – exceeded that awarded to the Arts Council, established in 1945 to encourage activities such as drama, music, painting and sculpture.[54] After Labour was forced into devaluing the pound in 1949, however, a new phase of retrenchment ensued, in which LEAs were urged to reduce spending under Section 53 of the 1944 Act. Capital grants for new building projects in particular were severely hit in consequence.[55] Yet it remained the case that the role of the Ministry of Education in sport was in sharp contrast to what it was before the war, and that this enhancement of the state's involvement came with the blessing of senior Labour figures. In response to a parliamentary question in July 1950 about the need for developing post-school training in athletics and sport generally to improve Britain's international performance, Attlee replied that the Minister of Education already had appropriate powers, through the administration of the 1937 and 1944 Acts. To this end the Minister supported the CCPR, youth organizations and national governing bodies, and provided financial assistance for the provision of playing spaces and facilities. The first aim of policy, the Prime Minister said, was to develop 'to the full each person's physical potentialities and not the fostering of success at competitive games, though I would hope that this might follow'.[56]

Conclusion

Attlee's rebuttal of the need for a separate ministry of sport, in reply to the parliamentary question of July 1950 and at other times, should not be taken to imply – as it has done in some existing literature – lack of interest or even opposition to the development of sport. In the government's eyes, the Ministry of Education possessed sufficiently wide powers to influence sport and to consider requests from sporting organizations for financial assistance, and could do so without violating the voluntary ethos that still underpinned British sport. In weighing up Labour's record, it must be conceded that the government's role was at times purely reactive, and on occasion treated sport as a by-product of more important concerns such as that of raising production levels in industry. Ministerial responsibility for sport, moreover, remained highly fragmented, spread across several Whitehall departments. But to set against this, there was clearly a supportive attitude towards sport in the upper reaches of the government, evidenced by the determination to make a success of the London Olympics despite the acute financial hardships of the day as well as by the much enhanced role of the Education department in stimulating sporting activity in schools and the communities they served. If rambling comes within the remit of a broad definition of sport, then the 1949 National Parks Acts also stands out from the Attlee years as a landmark piece of legislation, bringing long-term and lasting advances in the area of outdoor physical recreation.

Labour's record must be seen in a context where there were compelling reasons why the state might continue to have minimal involvement in sport, as was the case before 1939. Sport could not, for example, compare with the great themes of economic recovery and welfare which preoccupied and ultimately exhausted the Labour administration. After his parliamentary majority almost disappeared at the general election in 1950, Attlee struggled on as Prime Minister until he was defeated in a further election in October 1951, paving the way for Churchill to return to power to form his only peace-time administration. Sport did not feature at all in the election manifestos of the main parties in 1950 and 1951. This invisibility as an election issue reflected the absence of any systematic pressure either from sports administrators, who wished to run their own affairs, or from within parliament (apart from an occasional backbencher) to change the traditionally detached relationship between sport and the state. The widely held view in the late 1940s was that central direction of sport smacked of totalitarianism, whether of the Nazi or – increasingly as the Cold War got under way – the Soviet variety. Against this backdrop, it would be going too far to quarrel with Holt and Mason's verdict that 'the post-war Labour government did not have a sports policy'.[57] But the absence of a single, identifiable 'sports policy' (a state of affairs that remained the case, as we shall see, until the 1960s) should not disguise what was a creditable stance on sport, notably in relation to the Olympics, school sport and outdoor recreation. In view of the prevailing attitudes and circumstances of the day, the surprise was that Attlee and his ministers did so much in the field of sport, not that they did so little.

2 Britain in the World of Sport, 1951–59

Introduction

Britain in the 1950s is often associated with a sense of national well-being, in which sporting achievement played a key role. In the words of the election expert David Butler, writing in the mid-1950s, 'Everest had been conquered, an Englishman [Roger Bannister] had been the first to run the four-minute mile, and England had regained, and then held, the Ashes'.[1] As wartime rationing finally came to an end, the stirrings of an 'affluent society' – with many enjoying the benefits of consumerism for the first time – helped to underpin a period of Conservative domination of politics, reflected in three consecutive general election victories, each more emphatic than the previous one. Winston Churchill secured a narrow win by 17 seats in 1951, and improving world trade conditions meant he could retire and hand over to Anthony Eden in 1955 confident of electoral success; the government's majority duly increased to 59 seats. Eden's premiership proved short-lived, and he left office under a cloud early in 1957 after his handling of the Suez Crisis, but his successor Harold Macmillan engineered a renewed consumer boom. Voters were sufficiently persuaded by Macmillan's 'never had it so good' message that the Tories triumphed with a resounding majority of 100 seats at the 1959 election.

On closer inspection, the era of Conservative ascendancy after 1951 was more troubled for governments of the day than appears the case with hindsight. Far from being a decade of uninterrupted improvement, there were intermittent periods of economic stagnation, and with Labour still polling over 40 per cent of votes cast even in defeat, an easy electoral supremacy could not be taken for granted. In reality, Conservative leaders struggled for much of the time to synchronize the electoral and economic cycles and to reconcile the wishes of disparate groups of voters: natural middle-class supporters looking for tax cuts and reduced state spending, and working-class sympathizers reluctant to see any threat to full employment or welfare services such as the National Health Service (NHS). With much to occupy their attention, any prospect that Conservative ministers might build upon the interest in sport shown by their Labour predecessors soon receded. The 1950s was to witness a steady rise of concern about the condition of sporting facilities in Britain. At grass-roots level, it became fashionable to claim that better opportunities for recreation were required in an age where workers had more time than ever before to devote to leisure. On the international stage, criticism intensified (though was far from new) that British teams were falling behind in major sports such as football, tennis and athletics. But from whatever source concern emanated – whether it was lobby groups, MPs, sections of the press or academics, such as those who produced an influential booklet called *Britain in the World of Sport* – Conservative leaders remained unmoved. For Churchill, Eden and Macmillan, none of whom had any great regard for sport, it was business as usual: in line with pre-1939 thinking, they saw no need for anything more than minimal state involvement with the nation's sporting pastimes.

Hopes Deferred, 1951–55: Resisting Lobby Groups and Parliamentary Pressure

There was little sense of urgency in the Churchill government's approach to sport after 1951. Faced with inheriting the economic difficulties of the previous administration, tough cutbacks in public spending were quickly introduced by the Conservatives. With the prospect of austerity intensifying rather than disappearing (as was promised at the election), Churchill's friend Brendan Bracken wrote to Lord Beaverbrook that the Treasury was 'preparing to slaughter the do-gooders & easy spenders in Government service'.[2] The prevailing atmosphere of economic hardship during the first eighteen months of Churchill's administration made life difficult for the major pressure groups lobbying on behalf of sporting interests. In his history of the Central Council of Physical Recreation (CCPR), of which he was Secretary for many years, Justin Evans reflected on a period of mixed fortunes. On the one hand the CCPR, he wrote, had become 'an established and well-accepted

body', trusted by government to continue developing its programme of national and regional training courses and of seeking
to promote the benefits of recreation to the public at large. But,
on the other hand, Evans noted, the early 1950s were 'a time of
great national economy', and many hopes of progress 'had to be
deferred'. The CCPR made little headway, for example, in pressing
for the removal or at least the reduction of purchase tax on sports
equipment, which the Council saw as 'a tax on the instruments of
fitness'. The CCPR's own grants from the government remained
static from 1951 to 1954, with a modest improvement only in the
final year of the parliament, ahead of a general election.[3]

The Ministry of Education was also on the defensive in the early
1950s over its responsibilities under the 1937 Physical Training and
Recreation Act and the 1944 Education Act. The scale of the paral-
ysis was made clear in the figures contained in an internal Ministry
memorandum of 1953. These showed that under Labour total
spending under the relevant headings of the two Acts rose from
£386,672 in the financial year 1947–48 to £631,786 in 1950–51. But
after the Conservatives came to power expenditure fell, in three
successive years, to £536,274 in 1951–52, £420,497 in 1952–53 and
£309,434 in 1953–54.[4] One of the areas affected by this reduction
was the provision of new playing fields, a development that caused
particular concern for the lobby group the National Playing Fields
Association (NPFA). Established as a voluntary fund-raising body
in the 1920s (its role is discussed further in Chapter 10), the NPFA
sent a deputation to the Ministry of Education in 1952 but was sent
away without receiving any reassurances. In February 1954, a civil
servant advised Florence Horsbrugh, the Education Minister, that
it would be 'politic' to meet again with the NPFA to explain the
impossibility of resuming government grants to support the provision of new play areas. The Association was, the official noted, 'a
splendid example of voluntary effort which is so much part of the
British way of life'. Even so, at a time when Ministry expenditure
was directed towards dealing with greatly increased numbers of
children in schools following the raising of the leaving age and the
provision of 'all-age' secondary schools, the Minister should not
'follow the opposition's example and give pledges which she cannot be sure of honouring'. Horsbrugh duly took a conciliatory but
firm line when she met the NPFA.[5] Although she told the NPFA
deputation that she hoped restrictions might be removed soon, in

July 1954 she was still responding to parliamentary questions by saying she was unable to set a date for doing so.[6]

Until September 1953, nearly two years after Churchill returned to power, the Ministry of Education was not deemed sufficiently important (unlike in the Attlee era) to command a seat at the Cabinet table. This meant that, even if she had been so inclined, Florence Horsbrugh was unable to take up with senior colleagues in the manner that Bevin and Noel-Baker had the claims of the third long-established lobby group, the British Olympic Association (BOA), whose efforts were focused on preparing and financing a British team to attend the Helsinki Olympics in 1952. When asked in the House of Commons if she would consider making a contribution towards the expenses of the British team, the Minister's reply was unequivocal: 'No such contributions have been made in the past, and I cannot give any encouragement to the suggestion that a different policy should be adopted on this occasion.'[7] In approaching the Olympics, the Conservative administrations of Churchill and his successors reverted to the position adopted by the pre-war governments, namely that unless international sport raised issues pertaining to British interests overseas there was no cause for Cabinet attention or interference. This stance was to come under increasing pressure as time passed, in part because of a growing recognition that the detachment of the British government was becoming a minority practice among those who sent teams to the Olympics. A survey conducted by the Belgian Olympic Committee in 1952 found that of the 40 nations that replied to the survey, 13 provided direct government grants for Olympic purposes; 11 relied on a mixture of government grants and public appeals; 10 used various mixes of grants, lotteries and public appeals; and just 6 – including Britain – relied on fund-raising appeals only. For the foreseeable future the BOA had to make do without government assistance, even though its costs were rising inexorably; the 1956 Games were scheduled for Melbourne, requiring a huge effort to finance a team to travel and stay in Australia.[8]

In addition to casting around for fresh ways of finding funds for travel and subsistence costs, the BOA felt compelled to give attention to the issue of whether more could be done to improve standards among British athletes competing on the world stage. At the Helsinki Games Britain won only one gold medal, in the equestrian team competition, and its tally of eleven medals in total was the lowest in any of the modern Olympics since 1896. The correspondent of the *Times* reflected that Britain's effort 'cannot escape some odious comparisons, unfair or otherwise'.[9] In the light of what the writer called an 'extraordinary leap upwards in the standard of achievement all round', it was reasonable to conclude that the British team was the strongest ever sent to an Olympics. But this charitable view was not shared by all sections of the press. Sarcastic tabloid headlines jibed that Britain's prowess was dependent on a horse. As Commandant of the British team, Philip Noel-Baker, now on the opposition benches as a Labour MP, argued that based on London 1948 standards the British men would have come home with twelve gold medals in 1952. In a letter to the *Times*, Noel-Baker could not resist pointing towards a shortage of facilities that many in the sporting world believed was hampering British performers:

> We are still suffering in athletics from some serious disadvantages. We are disastrously short of tracks: America has, perhaps 100 tracks for every one that we possess; and they have indoor facilities as well. We have too few coaches and their status still leaves something to be desired.[10]

The fight for greater resources for sport was at the heart of a new initiative launched by Noel-Baker in 1952, the Parliamentary Sports Committee (PSC). With the Conservatives returned to power, Noel-Baker believed the best way to maintain the sense of momentum developed in the Attlee years was to work through an all-party body; this he felt might have more credibility in ministerial eyes than purely opposition-inspired ventures. Soon after the 1951 election he wrote to various interested MPs to test the waters.[11] Meeting for the first time in March 1952, the initial concern of the new group was to assist the BOA with fund-raising for the 1952 British Olympic team. With a view to providing a link in any discussions between the Association and government departments, the Secretary of the PSC, Sandy Duncan, was not a parliamentarian but a prominent member of the BOA.[12] Before long the PSC developed a wider focus than simply the Olympics. It drew membership from both the Commons and the House of Lords and was prepared to raise specific legislative issues relating to sport as well as initiating discussion on more general matters such as the financing of sport. Although it only tended to convene once or twice a year, with small numbers of MPs and peers in attendance (often less than ten), the emergence of the PSC marked a significant moment in the evolving relationship between sport and politics. Noel-Baker persuaded a Conservative MP, Wavell Wakefield, a former England rugby union international and President of the English Rugby Football Union, to become vice chairman of the PSC. As a result it developed into a genuinely cross-party vehicle, one that for the first time was in a position to consistently highlight in parliament both the broad and the particular concerns of the sporting community.

In testing economic conditions, the PSC proved at times more effective at influencing events than more established groups like the BOA and NPFA. This was the case particularly in relation to entertainment duty, a tax first introduced to boost government revenue during the First World War, and one long resented not only in the world of sport but also in other affected spheres such as theatre and cinema. In the 1952 budget the Chancellor of the Exchequer, R.A. Butler, announced a new uniform entertainment duty on gate receipts, a measure which particularly hit those sports like football, cricket and horse racing with a large spectator base. The PSC took up the cudgels against what Noel-Baker called the 'pernicious effects of the entertainment duty', and amidst the first signs of an economic upturn in 1953 the Chancellor agreed to exempt cricket and all amateur sport organized by non-profit making organizations.[13] The wisdom of working through cross-party channels was reflected in Noel-Baker's later admission that he owed a debt to Hubert Ashton, a Conservative MP, former Oxford triple blue and an active member of the PSC in its early days. Ashton was Parliamentary Private Secretary to the Chancellor, and so well-placed to persuade Butler that cricket should be treated separately.[14] Butler's assertion that cricket 'occupies a special place' in English affections met with resistance, however, on the Labour backbenches. Concerned that working men were being discriminated against, Labour MPs put forward an amendment to the Finance Bill, aimed at extending the abolition of entertainment tax to include football. 'Surely it would be better', one MP claimed, 'to encourage the national game of football rather than to build up cricket, which merely gives a sun tan and provides a social oasis ... for 1s 6d. or 2s'. Tory loyalists retorted that no proposals for replacing the revenue lost if football was exempted were forthcoming, and voted on party lines to ensure the defeat of the amendment.[15]

Although the economic outlook was far brighter in the second half of Churchill's administration than in the first, sport barely registered on the government's list of priorities. The existence of the PSC did allow for a greater airing of sporting issues in parliament than ever before, especially against a backcloth of concern about British failures on the international stage. In spite of Roger Bannister's breaking of the four-minute mile barrier in athletics, this individual achievement was set against the collectively poor showing at the Helsinki Olympics and the famous 6–3 win by Hungary at Wembley in 1953, a first ever home defeat for England in international football. In July 1954 the Labour MP for Stoke-on-Trent South, Ellis Smith, a member of the PSC, opened a two-hour Commons' debate on facilities for sport by referring to the 'severe shocks' of recent times, including the paucity of medals at the Olympics and the prowess of Hungary at football. This prompted an intervention from the Deputy Speaker of the House, presiding over the debate, who said he was unable to see how the Ministry of Education could be held responsible for the plight of British football. Ellis Smith retorted: 'I believe we can produce many more men like Roger Bannister ... and Stanley Matthews provided that we modernise our methods and profit by recent experience, that we organise to achieve our objectives and the Ministry of Education provides more financial support.' In the remainder of his speech Ellis Smith alluded to the wider benefits of sport, notably fitness for work and improved health, and argued that with the government taking several million pounds out of sport annually from various taxes, the Ministry's small and declining contribution to the improvement of facilities was 'disgraceful', even 'scandalous'.[16]

The short debate of July 1954 marked the start of what was to be a growing trend: parliamentary discussion of general sporting themes in a way that had not been evident before the war or even in the late 1940s. In October Churchill made a brief public reference to sport: his only contribution on the subject throughout the parliament. When asked by the Labour MP for Dartford, Norman Dodds (also a member of the PSC), whether he would consider appointing a Minister of Physical Education, Churchill's reply – though longer than his predecessor Attlee's when asked a similar question – was similar in tone and content: 'It is the declared policy of Her Majesty's Government to encourage the development of sport and physical fitness. I do not think, however, that the appointment of an additional Minister, presumably with a Department, is either necessary or desirable.'[17] A week later Dodds returned to the issue in an adjournment debate, saying he had at least raised the profile of sport, judging by the reaction to his question. Press critics, he said, accused him of favouring the worst type of state centralism, though the MP insisted in response that he had in mind not Communist regimes but western democracies where large sums of money were being diverted from central resources. In West Germany, Dodds noted, new facilities were being built with funds from the state-controlled football pools. The tendency to make comparisons with rival nations was becoming a staple feature in parliamentary discussion of sport, though it did not trouble Dennis Vosper, the junior Education Minister who replied on behalf of the government. Vosper (not known for his sporting credentials, though as one journalist quipped he was regarded as a 'serious gardener') played with a straight bat: as this subject had been tackled in the July debate, he said, 'there is not a great deal of fresh ground to be covered'. He made no mention of Britain's record compared with overseas rivals and he proceeded to list the various ways in which the Ministry of Education encouraged physical activity without promising any further resources.[18]

For a brief moment in the spring of 1955 the possibility of a more radical departure in the government's approach to sport hung in the air. At a meeting of the PSC in March, the Labour MP for Coventry South, Elaine Burton, a former teacher and county hockey player, proposed that ministers should be pressed to provide more direct financial aid to sport. Her reasoning was partly based on the theme that was becoming more commonplace in political discourse: facilities in Britain, she claimed, 'were lagging far behind those in many other countries in the world'. She also felt it 'wrong in principle' that teams for the Olympics had to be financed purely by public appeal, when this was out of step with practice elsewhere. In discussion PSC secretary Sandy Duncan said governing bodies did not want a Ministry of Sport, but might welcome something like a 'British Sports Council', receiving and distributing grants on the same lines as the Arts Council or the University Grants Committee. This was the first serious reference to an idea that was to loom larger in years to come, though was to take a decade to come to fruition. Hubert Ashton, the Tory MP with links to the Treasury, responded to the contributions of Burton and Duncan by asking for a memorandum to be drawn up, showing the sort of annual sums that might be required; this, Ashton said, could then be formally presented to the Chancellor of the Exchequer by the PSC.[19] But nothing came of this bold initiative. Within weeks Churchill announced his retirement, and his successor Anthony Eden decided the best way of securing his position was to call for an early general election. As the parties suddenly geared up for electioneering, the prospect of a consensual way forward for sport through the good offices of the PSC was lost.

The election of May 1955 witnessed for the first time formal references to physical recreation in the manifestos of the major parties. These references were fleeting, however, and never ventured onto the territory of direct government aid. The Conservative manifesto confined itself to a single sentence, placed under the 'Education' heading (in line with departmental responsibility for sport and recreation): 'Grants will continue to be given for playing fields, community centres and youth clubs'.[20] Labour's counterpart included two sentences: 'We shall provide more playing fields. We shall abolish the [entertainment] tax on sport and the living theatre'.[21] Noel-Baker tried to draw attention to this part of Labour's policy by attacking the Tory record in an election speech. 'There is no social equality more glaring', he said, 'than that in the facilities for games and physical education for poor boys in our towns and villages and for richer boys at Eton, Harrow and elsewhere.' As for the Chancellor, Noel-Baker claimed, he did not 'want to be the man who killed first-class County Cricket', but entertainment tax still applied to other sports and was having a crippling effect. 'Surely it will be a good investment to abolish the tax on sport, to provide more playing fields, and to build up the standards of our physical training. This is one more powerful reason for voting Labour.'[22] The electorate was not convinced. In practice sport hardly registered among voters, mostly concerned to see the upturn in the economy sustained. In the wake of a spring budget in which income tax was sharply cut, Eden easily won the election, exploiting divisions in the senior ranks of the Labour party. The outcome was summed up by the *New Statesman*: 'the nation felt comfortably satisfied and in no mood for a change'.[23]

The 1955 Parliament: From Eden to Macmillan

In several respects the pattern of the early 1950s was repeated in the 1955 parliament. The optimism surrounding Eden's election victory quickly disappeared, and by the autumn a deteriorating balance of payments led to a renewed sense of economic strain. Although Eden was replaced as Prime Minister by Harold Macmillan in January 1957, it was only in the second half of the parliament that living standards rose and government fortunes revived. 'Supermac', as he became known, became associated with a wave of rising affluence, bringing consumer goods such as television sets and washing machines into wider circulation than ever before. Commentators increasingly reflected that while recreational opportunities were being widened by private clubs, with new sports like badminton rising in popularity, there was much scope to expand public provision to cater for the growing leisure time available to the majority; such provision was deemed particularly important in alleviating growing concern about 'juvenile delinquency', socially unacceptable behaviour among groups of youths such as 'teddy boys'. But throughout the 1955 parliament, and especially during the economic downturn of 1956–57, the Conservative approach to sport remained resolutely in the mould that characterized Churchill's premiership. With no notable interest in sport among senior ministers, any change of direction looked unlikely. The major lobby groups, the CCPR, NPFA and BOA, continued with their core activities, largely in isolation from each other, and took comfort from whatever signs could be detected of a more progressive government stance, as when it was agreed to eliminate any remaining entertainment tax on sport in 1957.

Another feature of the landscape that remained familiar from the early 1950s was an occasional stinging critique of the government's approach in the House of Commons. In April 1956 Elaine Burton regretted that the Chancellor's budget made no mention of recreation, and she used her speech in the budget debate to expand on themes raised at the PSC meeting before the 1955 election. Her speech was important for looking to tie together the two dimensions – international and domestic – that motivated those pushing for greater state intervention. Governments should be alive, she claimed, to the need to support those amateur sports men and women who were ambassadors for Britain overseas; they were not paid for their endeavours and made great sacrifices to reach the pinnacle of their sport. If Britain no longer wished to be 'outclassed' at events like the Olympics, then rather than always relying on the BOA the Treasury should seriously consider funding for the Olympic team, as was the case elsewhere. The Italian Olympic Committee, she noted, received an income of £2 million per annum from receipts from football pools. 'Yet we still go round, cap in hand, begging for money to send our teams to every international event that comes about. That is defeatist, out of date and out of touch with public opinion.' At the same time Burton called for a government grant directed at improved facilities – more playing fields, running tracks, floodlighting and so on – that were 'not luxuries' but 'essential today as much for fitness and leisure as they are for the Olympic Games'. Another notable element in the speech was that, for the first time in open debate (rather than behind the scenes at the PSC), the call was made for an innovative way of delivering improvements to sport. It seems to 'some of us', Burton concluded, that it might be useful to consider 'the formation of a British sports council', or some type of similar body, to administer the annual grant provided by government.[24]

Elaine Burton was a vociferous campaigner for ideas which went beyond Labour's 1955 manifesto promises. But the chances of making headway with such an agenda in the Eden–Macmillan era were remote. Indeed in some respects the prospects of the government responding to burgeoning pressure to adopt a more proactive stance on sport were slimmer than before 1955. As we have seen, when the Parliamentary Sports Committee functioned as a genuine cross-party body it met with some success; Tory members were prepared to use their contacts to influence ministers. But after the 1955 election Philip Noel-Baker suffered from a succession of illnesses which kept him in hospital for lengthy spells, and in his absence no meeting of the PSC was convened for about three years. This affected the dynamic of how the parties approached sport. In January 1957 Noel-Baker wrote in frustrated vein to Sandy Duncan, PSC Secretary, to say it looked increasingly difficult to 'get more money for sport out of the government' on an all-party basis. Noel-Baker claimed that Hugh Gaitskell, Attlee's successor as Labour leader, was sympathetic towards considerably increased funding. 'But the present Government, with its deflationary policies and its search for economies, is, I am afraid, most

unlikely to give a farthing.' Noel-Baker, knowing he was not able
to get to Westminster frequently during his illnesses, hoped that
Wavell Wakefield might take over the chairmanship of the PSC;
this would allow for a renewed 'all-party push'. Unless Tories such
as Wakefield could be persuaded to 'take the lead', he concluded,
sport would suffer by being seen as a matter of party contention.[25]

In the event Wakefield never assumed the leadership of the PSC,
and Noel-Baker returned to the helm when his health improved
in 1958. By that stage a political stalemate on sporting issues had
been in place for the best part of the 1955 parliament. Without the
good offices of the PSC to lobby behind the scenes, ideas such as
those aired by Elaine Burton – who wrote in the *Daily Herald* that
lack of funding was 'starving and stifling British sport'[26] – were dismissed by ministers as the partisan and potentially expensive musings of the Labour opposition. Sport was now becoming a bone of
political contention in a manner alien to earlier periods. In reply
to the frequently asked question in the Commons about the desirability of appointing a single minister with responsibility for sport,
junior Education Minister Edward Boyle replied in the negative in
April 1957 and sought to make light of recreation as a suitable topic
for parliamentary debate. 'Having taken the duty off sport', Boyle
quipped, 'the Government do not consider it necessary to impose
a Minister on it'. Gaitskell from Labour's front bench asked the
minister to bear in mind that 'there is a strong case for assisting
sport and that his own Department could do a great deal more in
that direction'. To this Boyle responded with the standard official
line: it was policy of the Ministry to foster physical education in
schools and local authorities used their powers under Section 53
of the 1944 Act to do so.[27]

With party divisions blocking any way forward in parliament,
and key lobby groups ploughing their own furrows, any fresh
impetus for a change in direction for sport would have come from
elsewhere. In 1956 a tiny spark came from within academia, in the
form of the publication of a slim, 70-page booklet written by seven
members of the Physical Education department at Birmingham
University, entitled *Britain in the World of Sport*. With experience
of representing England or Great Britain in various sports, and of
studying the development of sport in several countries, the authors
focused, as the subtitle denoted, on 'an examination of the factors involved in participation in competitive international sport',

though there were also reflections on domestic British issues such as the level of facilities and financing. As Justin Evans of the CCPR observed, this was to be 'a short pamphlet but one of outstanding importance'.[28]

One of the reasons for the influence of *Britain in the World of Sport* was that it provided a calm, generally dispassionate, summary of sporting developments past and present. The early part of the booklet sought to test the idea that Britain was in decline on the world sporting stage. In this context, the authors noted that if there was a golden age of British sporting pre-eminence, it was short-lived. In tennis, for example, Wimbledon was dominated in the early years by English and Irish players, but after 1909 there was no British success in the men's singles for another 25 years. National defeats in sport were not the only regular occurrences in the past; so too were outbreaks of despondency occasioned by such defeats. When Britain won only 9 gold medals at the 1912 Stockholm Olympics, in contrast to 44 taken four years earlier, the Duke of Somerset, Chairman of the BOA, lamented 'our power is on the wane'. The association between international sport and wider national standing was therefore already evident before the First World War. In terms of measuring British sporting performance of the 1950s with that of earlier times, the authors believed this was subjective in many cases and made more difficult by technological developments or rule changes. But in some instances, such as track and field athletics, the measuring tape and stopwatch allowed for firm comparisons, and the record pointed to continuous progress during the twentieth century. Fourteen of eighteen native English track and field records in 1955 had been set since 1945, ten of these in 1954 and 1955 alone. On this basis British standards had risen steadily; the problem was that many other nations had begun paying more serious attention to sport than half-a-century earlier, so making it difficult to retain pre-eminence. The conclusion was measured: 'We have not gone to the dogs. We are competing in a vastly more crowded field.... Relative to our population, we do not do too badly; relative to our past we do.'[29]

Set against this international backdrop, the remainder of the booklet aimed to identify the characteristic features of British sport, and to contrast these with what was found overseas. In general, of course, Britain stood at one end of the spectrum where sport was organized piecemeal by voluntary bodies, largely free

to make their own decisions, rather than at the opposite extreme
where sport was integrated within the political system and was an
instrument of government policy, as in eastern block Communist
regimes. This, the writers claimed, needed to be borne in mind
when looking at the facilities available in Britain. The shortage
of playing fields, it was argued, had in some respects been exaggerated by the NPFA, which concentrated on publicly-provided
ventures and mostly ignored the thousands of clubs up and down
the country endowed with private facilities. The booklet did
though point to the 'real inadequacy' in the case of athletics. In
England and Wales there were 47 public and 83 private tracks in
1954, compared with 800 in Sweden and 500 in Finland; and both
Scandinavian nations had markedly smaller populations than
Britain. If outdoor facilities were 'just adequate', the same was not
true of indoor facilities. The spread of sports such as basketball
was being held back in Britain by a lack of indoor halls, which also
prevented much needed winter training for elite athletes. While
some towns and cities were well-served by public swimming baths,
many rural areas had no such facilities. West Germany had built
47 public baths (with 200 more planned) since the war; England
had built one. A similar pattern applied in relation to coaching.
Progress had been made in recent years, especially as a result of
the Ministry of Education's willingness to provide financial support
to national coaches appointed by the governing bodies, but there
remained something of a residual antagonism towards coaching
in Britain.[30]

Moving on to issues of finance, *Britain in the World of Sport* conceded that it was difficult to find precise and accurate figures.
The state certainly received a considerable income from sport.
Pool betting duty, for example, was now worth some £30 million
per annum, primarily from football pools but also from greyhound racing. In some other countries, it was noted, state-run
pools were used to devote sums directly to sport, but the British
tradition was that taxes raised went into general revenue. This
was one of the reasons it was difficult to calculate how much was
spent on sport. The government contributed directly, of course,
via the Ministry of Education grants for the training of coaches,
and also through grants for the capital cost of facilities under the
1937 legislation. Local Education Authorities, subject to ministerial approval, had the power under the 1944 Act to give financial

assistance towards the provision, maintenance and management of recreation facilities for children and those in further education, and spent an estimated sum of £4 million on such facilities in England and Wales during 1953–54. Local authorities also made important provision in other ways. The authors noted, drawing on figures for Birmingham, that the City Council in 1954–55 spent a net sum of over £200,000 on running their swimming baths and nearly £650,000 on parks, recreation grounds and golf courses. 'The Government takes a great deal of money from sporting activities but puts back directly only a very small sum', the booklet concluded: 'It does, however, support physical activities indirectly, by payments to Local Authorities and in other ways.'[31]

It was only in the final chapter that the detached, academic tone of *Britain in the World of Sport* gave way to a more controversial discussion of whether an 'uncoordinated' approach best served the interests of competing in international sport. It was no secret that opinion on this was divided. Some believed parallels with the United States (where private provision for sport was strong) indicated that a mix of financial approaches should be no hindrance to success, while others sought greater coordination and felt the government 'should put more back into sport'. The view of the Birmingham writers was that without greater central coordination, Britain might muddle through in international sport, but the situation would grow worse and teams such as those taking part in the Olympics would not be representative of the nation as a whole; competing at the highest levels required both time and money, and many from modest backgrounds were in effect debarred from competing because amateur rules prohibited anything beyond the barest financial support. It followed that if the 'extraordinary untidiness' of British sport was to be remedied, then some form of national authority was required, and here the basic choice appeared to be between a representative sports committee, an 'Advisory Council' instituted by the sporting bodies themselves, on Swedish or American lines, or 'a governmental or ministerial organisation on Russian lines'. The authors were in no doubt as to their own preference: 'Sport needs a lead which would best come from sport itself. We hope, most earnestly, that someone or some group will take the initiative and invite all sports organisations to take part in deliberations designed to establish a sports advisory or governing council.'[32] It was this closing salvo which, in a

roundabout way, was to have huge significance for the development of sport in Britain in the years to come.

Towards the 1959 Election

Britain in the World of Sport made little immediate impact on politicians. Its injunction, however, for 'someone or some group' to take
the initiative did act as a trigger for action. The Birmingham study
attracted wide interest in the sporting world, and following favourable publicity in the journal *Physical Recreation* a resolution was
proposed at a CCPR conference in January 1957, calling on the
Council's executive committee to respond to the challenge posed
in the conclusion to the pamphlet. The resolution was carried
and before long the CCPR was committed to referring the whole
subject of the development of physical recreation to an impartial
body, 'qualified to hear evidence and reach conclusions'.[33] By the
autumn of 1957 a new committee was in place with a broad remit:
'To examine the factors affecting the development of games, sports
and outdoor activities in the United Kingdom and to make recommendations to the Central Council of Physical Recreation as to any
practical measures which should be taken by statutory or voluntary
bodies in order that these activities may play their full part in promoting the general welfare of the community.'[34] The committee
was chaired by Sir John Wolfenden, who was chosen on the basis
of his distinguished record in public service. Wolfenden had been
a classics scholar and hockey blue at Oxford before becoming a
public school headmaster. He accepted the CCPR's invitation once
he was free from commitments associated with the Home Office-
sponsored report bearing his name on Homosexual Offences and
Prostitution, published in September 1957. Although the highly
influential 'Wolfenden Report on Sport' was not to see the light of
day until three years later, the committee's work was increasingly
the focal point for discussion from 1958 onwards.

One reason why the Wolfenden committee carried weight was
that its membership was drawn not from partisan party ranks
but from the 'great and the good' of the British establishment.
Wolfenden was known, Justin Evans wrote, as a man of 'unvarying
good humour', possessing an 'unequalled skill both as Chairman
of a meeting and as a master of lucid exposition and argument'.
Several other members of the committee shared Wolfenden's

distinction of having represented Oxford sporting teams in their youth: Dr Gerald Ellison, the Bishop of Chester; Jack Longland, Director of Education for Derbyshire; Sir Arthur Porritt, a surgeon and member of the International Olympic Committee; and the journalist Tony Pawson. Insider knowledge of the workings of government was provided by Sir Godfrey Ince, a former Permanent Secretary at the Ministry of Labour (and one time captain of the London University football team). In addition, specialism in physical education at school and university level came courtesy of Mrs Mabel Allen, a former inspector of schools, Miss Betty Clarke, headmistress of Benenden independent school and David Munrow, Director of the Physical Education (PE) department at Birmingham University and one of the chief influences on *Britain in the World of Sport*. Justin Evans, who was seconded from his role at the CCPR to act as secretary, noted that Sir John's group not only had the virtue of being independent, but also brought wide experience and knowledge to the issues under consideration.[35]

The careful working methods of the Wolfenden committee also served to enhance its credibility. The committee held its first meeting in London in January 1958, and in the two years that followed took oral and written evidence from hundreds of individuals and organizations, including representatives of all the major sports governing bodies. Political opinion was also deemed important: within months Sir John contacted Noel-Baker to request assistance from the Parliamentary Sports Committee. In December 1958 Wolfenden visited the PSC, meeting for only the second time during the 1955 parliament. He began by describing his work as that of 'a private and independent Inquiry', set up by CCPR, though one which he hoped would 'eventually reach the House of Commons'. Ahead of the meeting he wrote to Noel-Baker that 'we are not yet very near to finding the answers', though he revealed to the PSC that certain themes were recurring in proceedings.[36] The idea of a 'National Sports Council' was being widely mooted, to distribute funds for improved facilities and international competition, and to be run on similar lines to the Arts Council. The terms of reference and principles for distributing funds would need to be very carefully considered, Wolfenden added, as would the issue of whether a Sports Council would report to the Ministry of Education or the Treasury. Sir John's presence gave stalwarts of the PSC an opportunity to grind their particular axes. Elaine Burton repeated her demands for urgent government financial aid; from the Conservative angle Wavell Wakefield spoke of the need to learn from the operation of grant-giving bodies in other countries.[37] One outcome of the meeting was an agreement to consult parliamentary opinion more widely. A letter was subsequently sent to all MPs and leading peers inviting them to inform the Wolfenden committee of their views on questions such as the extent, if any, to which sport should be financed from public funds; an appeal that resulted in almost a hundred responses.[38]

While Sir John's work appeared to be gaining momentum, and was greeted with enthusiasm in many quarters associated with sport, the government's attitude was more reserved. An internal memorandum written by E. B. H. Baker, an Assistant Secretary at the Ministry of Education responsible for administering grants to sports bodies, described a polite but cool meeting with Wolfenden's committee in December 1958. Baker was invited to explain the statutory basis of the government's powers under the 1937 and 1944 Acts and gave figures for recurring grants made to voluntary bodies. 'It was clear', Baker believed, 'that the Committee have received ... a good deal of evidence claiming that the Government is not providing enough money for the provision of sporting facilities, or for coaching schemes or for the representation of the United Kingdom in international sporting events'. Some questioners, the memo recorded, suggested that the 1937 Act should be taken up more vigorously, and others felt that such matters might more properly be the concern of the Treasury than the Ministry of Education.[39] The implication of this tense encounter was that the Ministry was adopting a low-key approach to Wolfenden, neither obstructing the committee's work nor assisting it in any significant way. The absence of high-level representation was something that struck Justin Evans, who later wrote that 'no-one could be found to speak to the Committee with any real authority about the Ministry's policy'. Although the three representatives at the meeting, Baker and two Staff Inspectors of PE, showed 'no lack of conviction', their evidence 'could not conceal the fact that they had to work within severe financial restrictions and the development of sport was not high among the Ministry's priorities'.[40]

The appointment of the Wolfenden committee did not therefore herald a major shift in Conservative attitudes towards sport. The extent to which Sir John's work coloured discussion as a general election came closer was indicated when a short 1959 publication in the name of the study group the Conservative Political Centre, *The Challenge of Leisure*, proposed the use of government grants for a range of purposes: to facilitate the work of the CCPR (now at c.£130,000 per year and in need of raising further); towards coaching schemes; towards costs of sending representative national teams to events such as Olympics; and to local authorities and voluntary bodies, including the NPFA, for the development of facilities. The study group, which included the likes of Hubert Ashton, even called for the establishment of an independent 'Sports Council of Great Britain', operating under the purview of the Treasury and distributing a budget for all the purposes described that might grow towards £5 million annually.[41] But the views expressed by the Conservative Political Centre were a long way from becoming official party policy. In a rare parliamentary intervention on sport in November 1958, Harold Macmillan rejected a call from Labour's Ellis Smith to appoint a 'National Sports Council', saying he 'did not think that this would be appropriate'.[42] Government policy, in short, remained much as it had been throughout the 1955 parliament, content to confine itself to fulfilling but not significantly expanding upon statutory requirements. In the party's manifesto at the 1959 election, sport merited (as in 1955) only a single and imprecise sentence: measures would be taken to encourage 'more playing fields and better facilities for sport'.[43]

Labour's formal position was more advanced. As part of a revision of its 1955 stance, Noel-Baker submitted a confidential paper in the spring of 1959 outlining three reasons why a 'forward-looking British government' should make large-scale provision for physical recreation. These were the strong likelihood of increased leisure time for the generation ahead; the recognition of the right of all people, not just the wealthy, to participate in sport when they desired; and the contribution physical recreation made to remedying social evils such as hooliganism and juvenile delinquency.[44] Noel-Baker's views heavily influenced the relevant sections of the Labour party booklet *Leisure for Living*, the publication of which was delayed by a printers' strike until the autumn of 1959 (after the Conservative Political Centre's equivalent). This document more than any previous pronouncement fleshed out the aims and functions of a proposed 'Sports Council of Great Britain, analogous to the Arts Council'. This would be appointed by the Minister of Education and be accountable to Parliament through him or her; membership would include representatives of various forms of sport and 'laymen' interested but not identified with particular sports. The Council's role would be to cooperate with national sporting organizations in providing required facilities and coaching; to ensure fuller British participation in international events; and 'take such action as will raise the standard of games and athletics throughout the country'. A Labour government, it was asserted, would make available not less than £5 million to the Council for capital expenditure and administrative expenses, and 'thereafter such yearly sums as will enable it to do its job adequately'. While local authorities would still have direct access to Whitehall funds for their own initiatives (meaning that total spending on sport would be substantially higher than £5 million), it was imperative to act decisively. 'A change of outlook at the centre, expressed in a generous approach by the State, can bring new enjoyment and new health to millions of our people'.[45] Labour's election manifesto (in a lengthy section on leisure) confirmed the party's thinking, promising the creation of a Sports Council 'with a grant of £5 million'.[46]

Conclusion

In contrast to the Attlee era, the 1950s – more particularly the second half of the decade – saw striking changes in the terms of debate about the relationship between sport and politics. From various quarters, calls for state intervention were being heard that seemed unthinkable just a few years earlier, prompted by a mixture of concern about faltering international performances and inadequate sporting facilities in an era of rising affluence. The scale of burgeoning political interest was reflected not only in the publication of rival party documents on sport ahead of the 1959 election, but also in the unprecedented press coverage and strong reactions that followed. The *News Chronicle* claimed the short Conservative document, *The Challenge of Leisure*, indicated that cultural and sporting issues were of concern to the electorate as never before (especially young first-time voters, of whom there were an estimated three million).[47] Morgan Phillips, the Labour Party's General Secretary, was furious that the Tory document – a 'fraud' and 'hollow sham' he called it – was published four days ahead of

Labour's long planned but delayed *Leisure for Living*. His attack on the Conservative report was echoed in left-leaning publications such as the *New Statesman*, which described *The Challenge of Leisure* as opportunistic, bringing to mind 'a dead mouse arriving on a silver tray'.[48] Even the Tory-supporting magazine *Spectator* acknowledged that while it was amusing to see Morgan Phillips having an attack of 'political apoplexy' at the sight of the Conservative party stealing Labour's clothes with the prior publication of its thoughts on leisure, there was a serious point to be made: 'The simple truth is that the Conservatives have been in office since 1951 and have not done any of the things they now propose … and even if they carried out this entire programme it would still only be a drop in the ocean.'[49]

Those who felt electoral rhetoric was paramount appeared vindicated when the Conservative manifesto took a studiously cautious line on sport. In reality, although the terms of debate had shifted markedly, all the pressure exerted by lobby groups and in parliament had not fundamentally influenced the government's *laissez faire* stance on sport in the 1950s. Far from being part of an agreed political consensus, sport was the subject of sharp, ideologically driven party differences. Whereas Labour favoured greater state intervention, for Tory ministers sport rightly remained the province of independent governing bodies and those with special functions such as the BOA. Local authorities had a role to play, though this was carefully constrained for much of the period (as described in more detail in Chapter 10), and it was no coincidence that central government spending under the relevant sections of the 1937 and 1944 Acts rose only modestly under Macmillan. In late 1958 the Prime Minister informed the Commons that some £400,000 was being spent annually under the Physical Training and Recreation Act, while grants to local authorities and voluntary bodies under the Education Act came to about £200,000.[50] The combined total in 1958 was thus less than the figure of over £630,000 spent by Labour in 1950–51. When a Labour MP teased the Minister of Education in parliament about the need to rescue the provisions of the 1937 and 1944 Acts relating to sport 'from the deeper recesses of the Ministry' so that they might receive the prominence they deserved, he was expressing a sentiment that was broadly echoed among sports administrators. Sir John Wolfenden told the Parliamentary Sports Committee in December 1958 that during his deliberations hitherto one message had been received unequivocally: 'Sport was desperately starved of money, and it would seem this could only come from Government.' Sir John added that he had no doubt about the need for 'the right facilities and more of them, in the right places'.[51] But in the absence of a published report from Wolfenden ahead of an election it confidently expected to win, the government was spared any extra incentive to change course. As Macmillan returned to Downing Street following a comfortable victory at the polls in October 1959, it was not clear what impact, if any, Sir John's findings might have in the 1960s on the detached approach to sport practised by the Conservatives throughout the 1950s.

3 The Impact of the Wolfenden Report, 1960–64

Introduction

After lengthy deliberations, involving meetings on 58 separate days, the 'Wolfenden Report on Sport' was finally published in the autumn of 1960. The Report was quite short, at little over a hundred pages, but was immediately received as being erudite, balanced and wide-ranging. It began with an assessment of the value of sport, which was described as a contribution to 'decent living together in society', valuable in its own right but also delivering social benefits such as 'character building'. It covered several areas in depth, including the provision of facilities, coaching, organization, amateurism, international sport and the so-called gap, the break between taking part in games at school and participating as an adult. In weighing up the 'present picture', the Report acknowledged several positive features of the sporting landscape: the general rise in numbers taking part in many sports, the sterling work done by unpaid volunteers and the good quality provision in schools. But while not everything found overseas was worthy of imitation, 'we are convinced that we have a great deal to learn, particularly in the planning, construction and use of facilities'. For urgently needed requirements such as swimming pools, athletics tracks, all-weather play surfaces and indoor arenas, the Report suggested that restrictions on capital expenditure by local authorities, in place for much of the 1950s, should be relaxed as soon as possible. Increased state funding was also recommended for the headquarters administration of bodies such as the Central Council of Physical Recreation (CCPR), the British Olympic Association (BOA) and the National Playing Fields Association (NPFA). Arguably the most important among over fifty recommendations – certainly the one to attract most publicity – was the call for a Sports Development Council (SDC). The members of the Committee were unanimous (as they were on all proposals except over the future of amateurism) that there could be no 'new deal' in sport without such a body. It would consist of between six and ten distinguished individuals, and would be independent of the Ministry of Education, reporting to the Lord President of the Council or to the Chancellor of the Exchequer. The SDC would have under its control an annual sum of £5 million, to be distributed either as non-recurrent grants or in assistance towards the recurrent expenditure of 'composite bodies' like the CCPR and individual governing bodies. A similar, additional sum should also be allocated annually for capital projects by local authorities.[1]

The Wolfenden Report has been widely regarded as a landmark document in the relationship between sport and politics. Historians Richard Holt and Tony Mason describe Sir John's Report as a 'very significant moment in the history and development of British sport', one that 'did much to persuade both politicians and sportsmen and women that there ought to be an enhanced role in sport for the public sector'.[2] From a social science perspective, Maurice Roche wrote that 'much of subsequent British sport policy...stems from the influence of the views and positions established by Wolfenden'.[3] While several writers note that progress in implementing the Report was initially slow, much of the existing literature implies it was only a matter of time before politicians moved towards what the Report's author called the 'new deal' for sport. John Coghlan, a leading sports administrator in the 1980s, speaks of the Report as one that was 'to alter the face of British sport within the decade': it confronted the government with a challenge (to provide for sport as never before), governing bodies with an opportunity (to develop and expand) and the public at large with 'a formal recognition' that society had responsibilities in this field. It was, Coghlan claims, a document 'no government could ignore', and there followed a step-by-step process that 'moved inexorably forward to late 1964', when the decision was reached to introduce a Sports Council.[4] This chapter sets out to show that the impact of the 1960 Report has been exaggerated. Although without question a comprehensive and influential document, many of its ideas were not novel, including its most important suggestion; as we saw in the previous chapter, references to a Sports Council had been circulating for several years before 1960. The reception of the Report, moreover, indicates it was not launched into a political environment where there was ready-made acceptance of the required way forward in sport. In spite of Sir John's best efforts, his main recommendations were not acted upon by Macmillan or his successor, Sir Alec Douglas-Home, and the evidence points to the probability that a Sports Council would not have been introduced at all but for a change of government when Labour returned to power in 1964. The Report nudged the Conservatives only marginally in the direction of accepting an 'enhanced role ... for the public sector'; before 1964 there was to be no new deal for sport.

Two Cheers for Sir John

The Wolfenden Report was formally launched at a press conference in London on 28 September 1960. Introducing his work, Sir John spent much of his time addressing concerns which he suspected, from soundings already taken, would arise about the introduction of a Sports Development Council. In the eyes of his Committee, the Council 'is not a vast bureaucratic structure; nor is it a super-fluous piece of super-machinery'. He noted that an existing public body run along similar lines, the University Grants Committee (UGC), had a small but expert staff, and disbursed far greater sums of money than proposed for the SDC. The new body would not see itself as a 'Sports overlord', Wolfenden said, or look to take over managing individual sports from governing bodies, any more than the UGC ran individual universities. In effect Sir John knew, as was clear from the evidence given to his committee, that while the idea of a Ministry of Sport had few adherents, being too closely associated with the practice of totalitarian regimes, there was support in the sporting world for a body that would be aligned to but semi-independent from the state. On the question of funding, Sir John conceded that in the absence of detailed survey work (which he hoped the Council would encourage), the sums required could not be precisely calculated. But he suggested that the material contained in over thirty paragraphs relating to facilities in the Report indicated that a £10 million budget was 'not out of scale with the needs that were very emphatically brought to our notice'.[5]

The Report was warmly welcomed by sport enthusiasts. For the likes of Philip Noel-Baker, it gave wider credence to ideas he had long advocated. He wrote to friends that coming as it did in the wake of the 'immense success' of the Rome Olympics, the Report was well timed to push the government into providing 'big money' for sport. Noel-Baker told Sandy Duncan of the BOA that he was 'most ardently in favour' of this 'urgent social reform'; the Parliamentary Sports Committee (PSC) would do its best to support Sir John.[6] The CCPR, having appointed Wolfenden's Committee, was on the whole also delighted with the outcome. It produced a statement agreeing with the emphasis in the Report on the need for greater state aid, though there were divisions over the call for a SDC. The statement said an 'overwhelming majority' within the CCPR favoured introducing a Council, while a minority (including Phyllis Colson, a powerful figure at the CCPR for many years) believed the same ends could be achieved simply by increasing the sums channelled through the Ministry of Education.[7]

Sir John's Report had an impact well beyond the world of sport. After ten thousand copies sold out a further print run of five thousand was ordered. The Report was widely commented upon by the national and provincial press, and much of the coverage was favourable. This applied, as might be expected, in left-leaning newspapers such as the *Guardian* ('a sound, modest and readable Report'), *Daily Herald* ('a big cheer, you millions of sports fans') and *Sunday Dispatch* ('a monumental work'). More surprisingly, even the *Daily Telegraph* conceded that 'broadly speaking', the Report found the right arguments to justify spending public money on sport. At the extremes of press opinion a minority took the view that it either went too far (*City Press* thought governments 'had no right to use taxpayers' money in this way') or was not bold enough (the *Daily Sketch* described it as a 'timid affair'). Yet it was the *Daily Mail* whose response illustrated the general tenor: 'It is fair enough...the essential first step in the revitalising of British sport'. Acceptance of the Report seemed sufficiently widespread for the *Star* to comment that implementation was now the key. The Report, it warned, 'must not be shelved...The Sports Development Council should be set up and at work by Christmas'.[8]

For the first time since 1945, sport was not confined to the periphery of political debate. In the words of Justin Evans of the CCPR, Sir John's Report received 'a very rare amount of attention, which no Government could ignore'. But while immediate public reactions were positive, the Report did not decisively alter the preference of Conservative ministers to maintain an arms' length

approach towards sport. In the weeks after publication, the government did little more than give a cautious welcome to Sir John's
findings, while requesting more time to formulate a full response.
The central reason for this tardy reaction was simple: enthusiasm
for the Report was not shared in the corridors of power. While the
Conservatives had accepted since 1951 the need to preserve key
features of the welfare state such as the National Health Service
(NHS) and a social security safety net, Tory leaders were not in the
business of looking to extend state powers where voluntary provision was felt to be sufficient. Apart from some brief references
to combating juvenile delinquency, Wolfenden's Report did not
make a strong case (as was to later become fashionable) for invest-
ing in sport in order to deal with wider societal problems. This
reinforced the lukewarm Conservative response, as did knowledge
that a year on from Macmillan's resounding triumph at the polls
there appeared to be no electoral imperative for a sudden change
of course.

Ministers thus adopted a non-committal stance. Although not
prepared to say so openly for some time after publication, for fear
of a backlash in the light of favourable reactions to the Report, the
government was determined that the chief recommendation of a
SDC would not come to pass. The day after Sir John's press conference launch, the Minister of Education, David Eccles, wrote to his
Permanent Secretary:

> I am anxious to prepare public opinion for the rejection of
> Wolfenden's new Sports Council. If Local Education Authorities
> and the Ministry have been stingy in the past years it is not because
> they do not want to do more for sport, or had not the machinery to
> do it, but because Governments chose other priorities. If therefore
> Wolfenden persuades Her Majesty's Government to give sport more
> money in the future that is no reason for creating new machinery
> to give it.[9]

Having grown accustomed to playing a leading role in administering state aid towards sports and recreation, the Ministry of
Education was not prepared to see its powers suddenly usurped by
a body over which it had no control. Hence it suited the Ministry to
push the view, taken up by others in Whitehall, that a SDC would
perform no useful function. E. B. H. Baker, the official who led the

small departmental delegation giving evidence to the Wolfenden Committee, bolstered the Minister's view by writing in his response to the Report that 'we can obtain the same results by using our present machinery'.[10]

Within a week of Sir John's press conference, a strategy was taking shape aimed at limiting the impact of the Report. Eccles was sent a memorandum advising him to welcome the Report as a valuable contribution that would help the government in finalizing it own ideas on sport. In the meantime, the memo continued, the Ministry of Education should consult with the Ministry of Housing and Local Government (MHLG) – responsible for working with local authorities in this field – with a view to formulating a joint policy; this would set out how much expansion of present services was necessary while also showing that 'the Sports Council is a bad idea'. Eccles scribbled across the memo: 'I like this line'.[11] The determination not to be bounced by the Report into early action was shared at the Housing and Local Government department, where the Minister, Henry Brooke, was told by one of his leading officials that preliminary contact with the Ministry of Education indicated shared opposition to the introduction of a Sports Council. Brooke was advised there was some weight in the Wolfenden criticisms, notably over the lack of a coherent doctrine about the scale and type of facilities that ought to be provided for sport. There was also, it was candidly admitted, 'the well known difficulty that provision for sport and physical recreation has been starved of capital investment', and the fact that little real coordination existed between provision made by local authorities (sanctioned by the MHLG) and voluntary efforts (aided by the Ministry of Education).[12]

In mid-October 1960 the two ministries produced a draft paper to go to the Home Affairs Committee of the Cabinet. This noted that the Report's anxiety about inadequate facilities required a response, and – anxious not to lose the opportunity for raising the profile of sport – the paper suggested a supportive tone. 'With much of what the Report proposes we can agree', it was stated:

> In the provision of facilities for amateur sport, games and athletics – in spite of what has been achieved for school children in ten years of intensive building of new schools – we have done little since the war, especially in comparison with some of our continental

neighbours. And we have reason to believe that the local authorities would readily take up a much larger capital allocation than is now made for this purpose.

There was also a case for increasing the level of exchequer grant to support voluntary bodies such at the CCPR. It was therefore hoped that ministerial colleagues would regard the Report as a chance 'for a move forward', but not under the auspices of a Sports Council. Any development, the paper argued, 'can be done under existing machinery'. The arguments against a SDC, it became clear, were financial as much as administrative. The Education and Housing ministries did not wish to see the establishment 'without good reason' of another body, 'one of whose main functions would be to act as a pressure group on the Government for more expenditure'. Comparisons were often drawn with the Arts Council, but the paper argued this had been established to provide a channel for state assistance where none existed before, whereas a Sports Council would duplicate what government already provided. If there was a need for improved coordination, it might be best to further consider the idea of a central advisory group to represent governmental, local authority and voluntary interests, chaired by a minister.[13]

One of the reasons the government's response to the Wolfenden Report took a long time to finalize was the complex administrative framework in which recreation operated. It was difficult enough to reach agreement between the Ministries of Education and Housing and Local Government on the best way forward. Henry Brooke at the MHLG was warned at one point by an adviser: 'I cannot help thinking that Education intend to take this over, though in view of the dominant role of local authorities ... I do not think we could accept that'.[14] Over and beyond departmental rivalry, there was the whole question of securing the approval of the Treasury, ever on the alert as the keeper of the government's purse strings to restrict demands for increased spending. Reporting back to Eccles, one education official wrote that he was given the clear impression in preliminary discussions that the Treasury was determined to resist any notion that 'considerable extra funds should be made available for sport'. In the view of the Treasury, the real need appeared to be a small increase in funding from within the existing Ministry of Education budget.[15] With three separate departmental positions in play, it was not surprising that the Home Affairs Committee made little progress when it discussed Sir John's findings in December 1960. The Report was not rejected, but it was agreed that further study would be required by officials. In the meantime, by common consent 'there was no need for the establishment of a Sports Development Council'. Pending further investigation, the Treasury reserved the position of the Chancellor of the Exchequer on committing additional funds to sport and recreation.[16]

In mid-January the first meeting of a 'Working Party of Officials' took place, pointedly chaired by a representative of the Treasury. By this point concern was being expressed that the government was dragging its feet. When the whips office got in touch to say a debate was being proposed in the House of Lords, the Ministry of Education decided it would have to take the line that the government was not in a position to state its settled view on the Report and might not be for some time to come.[17] At the end of January David Eccles played for time in response to a question in the Commons about the setting up of a SDC: Sir John's findings were being carefully studied, he said, and he was not yet able to make a statement. Whether because of the tone of the Minister's reply or because of a leak, adverse newspaper headlines quickly followed. The *Telegraph* and *Express* both ran headlines claiming the Report was being shelved.[18] The Prime Minister was prompted to intervene, writing to his private secretary: 'I am not conscious that we have turned down anything. Has this gone to any Committee or the Cabinet?'[19] Macmillan's lack of awareness about the Report was itself instructive. He was put in the picture about developments by his advisers, but there were no efforts to inject greater urgency into the government's response. Ahead of the debate in the Lords, the government's spokesman, Lord Kilmuir, the Lord Chancellor, was extensively briefed, about what he should and should not say, by the Treasury civil servant in charge of the Working Party of Officials.[20]

When the first full-scale parliamentary discussion of Wolfenden took place on 15 February 1961, speakers from across the political spectrum agreed with BOA stalwart Lord Aberdare in hoping the government would soon act upon the Report's main recommendations, including the creation of a SDC.[21] But Lord Kilmuir prevaricated. The distinguished athlete turned journalist Chris Brasher, writing in the *Observer*, noted that Lord Kilmuir 'threw a smokescreen of figures about – and a sharp sprinkling of cold water – on proceedings'. There were promises of some additional funding, especially towards the maintenance of national recreation centres by the CCPR and for grants towards coaching schemes. But the total figure of £18 million spent on sport claimed by Lord Kilmuir was misleading, Brasher claimed. Half of this related to provision for schools under the Education Act and millions more of the total spent by local authorities were not part of any coherent government plan. Ministers had no framework for planning the provision of facilities, Brasher said, a situation that would remain unchanged until such time as a Sports Council carried out necessary survey work. Brasher's fear was that the government intended to do 'no more than slightly to relax the reins which have held back local authorities from spending what they would have wished during the last fifteen years'.[22]

Kilmuir's response did not allay the suspicions of those who felt the government was engaged on a containment exercise. In late February 1961 the *Times* reported that separate motions had been put down by 99 Conservative and 67 Labour MPs to indicate impatience with the government's 'evasive answers' on the Wolfenden Report. Conservatives, led by Wavell Wakefield and Hubert Ashton, urged ministers to give local authorities more leeway, while Labour backbenchers followed Ellis Smith in calling for the full implementation of the Report. Shortly afterwards the *Times* published a letter signed by the heads of the BOA, NPFA and CCPR asserting that 'the need both for funds and a new approach is very great'.[23] At the same time a meeting of the PSC agreed that an all-party delegation should seek to meet the Chancellor of the Exchequer. This meeting took place in March and the delegation 'left imbued with some measure of optimism'.[24] For a brief period, there was hope the deadlock would be broken. The Chancellor, Selwyn Lloyd, hinted that new funds for sport would soon be made available, and a memo written by a MHLG official claimed that it seemed likely 'we shall get some additional capital investment for Wolfenden purposes', with the Ministry of Education budget also being bolstered.[25] But by the time of the spring budget, the economic outlook was turning bleak, and with the Working Party of Officials still wrestling with the best form of administrative machinery to employ, ministers remained reluctant to make definite commitments. In April it was the turn of the House of

Commons to discuss the Wolfenden Report for the first time, but
E. B. H. Baker of the Ministry of Education wrote in advance of the
debate that all-in-all 'there is not a great deal' for the government
to announce 'in addition to what the Lord Chancellor said on the
15th February'.[26]

As in the House of Lords, the Commons debate of 28 April witnessed speakers from all sides calling for a Sports Council. From
the Tory benches Hubert Ashton claimed it would bring 'imagination and drive' to the whole enterprise. The debate was most
noteworthy for the first speech from Labour's frontbencher Denis
Howell, recent victor at a by-election at Birmingham Small Heath
and well known as a distinguished Football League referee. In his
memoirs, Howell wrote that party leader Hugh Gaitskell asked
him to do his best to raise the political profile of sport.[27] For many
years to come Howell was to take the leading role in formulating
Labour's approach, in effect assuming the mantle previously held
by Philip Noel-Baker, now too elderly to be considered for high
office. More so than Noel-Baker, Howell was known for a pugna-
cious and forthright style. He described the government's stance
as 'scandalous... it is scandalous that the Government should put
back into sport such paltry sums compared with what they take out
of it'. He claimed betting tax on football pools and purchase tax
on sports goods brought in £100 million per year, and he accused
ministers of 'cooking the books' in claims about what was being
spent on sport; most of what was happening was that 'local authorities are to be allowed to spend their own money'. Replying for
the government, Kenneth Thompson, Parliamentary Secretary at
the Ministry of Education, appeared rattled and hoped the debate
would not end with 'the country convinced that absolutely nothing is being done'. His defensive tone was reflected in his claim
that the idea of a SDC was 'fraught with all sorts of complications'.
The government required more time to devise the best form of
machinery to achieve the desired aim, but the clearest hint yet of
the Whitehall orthodoxy behind the scenes came in Thompson's
assertion that it 'would not be right for the Government to impose'
on existing bodies who controlled most forms of sport 'some ill-
defined or imprecise authority'.[28]

Justin Evans of the CCPR noted that the combined effect of
the parliamentary debates in February and April 1961 was 'a chill
of disappointment'.[29] Six months on from the publication of the

Wolfenden Report, there were few indications that Macmillan's government had departed from 1950s' orthodoxy. The Report was not entirely without effect. When the Working Party of Officials finally reported in June 1961, it confirmed that there was no wish to see a SDC or even an internal advisory council, but it did advocate higher levels of capital investment over the years to come. Local authority expenditure, it was argued, should rise significantly, from £4.3 to £11.5 million over a four-year period, half of this increase being accounted for by sanctioning proposals to build new swimming pools, costing an average of £200,000 each. While there was no accurate estimate of needs in Sir John's Report or elsewhere, 'the anxiety of local authorities to spend more than has to date been approved', the Working Party noted, 'suggests that there is an unsatisfied demand for facilities'.[30] On this evidence, the impact of Wolfenden was to push the government to go a bit further and faster than it might otherwise have done. But in the event, even the limited proposals of the Working Party were put on hold. By the time it reported in the summer of 1961 the economy was heading into a downturn which prompted new restrictions on public spending. On 26 July Chancellor Selwyn Lloyd outlined emergency measures and made a specific reference to the Wolfenden reforms as an area where fresh investment would have to wait. For sport, it was back to square one. Like many others, Noel-Baker's hopes had been raised by Sir John's Report only to be dashed. The government, he wrote to a friend in July, was 'certainly going to do nothing about the Wolfenden Report this year'.[31]

Enter Lord Hailsham

For almost a year after Selwyn Lloyd's emergency budget the issues raised by Wolfenden were on the back burner. One civil servant wrote that following the Chancellor's statement first the MHLG and then the Ministry of Education (the latter 'under Treasury pressure') cut back the local government investment programme.[32] This meant that half the maximum possible lifespan of the 1959 parliament passed without any practical change in the government's piecemeal approach to sports facilities, and the spotlight turned in the second half of 1961 to a separate issue affecting the sporting world: that of legislation on betting and gambling. In the

1955 parliament the Conservatives baulked at the prospect of acting on Royal Commission recommendations to streamline the law.
In particular the proposal to liberalize the system by legalizing
off-course betting on horse racing encountered 'moral and con-
fessional opposition' (including among the Tory rank and file),
persuading Macmillan not to act on 'so contentious' a topic.[33] But
the Betting and Gaming Act of 1960, coming into force in 1961,
finally went ahead on the grounds that restrictions on off-course
betting had been long abused and were unenforceable in law. 'In
many respects', historian Roger Munting notes, 'the Act satisfied
no interested party fully'. The Jockey Club felt its authority was
under threat; only a small proportion of off-course betting duty
passed back to racecourses and the racing industry. On the other
hand, anxious to appease anti-gambling sentiment in Tory ranks,
newly legalized off-course betting was faced with a host of restrictions. Betting shops were obliged to be unattractive environments
(e.g. with no televisions, comfortable chairs or refreshments permitted, and opening hours limited), though as Munting observes
'this did not appear to be a disincentive for a good many punters
to enter and linger'.[34]

From the spring of 1962 onwards, the financing of provision for
sport returned to dominate parliamentary discussion. Although
the economy remained in the doldrums, Macmillan's slide in
the opinion polls was followed by attempts to revive popularity
through a range of new measures, and in March a note by the
Prime Minister's private secretary claimed that the government
was 'going to do Wolfenden on Sport'.[35] Pressure was being applied
behind the scenes at this point by Noel-Baker and Wavell, who with
the backing of the PSC met the Chancellor to underline the extent
of cross-party backing for some increased funding in the budget
as an initial step towards full implementation of the Wolfenden
Report.[36] Selwyn Lloyd duly promised in the spring budget to
begin 'in a modest way' to remedy some of the deficiencies pointed
out by Sir John. In May 1962 the Chancellor gave more details
of what would follow: an extra one million pounds was added to
the capital investment programme for local authorities to spend
in the current year, and the Ministry of Education was provided
with an additional £200,000 under the Physical Training and
Recreation Act, up to a total of £670,000 per annum. On a Sports
Council, the government line was unchanged: it was still under

consideration. Contributors to a short debate in the Commons, led by Howell, attacked the 'very meagre' new provision outlined by the Chancellor. Lloyd replied that 'in my Budget speech I said that I would make a modest start to remedy certain deficiencies...and what I have said today comes within that definition'.[37] Noel-Baker, who took a more conciliatory line than many in the debate, was pleased that at least some progress was in the offing, and his grounds for optimism increased further when Chris Chataway was appointed a junior minister at the Education department. Noel-Baker wrote to Sandy Duncan that this could swing the argument in government circles in favour of the SDC: 'As you know, the chief opposition has always come from the Ministry of Education and we might now be able to smash it for good and all'.[38]

The merits or otherwise of a SDC were certainly being actively considered once more over the summer of 1962, both at Westminster and beyond. A powerful contribution to the debate came in the form of a pamphlet by Dennis Molyneux, a Birmingham University lecturer, entitled *Central Government Aid to Sport and Physical Recreation in Countries of Western Europe*. This short work echoed many publications in the early 1960s comparing Britain's performance unfavourably with developments elsewhere across a range of social and economic indicators. In addition to showing how much financial aid flowed into sport in European nations as a result of state control over football pools or other types of gambling, Molyneux contrasted the Wolfenden Report with the so-called Golden Plan for sport produced by the German Olympic Association in 1960. Whereas Sir John relied on written and oral evidence, the German report contained a detailed analysis of requirements and projected costs for more than a decade ahead. Two years on in Britain, the author noted, 'there has been little advance towards a realisation of the recommendations of the Wolfenden Report', while the Golden Plan had been adopted as policy in West Germany; the likely financial impact was for £28 million to be spent in direct subsidies for sport facilities over a four-year period. Although he held back from open advocacy of a Sports Council, the logic of Molyneux's case was clear. Britain, he noted, lacked a single voice for sport, whereas many European nations benefited from government-supported bodies with responsibilities very similar to those of the SDC championed by the Wolfenden Committee.[39]

Calls for a full statement of government intent also continued in parliament. In November 1962 Elaine Burton, now in the House of Lords as the Labour peer Baroness Burton, asked whether ministers were in a position to announce their 'long-delayed' decision about the establishment of a SDC.[40] A few weeks later, without much prior warning, the government finally – over two years after the publication of Wolfenden – made a definitive statement, issued jointly in both houses of parliament. In the upper chamber Lord Hailsham, Lord President of the Council and Minister for Science, spoke of the 'large and mounting expenditures' contained for sport in programmes spread between various departments such as Education and Housing. As normal divisions of ministerial responsibility did not apply, Hailsham argued, this was not a problem that could be solved, in the Government's view, 'by creating another agency that would be interposed between the responsible Ministers and local authorities'. While agreeing with the diagnosis of the Wolfenden Report about the need for improved facilities and coordination, the government did not agree with Sir John's proposed remedy of a SDC. As for how to improve coordination, Hailsham announced: 'I have now been given special responsibility for ensuring this.' He would, he reassured his somewhat startled audience, have access to expert advice from inside and outside of the government in securing his objectives.[41]

Was this, then, the moment that finally signified a more proactive Tory stance on sport? John Coghlan has argued that the willingness to assign a senior Cabinet figure to the task at hand was 'a sign that the argument for a new deal for sport was being won'.[42] Yet this assessment does not bear scrutiny if the background to the appointment is taken into account. Since the summer of 1962 the Wolfenden Report had been widely discussed by ministers behind closed doors, but at no point ahead of the end-of-year announcement was a Sports Council a serious possibility. What made the talks so protracted was lack of agreement over the best way to secure improved coordination of sport. At the Home Affairs Committee of the Cabinet in mid-July, it was agreed that Wolfenden's SDC proposal should be formally rejected and that responsibility for administering sport should remain largely as it was, though with some updating. Selwyn Lloyd was of the opinion that any modernization required the creation of an independent advisory council, made up mostly of sporting experts, able to offer impartial advice. But others on the Home Affairs Committee, including the Ministers of Education and Housing and Local Government – not wishing to see their powers diminished – objected to this proposition. An advisory council, it was claimed, would 'have no real job to do' and might develop 'either into a pressure group or become a visibly dead piece of wood'. The conclusion of the meeting was that the government would make a statement in the Commons after the summer recess, making no reference to an advisory council.[43]

In the autumn of 1962, just weeks ahead of Hailsham's statement in the House of Lords, the involvement of the Lord President was not on the horizon. It only became so when the matter was discussed in Cabinet on 1 November, and the feeling arose that the government would leave itself open to criticism if, two years on from Wolfenden, it could say nothing more than that existing administrative arrangements were largely satisfactory. The discussion in Cabinet proceeded on much the same lines as at the Home Affairs Committee in July. Ministers readily agreed with the view of the Treasury minister John Boyd Carpenter that a SDC was 'expensive and unnecessary'. When it was suggested that a Sports Council might work in the same way as the Arts Council, others retorted that the 'real difficulty was the pressure to spend money which would arise from the creation of an independent body'. There was some sympathy for an internal advisory committee, overseen by senior civil servants; if established on 'imaginative lines', this would help the government to 'carry conviction' in seeking to improve facilities for sport and recreation. But again other ministers felt even this type of innovation might become 'a channel for embarrassing demands for money which could not at present be afforded'. The Prime Minister summed up that it was right to reject the recommendation of a SDC and that the advisory committee idea could not be endorsed. He was anxious, however, that any statement of policy should strike a 'positive and practical note'. This meant emphasizing what was being done in the field of sport and possibly – bringing into play an entirely new idea – asking the Lord President to assume responsibility for coordinating action among the departments chiefly concerned. A revised statement was to be drawn up along these lines.[44]

It was this revised statement that was read out in December by Lord Hailsham, who was almost as surprised as his audience to find himself assigned his new role. Far from being a carefully thought

out strategy signalling a decisive new commitment, the announcement on 20 December bore all the hallmarks of a hastily contrived
expedient. The only reason Hailsham was landed with the responsibility was that he waxed lyrical when the subject was discussed in
Cabinet. As he later wrote in a book of recollections, 'quite unwit-
tingly I talked myself into the job'. He noted that problems of recreation could not be free from government responsibility and he
spoke of the need, not for a Ministry of Sport (which 'savours of
dictatorship'), but 'for a focal point under a Minister, for a coherent body of doctrine, perhaps even a philosophy of government
encouragement'. His musings were influenced by his experiences
as Minister for Science, in which capacity he made use of independent expertise while not seeking to impose central regulation.[45]
Macmillan was sufficiently impressed by these thoughts – in effect
the first time the cause of sport had been taken up in Cabinet during his premiership – that the coordinating role was created more
or less on the spot. Hailsham in his memoirs described this turn
of events as 'bizarre'; he indulged in no sporting pastimes beyond
climbing and walking and heartily disliked the 'chauvinism' that
surrounded so much competitive sport. His biographer Geoffrey
Lewis calls him 'perversely unsuited'. It was not of course necessary to have been a top sportsman to take on the new role, Lewis
wrote, but even so Hailsham could boast 'an impressive number of
disqualifications for the job'.[46]

Further confirmation that policy towards sport was being
treated in a cavalier rather than a considered way came in the
reaction behind the scenes in Whitehall. The two departments
most affected had little choice but to accept the Cabinet's decision, though both harboured suspicions of where it would lead.
One official wrote that the Permanent Secretary of the MHLG
appeared to think the proposal would cause 'the maximum of
trouble with the minimum of result'. The concern at the MHLG
was that if the proposals represented 'only a public gesture, no
one was likely to be deceived'.[47] Sensitivities over the new arrangements were equally apparent at the Ministry of Education, where
one civil servant wrote that the Minister had it in mind to go back
to Cabinet to say that if a new body was formed to assist the Lord
President it would almost certainly lead to expectations of more
funding for sport, well beyond the levels of increased capital investment already in the pipeline.[48] In effect the two main ministries

concerned, confident in previous discussions that their influence over sport and recreation was secure, were bounced into accepting a sudden change of arrangements. Lord Hailsham's emergence from the shadows was less an indication of a genuine commitment to sport but more a device to fill the administrative vacuum left by the rejection of a SDC and other alternatives such as an advisory council. At the end of 1962 a new deal for sport remained as elusive as when the Wolfenden Committee reported.

Hailsham's 'minor matter'

Whatever the motives for bringing Hailsham to the forefront, the opportunity presented itself, in the weeks and months that followed, for him to leave his mark on the development of sport. But by his own admission, he barely aspired to becoming a 'focal point' for sporting interests, still less to developing a coherent body of doctrine underpinning state support. 'This particular activity', he later admitted, 'was a minor matter, and I thought comparatively little of it at the time since it occurred at a time when other things were preoccupying my mind'. Hailsham described as 'far more important... and exciting' the mission to act with special responsibility for economic regeneration in the North-East of England, which Macmillan also entrusted to him at the start of 1963.[49] When he met in January with officials of the Lord President's Office and the Cabinet Office to discuss how to act upon his statement in the House of Lords, he opened by saying his new responsibilities for the North-East 'would necessarily reduce the time which he could give to sport'. At this point he hoped that Chris Chataway, with his knowledge and interest in this area, might act as a special adviser. Chataway, present at the meeting, hinted that his duties at the Ministry of Education prevented him from doing this in a formal way, and pointed to continuing administrative overlap between Education and the MHLG as an obstacle to progress.[50] One clarification that was agreed early in 1963 was that the Treasury, having been at the forefront of high-level discussions during 1961–62, would step back now that Hailsham had come to the fore. The Treasury role will revert, one official noted, 'to the normal one of controller of expenditure'.[51]

Although he was ambivalent about his responsibilities for sport, Hailsham did put in place some fresh administrative arrangements.

He appointed Sir Patrick Renison, former Governor of Kenya, as his Principal Adviser on Sport, and Renison presided over an 'Official Committee for Sport', an interdepartmental body of officials which reported in turn to ministers. The Official Committee made recommendations for increased spending which Hailsham duly adopted in a debate in the House of Lords in May 1963. These included higher grants for the administration of governing body headquarters, an increase in the Ministry of Education budget to support coaching schemes and better provision for voluntary single activity sports clubs, up to half the cost of facilities provided. According to the Lord President, government spending had been 'steadily rising' when combining provision for school sport, capital expenditure by local authorities and Ministry of Education grants to voluntary bodies. In total, expenditure had gone up, he claimed, from c.£21 million to £32 million over the period 1960–63. While presenting this as a defensible record, Hailsham was not inclined to boast of any sharp departures: 'I have from the outset held the view that significant help could be given at comparatively little cost' he concluded. 'I regard these measures as a modest but well-considered start in improving the method of Government support for sport activities and recreation.'[52]

The language employed by Hailsham reflected the Whitehall view that slow progress remained the order of the day. One civil servant noted the suggestions for increased spending that came forward from the Official Committee were 'quite modest', and accordingly acceptable to the Treasury.[53] The general tenor of the debate in the Lords was that Hailsham would need time to demonstrate any significant results. Baroness Burton, who initiated the discussion, asked for clarification which was not to be forthcoming for some years ahead: a detailed breakdown of the figures cited (e.g. to distinguish spending on playing fields from that on community halls) so that it would be possible to ascertain 'exactly what help is received for sport'. Although speaking from the opposition benches, Lady Burton was by no means the most critical of their Lordships. Lord Aberdare said bluntly that a SDC was still required, as was 'more Government money and some form of regional planning to make the best use of it'. And Lord Luke, voicing the concerns of the NPFA, argued that the situation in relation to the provision of facilities 'has got quite beyond the capacity of voluntary effort'. He very much hoped that the Lord

President would make a difference, 'because if we are to go on more or less as before, with a few minor changes, I think the disappointment will be very widespread. I feel that a new and vigorous chapter in the history of sport and recreation needs to be written here and now'.[54]

What followed in the remaining months of the 1959 parliament was difficult to construe as a 'new and vigorous chapter', though it was not altogether devoid of novel initiatives. The Official Committee looked at the issue of financial assistance for British sporting teams overseas, noting the orthodox view that if this was conceded, as Hailsham wrote to one colleague, 'public support would diminish'. The Lord President was, however, sympathetic to the idea of limited backing 'in suitable cases' such as the Olympics, especially as a contribution to the cost of running an appeal could be regarded as consistent with support for the administration of headquarters' organization. In early 1964 the Treasury wrote to the BOA offering a small grant towards its appeal for the 1964 Games in Tokyo (see Chapter 7 for more details). At the beginning of 1964 the influential and energetic Sir John Lang, a former top civil servant at the Admiralty, succeeded Patrick Renison as the minister's Principal Adviser, and in the spring Hailsham addressed a meeting at Shell House in London attended by about 250 representatives of governing bodies of sport and outdoor activity associations. This was a seminal moment, the first occasion on which a minister had addressed leading administrators about the government's view of sport. The Lord President used the opportunity to reiterate his claim that spending on sport was rising: the CCPR's grant from the Ministry of Education, for instance, had doubled since 1960, though some of this increase was due to a move to new offices.[55]

By the summer of 1964, it was evident that 18 months of Hailsham's stewardship had not silenced all the government's critics. Calls for the introduction of a Sports Council continued to be heard, led by Baroness Burton in a debate in the Lords in which she made a marathon six-hour speech. Five other speakers in the same debate followed her lead in asking for the government to reconsider its decision. The same theme was taken up in the Commons on 22 June when Bill Mallalieu, MP for Huddersfield and a former Oxford rugby blue, making his debut appearance on the opposition front bench, argued that if elected to power Labour would press for more active ministerial encouragement for the arts, sport and recreation. Quintin Hogg (as Hailsham was known after renouncing his peerage in order to vie for the Conservative leadership after Macmillan's sudden retirement in 1963) responded that it was a delusion to think a 'ministry of leisure' was a worthwhile enterprise, and he equally rejected renewed calls for a SDC. Hogg confessed he initially saw merits in the SDC idea, having experience of dealings with the UGC, but he had been 'steadily moving away from it'. How, he asked, could a SDC represent over 300 individual governing bodies without superseding the CCPR? Lady Burton wrote to the *Times* to argue that this was an inaccurate representation of majority support for a SDC inside the CCPR. She requested that he withdraw the remarks, but when she raised the matter further in the House of Lords she was told that Hogg had been stating an opinion, not making official policy.[56]

With a general election drawing close, the Commons debate of June 1964 was notable for a sharpening of party knives. From the government benches Chris Chataway chided Labour for promising all sorts of new government departments and for 'handing out cheques' which had already been stopped: a reference to the statement of shadow Chancellor Jim Callaghan that existing spending levels could not be responsibly exceeded. For Labour, Denis Howell jibed in return that Chataway had been in favour of a SDC in the past but had gone silent on the matter since being appointed to a junior role at the Ministry of Education. As for claims that government spending was rising, Howell said the numbers cited by Chataway include 'almost everything under the sun – cemeteries, flower beds, Royal Parks, youth clubs and education. It is not possible from analysing these figures to find what the Government are spending'. The core of Howell's critique was that there 'was no appreciation of the need for a coherent strategy in planning for leisure'. Hogg, he charged, with so many other duties to attend to, was inevitably unable to do justice to sport and recreation. 'The Government have taken a few halting steps ... but have made no real progress because they have no basic philosophy of the fullness of life ... In sport the great crime is to deny sportsmen the opportunity to develop the fullness of their potential and, for the nation, the great crime is for people to be unable to take intelligent choices. On each count the Government stand condemned.'[57] Hogg rounded off the debate in what the *Times* called a 'most docile speech', complaining that Howell had injected strong party feelings into a subject that required discussion in a 'more relaxed atmosphere'. In his memoirs, Howell wrote that the minister's contribution perfectly illustrated why 'a relaxed approach to this subject had achieved very little and was unlikely to do more in the near future'.[58]

Conclusion: Labour Returns to Power, 1964

The Wolfenden Report gave a focus to political debate that sport lacked prior to 1960. By reviewing all aspects of sporting endeavour from elite level to the grass roots, it helped – in the words of one academic assessment – to shape 'the context within which public involvement of sport was to be considered for the next generation'.[59] But two important reservations need to be emphasized when summing up Sir John's work. The first is that the 1960 Report crystallized and gave greater credence to ideas that had been circulating for some years, rather than outlining an entirely new agenda. As we have seen, advocates of closer involvement by the state in sport, particularly in terms of assisting with the growth of facilities such as pools, tracks and parks, were growing in number steadily during the 1950s, in parliament, the press and the sporting world. Much of what Sir John called for had been outlined by Labour in its 1959 policy document *Leisure for Living*, issued ahead of the Wolfenden Report. In preparing its 1964 election campaign, Labour established a Working Party on Sport which concluded that *Leisure for Living* was still as relevant as when it was first written; shortages of facilities were 'at least as acute' as in 1959, and the 'urgent and important task' was to update earlier thoughts to ensure that all who wished to could benefit from leisure in the more affluent 1960s. Labour, in short, had prefigured Wolfenden's views and channelled the Report's main thinking into the political mainstream; sport should be enjoyed primarily for its own sake, as well as for its benefits to individuals and society.[60]

While Labour under Harold Wilson's leadership moved to a serious consideration of 'quality of life' issues, ranging from technology to leisure, the same cannot be said of the Conservatives under Sir Alec Douglas-Home, who replaced Macmillan in 1963. Douglas-Home had more substantial sporting credentials than any of his predecessors since 1951; he actively engaged in countryside pursuits such as shooting and had briefly played county cricket in his younger days, retaining strong links with senior cricket administrators when he went to Number Ten. But his 'grouse-moor' image proved a political handicap at a time when the Tory government faced accusations of being outdated, especially when contrasted with the more energetic, modernizing persona projected by Wilson. Douglas-Home had little time to turn the spotlight on sport before Labour returned to power with a narrow election victory in October 1964. The second reservation to be noted in relation to the impact of the Wolfenden Report is that it remained largely unfulfilled when the Conservatives relinquished power. It did not, in other words, herald a decisive immediate or medium-term breakthrough. Throughout the 1950s sport, as we have seen, was of marginal concern to successive Conservative administrations, and this largely remained the case after 1960. As the Report was unofficial, a CCPR-sponsored rather than a government initiative, ministers did not feel obliged to take up its main findings. In the Douglas-Home era, as much as in Churchill's twilight years in power, sport for the Conservatives was a largely voluntary enterprise that should be left to run its own affairs.

Ministers did not, of course, entirely reject Wolfenden's findings, and the arrival of Lord Hailsham as minister with responsibility for sport in late 1962 opened up a phase of more intensive activity. But, as Hailsham readily admitted in his memoirs, sport comprised a small component of his extensive portfolio of duties, and he never used his status as a senior minister to showcase sporting concerns around the Cabinet table. He did secure the approval of colleagues to act to a limited degree on Sir John's call for increased state aid to composite bodies like the CCPR and the BOA, and he prided himself in his memoirs on how he adjusted the arrangements for ministerial oversight of sport. He sought, he said, to be a 'friend at Court' to the composite bodies, seeing himself as 'an honest broker rather than an administrator with actual powers'.[61] While this provided a novel measure of guidance from above, it left untouched a complex and cumbersome system in which numerous Whitehall departments continued to hold some degree of responsibility for sport: the Ministry of Education for school sport, administration and coaching, the Foreign Office for international sport, the MHLG for local facilities and the Treasury for the overall control of costs. Most crucially, this meant facing down Sir John's core proposal for a Sports Council, an idea which Denis Howell believed the 'formidable' Phyllis Colson of the CCPR persuaded the Lord President against.[62] Yet a wide body of sporting and political opinion continued to regard a Sports Council as essential. As one of its advocates, David Munrow (a member of the Wolfenden Committee) wrote in 1963, a Council would not sweep away every difficulty, but without one 'sport loses out all along the line because it seldom speaks with one voice and...society misses out (and will do to an ever increasing extent) because the contributions of sport are never viewed as an entity and never will be unless there is some machinery to make it possible'.[63]

In his book *Sport and British Politics* John Coghlan claims: 'It is idle to speculate...whether or not there would have been a Sports Council if the Conservative Government had been returned to power.'[64] Yet Coghlan acknowledges that Hailsham and his adviser Sir John Lang were both opposed to such a move. And, it should be added, the idea did not feature in the Tory manifesto at the 1964 election, which (in a brief paragraph where 'sport' appeared under a sub-heading in its own right for the first time) referred to the need for more facilities 'in and around towns and cities', promising that 'a substantial programme will be authorised'.[65] Whatever was pledged for the future, it remained the case that through to 1964 the Conservatives had no intention of acting upon the major recommendation of the Wolfenden Report, that of providing a Sports Development Council to act as a focal point for future development. The thrust of policy since 1960 makes it difficult to conclude that sport was heading in a predetermined fashion towards the introduction of a Sports Council. Instead of political approaches to leisure developing as part of a consensus around the importance of welfare principles, party differences based on differing views of the role of the state were as acute in the run up to the 1964 election as they had been in 1959. Labour's manifesto pledged that a Sports Council would provide a fulcrum for the facilities and funding 'that are so badly needed', and Hailsham later admitted that things 'developed on rather different lines' to what he had envisaged after the Tories lost office. Soon after coming to power in October 1964, Harold Wilson charged Denis Howell with the task of bringing a fresh dynamic to leisure and making the Sports Council a reality. At an initial meeting with Sir John Lang, who remained in Whitehall to advise the incoming administration, Howell was given what he called 'half a dozen of the thinnest files I have ever seen'. This, Lang told him without any trace of irony, 'represented the previous Government's thinking on sport'.[66]

4 Creating and Running the Sports Council, 1964–67

Introduction

Harold Wilson's term as Prime Minister between 1964 and 1970 has been viewed in contrasting ways by historians. Some point to the gradual fading of 1964 promises of a 'New Britain', with economic difficulties resulting not in economic regeneration but in a humiliating devaluation of sterling and a lower growth rate than in the so-called wasted Tory years. Others reach a more sympathetic verdict, arguing that despite various bouts of retrenchment, Wilson presided over some significant achievements: spending on education and health rose as a proportion of public expenditure; the Open University was created amidst a massive opening up of opportunities in higher education; and a raft of social reforms were introduced including equal pay for women and statutory redundancy pay.[1] The evidence presented in this chapter indicates that sport should also be added to this list of creditable advances in the early years of Wilson's premiership – a period when Labour secured a comfortable majority at the 1966 general election.

The aims of Labour in sport, educationists Peter McIntosh and Valerie Charlton have claimed, 'differed little from those of the previous government'.[2] Yet if some broad objectives overlapped, such as enhancing physical education (PE) for school children, earlier chapters have underlined that sharp differences existed over the speed and scope of any proposed change. It will be argued here that Labour's approach after 1964 was characterized not only by significantly greater urgency than anything that came before, but also by a novel attempt to widen the focus of government activity to embrace professional as well as amateur sport. State intervention of a sort alien to pre-1964 administrations became the order of the day. A Sports Council, resolutely opposed by the Conservatives, was quickly introduced, not with the intention of securing state control but aimed at creating a viable partnership between statutory authorities and voluntary sports organizations. In an age where it became realistic to talk of 'sport policy', rather than a series of uncoordinated government responses, there was even evidence that Labour regarded sport as a potential electoral asset; a far cry from the prevailing orthodoxy in the 1950s. Within six months of Labour coming to power in 1964 an official at the Treasury wrote (disapprovingly, in view of the financial implications) that 'there has been a marked increase of interest in sport'. And an internal report later in the decade by a Conservative study group, recognizing the need to make up ground, noted that whatever its failings in various directions, 'sport is one sphere in which the Government is thought by the public to have been successful'.[3]

Appointing a Minister for Sport and a Sports Council

The extent to which the new government differed from its predecessors on sport became apparent in a matter of weeks. Part of Harold Wilson's 'New Britain' appeal as he carried Labour back into office in 1964 was his promise to shake up the machinery of government. He was keen to introduce both new forward-looking departments such as the Ministry of Technology and to appoint within existing departments junior ministers with specialist functions. Sport fell into the latter category. Although not known as a sportsman in his youth, Wilson was a keen follower of football, capable of reciting all the names of Huddersfield Town's 1938 Football Association (FA) Cup final team. Ahead of the general election, there was talk in Labour circles of appointing a senior Cabinet figure, possibly the Lord President of the Council or the Lord Privy Seal, to oversee both the arts and sport, working through an expanded Arts Council and a newly formed Sports Development Council.[4] But on further reflection, Wilson decided it would be a simpler and more effective way forward to appoint – as he wrote in his later account of his 1964 administration – a number of junior ministers 'with special responsibilities for subjects essential to Britain's economic and social development which had not been given an adequate priority in the past'. In this vein he offered to Denis Howell the position of Under Secretary of State with special responsibility for sport at the renamed Department of Education and Science (DES). Howell, the Prime Minister noted, had 'an unrivalled knowledge of sporting problems', and was to become widely known as the 'Minister of Sport'. Aneurin Bevan's widow, Jennie Lee, was accorded similar responsibility as a junior minister for the arts, initially based at the Ministry of Public Building and Works, though before long also transferred to the DES.[5]

In his memoirs Denis Howell said he did not know in advance what role he would be asked to play in the new government. Junior ministerial appointments were delayed over the weekend after the election by intense private discussion between Wilson and senior colleagues about the huge scale of Britain's overseas deficit. The decision was taken that while it might be economically necessary, a devaluation of sterling would be politically disastrous for a new administration with a tiny majority of only four parliamentary seats. Although tipped off about being on a list of potential ministers, it was not until Monday lunchtime that Howell was summoned and told by Wilson that he wished him to go to the DES: 'You will be the first Minister for Sport, it will be very exciting.' After accepting the offer, Howell asked what approach the Prime Minister wished to see pursued. On this Wilson said (possibly covering for a lack of detailed knowledge) that policy was in the minister's hands: 'I think you know what needs to be done otherwise I would not be appointing you.' Feeling emboldened, Howell enquired if there was money to spend, only to be told not ('the country's broke'), but the Prime Minister was more receptive to the idea of including sporting figures in the forthcoming Honours List and also – when Howell mentioned the Olympics taking place in Tokyo – the possibility of a reception in Downing Street for the British team when they returned. To his surprise, Howell also received a positive response when, thinking out loud, the difficulties of England hosting football's World Cup in 1966 came to mind. He understood the previous administration had promised little more than police escorts for teams during the tournament, whereas Howell knew from conversations with football friends that there was much to be done by way of preparation. 'How much do you want?', Wilson asked. Howell recollected that at the time he had not the 'faintest idea', but reluctant to lose his opening, he suggested half a million pounds, to which Wilson agreed. 'I thanked him again and, assuring him of my full support, I left Number Ten, astonished at my good fortune and overwhelmed by my interview with the Prime Minister.'[6]

News of Howell's appointment was warmly received for the most part; British athletes in Tokyo were said to have cheered when they heard the announcement. In part this was due to Howell's sporting background, as well as his enthusiasm for the task ahead, though some found his personality overbearing. Neil Macfarlane, who was later to serve as Sports Minister under the Conservatives in the 1980s, wrote that to his detractors Howell had the 'earnest busy pomposity of Mr Magoo – he likes to call it dignity and any soccer referee will tell you that dignity is a most priceless asset'. In Macfarlane's eyes, Denis was 'a punchy but essentially amiable man', though he suspected Howell suffered the same frustrations as many who were to follow him, in that the post of Minister for Sport was 'rather like someone bicycling away on one of those keep fit machines; the pedals were going round at varying speeds, but not getting anywhere'. What Macfarlane had in mind was that there was no legislative framework or terms of reference upon which the minister might draw: 'The job is what you make it.'[7] Howell's interview with Harold Wilson confirmed there was no clear remit, and within weeks of being in office he was reminded that suspicions lingered about what precisely his role might be. The Marquess of Exeter, arguably Britain's most well-known sporting administrator, connected with the International Olympic Committee (IOC), British Olympic Association (BOA) and Amateur Athletics Association (AAA) among others, deliberately greeted him at a function as 'the Minister *for* Sport', adding: 'very important that little word'. Howell said he immediately recognized the implication. Although in the years to come many called him the Minister *of* Sport, Howell was always careful to avoid this label, which he knew signified in certain eyes the unwelcome levels of political control and interference associated especially with the Communist regimes of eastern Europe.[8]

The administrative framework put in place by Harold Wilson thus contained some inherent structural problems. The role of Sports Minister was created without any well-defined sense of the scope or limitations of the post, and for years to come sport and the arts were to find themselves competing for scarce resources rather than working together as part of an integrated approach to leisure in the wake of the arrangements chosen by Wilson. None of this, however, greatly concerned Denis Howell in the autumn of 1964, or detracted from the significance of what had taken place for the relationship between sport and politics. The idea of a considered government 'policy' towards sport was no longer a misnomer; the word itself was explicitly used in the meeting at which Howell was appointed, a notable departure from previous practice. 'At no other time in my life', he later wrote, 'have I known a period of such sustained excitement as in the months which immediately followed my appointment as Minister'. With an energy that was to be much lauded, Howell threw himself into the fray. On his first day at the DES in Curzon Street, he was greeted by Sir John Lang, available to continue as a part-time adviser on sport as he had been under the previous government. Howell asked if Lang would be prepared to work for more hours during the week than he did for Lord Hailsham – 'we were going to take sport seriously' – and was delighted that Sir John agreed, giving him an experienced and well-regarded ally in Whitehall as he embarked on the battle for 'new policies, new staff and new money'. Howell established from talking to the Permanent Secretary, Sir Herbert Andrew, that while he would have other responsibilities as a junior minister, for example in relation to the youth service, he was free to focus for a large slice of his time on sport. The only disappointment he experienced on his first day was to hear Sir John Lang saying that he was opposed to the introduction of a Sports Council, despite it being a Labour manifesto commitment. The Minister gave him a fortnight to put together a document setting out the arguments against such an innovation.[9]

While he awaited Lang's paper, Howell set about reinforcing the case for acting on Labour's pledge. He knew he needed to flesh out previous thinking if Whitehall opposition to a Sports Council was to be overcome, and just days after his appointment he invited two trusted allies from Birmingham University to a long Sunday afternoon talk. David Munrow was known to be among the staunchest of advocates of a Sports Council on the Wolfenden Committee, and Dennis Molyneux was author of the 1962 booklet that contrasted Britain's provision for sport unfavourably with that of European neighbours. 'When we met', Howell wrote in his memoirs, 'they could not contain their delight that a Labour Government ... intended to implement its policy document *Leisure for Living* ... At last sport, the arts and leisure were to be regarded as subjects of serious Government involvement'. Both his guests were 'resolute' in saying the Minister should himself chair the proposed

Sports Council, and that it would not get off the ground without this lead. The three men also agreed that – with Labour's small majority making another election likely in the not too distant future – it was important to act quickly; hence an advisory body was preferable to the legislation believed to be required for an executive council along the lines recommended in the Wolfenden Report. On personnel, Walter Winterbottom, former manager of the England football team and a key figure at the Central Council of Physical Recreation (CCPR) in the 1960s, was seen as an obvious choice for chief officer. Winterbottom's uniting influence, it was believed, would help to overcome sensitivities about how the new Council related to the CCPR, the body representing most individual National Governing Bodies (NGBs). By the end of the afternoon it was also agreed that a fourfold sub-committee structure would help the Sports Council to cover several areas of responsibility: facilities and planning; research; coaching and development; and international sport.[10]

In due course Sir John Lang produced what Howell called four pages of 'well-argued' points opposing a Sports Council. But the Minister was ready, and told his adviser he thought the election result had decisively changed matters. Lang's objection that other government departments with an interest in sport would oppose a body under the jurisdiction of the DES – especially the Ministry of Housing and Local Government – was met by noting that the Prime Minister was supportive of Howell's plan. Without a moment's hesitation, Lang changed tack and began to offer advice on how best to proceed. It was, Howell reflected, a 'classic' civil service response. Within minutes it was agreed Sir John would act as deputy chairman of the Council, and Howell left Lang to brief the Secretary of State for Education, Michael Stewart, who gave the initiative his blessing. Stewart said he was happy to leave policy for sport to his junior minister so as long as he was kept informed. Less than a month after Labour came to power, Howell therefore found himself in front of a Cabinet committee setting out the case for introducing a Sports Council. The move was speedily endorsed. As Howell noted, many ministers newly in office had time consuming projects in mind; when he made it clear he did not need to compete for precious legislative space by opting for an advisory group with himself as chair, colleagues were happy to give him the green light. He encountered a colder atmosphere, he noted in his memoirs, when he returned shortly afterwards to outline plans such as improvements to football grounds ahead of the 1966 World Cup. Unlike the creation of the Sports Council, this required the rapid injection of large sums of money, and the Treasury minister present pointed to the tricky economic backcloth. Howell was getting concerned about the outcome when the chairman of the meeting suddenly curtailed discussion and nodded the proposals through. 'Clearly, he had been well briefed beforehand', Howell reflected. 'Harold Wilson had kept his part of the bargain.'[11]

Wilson was also keen to exploit – in a way that had not concerned his predecessors – the publicity potential of sport, and just weeks after he came to power some 300 guests, including Olympic athletes, officials and doctors, attended a big party in Downing Street. 'There had never been a reception of this size and certainly not of this importance for sport', Howell noted. 'It really marked the new Government's determination to take sport seriously in a manner that was unprecedented.'[12] While not of course regarding sport as a front line election issue, the Prime Minister sensed it had potential electoral resonance, associating politicians with one of the nation's favourite endeavours. A further illustration of Wilson's alertness to the symbolic importance of sport came when the first Honours List of his new administration included a knighthood for the football legend Stanley Matthews. Wilson was later able to claim that the press welcomed moves to make the Honours system 'less stuffy' and representative of 'the kind of people who made Britain tick'.[13] Howell also enjoyed what he called a piece of good fortune in his early weeks in office, drawing parliamentary attention to his work. A newly elected Conservative MP, John Hunt, chose to use his position at the top of a ballot for private members to debate a motion urging the Government to give 'every encouragement to the fuller use of leisure time'. This allowed Chris Chataway from the opposition benches to complain that, whereas Labour spoke before the election of the need for oversight by a senior figure, in practice sport was being dealt with 'in this Government at a lower level than under the previous one'. Philip Noel-Baker retorted sharply that while Lord Hailsham was known to possess an 'athletic mind', his efforts on behalf of sport before 1964 had been 'most inadequate'. Howell joined in the opportunity to lambast the Tory record, adding that the Secretary

of State at the DES would speak for sport at the highest level in
Cabinet when required.[14]

At the start of the New Year, 1965, Howell's energies centred on
firming up the personnel and structure of the proposed Sports
Council. He met with leading figures on the CCPR who, as its
Secretary Justin Evans noted, were wary of how its role would
be affected by the introduction of the new Council. The minister's placatory tone proved reassuring, and within a week Walter
Winterbottom (who kept his existing ties at the CCPR) agreed to
act as Director of the new body.[15] The rest of the arrangements
fell into place much as the minister discussed at his home on the
Sunday afternoon following the general election. David Munrow
was confirmed as Chairman of the Sports Development and
Coaching Committee and the distinguished athlete and surgeon
Roger Bannister accepted an invitation to take the lead on the
Research Committee (with Molyneux as his deputy). Lady Burton,
the Labour peer, agreed to chair the International Committee,
and the Facilities Planning Committee was headed up by Lord
Porchester, Chairman of Hampshire County Council. Howell was
pleased with the appointment of Porchester, who was not only
experienced in the workings of local government, but who as a
prominent Conservative brought cross-party balance to the Sports
Council. With the key individuals in place, attention turned to
ensuring the remaining members of the Sports Council represented the geographical regions of the United Kingdom – notably Scotland and Wales – as well as a variety of social and ethnic
backgrounds. He was delighted that the lacrosse expert Kathleen
Holt joined the dozen or so members of the team, as did Sir Learie
Constantine, the former West Indian cricket captain and 'a won-
derful inspiration for his own people now settled here'.[16]

Although everything was in place for the Sports Council to go
ahead, feathers had been ruffled in some parts of Whitehall. At
the Ministry of Housing and Local Government (MHLG), H. H.
Browne, the official who spoke for his department on the Official
Committee on Sport set up by Hailsham, expressed concern
about the Sports Council being under the purview of the DES;
its functions included matters, notably in relation to the development of local authority facilities, for which 'we have departmental responsibility'.[17] One of Browne's colleagues wrote in an
internal memo that in the setting up of the Sports Council, 'we

have recently been left very much on the side lines!' Although not opposed in principle, the MHLG would at least like to have aired its views, particularly over having more representation on the Council of experienced local government figures. Mr Howell, it was said, seemed to have compiled the list of members 'more or less by himself'. The Minister for Sport had 'clearly been pushing ahead briskly', and had already asked if the Housing department could expand its capital investment programme for sports projects by local authorities. The tone of internal memos at the MHLG became ever more irate. The Permanent Secretary was told by officials that 'we consider we have been treated in a rather high-handed fashion about the Sports Council', and it was suggested a comment to this effect should be made when replying to Howell about capital investment.[18] The episode marked a small warning shot for Howell, and a reminder that responsibility for sport was not exclusively in his hands but remained dispersed across government departments. He was soon to discover that his missionary zeal was not universally shared in Whitehall.[19]

In the short term the Sports Minister remained in buoyant mood, and on 3 February 1965 he was ready to tell the House of Commons that the government was establishing a Sports Council 'to advise them on matters relating to the development of amateur sport and physical recreation and to foster cooperation among the statutory and voluntary organisations concerned'. In a brief statement Howell outlined the membership of the Council and indicated the key areas in which it would advise the government, including the provision of facilities and likely capital expenditure, regional planning, the development of coaching and participation by amateur British teams in overseas events such as the Olympics. From the opposition benches, Quintin Hogg wished those who were to serve on the Council well, but pointed out that as an advisory body with no direct responsibility for funding it ran counter to what Labour promised at the election. Howell responded that as the Wolfenden Report was a 'considerable distance away now', the government believed on balance it was right – given the need to act quickly – to set up an advisory group rather than bringing forward the legislation necessary for an executive body. Asked for a reassurance by Conservative MP Anthony Fell that the Council 'will not result in any cost to the taxpayer', the Minister replied briskly that it would be wrong to assume enhancing sport in society 'will not cost anything'. An accurate estimate of what funds were required, however, awaited surveys of national and regional priorities.[20] Howell wrote in his memoirs that the announcement was warmly received in the Commons and in press coverage, with the appointment of Winterbottom as Director being 'of cardinal importance in producing a helpful and constructive response'. Much of the newspaper reaction picked up not only on Labour's speedy action, compared with the way the previous government dragged its feet over Wolfenden, but also on the youthful composition of the Sports Council. Among those recruited were well-known sportsmen such as the international athlete John Disley, aged 36, the 26-year-old Welsh rugby captain Ted Rowland and the swimmer Ian Black, aged only 23.[21]

Two Steps Forward ... and One Step Back

For much of the remainder of 1965 Howell maintained the momentum of his early weeks in office, attempting to demonstrate that a new chapter was underway in the relationship between sport and the state. On 11 February, in a fresh indication that the sporting faternity was welcome in the corridors of powers, members of the Sports Council attended a reception in Downing Street, and were met in advance by the new Secretary of State for Education, Tony Crosland. Michael Stewart had been moved by Wilson to become Foreign Secretary, though the Sports Minister was not concerned about the change disrupting his plans. The new head of the DES, he wrote, was someone with a 'passionate interest in sport', known for absenting himself from dinner parties in order to watch football's 'Match of the Day' on BBC television. Like Stewart, Howell noted, Crosland 'left it all to me and whenever I called upon him for advice or for help in Cabinet he was first-class'. Howell was also confident by this stage that an enthusiastic team of officials was in place, the core of a 'sports division within the Education Ministry'.[22] The Sports Council met for the first time later in February at Richmond Terrace, near to the DES. By early April 1965 the four planned committees were functioning and Howell congratulated members of the Council on the alacrity with which they had got down to work. The minutes of the Council reported that criticisms in sections of the press, claiming the new body could not be fully effective unless it had executive authority, were 'completely refuted by Mr Howell; he considered the arrangement a very satisfactory one'.[23] While critics could be shrugged off at this point, in the years to come the question was to frequently resurface: what was the best system for government oversight of sport? Concern was to be increasingly voiced that the most appropriate framework should not centre on a Council which, though nominally established to represent sporting interests, was in practice closely yoked to party preferences via the chairmanship of the Minister.

While establishing the Sports Council was a major priority for Howell, he also quickly became a focal point for responding to a range of sporting topics of interest to MPs. Questions were asked in the Commons on issues as diverse as the sale of black market tickets for major events to the alleged taking of drugs by sportsmen and women – a thorny problem that was to loom larger in min-isterial thinking in later years. The Minister was also faced with Labour backbenchers looking to introduce legislation, in the form of a Sports Facilities Bill. The chief focus of this related to foot-ball. The financial basis of the professional game had been under pressure for some time, with attendances for top league matches falling at a time of increased wages costs following the abolition of the maximum wage. The Sports Facilities Bill proposed to set up a Board to control football betting, with profits being ploughed back into various sports. Howell had sympathy with the aims of the Bill but encountered strong opposition in Whitehall. In particular the Treasury regarded this as 'an invasion of the province of the Government'; if passed it would concede the principle of an inde-pendent body having the right to regulate betting and raise rev-enue.[24] By way of concession when the Bill was withdrawn, Howell announced in February 1965 a wide-ranging review of football organization and finance; on the same occasion he revealed to the Commons that the government would provide financial sup-port for the World Cup. The football enquiry was to be chaired by Sir Norman Chester, Warden of Nuffield College, Oxford, and a keen follower of the game. In March 1965 Howell also provided some figures in the House that underlined his success thus far in increasing the available government funding for sport. The level of direct Exchequer assistance to sport and physical recreation in England, Wales and Scotland, he reported, would rise from £915,000 in 1964–65 to £1,571,000 in 1965–66, an increase of 70 per cent. 'Not enough', he believed, 'but a good start'.[25]

Another of Howell's preoccupations in early 1965 was ensuring that the World Cup, second only to the Olympics in terms of global prestige as a sporting spectacle, 'should be staged in a manner which reflected credit on me and on the new ministerial post which I was proud to occupy'. Sir John Lang admitted to being 'incredulous' when he was told the Prime Minister had pledged half a million pounds. For Lang, conscious that previous regimes had been reluctant to spend taxpayers' money on amateur sport, the prospect of state funding to aid a professional sport – expected to pay its own way in the normal course of affairs – was inconceivable. Sir John agreed, however, to chair a small working group that included leading figures in British football such as Winterbottom, Stanley Rous of the FA and Alan Hardaker, Secretary of the Football League. With the blessing of the working group, Howell embarked on a highly publicized tour of the football grounds earmarked for World Cup group fixtures. He soon realized the need for a 'great uplift in standards'. This meant, among other things, more and better seating, hugely improved toilet facilities (especially for women spectators), dedicated training facilities for visiting teams and hospitality suites for the large numbers of overseas guests and journalists certain to attend. Some club officials, Howell recollected, were a little suspicious, partly he felt because they were unused to ministerial injunctions to improve their facilities and partly because the levels of assistance available were not confirmed at the time of visiting; the details were still being worked out by the Treasury. Lang eventually told Howell a formula had been agreed: the government would cover 50 per cent of the cost of substantive work of a permanent nature and 90 per cent for temporary installations. Confident that the required changes would be made, and that in the meantime the World Cup had received a major promotional boost, the Minister reported the details to parliament in May. 'We were on our way', he later wrote.[26]

Behind the smiling photographs taken at World Cup venues, the fight for state aid had been far from straightforward. Just as Howell upset some in Whitehall with his failure to consult the MHLG over the Sports Council, so his handling of World Cup funding did not go down well at the Treasury. Officials appeared to remain unaware for some time that Howell had secured the private backing of the Prime Minister. The Treasury view initially was firmly in line with pre-1964 practice: whatever the importance of the World Cup as a sporting event, it was 'important to avoid public expenditure in staging it here'.[27] In March 1965 one civil servant at the Treasury was surprised to be told about a conversation in which the Sports Minister spoke of being instructed by colleagues to 'seize the initiative about the World Cup, make as much political capital for the Government as possible and go up to an agreed figure of £500,000'.[28] Seeking to keep a measure of control over costs, the Treasury requested the DES make a formal request for funding, and pushed down the figure of c.£575,000 that came forward. In summing up its position, the Treasury noted that criticisms in the press illustrated there was no 'universal support' for public funds being used to subsidize professional sport, which after all was expected to live and die by its ability to generate profits. On the other hand, the Treasury conceded a case could be made in relation to the national prestige associated with the tournament and possible increased revenue from tourism and exports. In these circumstance it was 'fair and reasonable' to offer £400,000 in grants and £100,000 in loans, but no more. This was quite sufficient given that the taxpayer was effectively 'paying for the F.A.s earlier shortcomings'; the decision to host the World Cup in England had been taken in 1960 but the FA had not built up any reserves to cover the extra expenditure they must have known would be required. 'More generally the Treasury is in a very difficult position in relation to the pressures for expenditure on sport', one official wrote: 'Mr Howell regards himself as having a roving commission with responsibilities to no one except the Prime Minister.'[29]

In April 1965 Howell gave an important address to the National Playing Fields Association (NPFA), reflecting on his first six months in post. He began by saying that his role covered 'all sorts of things'. When asked a few days after his appointment about the boundaries of his responsibilities he admitted he did not know. 'The Prime Minister did not tell me, so I am proceeding on the understanding that I am responsible for everything until somebody says "No". Nobody has said "No" yet.' He therefore told the NPFA that he saw himself as having oversight of both professional and amateur sport. He took 'good care', he insisted, to talk about the establishment of the Sports Council, dealing with recreational aspects of leisure, before saying anything about the World Cup. 'I was most anxious to get the thing in perspective', and to show it was not the government's intention to 'run sport'. The lesson of his brush with the Marquess of Exeter had been learnt: 'This is the great distinction between having a Minister of Sport, as certain countries do, and a Minister for Sport, which I am'. The World Cup was a case in point, as his task was to ensure a successfully run tournament, and not to interfere with the team – so illustrating 'the distinction between what I am doing and where I wish to draw the line'. His major concern, he told his audience, was to widen opportunities 'for ordinary people to play for the fun of it', which might in turn create a greater reservoir of talent for elite sport. To this end the Sports Council had been set up and was working 'very fast'; regional councils were now being considered in order that plans could be drawn up from below rather than imposed from the centre. He concluded with a rallying cry, saying that much remained to be done: 'In my judgement, the nation cannot afford not to do it. The very people who complain bitterly about juvenile delinquency, which largely arises, as we know, from the boredom of young people, are usually the first to complain about spending money to alleviate boredom and juvenile delinquency. The two go hand in hand.'[30]

By the summer of 1965 the Sports Minister had developed a considerable public profile, junior though he was in the government hierarchy. His outgoing personality made him a favourite with many journalists, who were happy to report his claims in July that the Sports Council was proceeding with its work at a 'cracking pace'. Announcements about financial support for governing bodies arranging international events in Britain, extra funding for national teams competing overseas, and the imminent creation of regional councils were greeted by the *Daily Telegraph* as among the 'most significant and exciting ever uttered about British sport'.[31] But Howell's status and style continued to grate in some parts of Whitehall. One official at the Treasury wrote following the July announcements that the impression was being given that the 'Sports Council *itself* was making grants'. It was 'particularly annoying', the civil servant continued, to find this happening when the government was looking to restrain public expenditure, mindful that it needed to retain a reputation for economic competence.[32] From this point on the Treasury more actively sought ways of reining in the Sports Minister. It was decided to furnish the Chancellor, Jim Callaghan, with figures suggesting that total spending on sport (including that by local authorities) could rise from £45 million in 1965–66 to £56 million in 1966–67. Callaghan scribbled on the relevant memo: 'What is being done to keep this expenditure within bounds?'[33] Interpreting this a signal for action, Treasury officials stepped up the pressure on the Sports Council, referring to it as a body 'which spends its time pressing local authorities to spend money'; it might be necessary to enlist support in other departments 'to suppress the Sports Council if they work against us'.[34] By September 1965 Treasury pressure forced the DES into issuing a letter stating that in the wake of the Chancellor's pronouncements about holding down public spending, projects in the pipeline for new sports facilities built by local authorities would have to be postponed for the time being.

Although the new restrictions marked a step back after the swift progress made on the twin fronts of creating the Sports Council and preparing for the World Cup, Howell still had reason to be satisfied at the end of his first year in office. In DES discussions about estimated spending for 1966–67, Tony Crosland's backing for sport was illustrated when he compensated for local authority restrictions by approving a big increase in departmental funding. As the development of state funding was still in an 'embryonic' stage and the sums involved were 'relatively small' in relation to the total Education budget, the Sports Minister was offered a 20 per cent increase over the previous year.[35] Introducing a debate in the House of Lords in December 1965, Baroness Burton singled out Howell for praise ('he has done a first class job'), as did Lord Longford, speaking formally for the government. The minister's 'energy is quite phenomenal', he said, 'and I think that everyone feels he has infused a tremendous excitement in the sporting world'. Although the figures for spending were difficult to untangle, Longford claimed total public expenditure on sport and physical recreation was in the region (as claimed by the Treasury) of £45 million for 1965, suggesting that in spite of recently imposed restraints capital expenditure had about doubled over four years. The only dissenting voice in the debate came from Lord Aberdare, who noted that capital projects had been curtailed at a time when half a million pounds was set aside for the World Cup. It was 'extraordinary', he said (reflecting his lifetime commitment to amateur athletics), that this first-ever infusion of state funds into professional sport should go to football clubs who spent enormous sums on transfer fees but seemed unable to maintain their grounds in good condition.[36] Not all of the government's opponents took such a stern view. Justin Evans of the CCPR reported that when Howell addressed a packed meeting of representatives of governing bodies at Shell House late in 1965, there was some ironic cheering and amusement when Charles de Beaumont, a leading figure in the sport of fencing, 'rose to say that though he was not of the same political persuasion as the Minister, he felt bound to declare that the Government, through him, had done more for sport than any of its predecessors'.[37]

The 1966 Election and the World Cup

Although there were more high points to come, nothing quite matched the excitement of Howell's early months as Sports Minister. As well as grappling with internal Whitehall resistance, he was more and more faced with dissent towards aspects of his policy, not least from the Conservative opposition. In the aftermath of defeat at the 1964 election, Edward Heath, Douglas-Home's successor as party leader, bringing managerial efficiency to the role, sought to reassess Tory strategy across the board. Chris Chataway, a former minister at the DES and described by the *Times* as a 'crisp man ... sincere, well-informed', was put in charge of a Bow Group committee tasked with considering the broad field of leisure.[38] When the study group produced an internal report in July 1965 it provided without question the most thorough Conservative assessment yet of sport, much more comprehensive than corresponding earlier works such as the 1959 *Challenge of Leisure* pamphlet. This marked a key moment, in other words, when the Conservatives sought to develop a coherent sports policy, finally moving beyond the detached approach of the pre-1964 era. The report was clearly influenced by the need to respond to Labour. Mr Howell, it was agreed in the Bow Group report, 'gets a large press coverage and from the public relations point of view his appointment and the setting up of an advisory council liberally sprinkled with popular young sportsmen, has probably been a success so far'. The impact made by Howell made it difficult, at least in the short term, for the Bow Group to come up with popular alternative policies. Chataway could hardly propose – so soon after being part of an administration that resolutely set its face against such a move – the introduction of an executive Sports Council as recommended by the Wolfenden Committee. 'Another promise by a party in opposition to institute a Sports Development Council', the Tory report noted, would 'meet with justified derision'.[39]

With a difficult hand to play, Chataway's study group managed to be distinctive at least in two respects. The first was setting out a framework of principles upon which Conservative policy might be developed. A lengthy introduction to the July 1965 report noted that the very notion of public expenditure on sport remained unwelcome to those Tories who felt this was an area for individual choice and market forces. But among those who saw themselves as progressives, such as the Bow Group, increasing leisure time made some state involvement unavoidable; to deny this would be to 'render this a wretched country in which to live'. The hard question was how to ascertain the 'proper limits' of public spending. On this the Tory report claimed it was 'repulsive' to argue that the state should assume universal responsibility for providing free public recreation, in the way that it provided free health and education. The Bow Group report preferred to start from an awareness of the mixed pattern that had evolved in Britain where, for example, public parks were generally free amenities, athletes received small subsidies and golfers met the full cost of their activities. Hence the best course was to take a 'pragmatic line, and weigh each case for government subsidy on its merits'. Much of what followed in the way of firm recommendations, the report noted, could 'be self-financing; we do not envisage any great increase in public expenditure'. If this indicated that there remained important differences between the parties over sport – Labour advocating both improved planning via the Sports Council and higher expenditure – then so too did the finale to the opening section of the Tory report: 'We start with a prejudice in favour of private rather than public financing where recreation is concerned.'[40]

The second way in which the July 1965 report struck out in a fresh direction was in its key proposal for action: that government responsibility for sport, instead of being dispersed across Whitehall, should be concentrated in a newly formed 'Recreation Department' at the MHLG. Chataway believed this would be an improvement on both the 'Overlord' system operated by Hailsham and the 'Underlord' approach of Labour in which a junior minister at the DES sought to coordinate the work of several departments.

The problem with both approaches, it was argued, was that sport was 'dealt with in a piecemeal fashion and within the Civil Service at a relatively low level'. There was no need, the Bow Group argued, for a separate Ministry of Outdoor Recreation, but there was a strong case for a 'major change in the machinery of government', in particular a branch within a Ministry having some measure of executive authority and 'capable of seeing the problem as a whole'. Although under the jurisdiction of a junior minister, sport should also attract 'a good share of the time and interest of the Permanent Secretary and the Cabinet Minister in charge'. The obvious nucleus of a 'Recreation Department', the report concluded, was to be found at the MHLG, because it already dealt with the largest share of public sports provision, via the local authorities, and with town and countryside planning issues. The DES would continue to deal with PE in schools but oversight of most sport-related functions should in due course be transferred to the new Recreation Department, which was regarded 'as essential to the fulfilment of most of our other recommendations'.[41]

Party leader Ted Heath felt there was sufficient merit in the Bow Group's report for it to be published, which it was early in 1966 under the title *A Better Country*.[42] The timing was such that it became part of a general election campaign. Harold Wilson, hoping to escape the constraints of a small parliamentary majority, went to the country in March 1966 with the wind in his sails. He claimed that his government had both come through a financial storm and undertaken a legislative programme that 'stood comparison with the best of the Attlee years'. Among achievements he listed was the creation of the Sports Council.[43] Although the energy and profile of the Sports Minister meant sport was frequently in the news, it remained low down the pecking order in terms of party campaigning. The Conservative manifesto, drawing from *A Better Country*, made a single pledge: that if elected, the party would end the existing 'confusion and duplication of effort' between various ministries by creating within the MHLG a Recreation Department.[44] In confident mood, and so less inclined to make bold promises than in the past, Labour made only vague references to improving facilities for recreation in its manifesto, and Howell restricted his claim to success in office to having 'set the mood right and provided the momentum in sports thinking'.[45] In the event, Labour's optimism proved justified:

Wilson secured a comfortable overall majority of 96 parliamentary seats.

With the election safely out of the way, Howell returned to his post at the DES secure in the knowledge that Labour policy could be developed over the full lifetime of the parliament ahead. Although careful not to say so in public, Tory election charges of administrative muddle appeared to have struck a raw nerve. Eighteen months of contending with different Whitehall interest groups moved Howell towards accepting that the machinery devised in 1964 for dealing with sport was far from ideal. In April 1966 Crosland as Education Secretary wrote to the Prime Minister expressing his support for Howell's view that 'the present divided responsibility for closely related fields is making a coherent policy difficult to achieve and is hindering progress'.[46] Although Wilson was slowly becoming more receptive to the idea of concentrating responsibility for sport in one department, in mid-1966 he was not ready to embark on a fresh bout of reorganization. The Sports Minister was left to push for administrative reform behind the scenes. At a lunch with Richard Crossman, the Minister for Housing and Local Government, Howell complained that he was 'sick of the sabotage' he encountered from the MHLG, notably in slowing down local authority building projects for sport. Crossman recorded in his diary that he investigated this complaint and found some of his officials 'were fairly obstructive'. But having given the instruction that 'bits and pieces in the Department' might be relinquished to the DES, given that sport was not a leading priority for the MHLG, he found that when civil servants from the two departments got together their considered view was that that 'the whole of sport should be transferred from DES to Housing'. For Crossman the story illustrated the curious ways of Whitehall: he offered a colleague 'bits and pieces' and ended up being 'presented on a plate with the whole thing'.[47] But for Howell it was not what he wanted to hear; any thoughts of unifying the coordination of sport under his leadership at the DES had to be put to one side.

Exasperation with internal Whitehall politics in the summer of 1966 was offset by the excitement associated with the start of the World Cup, which got under way on 11 July. Sir John Lang, heading up the coordinating group, told Howell that all the improvements requested had been put in place, and as the tournament progressed the Minister was ever more persuaded that careful planning had been worthwhile. Everything went smoothly until Argentina, beaten in a close, controversial match by England at Wembley, took a huge amount of persuasion to attend a government reception for beaten quarter-finalists. The World Cup final between the hosts and West Germany on 30 July was, Howell wrote in his memoirs, 'something for all to savour and caught the imagination of the whole nation', much of which was watching on television.[48] England's 4–2 victory, after the drama of extra time, instantly became regarded as among the most famous occasions in sporting history. Stanley Rous later wrote that the publicity-conscious Prime Minister 'appropriated the World Cup as if it was his own, or the Government's achievement'. At the banquet in London on the evening of the match Wilson 'swept up the Cup' and went out with the players to wave the trophy aloft in front of excited fans. According to Rous, Denis Howell would have been a more appropriate figure for this celebration. It was he 'who worked hard to ensure all went off smoothly', taking 'a minute interest in every detail'.[49] The Sports Minister at least had the satisfaction of reporting to MPs that over £400,000 had gone to six clubs in grants and interest free loans to help ensure the success of the tournament. In view of the outcome, even those who felt professional sport should be left to its own devices were silenced. There was, Howell wrote, not 'a word of criticism inside or outside the House – no one dared!'[50]

There was, nevertheless, more than a 'word of criticism' still being voiced about the Minister inside the Treasury. One civil servant wrote irately in July 1966 of having learnt that the Sports Council was on the verge of publishing a major report, detailing its work thus far and its future plans, without anybody at the DES thinking to notify the Treasury. 'Yet another example, I am afraid', the official wrote, 'of the undisciplined way in which sports things are dealt with'.[51] The Treasury decided to 'lodge a forceful protest' about the lack of consultation, and as a result it was a further six months before the report finally saw the light of day. It was also notable that when Howell launched *The Sports Council. A Report* at a press conference in November 1966, he went out of his way to paint a balanced picture. On the one hand, he claimed that progress since he assumed responsibility had been 'remarkable, considering we were starting from scratch. It has exceeded my wildest expectations'. The creation of Regional Sports Councils in particular meant a clearer picture was emerging of what was needed in the way of improved facilities. On the other hand, he could not hold out the prospect of a British version of Germany's 'Golden Plan' for sport, setting out substantial state investment over a long period. He did not envisage big increases in the level of direct government assistance going to amateur sport and the pace of development in future would depend on a sustained improvement in the nation's finances. Sport, he was quoted as saying, 'could not divorce itself from what was happening to the rest of Britain'.[52]

A further indication that Howell's honeymoon period was at an end came when sport was raised during an adjournment debate ahead of the Christmas recess. In contrast to the upbeat verdicts offered in the House of Lords debate a year earlier, the tone at the end of 1966 was altogether more circumspect. The Labour MP Tam Dalyell, a staunch supporter of the Sports Minister, said there were urgent matters that warranted full discussion following the publication of the report by the Sports Council. In particular, while he recognized that housing and schools took precedence, he hoped that the budget for sport would 'no longer be the Cinderalla in our major Cabinet decisions'. Dalyell also felt a lengthier debate would provide an opportunity to clear up 'certain misconceptions' resulting from a recent article in the *Sunday Times* by Chris Chataway. Although no longer an MP, having been defeated at the 1966 election, Chataway delivered a broadside which according to Dalyell gave the impression that the government had done 'very little to help sport', whereas his own view was that 'great strides' had been made. Replying as Leader of the House of Commons, Richard Crossman agreed sport had suffered because of local authority cuts necessitated by economic circumstances, but he made no pledge to give MPs their first full-scale debate about sport since Labour came to power in 1964. The best he could do was to promise to convey Dalyell's views to the Chancellor, the Education Secretary and to the Minster for Sport.[53]

Conclusion

The period 1964–66 witnessed radical changes in the relationship between sport and politics. By appointing a Minister for

Sport, Labour provided a means of coordinating government policy and raising funding levels far more systematically than ever before. The newly introduced Sports Council, though not a full-blown executive group along the lines favoured by the Wolfenden Report, was in the words of John Coghlan a 'dynamic and promotional body', capturing the public imagination and giving a focus for the drive to improve sports facilities across the country.[54] In a way that seemed unimaginable before 1964, Howell also demonstrated how sport might be used an electoral asset. His willingness to make political capital out of the national game, using state funds to oil the wheels of a successful World Cup, contrasted with the lack of concern for Labour's working-class electoral base that exemplified Attlee's approach to issues such as the banning of midweek football fixtures in the 1940s. Howell's impact overall was such that the Conservatives felt compelled to treat sport far more seriously than they had in office during the 1950s. But at the same time, it would be misleading to claim that Labour had inaugurated what Wolfenden termed the much-needed 'new deal' for sport. After the heady early days following election victory in 1964, Howell found that the absence of a clear remit was a source of frustration as well as of opportunity. From his base at the DES, he was unable to galvanize into more urgent action colleagues at the MHLG, who with Treasury blessing kept a tight rein on local authority spending on sport. One Treasury memorandum in early 1967 noted that Mr Howell has at times pushed to 'be given control of the whole [sport] empire, whether within D.E.S. or M.H.L.G. But the Prime Minister has not blessed this'.[55]

Funding levels were of sufficient concern to the Sports Minister that in early 1967 he met with the Chief Secretary of the Treasury, Jack Diamond, to convey the strongly held feeling of the Sports Council – which he said he shared – that 'sport was getting less than a fair deal, especially compared with the arts, in the allocation of public funds'. He noted that various policy documents ahead of the 1964 election committed Labour to a direct expenditure on sport of £5 million per year; this contrasted with estimates for DES spending for 1966–67 of £1.6 million. Howell said he realized sport had seen advances over the past two years, but he was 'particularly embarrassed' by the big rises pencilled in for Arts Council spending. He felt it was 'ludicrous' that government estimates for

1967–68 projected (in the wake of an Arts White Paper) a £1.5 million increase for arts compared with a £150,000 rise for sport. Jack Diamond responded by reminding Howell that it was for the Secretary of State, who was as much responsible for arts as for sport, to decide on priorities within the total DES budget. It never had been the case, nor should it be, the Chief Secretary insisted, that expenditure in one particular area of spending should be levelled up or down to be in line with another area. Diamond ended on a more conciliatory note, pointing out that to redeem all party promises at once would stretch spending beyond 'tolerable limits'. Nor should it be forgotten that 'the present Government had done more in one and a half years than its predecessors did in four years'.[56]

Ahead of Howell's tetchy encounter with the Chief Secretary, officials prepared briefing notes reflecting the view at the Treasury – accustomed to battling with the Sports Minister to keep down costs – that Howell was a shrewd operator who had little real reason for complaint. One paper written in January 1967 by Peter Jay (Chancellor Jim Callaghan's son-in-law) argued that while arts was surging forward as a result of the White Paper, sport had done better taking into account the entire record since the last full year of Conservative government. According to Jay, whereas some parts of the DES budget had been cut since 1964, spending on sport had doubled, showing that the Secretary of State had allowed sport 'a faster growth within the education block than the block as a whole has enjoyed'. This was without the sums given in grants and loans for the World Cup, entirely separate from the DES vote, and the massive contribution made by local authorities; taking these into consideration, total public spending on sport easily exceeded that on arts. Jay warned the Chief Secretary, lest he not be aware, that the forcefulness of the Minister for Sport was the chief cause of this pattern of development. Howell was renowned for a tendency 'to encourage expectations of Exchequer support before obtaining Treasury agreement'. Efforts were continuing, Jay told Jack Diamond, to exert a greater measure of Treasury control, but 'exaggerated hope should not be encouraged'. If Peter Jay was right, there may have been no full-scale Wolfenden new deal, but the tenacity of the Sports Minister meant that central government involvement in British sport had been significantly extended. Jay's summing up for the Chief Secretary was that, all in all, sport had done 'pretty well' since 1964 and that if needs be, Mr Howell could be reminded that he himself said as recently as last November 'that "in one year we have achieved more than my wildest expectations" '.[57]

5 'Ballyhoo' about Sport in the Late 1960s

Introduction

In the summer of 1967 Denis Howell attended a meeting of the Parliamentary Sports Committee (PSC), chaired by the veteran Labour MP Philip Noel-Baker. In introducing the Minister for Sport, Noel-Baker spoke of the 'great work being accomplished by the Sports Council under the Chairmanship of Mr Howell'. In his comments, the Minister described some of the activities being undertaken by the sub-committees of the main Council: the International Committee was offering grants to unpaid amateur athletes for pre-Olympic training; the Coaching and Development Committee was giving support to the governing bodies of sport in preparing individual five-year plans; and the Facilities and Planning Committee was working harmoniously in conjunction with eleven regional councils, including one in Scotland and one in Wales. The reaction of the PSC to the minister's address illustrated that he continued to make a good impression at Westminster. When Howell asked for backing in pressing for the 'improved growth' of state funds for sport, the PSC – which represented all shades of political opinion in the Commons and the Lords – offered 'wholehearted support'.[1] But if sport now had an established foothold in central government, in contrast to earlier years, the second half of Wilson's spell in power was to bring fresh challenges and difficulties. Pressure grew for a streamlining of Whitehall machinery for dealing with sport, and financial constraints continued to thwart Howell's wish to see more rapid progress in the building of new facilities. From 1968 onwards, moreover, there was much 'ballyhoo', as one critic of the Sports Minister put it, over tangled questions involving international sport. One of the main features of the relationship between sport and diplomacy (discussed more fully in Chapter 7) was the speed and force with which crises might suddenly erupt, forcing governments to respond and adapt accordingly. For Labour in the late 1960s, controversy over links with South Africa was to bring an unwelcome public and political focus on international sport that persisted through to the end of the parliament and the general election campaign in 1970.

Sport on the Move: From Education to Housing and Local Government

Much of the Minister for Sport's energy after 1967 was channelled in the same directions as in earlier years. In the aftermath of England's World Cup triumph, football remained prominent in Howell's thinking. The Chester Committee, appointed by the Sports Minister to investigate the finance and administration of British football, published its detailed findings in 1968, making over thirty recommendations for reform. *The Guardian* described the Chester Report as 'an admirable document which was bound to meet resistance from some of the all-too-amateur worthies in positions of power within the game'.[2] When the House of Commons debated the report in October 1969 – with not a single Conservative MP in attendance – Howell struggled to conceal his impatience at the slow pace of change. Most of the issues arising from the Chester Report were for the relevant bodies such as the home nation Football Associations and the Professional Footballers' Association to decide upon; 'the Government cannot instruct them', the Minister said. While advances could be reported on some fronts, key recommendations continued to be resisted by the football authorities. These included the suggestion that an age limit of 70 be imposed for members of the Football Association (FA) Council or that a Football Levy Board be created to impose a small tax on the proceeds of pools betting. Howell conceded in his memoirs that it was difficult to build up a head of steam in favour of modernizing club finances at a time when transfer fees were rising sharply in the age of football celebrities such as George Best. The most he could offer at the end of the parliamentary debate in 1969 was to promise that ministers, whose job was not to interfere directly in professional sport, would keep 'probing and pressing' on behalf of 'all of us concerned with the health of this great game'.[3]

As he sought the continued development of amateur sport along lines laid down since 1964, Howell was likewise faced with familiar Whitehall inertia. The Treasury did its best to slow down efforts to depart with tradition by offering small-scale expenses to athletes representing Britain abroad at the Olympics. And in looking to persuade his Secretary of State to prioritize sport, Howell was not helped by frequent changes of leadership at the Department of Education and Science (DES). Crosland moved to the Board of Trade in 1967 and was followed in quick succession by Patrick Gordon Walker and then by Ted Short, both of whom Howell found supportive but not evangelists for sport.[4] The major constraint the Sports Minister faced was undoubtedly financial. Philip Noel-Baker, who owing to illness and advancing age was looking to relinquish the chairmanship of the PSC, told one possible successor that the group still had an important role to play in campaigning for more funds: 'Denis Howell is confident that he could use a lot more money and thinks he has been unfairly treated compared with Jenny [*sic*] Lee'.[5] This observation, indicating that sport's treatment compared with the arts was a running sore for Howell, came shortly before the government suffered the humiliation of a large devaluation of sterling in November 1967: an event that was followed by a sharp slump in Labour's popularity and led to fresh restrictions on public spending during 1968–69. The government faced accusations that it continued to take far more out of sport than it put in, especially in the wake of a new tax on gambling that was soon bringing in hundreds of millions a year.[6] In 1969 the Sports Council prepared a second major review of its work for publication. The document was criticized in draft by civil servants at the Ministry of Housing and Local Government (MHLG) for containing 'expansionist statements which should be avoided at the present time'. When published, although Howell wrote a foreword alluding to the Sports Council 'inspiring a new outlook for sport', commentators were struck by the sober tone of the review: fresh advances in sport were dependent on the return to a more favourable economic climate.[7]

Despite the frustrations he encountered, Howell reflected in his memoirs that he continued to greet 'every day with relish'. He gave little thought, he maintained, to his future prospects, though he recalled this came up in a conversation initiated by Sir Herbert Andrews, the Permanent Secretary at the DES, late in 1968. Sir

Herbert commented on how the Minister had been in the same role for four years, twice the average tenure in many departments, adding that some believed promotion was overdue. 'All this was a pleasant surprise but embarrassing', Howell wrote:

> I could not be happier than I was in my post as the Sports Minister; it was unique and as far as I could judge I was filling it successfully. The support I received from the Prime Minister certainly led me to believe so and I was conceited enough to believe that the partnership which I had established with British sport was an advantage to the Government.

Howell told Sir Herbert that promotions and demotions were a matter for the Prime Minister, though he went away thinking he was really being asked how he felt about remaining a 'one-subject Minister', even at the expense of personal advancement. With a devotion to the role that was not to be shared by some of his successors, he concluded that he 'did not feel disposed to suggest any change'.[8]

Several months after this conversation, in the autumn of 1969, Howell was finally promoted. As part of a general restructuring of departments, he was moved and raised in status to Minister of State level (one rank below that of Cabinet minister), though without severing his ties with sport. In discussing this development, the Prime Minister gave the impression that he acted on the spur of the moment. According to Howell, Wilson was in a 'chirpy mood' when they met to talk it over and said the 'solution' came into his mind while playing golf. The proposal was that Howell should be transferred to the MHLG, which would become the lead department for tackling sport. The Prime Minister said: 'You will be the first man in history to take a Ministry with him when he moves.' This transfer of ministerial oversight for sport had of course been mooted for several years. The Wolfenden Report of 1960 questioned whether 'sport in the community' should be the preserve of the DES, and as we have seen the Conservatives pledged at the 1966 election an enhanced role for the MHLG, mindful that recreation was a well-established function of local authorities who operated under the auspices of that department. In his memoirs Howell noted there was no way of ascertaining the decisive factors in the Prime Minister's thinking. It could have been that Sir Herbert Andrews (wishing to see Howell promoted) exercised influence behind the scenes, or that Wilson was finally persuaded it was the most rational solution. Or there was always the possibility, Howell concluded, in the light of the Conservative promise in 1966, that the Prime Minister wished to 'steal the Tory clothes, a ploy which was not unnatural to Harold'.[9]

Whatever the balance of motives, it seems certain that Wilson's decision resulted from more than just what Howell called 'the satisfaction of a long drive down the fairway'. In a later account of his premiership Wilson referred to 'many discussions' that preceded the departmental reorganization of 1969, including consideration of why sport would be better placed at the MHLG.[10] As Howell had bridled about opposition from the MHLG to his plans prior to 1969, it was not surprising he welcomed the Prime Minister's move when it came, especially as it was accompanied by a rise in status. The new arrangement was, he claimed in his memoirs, 'tailor-made' for him. As Minister of State, he found himself with a broader range of duties than before, taking on onerous responsibilities such as local government finance. But the 'sports department', he wrote, the small group of officials who assisted him, was transferred 'lock, stock and barrel' from the DES, which in the meantime retained control of school sport. Sir John Lang was also allowed to accompany the Sports Minister and the Permanent Secretary at the MHLG, Sir James Jones, 'was in every way agreeable and supportive'. The senior minister at Housing and Local Government, Tony Greenwood (chair of Labour's working party on leisure before the 1964 election), suffered from poor health, which meant his number two often had to deputize at Cabinet meetings, but in spite of the heavier work load Howell reflected that his time as Minister of State was 'an agreeable experience'.[11] From the vantage point of the sporting world, Howell's retention of his earlier brief was a welcome sign of continuity. Justin Evans noted that the Minister was well received when he told the Central Council of Physical Recreation's (CCPR) annual general meeting in 1969 that his move 'denoted no change in the Government's attitude to sport'.[12]

'The D'Oliveira Affair'

By the time Howell moved to the MHLG – settling the question of where within Whitehall sport was best placed for twenty years to come – he was embroiled in a protracted and messy controversy over cricket. Aided by mass audiences on television, global events such the Olympics and the World Cup had raised the profile of international sport considerably in public consciousness by the mid-1960s. As we saw in the previous chapter, the Sports Minister took a deliberately assertive approach to the World Cup, helping to ensure the smooth running of the tournament. But in relation to cricket, England's pre-eminent summer game, ministers were dragged more reluctantly into a dispute which highlighted the sometimes fraught relationship between sport and diplomacy. The issue first made major headlines with the eruption of the 'D'Oliveira affair' in the summer of 1968. Basil D'Oliveira, a talented coloured cricketer, moved to England in the early 1960s to develop a career stunted by the apartheid regime in his native South Africa. In 1968 he played a decisive, match-winning innings for England against Australia at the Oval, making himself a strong contender for inclusion in the team to tour South Africa the following winter. When his name did not feature, there was widespread incredulity in the press. Rumours spread that selectors at the Marylebone Cricket Club (MCC) had bowed to pressure from the South African government not to include D'Oliveira on the basis of his skin colour. The protests were loud and long, and when one of the England team withdrew through injury, the MCC declared that D'Oliveira would, after all, come in as replacement and be among the touring party. This drew a furious outburst in turn from the South African Prime Minister, John Vorster, who in a speech shown on TV claimed South Africa was facing not the team of the MCC but 'the team of the Anti-Apartheid movement'. Positions quickly became entrenched. The MCC decided it was not acceptable to be dictated to from outside, and in the knowledge that D'Oliveira would be unwelcome in South Africa the proposed tour was scrapped.[13]

The furore over the D'Oliveira affair can only be understood in the broader context of Anglo-South African relations in the 1960s. Apartheid (or 'separateness') had been enforced in law by the ruling National Party in South Africa since 1948. This enshrined the political, economic and social power of the white minority over those classified as 'blacks', 'Indians' and (like D'Oliveira) 'coloureds'; segregation was applied rigidly in sport as across South African society as a whole. Although racial discrimination was evident in many parts of the world, the strict enforcement of the

law in South Africa attracted widespread international condemnation, much of which was channelled through the British-based
pressure group the Anti-Apartheid Movement (AAM). Labour
adopted a strong anti-apartheid stance in opposition before 1964,
but in government the importance of South Africa as a trading
partner – at a time when sterling was in a parlous state – was difficult to ignore. Britain benefited from the import of fruit, precious
metals and minerals, while British companies provided two-thirds
of all foreign investment in South Africa. Harold Wilson made
plain in public his loathing of apartheid, but at the same time he
had little truck with those like the AAM calling for the imposi-
tion of sanctions, as this would damage trading relationships. In
sport there were many advocates of continued links with South
Africa. Although the International Olympic Committee excluded
South Africa from the Games of 1964 and 1968, the MCC had
long-standing ties with their southern hemisphere equivalents and
had never expressed opposition to the whites-only selection policy
employed in South Africa. In a fluid situation, Wilson's government was faced with charges of hypocrisy: on the one hand taking a conciliatory line towards South Africa whenever economic
interests were at stake, but striking a firmer pose in sport when
financial concerns were generally not paramount.[14]

The sensitivity of the issue was such that Howell was alive to the
dangers well before the summer of 1968. Almost two years before
the England touring side was due to visit, hints emerged from
South Africa that any team containing Basil D'Oliveira would not
be allowed to enter the country. Questions were asked in the House
of Commons and in January 1967 the Sports Minister made a statement which made clear his abhorrence both of apartheid and of
political interference in team selections. Howell said that while
financial assistance was made available in some cases for amateur
teams to take part in international events, 'the Government do
not aid teams wishing to participate in events overseas in circumstances involving racial discrimination, and no application for
Government financial assistance towards sports visits to South
Africa has been agreed to, or will be entertained'. According to
the Minister, six such applications had been turned down. In
relation to the proposed cricket tour of 1968–69, Howell made
it clear that the government had no responsibility ('nor do they
wish to have responsibility') for the decisions of the MCC. He had,

however, taken part in some informal discussions, in which the Secretary of the MCC intimated that the team for South Africa would be chosen on merit; 'in this respect any preconditions that the host country lay down will be totally disregarded'.[15] In a confidential note written sometime later, Howell confided to the Prime Minister that MCC members did seem in conversation to be 'very naïve about the potential political repercussions', though firm on the point that the tour should be cancelled if there was any South African attempt to influence team selection.[16]

Howell felt his parliamentary statement in early 1967 helped to calm troubled waters, and little more was heard for the next 18 months. The Minister was as surprised as many others when, initially, D'Oliveira's name was not included in the touring team announced in mid-1968. He told Wilson he found the decision 'incomprehensible', but knowing the selectors as 'men of integrity', he did not doubt they reached their conclusions on cricketing grounds alone. Although the Commons was in recess at the time, the Minister was inundated with requests to intervene. In response he reiterated the 'twin planks' of his earlier statement: it was not his job to play any part in team selection and he accepted MCC assurances about the squad being chosen on merit.[17] On the surface, events played out much as Howell anticipated in his 1967 statement. When an injury brought D'Oliveira's name into the equation, the South African Cricket Association made it clear the England team was not welcome and in response the MCC unanimously called off the tour. But this was not the end of the episode. Recriminations continued and at a special meeting of the MCC in December 1968, David Sheppard – a former England captain, later to be Bishop of Liverpool – moved a vote of censure attacking the MCC for 'mishandling' the affair. He claimed that the MCC had been influenced in its views by advice from a 'prominent professional politician'. Sheppard refused, however, to put a name on the record and his vote of censure was soundly defeated.[18]

In April 1969 the issue flickered back into life again when press stories revealed that Lord Cobham, a former MCC President, visited South Africa six months before the England team was announced to be told emphatically by the authorities there that D'Oliveira was *persona non grata*. Howell wrote to the Prime Minister at this point that he had no prior knowledge of Cobham's involvement; while government policy was not to intervene he felt the cricket authorities might at least have put him in the picture. 'The line I have taken on press enquiries', he added, 'is that this is primarily a matter for the MCC... though I have not concealed my view that if the MCC were aware of what had been said to Lord Cobham they would have been wise to think twice before proceeding with the tour'.[19] In his memoirs Howell reflected that Cobham behaved properly in the whole matter, simply passing on the information he was given. Howell was more critical of another key figure whose involvement only came to light later still. The 'prominent professional politician' to whom David Sheppard referred was the former Conservative Prime Minister and influential member of the MCC, Sir Alec Douglas-Home, who met with South African leaders ahead of Cobham's visit. The Secretary of the MCC in due course told Howell: 'We took Alec's advice. We did not think we could possibly do better'. The full executive of the MCC was never told of the visits by Home and Cobham and so what happened, Howell summed up, amounted to a 'monumental miscalculation – an attempt to appease the South African Prime Minister... And one must assume Douglas-Home did not see fit to advise the MCC that they had some responsibility towards their own Government. It was an episode from which few could claim credit'.[20]

The 'Stop the Seventy Tour' Campaign

The D'Oliveira affair turned out to be only the prelude to apartheid-related protests in Britain that continued until the eve of the 1970 general election. In early 1969 the MCC, looking to mend some fences, invited the South Africans to take part in a tour of England in the summer of 1970. This decision galvanized the AAM, which increasingly regarded sport as an ideal campaigning arena. The AAM pledged itself to oppose the South African cricket tour, though it was soon eclipsed by a new group led by the Liberal student activist, Peter Hain. In July 1969 four young Liberals, including Hain, were arrested after staging a sit-in at a Davis Cup tennis tie between Britain and South Africa. Hain, a native of South Africa, was impatient with the constitutional methods of the AAM, and keen to engage in direct action. Student protests at several British universities attracted enormous publicity in 1968, and encouraged by this, a 'Stop the Seventy Tour' (STST) group was formed in the autumn of 1969. At a press launch Hain declared the aim was to 'mount a sustained campaign against apartheid in sport', and in particular to prevent the 1970 cricket tour from going ahead. Writing about the episode in 1971, Hain noted that he started out as 'spokesmen', but was soon dubbed 'Chairman'. Most of his fellow committee members had no experience of politics, and initially the group was looked upon warily by sections of the AAM. The national press, Hain added, also paid little attention to STST at this point, although this changed once the group began to gather momentum.[21]

The catalyst came in the form of a rugby tour by the South Africans, starting in October 1969. Rugby was as much a passion in South Africa as was cricket, and the arrival in Britain of an all-white 'Springboks' team provided STST with a ready-made opportunity to trial protest methods that it hoped to employ in opposing the subsequent cricket tour. The opening fixture at Oxford University was scheduled for 5 November, but was cancelled after STST activists sprayed weedkiller on the pitch. Hain believed this action was 'absolutely crucial to the fantastic growth ... of the campaign'; with trouble afoot, the national press began to take notice.[22] The first match was moved to Twickenham and played in eerie silence in front of a tiny crowd. The visitors were far from comfortable and were beaten by moderate opposition, a portent of what was to be a difficult tour ahead. Initially STST activists confined themselves mainly to prolonged chanting inside and outside of rugby venues. But in the fourth match of the tour, at Swansea on 15 November, ugly scenes occurred when protestors invaded the pitch and were met with a fierce response from 'stewards', who it turned out were mostly local rugby players encouraged by the police to remove demonstrators forcefully. Several STST campaigners were hauled off the pitch and beaten up. The incident made front page news the following day, and indicated that the South Africans had strong support in the rugby community. *The Guardian* quoted a former Swansea club player saying that after the match he 'heard the stewards openly boasting' about their tactics in a local hotel 'while they caroused with the Springboks'.[23]

The challenges posed by the rugby tour for law and order meant the issue moved beyond Howell's remit, requiring consideration by other departments such as the Home Office. Calls in the House of Commons for a public enquiry into the Swansea match and the curtailment of remaining fixtures came to nothing. The

Prime Minister stayed aloof from the controversy and the Home Office stuck to the line that it was up to the rugby authorities to take the lead, though it was agreed that a match due to take place on Ministry of Defence land would be cancelled. Roy Hattersley, a junior defence minister, advised that to allow the game to go ahead 'would be tantamount to Government intervention on the side of the South Africans in a matter of considerable political controversy'.[24] The publicity accorded to the Swansea incident helped STST to attract many new young recruits, often students, and other local anti-apartheid groups were also galvanized into action. As a result, the Springboks found themselves hounded for the remainder of the tour. In some places the team coach was blockaded or pelted with eggs; at some venues further pitch invasions were attempted, and smoke bombs were released. The players were clearly distracted on and off the pitch. The tourists failed to win any of their four test matches, and the players were only prevented from returning home early when team managers insisted on staying to fulfil contractual obligations. Although several newspapers attacked the protestors for infringing the rights of sportsmen, by the time the Springboks left in February 1970 STST felt vindicated in using sport to highlight the injustices of apartheid. Peter Hain summed up what he saw as the achievements of his fledging group: some 50,000 demonstrators turned out during the 25-match tour; one match was abandoned, and two others were moved from their original venues. 'The Springboks', he concluded, 'had the worst tour in their history'.[25]

Disruption to the rugby tour did not, however, persuade the English cricket authorities to rethink. Jack Bailey, an influential figure at the MCC, wrote that the majority view remained that South Africa, with arguably the strongest team in the world at the time, had contributed much to the international game and deserved to be seen by cricket fans in the summer of 1970.[26] A meeting of MCC's Cricket Council, charged with oversight of the proposed tour, agreed to reduce the number of fixtures, but did so purely to assist police in helping to minimize potential disruption. The stance of the Cricket Council attracted considerable support. In Conservative party ranks many MPs believed engagement was the best approach to South Africa – in sport as in other spheres – and there was great resentment at the likely cost to the taxpayer of policing cricket grounds. Peter Hain's direct action methods became a particular target for abuse, with one letter writer to the *Times* attacking the 'thugs and hooligans who attach themselves to any cause which gives them an excuse for vandalism'. There were echoes here of the white South African view of STST members as, in the words of the pro-government *Die Beeld*, a 'bunch of left-wing, workshy, refugee long-hairs'.[27] To set against this, backing for an abandonment of the cricket tour grew apace. STST campaigners argued that a pro-engagement attitude equated to backing for apartheid, even if dressed up in concern for maintaining law and order. The AAM weighed in by organizing a 12,000-signature petition calling for a scrapping of the tour which it presented to the International Cricket Council. Over one hundred MPs signed a letter urging the MCC to take decisive action, and David Sheppard, now Bishop of Woolwich, led protests among former players by launching a 'Fair Cricket Campaign', backed by prominent figures such as the Tory ex-minister Sir Edward Boyle.[28] On a wider sporting stage, the stakes were raised as a steadily increasing number of African and Asian nations threatened to show their displeasure at the cricket tour by boycotting the Commonwealth Games, due to be held in Edinburgh in July. As Peter May notes, the 1970 cricket season in England got under way in 'the unlikely eye of a global political storm'.[29]

The polarization of opinion and heightening of tension caused mounting concern for the government. In early March a meeting of senior Cabinet ministers gathered at Chequers, where a key item of discussion – according to Tony Benn in his diary – was the 'extremely difficult problem of the visit by the South African cricket team, and the fear this would trigger off demonstrations all summer'.[30] Wilson was giving serious consideration to a June general election, but dreaded the prospect of polling taking place at the same time as large protests at barbed-wire protected cricket grounds. One minister at least, Richard Crossman, was less than impressed by the threats of STST activists, claiming they had 'damaged their own anti-apartheid cause' by hardening the views of those who thought sport should operate independently of politics. 'We have to oppose both the disruption of sport and apartheid and this double role is extremely difficult', Crossman noted.[31] During April Denis Howell was asked by the Prime Minister to chair a small committee to keep him abreast of the developing situation, notably the growing number of nations declaring their

intention to boycott the Commonwealth Games. Howell's committee reported back that there were no legal grounds for denying the
South African team entry to Britain. As a result the best course was
for the government to refrain from direct intervention but to give
'tacit support' to any moves that 'might achieve a useful result'.
Jim Callaghan, the Home Secretary, confirmed the legal position
while telling Wilson in more blunt terms: 'Our present objective is
to intensify the pressures by all the unofficial means we can find in
the hope that the nerve of the Cricket Council will crack.'[32]

By April 1970 the cricket tour had become, as Peter Hain noted,
'a major national political issue'.[33] Indeed not since the Wolfenden
Report briefly captured attention in 1960 had sport occupied so
prominent a place in political discourse. Although Hain believed
STST campaigning had much to do with this, party tensions in the
run-up to a general election were arguably of greater significance.
In mid-April Wilson made a speech in which he sought to test the
resolve of the Cricket Council by calling the decision to invite
the South Africans 'very ill-judged'. Although the Prime Minister
explicitly said he did not support 'violent methods' or disruptive
tactics such as digging up pitches, his assertion that protestors
had the right to demonstrate against apartheid was interpreted
by the Conservatives (and several newspapers) as an incitement
to law breaking. At meetings of the Shadow Cabinet Iain Macleod
said it was important to take the matter up on behalf of the 'silent
majority', those who 'detested apartheid' but also wished to see
the matches played. Sir Peter Rawlinson, who appeared on a
'Panorama' TV special to present the Tory case, argued that the
'major principle' at stake was the responsibility of the state to
maintain law and order and 'not to provoke disturbances'; if disruption did take place, 'the responsibility for this should be laid on
the Prime Minister and the Home Secretary'. Some concern was
expressed in the Shadow Cabinet that if attacks on Wilson were
taken too far 'we might... give people the wrong impression that
we were complacent about apartheid'.[34] But the die was cast. When
the Prime Minister appeared on television on 30 April to urge the
Cricket Council to reconsider its stance, Ted Heath quickly countered by backing the tour. Wilson, writing in 1971, believed there
was a big element of political expediency in the line taken by the
Tories. The opposition, he claimed, 'could barely conceal their
pleasure' at the prospect of an election dominated by the theme

of law and order; 'our opponents hoped that the General Election of 1970 would be fought and won on and around the cricket-pitch at Lord's'.[35]

With the tour due to start on 1 June, all sides remained intransigent. Whenever another nation (up to nearly 20 by mid-May) declared an intention to boycott the Edinburgh games, the Cricket Council reaffirmed that the South African tour would go ahead. The Sports Minister drafted a Cabinet paper on 6 May arguing that the best course for the government was still that of applying pressure through indirect means. Direct intervention, for example a personal appeal from the Prime Minister to the Cricket Council, could be counterproductive; if rebuffed, the government's credibility would be greatly damaged in the run-up to polling.[36] Tempers among ministers frayed, with Howell resisting pressure from Dick Crossman to take a stronger line with the MCC. 'We may have to interfere', Howell argued, 'but that moment was not today'. In a heated Commons debate on 14 May, Philip Noel-Baker opened proceedings by reminding the Cricket Council that they had responsibilities to sport as a whole, but he was followed by Tory ex-minister John Boyd-Carpenter, who argued that to cancel the tour would be to deny freedom. Outlining the government position, the Minister for Sport spoke of unique discrimination on grounds of skin colour that was the 'root cause of the offence South Africa gives to the world'. Howell was also able to report that a specially convened meeting of the Sports Council had been unanimous in calling on the cricket authorities to scrap the tour. Home Secretary Jim Callaghan (who afterwards said it was the most effective speech he had heard Howell make) concluded by insisting it was 'not unfair to the Cricket Council to throw responsibility upon them. They invited the South Africans, and they can uninvite them if they choose to do so'.[37]

What finally broke the deadlock was the announcement on 18 May that a general election would be held a month later. After Cabinet discussions to finalize the date the day before, Tony Benn wrote in his diary: 'Jim [Callaghan] has this terrible problem of the South African cricket tour, where the Cricket Council have so far absolutely declined to change their attitude.'[38] Any prospect that the election announcement would immediately alter the dynamics of the problem appeared to have passed when the Cricket Council, holding an emergency meeting on 19 May, declared that any future tours would not be sanctioned until South Africa selected its team on a multiracial basis, but that the impending visit would not be affected. Peter Hain was not alone in attacking this compromise, describing it as 'tinged with illogicality and hypocrisy'; the cricket authorities accepted the principle of severing ties 'but apparently wanted one last bite of the white South African cake'.[39] Once it was clear that the Cricket Council was not going to have a last-minute change of mind on its own account, Callaghan decided the time had come to make a direct appeal. With the cricket tour looking set to overshadow the election campaign, the traditional ministerial practice of maintaining distance from the decisions of sporting authorities was set aside. On 21 May the Home Secretary met with the Chairman and Secretary of the Cricket Council, J. C. Allom and Billy Griffith, and told them that while the government had no power to prohibit the matches, it felt that on the grounds of 'broad public policy' the cancellation of the tour was preferable. In particular Callaghan referred to the divisive impact of the visit, the consequences for race relations in Britain, the effects on the Commonwealth games and the additional burden placed on the police. Allom and Griffith agreed that, faced with this formal request, the full Cricket Council would feel it had little choice but to respond. The following day a hastily convened meeting of the Cricket Council, without recourse to a vote, called off the tour with 'deep regret'.[40]

Reaction to the news of the sudden abandonment of the tour was varied. Some cricket enthusiasts were aghast, and the Cricket Council sought to regain a measure of credit by hastily arranging a series of matches between England and a 'Rest of the World' team, which included prominent South Africans. By contrast, Peter Hain was jubilant, praising the government in a TV interview on 22 May for what he described as its courageous action. In later reflections, Hain argued that it was primarily STST which acted as the catalyst, engineering a position where the government had no option but to intervene. With the exception of individuals such as Edward Boyle, the role of the Conservatives was 'squalid', Hain believed, particularly when it sought to exploit the situation for 'narrow political ends'. According to Hain, it was his group which 'created the public interest and atmosphere of opposition; which forced the Government's hand; which in the end, stopped the Seventy

Tour'.[41] This conclusion did less than justice to the work of other bodies such as the AAM and the Fair Cricket Campaign, as well as the contribution made to the final outcome by nations threatening to cold shoulder the Commonwealth Games. On the other hand, Hain was no doubt right to celebrate a victory that left South Africa increasingly isolated in the sporting world, excluded from international events such as the Olympics and the Davis Cup and finding it difficult to proceed with cricket or rugby tours. Although the National Party remained implacably opposed to racially mixed sport, international isolation did persuade sports administrators in South Africa to begin seeking at least cosmetic changes during the 1970s.[42]

In British political circles responses to the scrapping of the tour were similarly mixed. Denis Howell was uneasy that, for the first time in the post-war period, the principle of not interfering in the decision-making processes of sporting authorities had been breached. He wrote in his memoirs that the Cricket Council demonstrated 'right to the end that they preferred to rest their decision upon the Government's advice rather than upon an acceptance of sporting responsibility'.[43] But the Sports Minister was also no doubt relieved, like his colleagues, that the issue would no longer influence the election campaign. For the Conservatives, Quintin Hogg indignantly attacked what he described as Labour's incompetence in preserving rights of freedom. In the view of the Prime Minister, senior Tories who rushed to denounce the decision to call off the tour were 'expressing a sense of deprivation – not of the opportunity of seeing some lively cricket, but of the prospect of Britain's television screens portraying anti-apartheid demonstrations'.[44] Public opinion polls indicated that a majority of voters were opposed to the cancellation of the tour, though there was no indication that it continued to resonate once the election campaign got into full swing. Howell was told by the cricket commentator John Arlott that some MCC insiders believed the government's position would cost Labour half a million votes at the election. This may have had some credence if the tour had gone ahead, resulting in endless media stories associated with violence and disruption. But in the event, agents for all parties were able to report that the cricket tour was not an issue on the doorstep; an opinion poll immediately after the election found that less than one per cent of voters mentioned it.[45]

Sport and the 1970 General Election

The settling of the controversy over the South African cricket tour paved the way, it seemed, for internal rather than external sporting matters to return to the fore in the run-up to polling day. The latter stages of the Wilson government had witnessed a nagging dispute about the status of the Sports Council. Alongside arguments over which Whitehall department should have priority, the DES or the MHLG, there was mounting concern after 1967 that as an advisory body, the Sports Council did not provide the best mechanism for delivering improvements in sport. Behind the scenes initially, two particular criticisms gained in force. One was that with Howell as its Chairman, the Council lacked the ability to speak independently on behalf of sport; the second and related argument was that at a time of economic restraint, the Council might be able to negotiate increased funding more effectively if it had full-blown executive authority, free from direct ties to the government of the day. In March 1968 the Minister confronted the issue head on by discussing with the full Council the idea of moving from advisory to executive status. Howell made clear that while this option was not ruled out if colleagues believed it to be right, his view was that it was undesirable. He argued that Regional Sports Councils, for example, forging ahead with activity across the country, valued partnership with the government. Several members of the full Council, however, made the case for reform: it was possible that an independent body would secure greater funding; the public had difficulty in distinguishing between the Council and the Minister; and some members felt inhibited under existing arrangements about criticizing government policy.[46] By encouraging debate, Howell drew some of the sting from the issue. In 1969 key players including leaders of the CCPR and heads of Regional Sports Councils were consulted, and a majority agreed that the advisory nature of the Sports Council should be maintained. A similar conclusion prevailed at a two-day conference of leading sports administrators held in the spring of 1970, which backed the minister's claim that the existing arrangements 'were proving efficient and satisfactory in practice'.[47]

Even so, this was not the last word on the matter. The functioning of the Sports Council was an increasing priority in the thinking of the Conservative opposition. Following Chataway's loss of his parliamentary seat at the 1966 election, the lead in framing Tory policy had been taken by Charles Morrison, MP for Devizes. Morrison had connections with football and hockey in Wiltshire, and although only in his mid-30s was appointed Chairman of the South West Regional Sports Council. After meeting on 11 occasions – taking evidence from bodies such as the CCPR and National Playing Fields Association (NPFA) – an eight-strong study group chaired by Morrison submitted a detailed report to Ted Heath in June 1969. Echoing the Bow Group findings of 1965, Morrison's report, which was meant initially only for internal consumption, conceded there was electoral ground to be made up by the Conservatives on sport:

> To a very considerable extent, the Government's reputation stems from the activity of Mr Denis Howell. He was responsible for the establishment of the Sports Council, the Regional Sports Councils and numerous local sports advisory committees. Although there is now some disillusionment amongst people serving on these committees, since promised resources are not being made available, the picture which Labour has nurtured is one of great benevolence to sport.

While acknowledging the need for the Tory party 'to demonstrate its own good intentions', the report believed the weakness of Labour's approach was a 'clumsy and muddled' administrative framework. This opened the way for a new initiative based on several proposals: Whitehall responsibility to be concentrated in a single department; more money for sport to be attracted from private sources; and an executive Sports Council to be established, taking over the grant-aiding functions of DES.[48]

In spite of the strong opposition in Conservative ranks to an executive Sports Council when it was proposed by Sir John Wolfenden in 1960, Morrison's group believed such a body was now essential to provide a 'focus of sports and recreational development'. When the Shadow Cabinet discussed sport in July 1969, Morrison described the need for an executive Council as his group's central recommendation. In the absence of Heath, most speakers who contributed to the ensuing discussion expressed the view that in sport, as in plans for the arts, a watchful eye needed to be kept on 'too much Government control'. Keith Joseph expressed himself 'against the use of public money' where possible. Others welcomed the report in broad terms but felt it would be unwise to abolish the role of Minister for Sport. This, Morrison's group found, would be the logical consequence of establishing a strong, independent Sports Council, 'since much of the work which he [Howell] now undertakes would have been removed'. Chairing the Shadow Cabinet, Reginald Maudling summed up that the recommendations of the study group could be carried forward subject to the reservation about abolishing the role of a Sports Minister.[49] At a meeting of the Conservative Advisory Committee on Policy shortly afterwards, Maudling expanded on the case for keeping such a position, whether at the DES or the MHLG. It had to be conceded that Howell 'made a good impression as Minister of Sport because he was a well-known personality', and this would have been the same irrespective of his departmental home.[50] By the end of 1969 Labour, as noted above, carried out a restructuring of Whitehall machinery which, by transferring responsibility for sport to the MHLG, undercut one of Morrison's main proposals. The result was that the recommendation to create an executive Council was left to become the centrepiece of the Tory election manifesto in this field in 1970: 'We will make the Sports Council an independent body, and make it responsible for the grant-aiding functions at present exercised by the Government.'[51]

The Conservatives thus went to the country with a distinctive policy position and even flirted with the idea of raising the profile of sport as a campaigning issue. In April 1970 the Shadow Cabinet considered a paper which started from a different basis: it claimed that while many believed the Sports Council had made 'worthwhile progress', the real weakness of Labour policy was a lack of sustained investment. Direct grant aid under the 1937 Act had 'increased substantially', it was conceded, but loans by local authorities had dipped, making it 'impossible for the Labour Party to claim that they have ended the parsimony in the supply of funds for recreation'. The main figures cited in the paper for loan expenditure were £29.5 million in 1963–64 and £24.77 million in 1968–69, though the small print conceded the basis of calculating the statistics had changed; the latter related to facilities used exclusively for sport, whereas the former included items for general recreation such as community halls.[52] Charles Morrison told colleagues that Labour's spending on sport 'was not equal to the amount said about the subject'. But in the Shadow Cabinet discussion that followed the case for prioritizing sport as an election issue was described 'as a marginal one'; the statistics could be read in various ways and the further back one went in time 'the less advantageous they would be to us'. Summing up, Ted Heath concluded that sport was not, after all, 'a very good subject' for parliamentary exposure in the run-up to the election.[53] Unwilling to adopt a strategy that promised higher public expenditure, the Tories retreated to a position that focused on the need for the creation of an executive Sports Council. This left Labour, as in 1966, believing it held the upper hand on sport as the election campaign got fully into swing. Labour's manifesto claimed the government's support for leisure over recent years had been 'immense' and that such support would continue into the 1970s.[54]

But unlike in 1966, a generally serene campaign for Labour was not to be followed by re-election. The prospect of prolonged protests against the visiting South African cricketers may have gone away, but in the final days of the campaign ministers were confronted with another unwelcome development on the international sporting front: England's exit from football's World Cup. The tournament began in Mexico on 31 May, and confidence was high as the defending champions progressed through the group stages, each England match attracting huge audiences on television. But on Sunday 14 June, just four days before polling, England squandered a two-goal lead to lose 3–2 to West Germany in the quarter-finals. The blame was put on a mixture of goalkeeping errors in the absence of the bug-stricken Gordon Banks and the decision to withdraw key players to preserve their energies for an anticipated semi-final.

After recovering from its dip in 1968–69, Labour had retained a small but steady lead in opinion polls for several months ahead of the election. In their study of the 1970 campaign David Butler and Michael Pinto-Duschinsky wrote that on 15 June there was a short break in the glorious summer weather: 'the change, like the World Cup defeat, may have contributed to a switch in mood'.[55] There was to be much talk in due course of a late swing to the Conservatives, sufficient to give Heath a surprisingly comfortable 40-seat majority. Howell was among those who believed the defeat in Mexico was a contributory factor. He wrote in his memoirs of a definite mood shift in the final days of campaigning, with

England's abrupt defeat the talk of the factories as he toured his constituency. Tony Crosland echoed this view, blaming Labour's slide on 'a mix of party complacency and the disgruntled Match of the Day millions'.[56] Butler and Pinto-Duschinsky argue, however, that if there was a late swing of public opinion it was more likely to have resulted from the announcement, the day after the World Cup exit, of adverse trade figures. After nine months of good returns, a large deficit for May was immediately seized upon by Heath in a strong TV performance. With the benefit of hindsight, about half of all Tory and Labour candidates at the election agreed with the notion of a late movement of opinion. Of those among this group who reflected on the causes, most put it down to the trade figures, with just a handful agreeing with the Labour MP who bemoaned 'the damned germ in Gordon Banks' tummy that punctured the mood of euphoria'.[57]

Conclusion

When Labour lost office in 1970, there could be no doubt that links between sport and politics had been put on a new footing. Before Harold Wilson entered Downing Street as Prime Minister in 1964, the approach of both Labour and Conservative administrations towards sport had been largely uncoordinated, ambiguous and low key. But under Wilson sport established itself as a legitimate area of government concern and claimed a political profile unimaginable in the 1950s. Much of this profile arose from growing commercial and media interest in international and professional sport. Against this backcloth, government involvement sometimes reflected positively on ministers (as in the hosting of the 1966 World Cup), though at other times it caused unwelcome and protracted anxiety, notably over the anti-apartheid protests associated with rugby and cricket during 1969–70. Looking back on the record of his government, Wilson felt especially confident in claiming that on the domestic front sport had been prioritized in an unprecedented manner. A long-awaited Sports Council finally became a reality, providing a vital focus, and Howell had served as Sports Minister with 'great force and equal acceptability'. Wilson noted that twice as much was being spent by central government in direct grants on sport in 1970–71, around £2.5 million annually, as in 1963–64, and that in consequence facilities for the likes of swimming, athletics and cycling had been 'revolutionized'.[58]

The attitude of the Prime Minister in establishing a benevolent environment for sport was crucial in the second half of the 1960s; not all of his successors, as will be seen in later chapters, took on such a supportive role. But the lion's share of responsibility for the higher profile of sport in political circles by the end of the decade clearly rested with Denis Howell. Justin Evans of the CCPR noted that after Labour's defeat at the 1970 election tributes to the work of the Minister for Sport and Chairman of the Sports Council 'were genuine and widespread – his energy, enthusiasm and friendliness had won him many friends in the world of sport'.[59] Howell's 'energy and enthusiasm' was the product of both ideological conviction – the belief that the state needed to actively assist the sport without directly controlling it – and a pragmatic sense that his party's image would be enhanced through a progressive policy. It was a testimony to his 'friendliness' that some of the tributes paid to him in 1970 came from his political opponents. Discussing the 'ballyhoo' created by Howell, Conservatives acknowledged in the run-up to the election that it was no longer possible to simply sideline sport, or to retreat to a stance of non-intervention.[60]

Yet in spite of all that had been achieved, when Wilson departed from Downing Street in 1970 the future relationship between sport and the state remained uncertain. Although the transfer of responsibility from the DES to the MHLG in 1969 provided for greater coherence in Whitehall, concerns about the most appropriate administrative machinery for developing sport remained a matter of contention. The parties went into the 1970 election divided over the future status of the Sports Council, in particular the vexed question of how far it should be tied directly to ministerial wishes. Wilson's claim that sporting facilities had been 'revolutionized' was also difficult to square with the reality on the ground and the scale of funding. Direct exchequer spending on sport had risen sharply but still not reached the levels proposed by the Wolfenden Report in 1960, and local authority funds had been continually squeezed. In its various guises state investment in sport remained only a tiny fraction, less than one per cent, of total public expenditure.[61] And Labour had not devoted much attention, as Howell promised in 1964, to explaining where sport fitted into a 'basic philosophy of the fullness of life', and whether it deserved government investment as of right or in order to serve other social purposes such as tackling youth crime or improving public health. In the 1970s, as the British economy lurched from one crisis to the next, sport would be faced with great difficulties in preserving the fragile and hard-won gains of the 1960s.

6 Battling for 'Sport and Recreation' in the 1970s

Introduction

'Almost everyone who has reflected seriously about Britain in the 1970s agrees that the decade was little short of a disaster', writes the historian Nick Tiratsoo. The charge sheet is long and well-known. This was a period in which successive governments, Conservative from 1970 to 1974 and Labour from 1974 to 1979, appeared to be overwhelmed by one economic disaster after another. Trade union militants were said to have become 'robber barons', holding the country to ransom with excessive wage demands, precipitating Heath's fall from power in 1974. A massive rise in world oil prices heralded an era of relentlessly high inflation, necessitating the humiliation of intervention by the International Monetary Fund (IMF) to 'save' the British economy in 1976. It seemed fitting that the decade ended with sustained and sometimes violent industrial unrest in 1979, when Prime Minister Jim Callaghan (who replaced Harold Wilson in 1976) was rendered helpless in the face of trade union power during the 'winter of discontent'. 'Nobody could sensibly claim that Britain was at its finest in the 1970s', Tiratsoo concedes, but he goes on to argue, in an attempt to modify conventional perceptions of the period, that 'the country's problems have frequently been exaggerated and distorted'. The government never had to draw on more than half the credits made available by the IMF, and there were short phases of economic optimism amidst the regular downturns. There were also some important landmarks in social reform, with legislation passed on topics including racial and sexual discrimination.[1] Any assessment of the relationship between sport and politics during the 1970s must therefore aim to get behind the stereotypes of the decade. For sport, as for society at large, this was a period of great stresses and challenges, but as will be shown, the trend towards closer

governmental involvement in sport evident since 1964 was not ruptured and was in some respects enhanced. In 1974 the author of
the first full-scale review of sport by parliamentarians, while critical of the low level of state investment, praised those who battled
for resources and claimed the real surprise was that any progress
was being made at all given the harsh economic climate and the
fact that until recently governments 'took scarcely any part in the
provision of sport or recreation facilities'.[2]

The Move to an Executive Sports Council

The new Conservative Prime Minister in 1970, Edward Heath, had
sympathy with sporting concerns as a proficient yachtsman (winning the prestigious Sydney to Hobart race on his boat 'Morning
Cloud' in 1969), and in line with pre-election party discussions
Heath continued with Labour's practice of appointing a Sports
Minister. The person chosen was not Charles Morrison, who shadowed Denis Howell from 1966 onwards, but rather Eldon Griffiths,
MP for Bury St Edmunds. Unlike Howell, who in the latter stages
of his stewardship operated as a Minister of State, Griffiths was to
remain a junior minister (Joint Parliamentary Under-Secretary) at
the newly created Department of the Environment (DoE) for the
full term of the Heath administration. John Coghlan, a leading
figure at the Sports Council in the 1970s, observed that Griffiths
was a good public speaker, though more hands-off towards sport
than his predecessor Howell; the new minister devoted the bulk of
his time to other responsibilities at the DoE.[3]

From his vantage point on the opposition benches, shadowing
sport and the environment, Howell was not the only one who found
the appointment of Eldon Griffiths a surprise; the latter's only
sporting connection seemed to be the presence of Newmarket and
its horse racing fraternity in his constituency. Howell later ascertained that Charles Morrison was told he was passed over because
Griffiths had strong links with Heath's inner circle and needed to
be accommodated in ministerial ranks. Howell also claimed he
wrote to Griffiths offering him good wishes in his new post and
full cooperation 'in all matters in which bi-partisan policies ought
to be followed'. But, he added, this offer 'was never taken up'.[4]
As well as illustrating that sport continued to be more politically
divisive than historians have usually acknowledged, Howell's terse

comment pointed to the acrimony that developed in the early 1970s over one issue in particular – the desire of the Conservative government to reconstitute the Sports Council as a body with executive powers, responsible for the grant-aiding functions hitherto exercised by government departments.

In July 1970 Griffiths, chairing his first meeting of the advisory Council he inherited from Labour, said that change would only follow after 'the fullest consultation with all interested parties'. For several months thereafter, the minister familiarized himself with the sporting scene, travelling the country and meeting key administrators and officials. He found opinion was sharply divided over the status of the Sports Council. Some felt reform would be beneficial, but others believed existing arrangements worked satisfactorily. Any change would have major implications especially for the Central Council of Physical Recreation (CCPR), the umbrella group representing national governing bodies, where the majority view was in favour of continuing with the status quo. Finding any consensus elusive, Griffiths decided to take the bull by the horns and press ahead with his party's 1970 election pledge. After almost exactly a year in office he announced his decision in a written parliamentary answer:

> It is the Government's intention to foster the development of sport in all its aspects…The Sports Council has a leading part to play in this; but it is not enough for the Sports Council to merely advise. Accordingly the government has decided to enhance the Council's status, give it independence and extend its role…The new Council's functions will include the provision of appropriate grants for sporting organisations, activities and projects; assistance to British representative teams competing in international sports activities…; the provision and management of national sports centres; and the forging of closer sporting links with and among local authorities, the armed services, private enterprise and the large spectator sports.[5]

The statement confirmed that Scotland and Wales would have their own equivalent Councils and that Dr Roger Bannister would chair the executive Council on a part-time basis. Bannister was famous as the world's first sub-four-minute miler in 1954, and in his professional life was an eminent neurologist. He headed the Research Committee of the advisory Council in the 1960s and was to bring, in the words of John Coghlan, 'a formidable intellect, style and sense of leadership' to the reconstituted Sports Council.[6]

The means chosen for changing the status of the Council was a Royal Charter, a device which Denis Howell claimed had never been mentioned by civil servants in his time as minister. Arguments about the functioning of the Council had, as we have seen, grown in intensity before 1970. Advocates of reform believed an executive Sports Council, as well as potentially receiving higher levels of funding, would also be free from government interference (an important principle for many Conservatives), operating in the same way as the Arts Council. Howell's view, however, was that the advisory nature of the Sports Council was not a handicap but a benefit; with a minister in the chair it proved a vital way of relating 'sport to government', creating an effective partnership between the two. In the absence of any approach from Eldon Griffiths – despite the promise of the 'fullest consultation' – Howell arranged a meeting with the Lord President of the Council, Willie Whitelaw, who had oversight of Royal Charters. He told Whitelaw that Labour would oppose the creation of a chartered Council, and would advise the CCPR to do the same. If Howell hoped this threat would stop the government in its tracks, making the issuing of a Royal Charter unusually contentious, he was disappointed. He assumed the CCPR, the 'democratic assembly of sport' he called it, would not surrender its position. But this seemed increasingly likely when the government offered CCPR staff the chance to become professional employees of the new Sports Council. The CCPR was also rumoured to be willing to relinquish its ownership of national sports centres such as those at Crystal Palace. 'I was incredulous that a voluntary body of sport would even contemplate such a proposition', Howell recollected in his memoirs. He knew that if the CCPR was not going to put up a fight to retain its independence, then the government's comfortable majority in the Commons meant there was little to prevent the Royal Charter coming into force.[7]

The knowledge that Griffiths would get his way may explain the particularly querulous tone adopted by Howell when parliament discussed the government's plans in July 1971. Coghlan described this debate as 'sharp, to the point and stormy'.[8] Howell began by asserting that anyone whom the minister bothered to consult was opposed to an executive Council. He wished the new body well but admitted to 'grave doubts'. What, he asked, 'does the Minister of Sport do if he is not Minister of Sport?' He would have no responsibility for the reconstituted Sports Council and would presumably not be answerable to MPs on the grounds that any enquiries should be directed to the Council. As a result there would be no public accountability for policy. Griffiths responded that the new Council would be more effective: it would work as a board of directors, making strategic decisions, rather than ploughing as the old Council did through the minute details of thousands of individual applications. It would also, he claimed, be accountable through annual reports and crucially, it would be independent. The idea of a Sports Council beyond the reach of ministerial diktat was a key attraction for Tory backbenchers, one of whom welcomed the fact that 'the Government are now dealing at arms' length with sport and are not directly interfering with it'. The fractious nature of the debate continued to the end with Tam Dalyell, summing up for Labour, welcoming the appointment of Roger Bannister but warning: 'the notion that he can do in two days a week the job that my hon. Friend the Member for Small Heath did seven days a week is simply fanciful'. In an unusually high turn out for a debate on sport, MPs voted by 190 votes to 161 in favour of a motion to introduce 'an independent sports council with enhanced status, wider powers and larger funds at its disposal'.[9]

Once MPs had agreed that Her Majesty be asked to grant a Royal Charter, it only remained to work through the details of how the new Council would operate. The most contentious remaining question was the future of the CCPR. Although the parliamentary statement by Griffiths on 10 June referred to ongoing consultations, later the same day the minister met the CCPR Executive and said he wished to see an 'amalgamation'. Griffiths sought to reassure his audience by saying CCPR staff had a vital role to play in the new system; they would be sifting the many applications for grants at London headquarters and would also provide the professional face of regional councils. Within a month of this meeting the CCPR through its Executive agreed to go into voluntary liquidation. Negotiations from this time on focused on securing the best possible terms for staff transferring from the CCPR to the Sports Council. Justin Evans, who retired at this time after many years of service at the CCPR, wrote that while some lamented the outcome, it was mostly felt to be unavoidable. By becoming progressively closer to government in recent times, 'seconding' its Director and providing secretarial services to the advisory Sports Council in the 1960s, 'the CCPR Executive had itself created a situation from which a retreat was impossible even if one had been desired'.[10] After many years as CCPR Chairman, Stanley Rous bowed to what seemed inevitable. 'On reflection', he commented, integration was 'the logical solution' because it helped to facilitate the Sports Council becoming 'fully effective'. Although not thanked for saying so, Rous felt the main achievements of the CCPR were in the past. The key thing was to create for the future a single body to coordinate efforts on behalf of sport 'and so I was content to step quietly aside when the effective power was transferred to the Sports Council'.[11]

The story of the CCPR took a surprise twist, however, when its long-standing President, Prince Philip, intervened at the AGM in November 1971 to say he was opposed to the body committing 'voluntary hara-kiri'. While welcoming the proposed Sports Council, and having no qualms about the transfer of staff, he objected to the possibility that the CCPR might be disbanded altogether and replaced by a standing conference of sports organizations. To his mind 'such a standing conference already existed and had been functioning as such for the past 35 years'. The Prince felt the CCPR should continue in that vein in future, having the necessary membership and methods of functioning, and requiring only a secretariat from the Sports Council to enable this to happen.[12] Although his opposition was widely reported in the press, Prince Philip did not stand in the way of a formal merger between the CCPR and Sports Council taking place when 'Heads of Agreement' were signed in 1972. At this point, as Justin Evans notes, the history of 'the original CCPR' came to an end, replaced by what Eldon Griffiths in a slip of the tongue referred to as 'the residual CCPR'.[13] A few months later Denis Howell was called to Buckingham Palace, where the Prince made clear his disgruntlement. In the wake of this encounter Howell devoted considerable time to a campaign to 'rescue the CCPR from oblivion'. In the spring of 1973 he was unanimously elected chairman of the reconstituted body, and set about exploiting the wording in the 'Heads of Agreement' under which the Sports Council agreed to make resources available to the CCPR 'as may reasonably be required'. This led to clashes with the Sports Council, which was reluctant to direct precious funds to staffing the CPPR, but Howell was hugely experienced in fighting this type of battle. By the time he relinquished the chairmanship in 1974, Howell was confident that 'the new CCPR...was beyond the destruction of the Government'.[14]

The CCPR lived on, but after the granting of the Royal Charter in December 1971 it was the executive Sports Council – formally constituted on 4 February 1972 – that was centre stage. Its twenty-strong membership included stalwarts of the earlier advisory Council like David Munrow, as well as fresh faces from the sporting world such as the footballers Jimmy Hill and Bob Wilson. The Council's first annual report gave a detailed account of its objectives, which were summarized as promoting understanding of the importance of sport and physical recreation, increasing the provision of new facilities to serve community needs, encouraging wider participation and raising standards of performance.[15] Based on the experience of other western European nations, Bannister launched a 'Sport for All' campaign, aiming to heighten awareness of the value of sport to people of every age and background. Free to determine how to spend its annual government grant, the Council in its early years supported a wide range of projects. Roughly one million pounds a year was devoted to assisting voluntary sports clubs in developing their programmes and infrastructure, and financial support was directed towards statutory bodies, including local authorities, for capital costs and the building of new facilities, such as a National Water Sports Centre at Holme Pierrepont. The encouragement of a major building programme of multipurpose indoor sports centres was a development Bannister particularly valued. 'I rate these as the most important Sports Council achievement', he later wrote.[16] In the eyes of many observers, any doubts about the value of an executive Council quickly disappeared. According to John Coghlan, the constitutional independence of sport seemed assured provided the Council was led by strong figures – such as Roger Bannister – capable of withstanding 'the considerable pressures from Government and Whitehall'. A crucial benefit, Coghlan claimed, was that sport was no longer prey to 'political mood and fashion, except for the all-important annual vote of financial resources from Parliament'.[17]

Finance and Policy Under Eldon Griffiths, 1972–74

The creation of the chartered Sports Council undoubtedly provided a fresh sense of momentum, but ultimately it did not make
sport immune to 'political mood and fashion', or bring an end
to arguments over the most appropriate relationship between
government and sport. All sides were agreed on the need for a
partnership, but the nature of the alliance remained in dispute.
Labour's view was that a Sports Minister, without dictating, should
be actively involved across a range of issues; in the Commons
debate of July 1971 Howell lamented that the Minister for Sport
had no real function if all responsibility for determining priorities and polices rested with the executive Sports Council. Whereas
Howell, in the words of John Coghlan, sought to maintain 'a high
profile both in and out of office', Eldon Griffiths, 'having set matters on the road' – by pushing ahead with the Royal Charter –
'largely withdrew' from direct intervention in policy-making.[18]
The principle adopted by Griffiths was that sporting authorities
should be free to determine their own needs as much as possible,
though not all his Tory successors were to be so willing to stand
aside, and Griffiths himself found himself increasingly drawn into
controversy over the scale of funding for sport: the 'all-important'
annual grant to the Sports Council that required Cabinet and parliamentary approval.

During his first year in post, Griffiths adopted a bullish
approach, claiming the Conservatives were determined to remedy years of under investment by Labour. One of the reasons tem-
peratures rose in the Commons debate on the introduction of the
new Sports Council was that Griffiths – more aggressively than
Tory spokesmen in the past – spent much of his speech seeking
to wrestle back Labour's perceived electoral advantage on sport.
He conceded that central government funding for sport rose
during the Wilson years, but claimed that in the wake of local
authority cutbacks after devaluation in 1967, combined central
and local government spending on sport was lower than when
the Conservatives relinquished office in 1964. 'The plain fact is
that Labour promises were not matched by Labour performance.'
Howell repeatedly interrupted this part of the Minister's speech,
which he claimed was 'beyond belief'. For Howell it was particularly 'contemptuous' to insinuate that during his time as Sports

Minister he had short-changed governing bodies over grant applications.[19]

It was one thing for Griffiths to lambast Labour's record; another to deliver on a promise in the same debate to more than double the direct Exchequer contribution to sport. In the last full year of the advisory Sports Council, 1970–71, central government spending ran at £2.53 million, a sum which rose to £3.26 million for 1971–72 and to £3.60 million during 1972–73.[20] John Coghlan reflected that these 'low-base' figures, where increases only kept pace with inflation, were an albatross around the neck of the executive Sports Council for years to come. Any thoughts of a rapid 'break out of the strait-jacket of public expenditure budgeting' were soon being scaled down.[21] The allocations were certainly not enough to satisfy the Council Chairman Roger Bannister, who before long was saying in public that the annual grant was insufficient to achieve a meaningful programme of development. The result was one the Conservatives had not anticipated in establishing a new administrative framework. Whereas Howell, by chairing the advisory Sports Council, could mostly keep arguments over funding behind closed doors, a strong head of the executive Council like Bannister had no qualms, indeed saw it as his duty, to vociferously demand increased funding. As well as making his case through speeches, giving the impression of the government dragging its feet, Bannister regularly lobbied ministers with a view to securing substantially higher investment. The response of the DoE in the summer of 1972 was that a 'more solid case' would have to be made if the Department was to 'approach the Treasury with any hope of success'.[22] In spite of his sniping at Labour's record, Griffiths was obliged to sing a different tune in responding to Bannister's requests: economic difficulties meant the time was not ripe, he wrote, for bids requesting additional public spending. The Sports Minister did, however, agree that officials working in his department should liaise with representatives of the Sports Council, with a view to reviewing where shortages of facilities were most acute and drawing up a list of key priorities that would require fresh finance in order to be successfully completed.[23]

By the beginning of 1973, having been in post for over two years, Griffiths was ready to press upon his Secretary of State at the DoE, Geoffrey Rippon, the case for significantly increased spending on sport. Initially he made little headway. Employing the language

Griffiths himself used in talks with Bannister, Rippon said 'this may not be a good moment to ask for more money'. The Sports Minister was encouraged to prepare a document setting out his views, and in this he began by alluding to the social benefits of sport, such as the promotion of physical and mental health and the part it played in countering juvenile delinquency. Here was a theme that to was occur with growing intensity from the early 1970s onwards: the notion that sport required state support not so much because of its own intrinsic worth but as something that contributed to other aspects of welfare policy. Griffiths noted that the government's existing figures projected an increase in the Sports Council grant from £5.0 million for 1973–4 to £5.7 million for 1975–6. He hoped, however, that they 'could go much further towards' Bannister's targets, which sought a rise from £5.75 to £11.0 million over the same period. The extent to which Heath's administration had been thrown on the defensive over sport since 1970 was illustrated when Griffith alluded to the electoral context against which his demands were set. 'There is an impression throughout the country, fed and fanned by the Press', he wrote, 'that the provision which the Government makes for sport is niggardly compared with the level of grant in aid to the Arts Council, for what some choose to regard as chiefly for middle class benefit'. There was, Griffiths concluded, a political imperative to act: criticism was not easy to refute and 'could be much reduced by announcing a provisional intention to embark on a steeply rising programme broadly as advocated by the Sports Council'.[24]

Geoffrey Rippon was not persuaded to accept the ambitious demands of the Sports Council. He did, however, press for some increase in the projected figures, bringing him up against the formidable barrier of the Treasury in the summer of 1973. The Environment Secretary argued that because the DoE had accepted tighter spending restrictions than many other departments, it had been agreed there might be some off-setting increases to 'sugar the pill'. In this vein he asked for a 'modest increase' of half a million pounds in the grant to the Sports Council for 1974–75, up to a total of £5.8 million, in order to 'avoid politically unacceptable consequences'.[25] When ministers and officials at the DoE met to discuss progress in August, Griffiths urged his superior to continue pressing the Treasury for more money. Other European nations were giving higher priority to spending on sport than was

Britain, he claimed, 'where such expenditure was in real terms no greater than in the early 1960s'. The Secretary of State, echoing the arm's length approach of his junior minister, said that once settled, the Sports Council should have a 'high degree of freedom to use at discretion the funds placed at their disposal; it should not be necessary for the Government to concern itself with how the Council spent modest sums'.[26] The Treasury was still not ready to relent. At a time of severe restraint, Rippon was told it looked bad to sanction increased spending of any sort, and a compromise figure of £250,000 was proposed. The Environment Secretary felt this was miserly. He had, he pointed out, recently postponed a major £30 million building project; it was only by putting spending levels on sport into this broader perspective that his request for an extra £500,000 was conceded.[27]

Part of the reason ministers felt under siege about spending levels on sport during 1973 was the publication of a substantial report by a Select Committee of the House of Lords. Although sport had been a regular topic for discussion in the upper chamber for many years, this was the first time a special committee – appointed in 1971 – set out to thoroughly review the public demand for sporting facilities. The Select Committee was chaired by Viscount Cobham, a former cricket captain of Worcestershire, and included among its membership Lord Greenwood, architect of Labour's *Leisure for Living* strategy in the early 1960s. The Report (divided into two, a short document in March 1973 followed by a fuller version in July) made over 60 recommendations under a range of headings, including administration, provision of facilities, finance and dual use. The final pages in particular – reflecting the message Greenwood first propounded in *Leisure for Living* – made uncomfortable reading for the government, arguing that the major obstacles to progress were the 'feeling that leisure is an optional extra' (whereas the Report believed 'recreation must be treated as a social service') and the fact that 'too little money is being invested in facilities'. The ending was emphatic: 'Public expenditure so far has been wholly inadequate to provide facilities on the scale that is, and will be, required.'[28] When he later introduced his findings in a House of Lords debate, Viscount Cobham acknowledged that in tough economic times it was tempting to relegate sport to the bottom of the pile; it was unrealistic to suggest it could take precedence over spending on housing, education or pensions. But, he continued, 'we have been told on the highest authority that man cannot live by bread alone...Surely, my Lords, it is time to make a start' on remedying past deficiencies.[29]

The government was in no hurry to make a formal response to the Select Committee. By the end of 1973 it had though – in a notable exception to its broadly detached approach to detailed policy – initiated legislation designed to improve safety at football stadiums. Amidst rumours that Heath planned a sudden general election with Britain in the grip of a three-day working week, in January 1974 parliament discussed the Safety of Sports Grounds Bill. This resulted from a willingness to act on the findings of an official enquiry that followed the death of 66 spectators at a Glasgow Rangers match in 1971: until that time the worst single tragedy experienced at a British ground. Among other provisions, clubs were in future to be required to obtain safety certificates from local authorities. On behalf of the opposition, Howell welcomed the move though with reservations, notably the absence of any financial support to help clubs with the expensive modifications recommended.[30] Although the measure later became law, its progress was delayed when Heath announced on 7 February that the nation would go the polls at the end of the month. In a campaign dominated by the threat of all-out industrial action by the miners, sport was confined as was usually the case to the margins. With the election coming only three and a half years into the parliament, all parties looked ill-prepared. The Conservatives pledged to provide 'further impetus' to the Sports Council, 'whose powers and funds we have already greatly expanded'. Labour promised nothing more than working to improve the environment in which people 'spend their leisure', and the Liberals were silent on recreation.[31] When the election results were announced, Labour emerged as the largest party but without an outright majority. In answer to the Prime Minister's question 'who governs', the electorate had responded that 'the answer shouldn't be Mr Heath'.[32] After failing in attempts to form a new coalition, Heath resigned and Harold Wilson found himself back in Downing Street as head of a minority Labour administration.

Denis Howell Returns to the Helm

Shortly after the election, Denis Howell was summoned to Number Ten and asked by Wilson to resume his role as Sports Minister. Howell was pleased to hear he would return as a Minister of State (at a higher rank than Eldon Griffiths), though surprised by an offer from the Prime Minister to create a separate Sports Ministry, with its own residence and officials. Howell was not sure if this was a serious idea, but the tantalizing prospect of a new department disappeared when he expressed concern that he would be at the bottom of the pecking order in Cabinet. His preference, as before 1964, was to be attached to a department with a Secretary of State who could fight the corner for sport when needed. Asked which department, Howell – knowing that his old friend Tony Crosland was to be in charge – 'without hesitation' plumped for Environment. The Prime Minister concurred, and also agreed with Howell's suggestion that it would be beneficial to bring together those branches of the DoE dealing with 'quality of life'. In his first meeting with his ministerial chief, Crosland confirmed that Howell would assume responsibility for areas such as the Countryside Commission and National Parks, as well as sport. Building good relationships with officials at the DoE was less straightforward. Howell inherited 'a very fine private office and a very competent sports department', headed by David Sharpe. Even so, there were initial tensions. His desire to take a lead came as a shock to some senior civil servants, accustomed to the more detached style of Griffiths. At one point Crosland was asked by officials to go to the Prime Minister to seek the removal of Howell, only to be told that if there was one member of the government who would not be moved it was the Sports Minister. Before long, Howell wrote in his memoirs, the air was cleared and we were all 'getting on famously'.[33]

It took longer to find a solution to what Howell regarded as the central problem confronting him on his return to office: where he stood in relationship to the executive Sports Council. According to John Coghlan, Howell 'hankered for the days between 1965–1970 when he was both Minister and Chairman of the advisory body, not for any purposes of self-aggrandizement but simply because he genuinely thought this to be the best way to promote and develop sport in Britain'.[34] Quite how Howell would assert himself in 1974 was a thorny problem. Howell was advised by officials that it would be inappropriate for him to resume Chairmanship of the Council; it was not clear he was even entitled to attend meetings. To alter its status would be time-consuming, requiring an act of parliament, and Labour whips made clear this was both unlikely to succeed and a very low priority. Despite his wishes, the Royal

Charter looked set to stay, leaving Howell to ask officials in frustration what his purpose was supposed to be in a situation where 'all...authority' had been 'surrendered' to the Sports Council. The scene was set for a fraught relationship between the Minister and Roger Bannister, who had become accustomed to setting priorities. Bannister, Howell noted, appreciated the way he worked with Griffiths and was insistent about maintaining 'at all costs' the structure introduced by Heath's government: 'When I asked Roger what he thought my role should be he replied to the effect that my job was to fight the Treasury for as much money as possible and to make this available for the Sports Council to distribute as they determined. I had to tell him that as he knew from previous experience, this was not how I operated.'[35]

In the event the deadlock was broken quite abruptly. Aware that the government's precarious position made another election likely before too long, Howell cast around for a proposal that would at least signal Labour's commitment to sport. He alighted upon the idea of improving facilities at Crystal Palace by building a new stand (one side of Britain's premier athletics track still lacked a stand for spectators), and with difficulty he persuaded the DoE finance officer to find £250,000 to put towards this project. The Minister planned to include the announcement as part of a public lecture, but when he told Roger Bannister of his intention, Bannister said he could not accept the money: 'It was my job to give him the money and for the Sports Council to decide how it should be spent.' Howell argued that there was an important distinction between existing sums, already allocated to the Council and which he had no desire to influence, and additional funding of the type proposed. With both men entrenched in their views, Howell said he would go ahead in his lecture and Bannister could reject it publicly should he wish. Although he did not do so, Bannister visited Howell within a week to say he could not accept the Ministry's way of doing things. 'It was an honourable resignation', Howell reflected.[36] Although in his departing speech Bannister spoke of retiring from the fray at a time in the autumn of 1974 when 'we are well on the way to achieving certain national targets in sports facilities', journalists suspected there was more to the resignation than met the eye. The sports editor of the *Times* claimed the decision was expected, 'but not for the reasons given'. It was widely believed Dr Bannister's position was not secure after Labour's return to power 'because of a lack of rapport between him and Mr Howell'. It was likely, according to the *Times*, that Bannister 'held his hand' to see if the government would survive; the return of a Conservative administration could change the picture again. But once Labour squeezed back in, securing a tiny majority at the October 1974 election, Bannister was reluctant to soldier on under a 'longer period of subordination to Mr Howell'.[37]

As a result of Labour's two election victories in 1974 the framework for government oversight of sport thus changed once more. The introduction of the chartered Sports Council in 1972 seemed to have provided a fixed relationship in which independent experts on the Council took the lead on details while politicians decided on appropriate levels of funding. But Labour's return to power meant a fresh twist to what Howell called the evolving 'partnership between sport and Government'.[38] In effect he tilted the balance in the partnership further back towards political influence than was the case under Heath's government. One key step in this direction came in July 1974, ahead of the resignation of Roger Bannister, when the Prime Minister informed parliament that Howell would henceforth be called the 'Minister for Sport and Recreation'. This broadening of the Minister's remit was in line with the House of Lords 1973 Select Committee Report. Wilson told the Commons that without infringing on the duties of other departments, Howell's appointment would 'facilitate the coordination of the recreational aspects of the Government's policies'.[39] Howell also actively sought a Chairman of the Sports Council with whom he could 'do business' following Bannister's departure. The post was offered to Sir Robin Brook, a former Olympic fencer and treasurer of the CCPR, who readily accepted the Minister's right to attend Council meetings when the occasion warranted. Although the new arrangements were satisfactory, Howell's feelings on the subject were clear in his reflection that 'it would have been better if I had chaired the Sports Council myself'.[40] John Coghlan, working as an employee of the Council, confirms that Howell and Brook 'got on well'. With this key relationship on a more even keel, the next few years, according to Coghlan, 'brought the Sports Council to a pinnacle of prestige and effectiveness in the field'.[41]

If the Sports Council was highly regarded in the mid-1970s, it was not on the basis of rapidly rising funding. In a period of alarmingly high inflation sparked by a global hike in oil prices, public spending was under intense scrutiny, and Howell faced an even greater task than he had in the 1960s in persuading the Treasury to loosen the purse strings. In December 1974 Labour's Chancellor, Denis Healey, asked for details of spending on sport in the wake of newspaper agitation about facilities being inadequate to match a boom of interest in leisure over recent years.[42] The DoE was told not to regard the exercise as a full-scale review, though this did not prevent Howell's officials submitting a paper with the message: 'sport needs a major injection of funds'. Howell followed this up by airing a familiar complaint to the Financial Secretary of the Treasury, John Gilbert. It was 'absurd', Howell argued, for the grant of the Sports Council to be only one-third of that offered to the Arts Council. Aside from the beneficial effects of recreation on reducing crime, Howell underlined the political dimension in all this: 'the followers of sport compose a substantial section of the rank and file of the Labour Party'.[43] But the Treasury had long experience of wrestling with the Minister for Sport. The Financial Secretary wrote a memo for the Chancellor claiming that much of the agitation for increased funding came from professional football clubs, anxious about the cost of carrying out ground improvements under the Safety of Sports Grounds Act. Objections to a special levy along the lines of that granted to horse-racing were considerable, and the best solution was for the football authorities to make modest increases in admissions charges. Amateur sport might feel hard done by in relation to the arts, Gilbert added, yet there was no real reason why funding for the two spheres should be related. On the basis of this advice, Healey bluntly told Labour MPs in a private meeting that there was no case for higher government spending on sport.[44]

Healey was a sufficiently tough customer that, having made up his mind, he even faced down pressure from the Prime Minister. In late February 1975, anxious about ongoing press attacks, Wilson wrote to the Chancellor about the 'genuine concerns' of those in sport: 'If we do not show that we have done something for sport, we shall hear the criticism that we have discriminated against the area which is of greatest interest to the majority, including those among whom our political support is concentrated.'[45] One of the Chancellor's aides hinted that Wilson appeared to be susceptible to the wily ways of the Sports Minister.[46] The Treasury may have played a part in a *Sunday Times* feature in March, which poured cold water on Robin Brook's claim that the Sports Council budget for 1975–76 did no more than keep pace with inflation, at £7.85 million, compared with £26.15 million for the Arts Council. As the *Sunday Times* noted, in 1972–73, the last year for which full figures were available, local authorities spent c.£68 million on sport, more than four times the amount devoted to the arts.[47] A couple of days later Healey formally responded to the Prime Minister. 'I should of course like to have been able to help', he wrote, but that it was too often overlooked that local authority financing of the arts was 'very small compared with support for sport'. In the light of sport already having a greater share of public expenditure in totality, there was little scope for more assistance. Howell was left to grumble that it was small wonder the Conservative opposition chose sport as an area to attack the government in parliament.[48]

The 1975 White Paper and After

If Labour was to take the initiative on sport during the course of the 1974 parliament, it would need to do so without injecting significant extra funding. It was therefore important to Howell's strategy that in 1975 he was ready to publish a White Paper, a comprehensive statement of official policy and the first document of its type since the equivalent which preceded the 1937 Physical Training and Recreation Act. The White Paper was more than a year in preparation, being initially mooted soon after Labour returned to power in February 1974 by Sir Robert (Bob) Marshall, one of two Permanent Secretaries at the DoE. Although Howell knew a broad statement was likely to be a slow burner, rather than having an immediate impact, he saw the merits of Labour setting out its stall, and he later described the White Paper as 'the blueprint' for the remainder of his term in office. It was, he said, an 'exhilarating experience' to spend many hours discussing and thinking through ideas with key figures involved in the project – Bob Marshall and David Sharpe of the DoE, sport adviser Sir John Lang and Walter Winterbottom, the chief permanent officer at the Sports Council. Much of the document was written by his colleagues, though Howell claimed that he penned the conclusion himself, outlining what he called a 'Government philosophy for sport and recreation – a leisure service'.[49] Published in August 1975 under the title *Sport and Recreation*, consciously highlighting how his ministerial remit had been broadened, Howell saw the statement of first principles as a vital means of underlining Labour's commitment in this field. 'The Government believes', the White Paper concluded, 'that sport and recreation provide enormous benefits for the individual in society, and recognises the part that they can play in the enhancement of personality... Where the community neglects its responsibilities for providing the individual with opportunities and choice in the provision of sports and recreational facilities, it will rarely escape the long-term consequences of this neglect'.[50]

The declaration of a 'philosophy for sport and recreation' was a novel departure. Even so, much of the detail of the White Paper was derived – as was openly acknowledged in several places – from the recommendations of the Lord Cobham's 1973 Select Committee Report. Whereas state involvement prior to 1974 centred primarily on organized sporting activity, both for elite performers and keen club-level enthusiasts, interest was now turning more to the importance of leisure provision for the masses. From this time on, there was to be much concern about how to balance scarce resources between competing needs. The list of priorities contained in the White Paper suggested that for the time being the emphasis should be on casual users. Particular prominence was given to the need to develop facilities in deprived urban areas, including the provision of designated 'kick-about areas' for youngsters. Only at the end of the priority list was there a pledge to encourage universities and colleges to develop training schemes for gifted sportsmen and women. The commitment to seeking more bursaries from business and commerce led before long to the creation of the Sports Aid Foundation, a charity which in time raised millions of pounds to support international athletes. Aside from the conclusion, one particular element of the White Paper bore the hallmark of Howell's imprint, indicating he had reluctantly come to terms with the structure bequeathed by his predecessor. It was confirmed that the executive Sports Council would continue as the lead authority at a national level, though a higher proportion of its membership than before (a quarter) was reserved for nominees of the CCPR, the body Howell fought strenuously to revive.[51]

John Coghlan describes the White Paper as 'a guideline for much of what was to follow'. His brief comment that it was published 'in the teeth of opposition from HM Treasury' can be verified by government records (not available at the time Coghlan was writing).

These show that in July 1975 Joel Barnett, the Chief Secretary at the Treasury, wrote to Harold Wilson proposing that in view of the seriousness of the economic situation 'we should not proceed with present plans to publish this White Paper'. Barnett acknowledged that the draft document was careful to avoid encouraging more expenditure in the short term and that the balance of opinion among ministers consulted at the relevant committee was in favour of publication. Nevertheless, he felt the government could not risk giving an impression 'which inevitably implies the desirability of extra expenditure on Sport and Recreation'.[52] Howell entered the fray by penning a forceful memo of his own to the Prime Minister. In hard times it was important to establish clear priorities, 'and this is precisely what we are seeking to do in the White Paper'. In particular it was of 'enormous social importance', Howell argued, to declare that recreation in deprived urban areas was top of the agenda. It was feasible, as was mooted by some, to announce over the course of a couple of weeks separate government initiatives in written parliamentary answers, but this would 'deprive ourselves quite gratuitously of the benefits of explaining in a connected way the "philosophy" which underlies and informs them; and so lose much of their positive impact'.[53]

The Prime Minister was briefed that both sides of the arguments had a strong case. The severity of the economic situation meant extra spending was simply out of the question, but on the other hand the Environment Secretary Crosland was known to be supportive of pressing ahead, and the White Paper was widely expected among interested parties in the sporting world. On 1 August Wilson scribbled approval on a note from the Treasury informing him that agreement had been reached on final changes to the text which went a long way to meeting the concerns of the Chief Secretary; on this basis it was recommended publication should go ahead.[54] Howell's persistence thus eventually won the day. 'It was only the political "clout" and determination of the Minister for Sport', observed John Coghlan, 'that ensured the White Paper saw the light of day'. But victory came at a price, including acceptance of Treasury briefing notes for the press launch. These insisted that Howell first refer to the absence of any guarantees about when spending restrictions might be eased; only when this was done could the Minister talk about his philosophy of sport and recreation.[55] The constraints imposed on Howell inevitably influenced reaction to the White Paper, which was not generally lauded as a significant breakthrough. In the *Times* Sir Robin Brook welcomed the document on behalf of the Sports Council but was quoted as saying: 'Policy alone is not enough. There must be adequate resources...Sport and recreation should be considered alongside housing and health and not rated as an optional extra'.[56]

Allegations that the White Paper contained more rhetoric than substance were made by Conservative spokesmen when parliament discussed the document in April 1977. This debate was another bad-tempered affair, confirming that sport was considered sufficiently important for the parties to engage in bouts of point-scoring. Mud slinging took place firstly on why it had taken twenty months since the appearance of *Sport and Recreation* to arrange a debate, though one MP pointed out that the small numbers in attendance did not suggest a widespread urge to discuss the topic; the motion to welcome the introduction of the White Paper was carried by 34 votes to 7. The minority included three vociferous Tory critics. Although no longer shadowing sport, Eldon Griffiths weighed in by claiming Howell had been wrong to tinker with the Sports Council (and to lose the services of Roger Bannister), and added that Labour's mismanagement of the economy had led to a decline in resources going into sport since 1974. The latter theme was echoed by the official opposition spokesman on sport, Hector Monro, MP for Dumfries. The White Paper might be a novel document, Monro argued, but without further resources 'much of it will become a non-event'. The debate ended in acrimony when Neil Macfarlane, Conservative MP for Sutton and Cheam, attacked the 'role, the direction and the general trend in which the Sports Council is leading sport and the moment', appearing to suggest that Robin Brook was not the right person to lead the Council. The Minister was goaded into intervening, saying this contribution was 'very wide of the mark' on several counts, especially the insinuations about Brook. For Howell, Macfarlane's 'whole speech was beset by confusion'.[57]

Eldon Griffiths touched a raw nerve when he said in the course of the White Paper debate that while he admired Howell's continuing dedication, 'his second innings is less impressive than his first'. Aside from perennial problems with finance, Howell discovered that more so than in the 1960s – when there was a freshness and urgency about much that he did – adverse publicity was difficult to avoid by the mid-1970s. Although still regarded as having the common touch, as he showed when called upon to become 'Minister for Drought' in the dry summer of 1976 (his portfolio of duties at the DoE included the water industry), Howell was forced on to the back foot by unwelcome developments such as rising levels of football-related hooliganism. The trouble associated with top teams such as Manchester United, Leeds and Chelsea attracted much critical attention on television and in the newspapers. The hooligan problem intruded significantly in the parliamentary debate of April 1977, when several speakers, rather than focusing on the White Paper, vied with each other in calling for tough measures against the culprits. The Minister's initial response was to establish a committee including representatives of the Football Association (FA), the police and the transport authorities, which came up with a code of conduct adopted by the various agencies. This was followed by the introduction of measures such as the segregation of home and away supporters, enforced by perimeter fencing at many grounds. With heightened vigilance on all fronts, Howell felt the situation improved by the time he left office in 1979. He reflected in his memoirs that it was a matter of great regret that the committee he established was not maintained by his successors. All of those who contributed to its work believed its recommendations were helping to improve crowd control and behaviour, and it 'was wrong of the incoming Tory Government to drop its guard ... I have no doubt that this lessening of vigilance contributed to the [1980s] resurgence of the problem'.[58]

Another episode which attracted adverse headlines was the controversy over finding a replacement for Walter Winterbottom, who announced his decision to retire as Director of the Sports Council late in 1977. Several well-known figures were touted as possible successors, but without consulting the Minister, the Council decided to appoint Nicholas Stacey, a former sprint finalist at the 1952 Olympics. In his memoirs Howell wrote that many in the sporting world shared his reservations about this development, which he felt highlighted the excessive influence of ex-Oxford athletes on the Sports Council. While he had the power to veto the appointment, Howell knew that to do so would lead to accusations of unnecessary political interference. His fear that dislike of the Royal Charter was coming back to haunt him was borne out when his decision to block Stacey was followed by criticism in several newspapers.[59] Fortunately for Howell the Sports Council, instead of digging in its heels, agreed to consult over the composition of a new short list. In this instance Howell was happy to approve all the contenders, and the post duly went to Emlyn Jones, director of the National Recreation Centre at Crystal Palace.[60] His arrival in the summer of 1978 marked the start of a new era for the Sports Council, with Robin Brook stepping down around the same time as Chairman, to be replaced by Richard ('Dickie') Jeeps, a farmer and President of the English Rugby Union. John Coghlan was among those who felt the changes were not for the best. Jeeps, he felt, was a vocal publicist but lacked Brook's understanding of how to negotiate with Whitehall, while the 'Stacey affair' he felt damaged the standing of the Council 'in the eyes of many who were dismayed at the squalid manoeuvring that had taken place'.[61]

Coghlan's verdict may have been influenced by personal disappointment at being passed over for the top post at the Sports Council; as Deputy Director since the mid-1970s he was seen by many as an ideal candidate to succeed Winterbottom. Notwithstanding problems of leadership, the Council could in fact claim to be making a good fist of realizing its objectives. Between 1973 and 1977 facilities for indoor sport in Britain almost trebled, and on a decade-long time scale there were notable advances particularly in relation to the construction of sports centres (up from 12 in 1971 to 449 in 1981) and swimming pools (up from 440 in 1971 to 524 a decade later). While content to accept that the Sports Council deserved much of the credit, Howell was as determined as ever to show that he was more than a benevolent bystander, nodding approval from the sidelines. His desire to maintain a high level of involvement, and to reap any potential electoral advantage to be gained, was evident in two notable examples towards the end of his tenure. First, he allied himself closely with the emphasis on promoting recreation in areas of social deprivation. With DoE officials providing figures on indicators such as population density and unemployment, the Sports Council introduced a £750,000 scheme in 1976 involving 120 projects. Following up this initiative, Howell ensured the government's 1977 White Paper *Policy for the Inner Cities* made reference to the importance of sport in improving the quality of life among those who might otherwise be drawn into lives of vandalism and petty crime. Second, the Minister continued to fight his corner with the Treasury to the last. With a general election in sight, he persuaded the Chancellor to provide an increase in Sports Council funding that more than simply kept pace with inflation. The budget for 1978–79 was set at £15.2 million, compared to £11.5 million the previous year; a 32 per cent increase at a time of 13 per cent inflation.[62]

Conclusion

A belated above-inflation injection of funds into sport could do nothing to arrest the tide that swept Labour from power at the general election in May 1979. For many contemporaries the disruption associated with the winter of discontent marked the culmination of a dismal decade. With Heath's successor as Conservative leader, Margaret Thatcher, coming to power describing Britain as 'the sick man of Europe', in need of drastic remedies, the temptation is to conclude that sport and recreation conformed to a broader pattern of stagnation in the 1970s. At the heart of the malaise lay low levels of investment; sport continued to receive only a tiny proportion of total public expenditure. From the perspective of a Sports Council insider, John Coghlan believed the annual allocations from parliament were 'woefully short of what was needed'; neither Heath's administration nor the Wilson–Callaghan government 'made any serious or meaningful effort to meet the budgetary demands made upon them by the Council'.[63] This was also the view of Sports Council Chairmen. Shortly before he left the post Robin Brook spoke of how in absolute and relative terms Britain still lagged behind its European neighbours in providing facilities for sport and recreation, as it had done when adverse comparisons were first given wide publicity in the 1950s.[64] A similarly bleak conclusion was reached by the sports administrator and writer Don Anthony, who noted in 1976: 'The cry "Sport for All" is a voice in the wilderness for much of our population ... If "Sports for All" is to be a right, like "education for all", governments – both national and local – must take more interest in sport, not less.'[65]

The policy-making framework for sport, as much as the economic situation, was not conducive to rapid progress. Fractious party disputes took place over the functions of a Sports Minister and the status of the Sports Council, which in its reconstituted form after 1972 often found itself at odds with the CCPR, struggling to carve out a new role for itself in the 1970s. In the corridors of power in

Whitehall attachment to sport still had shallow roots. The Treasury in particular acted as a block on ambitious developments, aided by the absence of a powerful sports lobby at Westminster. Whereas the cause of the Arts Council was bolstered by sustained interest among parliamentarians, especially in relation to London-based arts provision, sport was less well served. Lord Cobham, a powerful advocate in the House of Lords, died before being able to push far forward with his 1973 Select Committee Report. Among MPs, some were absorbed only in single issue campaigns. After years of quiescence, backbenchers opposed to hunting secured the passage of an anti-coursing bill through the House of Commons in 1975, but it foundered in the Lords after a Tory-dominated Select Committee concluded that 'the Bill should not proceed'.[66] In the absence of its original founder and inspiration Philip Noel-Baker, who retired as an MP in 1970, the Parliamentary Sports Committee became less influential. Although it met regularly with Sports Council officials to keep abreast of events in the first half of the 1970s, it lapsed by the end of the decade. Through no fault of a small number of devoted MPs and peers, parliamentary pressure on behalf of sport lacked bite and a sharpness of focus; aside from on occasional questions of wide topical concern, the sports lobby consisted – in the words of John Coghlan – of a 'handful of individuals rather than a solid cohort'.[67]

Yet despite many constraints and setbacks, political involvement in sport during the 1970s did produce some dividends. Of the two Sports Ministers in post during the decade, Eldon Griffiths left the legacy of an autonomous Sports Council with a professional staff numbering over 500, capable of pushing forward on numerous fronts. And Denis Howell reflected after leaving office in 1979 that his total of 11 years as Minister for Sport produced 'some solid achievements'.[68] In terms of his 'second innings', the claim in the 1975 White Paper that sport should be regarded 'as part of the general fabric of the social services' (echoing Lord Cobham's 1973 Report) was largely wishful thinking. In practice Labour's intention to use sport as an instrument of welfare policy never extended much beyond small-scale projects confined to deprived inner city areas. The White Paper nevertheless marked a symbolic commitment to the state using sport for broader social objectives; it was delivered in the face of intense Treasury hostility and influenced the policy agenda for more than a decade to come.

By battling tirelessly for more funding, Howell also ensured that rises in Sports Council expenditure were not all entirely eroded by inflation. Away from Westminster, local authorities continued with carefully planned programmes first initiated in the late 1960s to construct a new generation of indoor swimming pools and sport centres, and municipal initiatives were supplemented by the rapid expansion of private provision for newer sports such as squash and badminton. Even those like John Coghlan who were impatient at the rate of change had to admit that, all in all, there were reasons to be cheerful in the 1970s: 'The inertia of the fifties and early sixties was a thing of the past; there was now a new and exciting mood in the air that at last Britain was once again on the move in sport as users flooded to take advantage of the new facilities that appeared in their neighbourhoods.'[69]

7 The Olympics and International Sport

Introduction

Links between international sport and politics have a long pedigree. The political scientist Trevor Taylor has noted that while sport rarely if ever dominated interstate relations during the twentieth century in the same way as security or economic issues, there were obvious connections between sport and diplomacy. Among the reasons for this, Taylor pointed to sport becoming an organized global phenomenon, one that aroused considerable emotional commitment; on this basis alone, contentious questions concerning relations between nations were bound to arise. In addition, sport was consciously employed by some regimes as a tool of foreign policy, and the international controlling authorities of sport, who set the rules and organized worldwide events, were frequently drawn into political processes by having to interact with governments, corporations and the media. Taylor went on to describe why – despite claims to the contrary – the Olympic Games, the most high profile of all global sporting endeavours, was particularly vulnerable to political involvement and interaction. The use of the Olympics for propaganda purposes, divisions within the Olympic movement and the interaction of the International Olympic Committee (IOC) with participant nations: all contributed to what Taylor calls 'the politics of Olympism'.[1] Lord Killanin, reflecting on his experiences as President of the IOC in the 1970s, lamented that nearly all problems he encountered arose from issues in national and international politics: 'politics are "in" sport and have always been. Everything in our lives is governed by political decisions'.[2]

Not all nations, of course, approached sport on the international stage in the same way. In Britain, with its strong voluntary tradition in the organization and control of sport, there was widespread disdain for the crude exploitation of sporting events to demonstrate national prowess, whether in the case of Nazi Germany in the 1930s or east European Communist regimes after 1945. One common view across the political spectrum in Britain, voiced in the 1960s by a government minister, Baroness Phillips, was that it was best to separate sport and diplomacy wherever possible: 'it would be fair to say that the British do not bring international politics into sport, but that some other people, unfortunately, have done so'.[3] Yet, as the work of historian Martin Polley has shown, from the time of the first modern Olympic Games in 1986 onwards, British politicians were aware of the value of sport as a medium for diplomacy or as a form of cultural propaganda. Polley cites, for example, the 1930s National government resisting a bid for London to host the 1940 Olympics in order to let Tokyo succeed in the interests of improving Anglo-Japanese relations.[4]

This chapter sets out to explore how and why the relationship between politicians and officials and international sport became closer in the 1945–80 period. Some topics with a bearing on this question, notably controversies over sporting contacts with South Africa, have been introduced in previous chapters, and the post-1980 ties between politics and international sport will be addressed in the chapters that follow. Here the emphasis will be on demonstrating that the generally low-key British approach of the early post-war years – being drawn into diplomatic issues arising through sport largely when unavoidable – increasingly gave way to a more interventionist stance, mirroring what we have seen occurring in sport domestically. The number and intensity of global sporting controversies rose sharply, making greater engagement with international sport inevitable, though from the mid-1960s onwards ministers also became involved more willingly by sanctioning expenses to top amateur athletes for the first time. By the 1970s any notion that British governments could stand apart looked untenable, though the trend towards closer ties was to be abruptly halted in a bitter dispute over British participation in the 1980 Moscow Olympics.

Football and Post-War International Relations

While the amateur-dominated Olympics were at the heart of the relationship between politics and international sport, professional football also played a significant role. Even before massive television audiences led football's World Cup to rival the Olympics as a global sporting spectacle from the 1960s onwards, Britain's most well-supported game – an obsession for millions of working-class men especially – was capable of causing diplomatic ripples. In 1938 controversy arose when the Foreign Office (FO) insisted that England's players offer a Nazi salute as a mark of respect to Hitler when playing a match against Germany in Berlin. And within months of Labour coming to power in 1945, the potency of football to shine a spotlight on international relations was illustrated during a fractious visit to Britain by the Russian football champions, Moscow Dynamo. As a Communist dictatorship, the Soviet Union was largely ostracized in international sport before 1939, and Stalin's secret police – which sponsored the Moscow Dynamo team – had twin aims in allowing this first-ever visit of one of its top sports team to Britain. On the one hand, it might help to cement the Anglo-Soviet wartime alliance, which quickly came under strain after the war ended over spheres of influence in defeated Germany. At the same time, by sending such a strong side (second only to the Red Army team), the Soviets hoped to demonstrate the virtues of Communism in the world of 'bourgeois' football. In this light, the tour marked the first major example of what was to be a recurrent theme in the post-1945 era: the Soviet regime's explicit use of sport for political purposes.[5]

From the British side, the fact that the tour went ahead at all owed much to the influence of the Labour minister Philip Noel-Baker, Bevin's deputy at the Foreign Office. As noted in Chapter 1, Noel-Baker was an evangelist for the power of sport to improve international relations. 'In the nuclear age', he once remarked, 'sport is mankind's best hope.'[6] Approached by Stanley Rous of the Football Association (FA) early in 1945 over a possible Anglo-Soviet fixture, Noel-Baker – at the time a junior coalition minister at the Transport department – wrote to the Foreign Secretary, Anthony Eden, arguing that a 'soccer international of the kind which Rous proposes' would be a good way of improving relations with Russia. The Foreign Office agreed about the 'political desirability of broadening our contacts with the Soviet Union', though Eden preferred not to arrange anything hastily with the war still unfinished. Behind this caution was the view of FO officials, conscious of the discord created by the likes of the bodyline controversy in cricket and the Berlin Olympics, that sport was not necessarily a solvent of diplomatic tensions. As one wrote, it would take 'much more than a football match to break down the real barriers' which the Soviet system erected. Historian Peter Beck notes that Noel-Baker's idealism was not widely shared in Whitehall: 'officials in the Foreign Office treated international sport as a potential problem rather than a policy opportunity'.[7]

The Soviets, having made no reply for many months to the FA's invitation, issued in the spring of 1945, agreed to visit Britain at short notice in the autumn. The stakes suddenly seemed high. The British embassy in Moscow informed London that Stalin's regime attached 'considerable importance' to the visit 'on the grounds of prestige'. Embassy officials were unable to resist the comment that because the British, pioneers of the game, were 'still regarded as the world leaders in football', it was crucial to show 'that our star is not waning in this sphere'.[8] In view of this background and the public popularity of football, it was not surprising that the four matches played by Moscow Dynamo attracted enormous attention in Britain. But from the time the visitors arrived in November 1945 the tour was marred by tetchy claims and counterclaims: over accommodation arrangements, over which fixtures should be played at what venues and over the acrimonious nature of the games, in which the Russians remained undefeated. The Soviet press lauded the team's success, claiming it underlined the superiority of Russian training methods, organization and collective spirit. Everyday arrangements were the responsibility of the FA, but it was left to Noel-Baker, as the key figure in facilitating the tour, to represent the government at a farewell dinner in London on 4 December. Glossing over the various difficulties, he thanked the visitors and hoped the experience would provide a foundation for good working relations between governments and peoples.

The fractious nature of the tour, however, prompted a celebrated attack by the left-wing author George Orwell, who wrote shortly afterwards in *Tribune* about international sport as 'an unfailing cause of ill-will'. It was ironic that the firebrand socialist Orwell gave voice to the sentiments – usually expressed behind closed doors – of cautious civil servants. Looking at the Soviet tour and other pre-1939 examples, Orwell reached the conclusion that high-level competitive sport amounted to 'war minus the shooting'.[9] This article sparked what was to be a long-running debate about the virtues and shortcomings of international sport, one in which the balance shifted according to the perceived success or failure of particular sporting events. In late 1945 many no doubt shared Orwell's view, though some respondents to his article in *Tribune* complained he had not attended any of the matches and accused him of intellectual snobbery; he was showing 'highbrow' contempt for the working men who turned out in huge numbers to watch sport with little concern for the political implications. Studies of the Moscow Dynamo tour generally conclude that, while it caused a short-term stir, it played a negligible role in the broader deterioration of Anglo-Soviet relations during 1945–46. 'Favourable or unfavourable inclinations towards the Russians may have been confirmed', notes one such study, 'but no more'.[10]

In spite of a declining reputation – marked by a poor showing of the English team when it made its debut appearance at the World Cup in 1950, followed by the first-ever loss on home soil to the Hungarians in 1953 – football was not of undue concern to the Foreign Office again until the time of the 1966 World Cup. As we saw in Chapter 4, England's hosting of the tournament witnessed a novel departure for a British government when, following the lead of Labour's Minister for Sport Denis Howell, it was decided to invest taxpayers' money into professional sport. While this development caused anxiety at the Treasury (which reluctantly sanctioned the funding), the Foreign Office was more preoccupied with the involvement in the tournament of North Korea, a Communist regime not recognized by the British government since the time of the Korean war in the early 1950s. The FO official D. K. Timms wrote a briefing paper late in 1965 noting how the unexpected qualification of the North Koreans for the finals presented a 'difficult problem' (described by another civil servant as 'sitting on a volcano'). For one thing, England would now have to admit to its shores sportsmen from a nation it refused to recognize, a move that was certain to antagonize Britain's ally South Korea. If this happened, an unwelcome precedent would be set in relation to sportsmen and women from other hostile Communist states, most of whom had been barred from competing in Britain since the deterioration of East-West relations in the Cold War.[11]

In line with its tradition of allowing sport to operate free from political interference wherever possible, the Foreign Office weighed up how it might solve the problem without being seen to jeopardize the World Cup. The 'simplest way' to tackle the issue, Timms wrote in his paper, would be to deny entry visas to the footballers, but the consequences were likely to be profound: 'You can imagine what the papers would make of this. We would be accused of dragging politics into sport, sabotaging British interests and so on.'[12] The head of the Far Eastern Department at the Foreign Office, Edward Bolland, quickly realized that practical politics ruled out denying the North Koreans entry, which could only be done on security grounds: 'British public opinion would not tolerate an attempt by H.M.G to prevent the arrival of a football team for political reasons.'[13] Instead Bolland pressed for what a colleague called 'as much discrimination ... as possible' against North Korea. The team would have to take the simple name 'North Korea' (instead of the self-styled name the 'Democratic People's Republic of Korea', or DPRK); the flying of North Korean flags or playing of a national anthem would not be permitted during the tournament; and British ministers would reiterate that they did not recognize the North Korean government. The Foreign Office did not entirely get its way. Having invested so much into ensuring a successful World Cup, Howell sided with the international football authorities who insisted that the flags of all participant nations should be on show. But in the spring of 1966 an FO memorandum could still claim 'considerable success' in securing its objectives. The non-recognition of North Korea was made clear in parliament, alongside a firm rebuttal that the episode marked a precedent for the future, and while the department 'very reluctantly' gave way over flag-flying, the North Korean anthem would only be played if the team reached the final, which 'we have every reason to believe will not happen'.[14]

In his memoirs Howell recounted that the drama was far from over. He claimed that the Foreign Secretary, Michael Stewart, approached him privately some six weeks before the World Cup was due to commence in July. Stewart told him senior figures within the North Atlantic Treaty Organisation (NATO) objected to the participation of North Korea and wondered if it could be prevented at the last minute. Howell insisted nothing could be done, adding there would be uproar if the flags of all competing nations except North Korea were flown; the World Cup would be in crisis and likely to be called off, leaving NATO looking 'very silly'. Stewart was mollified by the news that national anthems would only be played at the opening game and the final, agreeing that he could at least tell NATO colleagues that there was almost no danger of the North Korean anthem being used.[15] But once play got under way, the North Koreans confounded those who regarded them as minnows. Despite their previous lack of pedigree, they pulled off a huge surprise by beating Italy to qualify for the quarter-finals. The prospect of a major embarrassment for the British government remained a real one. In August 1966, after England had won the tournament, J. B. Denson of the Foreign Office wrote to the British ambassador in South Korea to describe the tension of the moment. At one point North Korea led by three-nil in their quarter-final with Portugal, but 'thank heavens', Denson recollected, Portugal came through in the end, 'and we were spared an England/North Korea match at Wembley'. Denson also recounted how General Lee, the South Korean representative in London, finding a North Korean across the table from him at an official lunch during the tournament, threatened to return home in protest. Lee only relented when given soothing reassurances about the value to Britain of its links with South Korea. With the benefit of hindsight, once the North Koreans were defeated, Denson was able to conclude that the whole episode was finally 'sinking into oblivion and with it, we hope, this minor strain on Anglo-Korean relations'.[16]

The Foreign Office and the Olympics after 1945

The North Korean issue in 1966 provided an object lesson in the Foreign Office's handling of post-war sport. In the words of Martin Polley, it dealt with a problem not of its own choosing 'tactfully and diplomatically'. FO officials worked harmoniously with Howell and the football authorities, compromised where necessary (over the flying of flags), kept the issue mostly out of the press and brokered 'a satisfactory solution to a potential crisis', doing so 'without laying the government open to the charge of politicising sport'.[17] This restrained approach also characterized the Foreign Office's handling of diplomatic concerns associated with the Olympics after 1945. Despite the success of the London Games in 1948 (described in Chapter 1), the view persisted among some FO officials that, as one wrote in 1949, major international sporting contests 'often do more harm than good'.[18] As the Olympics were not likely to return to Britain for many years to come, it was possible for the Foreign Office to revert to its preferred policy: keeping a watchful eye on the Games to gauge the implications for British national interests. With Conservative ministers showing little interest in sport during the 1950s, civil servants were content to be kept abreast of developments via consular representatives across the globe, liaising when appropriate with influential figures such as Lord Burghley, the Chairman of the British Olympic Association (BOA). Shortly before the 1952 Olympics in Helsinki, Burghley telephoned the Foreign Office to seek guidance on the issue of Chinese participation. Burghley was also a key member of the IOC, the controlling authority of the Games, and he was advised that it would be best to take a cautious line, following the majority view, at a crucial meeting discussing which of the rival regimes in China to admit to the Olympics. In passing on to a superior a note about his dealings with Burghley, the official concerned wrote: 'I hope this reflects the line we would wish Burghley to take. Sport and politics are not necessarily the same, but in this case the Russians and Americans are likely to make this into a major political issue.'[19]

The case of Chinese participation illustrated that the Foreign Office was particularly attuned to any Olympic-related matters with a bearing on the rival power blocs in the unfolding era of the Cold War. The IOC decided that, having barred Germany as a result of its Nazi past in 1948, an invitation would be issued for the Helsinki Games. IOC practice was to issue only one invitation per nation, but this posed serious difficulties in relation to post-war Germany. Soviet-dominated East Germany refused to accept the right, granted by the IOC at a meeting in Lausanne in 1951, for Allied-controlled West Germany to take the lead in the selection of an Olympic team. Lord Burghley was once more to the fore. G. E. Hall, a Foreign Office official, wrote to Burghley in February 1952 expressing gratitude 'for the help you were able to give us at Lausanne over this wretched business'.[20] Shortly afterwards Hall reported to the British authorities in Berlin that Burghley had sent a telegram to the relevant authorities in both countries asking them to form a single committee to decide on 'an all-German team on merit alone'. It was not known if either side would accept this, Hall wrote, employing language which demonstrated that the Foreign Office was far from a neutral bystander. The key thing, Hall believed, was to resist 'communist infiltration'; if things went well, 'this could be turned into admirable propaganda for the West'.[21] In the event talks about forming a joint West–East committee broke down amidst mutual recriminations, leaving only West German athletes to appear in Helsinki, though four years later discussions were to prove more fruitful and a single German Olympic team was formed.

The main item of interest for the Foreign Office at Helsinki was the first appearance in the Olympics of the Soviet Union, which reaped the benefits of enormous state investment in sport by winning a total of over seventy medals. This rivalled the American performance, marking the start of intense competition between the superpowers at the Games. The British embassy in Moscow sent a series of reports to London gauging the reaction of Soviet newspapers as the Helsinki Games progressed. At first it was claimed there was plenty of 'national pride' in Soviet accounts, though little gloating when Russian athletes triumphed over Americans. But the mood appeared to change as Soviet team managers indulged in some criticism of judging in certain sports. On 1 August the embassy summary noted that 'the assumption of complete Soviet perfection in all things is as irritating as usual'. A week later the tone was firmer still. In the absence of an officially published medals table, the Russians declared themselves 'overall champions of the Games' and 'politics have featured more prominently than before', notably with claims that American officials sought to prevent their athletes associating with Soviet counterparts.[22] From observing the Games close up, the British ambassador in Finland took a more relaxed view of proceedings, writing to the Foreign Secretary Sir Anthony Eden to say the whole event had passed off smoothly. Although they complained about inadequate training facilities and some poor judging, Eden was told, on the whole the Soviet team soon settled down and its athletes, like those from other Iron Curtain nations, 'accepted victory or defeat with equal grace'.[23]

A strategy which respected the independence of sporting authorities such as the IOC and BOA remained the order of the day at a time when – compared with the tensions created by the 1936 Berlin Games – the Olympics were not the occasion of huge controversy. Following on from the successes of London and Helsinki, commentators were united in writing appreciatively of the friendly atmosphere at the Melbourne Games in 1956. Jesse Owens, the black American who defied Hitler with his sprinting triumphs in 1936, was quoted as saying he wished representatives of the United Nations were present in Australia to witness the extent of goodwill. For the Olympic correspondent of the *Times*, this was an exaggerated view; against a backdrop of the Suez crisis and other Cold War tensions, the Games could 'hardly help statesmen to settle anything'. Even so, it was worthwhile setting aside weighty global issues for a fortnight in the warm sunshine.[24] At the end of the Rome Olympics in 1960, the British ambassador in Italy was able to make a similarly positive assessment, writing to the Foreign Secretary in London that the Games had been a 'great success'. Although Communist regimes had sought at times to introduce 'a political element', there were in the end 'no serious international incidents'.[25] Commenting on the ambassador's letter, FO official C. R. Brooke noted that the press had depicted the outcome of the Games as an honourable draw between West and East, with both the United States and the Soviet Union putting in their usual strong showing. Reflecting on a slightly weaker performance by Britain than in Melbourne, Brooke used wording which summed up Whitehall's detachment about the value of sport: 'For the UK as for most countries', he wrote, 'the choice seems to be between a certain amount of disappointment every four years and the horrors of Government sponsorship of athletics'. Brooke added that he was in favour of more being done to help British athletes in future, 'but less, I hope, than in countries where athletic achievement is accorded a totally disproportionate status'.[26]

Pressure for Change: Funding for International Sport

The first signs of the state establishing a more hands-on approach to international sport than was evident in the 1945–60 period resulted from growing concern about British performances on the world stage. From the time of the London Olympics onwards, many were reluctant to accept what C. R. Brooke called a 'certain amount of disappointment every four years'. In the eyes of critics, Britain was trapped in a time warp, its athletes finding it ever more difficult to compete on equal terms. The United States was known to offer generous college scholarships to allow its best athletes to compete with a measure of financial backing, while the Soviets saw sport as a means of instilling patriotism at home and demonstrating to the outside world the benefits of its political system.[27] In Britain, by contrast, financial incentives in amateur sport were frowned upon. While the organization of the 1948 Olympics was much commended, it did not go unnoticed that for the first time in the modern Games Britain failed to provide a single winner in track-and-field events. In 1951 the journalist Hylton Cleaver made a scathing assault in his book *Sporting Rhapsody* on Britain's attachment to amateur principles. One well-known long jump hopeful, Denis Watts, had been selected for the Olympic team in 1948 but then barred from representing his country when it was ascertained he had applied for a job as a sports teacher, sufficient according to the amateur rule book to classify him as a professional. Hylton Cleaver lamented that, despite evidence to the contrary, 'we persist in regarding ourselves', in approaching the Olympics, 'as the only ones in step. We know that nearly every other country taking part is semi-professional, heavily subsidised by its government ... But in our own quiet, phlegmatic, insular and almost arrogant way we still pursue our own ideals; no sport is subsidised; only those who can afford to meet their own expenses can attain championship rank; ... and we are obsessed by the belief that to win is not the object of taking part'.[28]

As we saw in Chapter 2, disquiet built up during the 1950s, with a small though growing number of MPs and sections of the press bemoaning Britain's failure to perform better in major sporting events. Concern was expressed about a range of amateur sports (in tennis, for example, Britain failed to match the Fred Perry-inspired Davis Cup triumphs of the 1930s), though the Olympics remained a prime focus. In the run-up to the 1960 Games in Italy the journalist J. L. Manning fumed in the *Sunday Dispatch* about the 'folly bizarre of British sport'. Britain's fine athletes, he complained, suffered under the twin handicaps of inadequate training facilities and a bar on financial incentives.[29] The prospect of something being done came closer with the Wolfenden Report, published to coincide with the Rome Games in 1960. The Report accepted that international sport was 'a force for good', but in a sideswipe at excitable press coverage, it argued that patriotic sentiment should 'be kept in reasonable bounds. It is not the end of the world if British teams are defeated, still less is it a symptom or proof of national decadence'. Even so, the status quo was not considered satisfactory, and more consideration needed to be given to how amateur athletes – striving for international success while holding down jobs – could be given more assistance. The Report explicitly referred to national amateur teams needing subsidies for equipment, travelling expenses and a 'reasonable period' of preliminary training; but though what was reasonable 'must be the subject of close scrutiny'. Because governing bodies were of such variable size and wealth, it would be best for each to review how far successful competition in world sport was feasible without changes to existing practice. Fresh statements of policy from each National Governing Body (NGB), the Report argued, 'could do much to make clear our national philosophy and attitude on this difficult question'.[30]

Although hardly a clarion call for urgent intervention in international sport, the Wolfenden Report did pave the way for new departures on funding. The Report came too late to influence the Rome Olympics, but ahead of the Commonwealth Games in Perth, held in 1962, the Conservative government broke with the past by sanctioning a grant of up to £12,000 for expenses and costs. The grant was intended to supplement not replace private fund-raising, and only a third was ultimately used. The Treasury justified the move both in terms of responding to Wolfenden and in order to ensure strong British representation in Perth at a time of difficult relationships in the Commonwealth.[31] In planning for the Tokyo Olympics of 1964, the BOA requested over £20,000 for expenses associated with organizing a public appeal and with the running of its headquarters. Lord Hailsham, as minister with special responsibility with sport, was concerned that 'public support would diminish' if too much subsidy was provided. But in line with moves he was undertaking to enhance the efficiency of governing bodies, he gave ground and backed the Treasury in accepting the BOA request. At the same time it was made clear the grant was not intended to replace traditional 'voluntary effort' or the prime responsibility of the BOA for supporting Olympic athletes with their costs.[32] More broadly, in relation to assisting amateur British teams at events other than the Olympics, the government announced in late 1963 that it would consider proposals submitted via individual NGBs. A Whitehall committee established to formulate working rules for the new system concluded early in 1964 that any application coming forward must demonstrate 'need', be a supplement not a replacement of other funding and be confined to covering no more than half of all travel costs.

From a modest start, government subsidies to amateur teams travelling overseas were gradually extended after 1964. Labour's Sport Minister, Denis Howell, engaged in a series of running battles with the Treasury in order to secure more generous and extensive assistance to national teams. The working rules adopted by the previous administration remained in place, though set within a different framework with the creation of the advisory Sports Council, which under Howell's chairmanship included consideration of bids for overseas support as part of its remit. While the Department of Education and Science (DES) at Howell's prompting adopted a sympathetic approach, this was not evident elsewhere in Whitehall. Writing in 1967 one Treasury official, Miss Startin, wrote to her superior: 'we have as you know had several arguments with DES on the status of particular events that they wish to support'. An example of the type of tussle that developed centred upon a request for a grant of £10,000 towards expenses for the 1966 Commonwealth Games in Jamaica. The Treasury approved the grant, but the DES then came back, via the Sports Council, with a bid for additional money to cover personal expenses for competitors such as laundry, postage and bus fares. 'This was turned down', Miss Startin reported, 'on the grounds that it was wrong at that time to extend the scope of grants for international sport, let alone to provide pocket money for competitors'.[33]

The Minister for Sport was not to be easily deflected. He threw his weight behind a bid for assistance towards the travel and subsistence costs of athletes and team officials invited to visit the French Pyrenees, looking to train at high altitude in preparation for the acclimatization problems of holding the 1968 Olympics in Mexico. The request was initially rejected by the Treasury, which did not wish to extend assistance to preliminary training, to subsistence or to non-competitors – all of which were excluded from the terms of the 1964 rules. Howell took up the cudgels by pleading with the Chief Secretary, Jack Diamond. In a briefing note for Diamond, Treasury official Peter Jay wrote in an exasperated tone that the Sports Minister was calling again, 'this time' to argue that the Olympics deserved special treatment, that altitude training was vital, and the French might veto British entry to the Common Market if their invitation to use special training facilities was not taken up. Jay described the latter argument as 'absurd', and noted that a precedent might be set which could be exploited by other sports such as skiing teams, for whom training conditions in Britain were not ideal. Diamond was advised that he would be perfectly entitled to reject the bid outright, though when confronted by a persuasive Sports Minister he opted for a compromise; as this was a special case, 90 per cent of travel costs for competitors only would be offered.[34]

In the run-up to the Mexico Olympics Howell secured further concessions, despite Treasury concern that it was being asked, in the words of Miss Startin, to 'connive in evading such rules which are presumably designed to ensure that [athletics] is a truly amateur sport'.[35] In January 1968 Howell announced that as well as helping British squads 'for the first time' to undertake pre-Olympic training abroad, assistance was also being offered to enable teams to subsidize up to two weeks of preparatory training at home.[36] The following month a further government statement underlined how policy had changed in a short period of time. Agreement had been reached, it was announced, on a grant to the BOA for the Mexico Games based on half of the travel costs of competitors, coaches and managers, all of whom – in a further break with the past – would be offered modest out-of-pocket expenses. Money would also be made available for the travel costs of technical officials accompanying the British team.[37] In his memoirs Howell recorded how, when he attended the Mexico Olympics, he was pleased to find that several athletes, used to travelling and competing on a shoestring, appreciated the gesture of pocket money, amounting to about ten shillings a day. This allowance was 'modest enough', Howell wrote, but it brought British athletes somewhere closer to the conditions enjoyed in the Olympic village by their American and other counterparts.[38]

Before 1964, Conservative ministers were reluctant proponents of state assistance for international sports teams. But after 1970, spurred into action by Howell's success in associating Labour with reform, Heath's administration sought to emulate its opponents in promising an expansive approach. The Westminster battle for international funding was not just won; it was moving on to new territory. In an ill-tempered parliamentary exchange in July 1971, the Tory Sports Minister Eldon Griffiths claimed that 'substantially more money' than ever before was being contributed towards this aspect of policy. The Minister talked of a 'quantum leap' in aid for international teams, arguing it totalled £75,000 in 1969–70 (the last year for which Labour was responsible), compared with £125,000 in his first year in office and £168,000 in the current financial year. From the opposition benches Howell intervened furiously, angry that the Tories chose this ground to attack after the energy he had invested in prising more generous funding from the Treasury. He particularly resented the accusation that Labour had 'short-changed' British teams by not fully using up the budget set aside for international sport, which went up and down in different years between 1964 and 1970. Howell pointed out that the figures fluctuated according to the proximity of the Olympics, and the fact that the sporting bodies did not come forward with sufficient proposals to use up the budget was not evidence of short-changing; rather 'we were prepared to meet every demand made upon us, and we did'.[39]

The creation in 1972 of an executive Sports Council, with responsibility for oversight of funding for national amateur sports teams, distanced the issue from the direct political bickering engaged in by Griffiths and Howell. John Coghlan, from his vantage point as a senior administrator, later wrote that there were solid foundations on which to build by the time the Council changed from advisory to executive status. 'For the elite it was … largely but not wholly', he noted, 'a case of trying to do more of what had already been started'. As a token of its determination to press ahead, the reconstituted Sports Council quickly doubled the scale of funding for overseas travel grants, from under £200,000 in 1972–73 to over £400,000 in 1973–74. The most novel development came as a result of the Council's belief that more should be done to enhance provision for governing bodies to support individual athletes. NGBs, the argument ran, knew best what was needed for elite sportsmen and women, whether in terms of facilities or coaching and development schemes. With international competition in mind, funding for NGBs rose sharply even allowing for inflation, climbing from £0.6 million in 1972–73 to £4.0 million in 1979–80. Labour's 1975 White Paper also pledged support for 'high-level sport', and by 1978 the Sports Council was able to report that centres of excellence had been created in all the regions of England, catering for over twenty Olympic sports. In addition, some of Britain's national sports centres were developed with central funding to sufficiently high standards to be able to host major international events, as when the World Rowing Championships were held at the National

Water Sports Centre at Holme Pierrepont in Nottingham.[40] Before 1964 state backing for Britain's elite performers had been negligible. Fifteen years on, as amateurism gave way to growing professionalism in top-level sport (in cricket and tennis, for example, if not yet in athletics), it had become an accepted feature of the sporting landscape. Britain's Olympic performers, though still having to combine training with paid employment, could at least count on some financial aid to enable them to compete for gold medals.

Pressure for Change:
The Rise of Global Sporting Controversies

In the case of funding for elite athletes, politicians chose from the mid-1960s onwards to forge closer ties with international sport. At the same time, British governments continued to be drawn reluctantly into diplomatic issues arising from global sport. Whether these issues manifested themselves as short-term problems (such as anxiety over North Korean's involvement in the 1966 World Cup) or more protracted concerns (like the running sore of sporting links with South Africa), the regularity and scale of such occurrences hinted that a permanent change was taking place in the sport–diplomacy relationship. The Olympics in particular entered a phase of intense politicization which no government could ignore. The Mexico Games were marked by 'black power' protests, and the 1972 event in Munich was infamously overshadowed by an attack on the Israeli team, resulting in the death of 12 athletes at the hands of Palestinian militants. A Palestinian spokesman claimed the Games were deliberately targeted to attract worldwide publicity; 'sport is the modern religion of the Western world'.[41] IOC officials were left with the immensely difficult decision as to whether, in the words of the *Times*, this 'tragic and dishonoured festival should be played through to a grim conclusion or should be abandoned as a memorial to those who died'. Opinion in Britain was divided. Although the *Times* criticized the eventual IOC insistence that 'the show must go on', following a 24 suspension, the same newspaper attacked Harold Wilson as opposition leader for calling on ministers to urge the withdrawal of the British team. The Foreign Secretary Sir Alec Douglas-Home called Wilson's remarks deplorable, especially any implication that the Tory government was dragging its feet on counter-terrorism measures. Douglas-Home accepted there were differences of opinion over continuing with the Games, but this was not the point: 'The simple fact is that the decision to remain in Munich was for the British Olympic Committee and not for the Government. We do not run our sport here by Government decree.'[42]

In view of the suddenness and brutality of the killings in Germany, it was tempting to see Munich as another one-off case where politics and international sport accidentally collided. Yet as the *Times* noted, the Olympics had become such a huge global showcase (the BBC alone had nearly 100 journalists in attendance) that they were 'magnetic to political advertisement'.[43] This theme was taken up by the British Ambassador to West Germany, Nicholas Henderson, who in a despatch to London after the Games noted that while the actions of 'Arab terrorists' inevitably dominated proceedings, they were not alone in looking to exploit the event for purposes that had little to do with sport. The West German organizers, Henderson wrote, hoped through a friendly festival to 'expiate the sins of 1936', while Communist regimes as usual regarded the Olympics as an 'opportunity to pursue the Cold War by other means'. As for the British performance, the Ambassador noted an improved showing compared with Mexico in 1968, but 'no-one can say that for us to come eleventh in the medal table is impressive, bearing in mind our tradition as a sporting nation'. This did not mean Henderson advocated a radical shift in the British approach to sport. Although the Sports Council chairman Roger Bannister supplied him with figures showing that other European nations invested considerably more public money, the Ambassador said he remained unconvinced about arguments in favour of Britain changing course. Improved 'prestige' was often cited as a product of success in sport, but for Henderson there were 'many leisure activities outside the Games that are equally valuable from the social and health points of view'.[44]

In looking to the future, the British Ambassador also made two predictions that were borne out in subsequent years, both of which pointed to growing structural ties between sport and diplomacy. The first was that because the Olympics had become so large – costing some £200 million and involving over 8000 competitors in 1972 – without some reduction in scale in future, 'political exploitation is unavoidable'. This was certainly the case in Montreal in

1976. There were arguments between the Canadian government and the IOC over the participation of Taiwan and a boycott of over twenty (mostly African) nations took place in protest at a high-profile rugby tour by New Zealand to South Africa. Although not considered to have seriously damaged the Games, it was widely realized a similar boycott could completely undermine the smaller scale Commonwealth Games, due to take place in Edmonton in 1978. From a British perspective, the High Commissioner in Ottawa, J. B. Johnston, wrote to London saying that although the Queen's presence in Montreal was a personal triumph, it did not change 'the attitude of Quebecers to the Canadian monarchy as an institution'. The performance of the British team, according to Johnston, was 'about average', though disappointing in track and field events, with only one bronze medal won. This however needed to be seen (as Henderson pointed out four years earlier) in the context of resources and commitment. On this the existing global pattern looked set to stay: 'The totalitarian states will continue to run their factories for the production of gymnasts, weight-lifters and the like, and those Western states who can afford to will continue to try to prevent them from having things all their own way.' It was an encouraging feature of the Games, the High Commissioner wrote, that gold medals could still be won by those, including from Britain, who were products neither 'of great wealth or of a soulless State machine'.[45]

The second prediction made by Nicholas Henderson in his ambassadorial reflections on the 1972 Games was that policy towards sport, as with other activities, would increasingly be set within a European rather than exclusively British context. The Council of Europe, a pan-European anti-Communist alliance, had been active for many years in promoting the virtues of recreation, and in the mid-1970s it decided to establish a Committee for the Development of Sport (CDS). This grouping outlined a European 'Sport for All' policy, emphasizing the need for public authorities to take a lead in financing new initiatives; a policy that was endorsed by the Council of Europe in 1976. Britain played a leading role in this sphere, with Walter Winterbottom, Director of the Sports Council, being appointed as Chairman of the CDS when it became fully operative in 1977. Winterbottom's enthusiasm was such that the Foreign Office sought to impose some gentle restraint, insisting that the British delegation in Strasbourg included in CDS development plans the wording 'as and when resources can be made available'.[46] Winterbottom persuaded Denis Howell that it would be beneficial if sports ministers from across the continent met regularly to discuss common problems. Britain's Sports Minister discovered that with longer experience in this sphere than many of his counterparts, he was regarded as the figurehead, and he was asked to chair a formal conference of European ministers for sport at Lancaster House in London in 1978. For Howell, the European dimension provided a platform to influence the politics of sport on a wider stage. In alliance with like-minded non-Communist ministers in Germany and France, he put his weight behind efforts to hold back moves by Warsaw Pact countries and assemblies of African politicians to alter the dynamics of global sport, notably when the United Nations body UNESCO initiated moves to usurp the authority of the IOC.[47]

A further indication that international sport in the 1970s had broader ramifications than in the past came with ongoing controversy over the question of contacts with South Africa. Despite widespread condemnation of apartheid, and banishment from the Olympic Games, South Africa continued to seek international competition, particularly in its traditional non-Olympic sports of rugby union and cricket. Anxious to avoid any repeat of the messy battles over the proposed South African cricket tour to England in 1970, Denis Howell pressed for a clear statement of policy when he returned for his second spell as Minister for Sport. In December 1974 the Foreign Secretary Jim Callaghan set out Labour's position: 'The Government regard sporting contacts with South Africa, so long as selection on the basis of race and colour is maintained, as repugnant, and they will receive no official support or approval.' In 1976 Howell reminded the Sports Council that its funding was based on the understanding that it would not provide grants for any visits by national teams to South Africa. While urging the Council to back the government line, Howell admitted there were limits to what could be achieved. It was difficult, for example, to ban individual South Africans from taking part in events in Britain; sportsmen and women did not require work permits to visit unless they intended to stay for an extended period.[48] By this point Britain could not operate in isolation on the apartheid issue. Just as the European context of sport policy was becoming more pronounced, so too was the Commonwealth dimension.

Sport provided an important cultural bond for Commonwealth nations, several of whom shared Britain's long history of competing with South Africa in cricket and rugby especially. The pressure for a broad new initiative mounted when the New Zealand leader Robert Muldoon came to power as a strident supporter of links with South Africa. His vocal backing for the rugby tour of 1976, which took place against a backdrop of rioting by disaffected blacks in Soweto, prompted the extensive African boycott of the Montreal Olympics. The prospect of African nations adopting the same stance at the 1978 Commonwealth Games threatened to fatally compromise the whole future of those Games.[49]

While in Montreal for the Olympics, Denis Howell was reassured by talks in which colleagues from Africa said they appreciated Britain's position on apartheid in sport, 'which indeed we have reiterated many times'.[50] In some quarters Howell has been credited with a major new initiative in 1977. According to John Coghlan, it was Labour's Sports Minister who 'devised' a Commonwealth agreement on sporting contacts with South Africa.[51] In reality, the background to this development involved several key figures in Britain and elsewhere. Aware that this thorny problem could sour Commonwealth relations, a one-off meeting of British ministers in May 1977 recommended that Prime Minister Callaghan press for an agreed statement when Commonwealth leaders came to Britain in July. This would refer to sporting links with South Africa as 'offensive', adding that 'no official support, financial or otherwise', would be given to such contacts. It was also recommended that rather than Britain taking the lead (which could provoke opposition in some quarters), broader support might be forthcoming if responsibility for finalizing any agreement was left with the Commonwealth Secretariat.[52] From this point on a major role was played by the Secretary General of the Commonwealth, 'Sonny' Ramphal, whose staff prepared the ground and worked on a new form of wording. In the informal atmosphere of a weekend retreat at Gleneagles Hotel in Scotland, a small group of Commonwealth leaders – including crucially Robert Muldoon – accepted a 500-word statement referring to the 'urgent duty' of governments to fight apartheid by 'withholding any form of support for, and by taking every practical step to discourage, contact or competition by their nationals with sporting organisations, teams or sportsmen from South Africa'. When the wider group of Commonwealth leaders resumed their meeting in London after the weekend retreat, formal approval was given to what soon became known as the 'Gleneagles Agreement'.[53]

For a while at least the Agreement succeeded, in the words of political scientist Anthony Payne, in getting Commonwealth leaders off 'a nasty hook'.[54] Muldoon reluctantly came into line and the number of sporting links with South Africa fell, though they were not eliminated altogether. Britain continued to have its share of adverse publicity. Some Commonwealth leaders were aghast to discover that with the ink barely dry from Gleneagles, South African women tennis players were taking part in the Federation Cup competition in England. Callaghan reiterated his position and revealed that Howell and other senior ministers 'did their best' to prevent the Lawn Tennis Association from issuing an invitation to South Africa, but to no avail.[55] The Prime Minister promised that governing bodies of sport would be made aware of 'the importance of the Commonwealth statement', and in October 1977 Howell wrote a forceful letter to the Sports Council expressing concern that a 'small number' of governing bodies continued to condone and even encourage sporting links with South Africa. He wished to make it clear that while he firmly supported the principle of individual sports being left to make their own decisions, 'independence carries with it responsibility'. He requested that the Council bring to the attention of all governing bodies the terms of the Gleneagles Agreement, and urged them to 'act within its spirit'.[56] The most obvious vindication of the Agreement in the short term came when the Commonwealth Games went ahead in Canada in 1978 without any notable controversy. Confident that the spotlight would be on sport rather than politics, Callaghan wrote to Secretary General Ramphal shortly before the Games started saying they agreed that all Commonwealth nations 'have done their best to honour their obligations under the Gleneagles Agreement'. Ramphal made the point that although occasional breaches of the agreement were still taking place, this was despite the best efforts of the individual governments concerned.[57]

Conclusion: The Moscow Olympic Boycott

By the late 1970s Whitehall's traditional detachment towards top level sport, punctuated only by occasional exceptions where there was no choice but to intervene, appeared to be on the way out. But the trend towards closer ties between politicians and sport, epitomized by Britain taking a leading part in formulating international policy on sporting contacts with South Africa, was abruptly interrupted in 1980. The fragility of the developing links between global sport and politics (and the power of a prime minister to dictate policy) were illustrated when Margaret Thatcher, head of the Conservative administration which replaced Labour in 1979, sought to persuade British athletes not to attend the Olympic Games, due to be held in Moscow in the summer of 1980. Following the lead of American President Jimmy Carter, the Prime Minister advocated a boycott of the Games in response to the Soviet invasion of Afghanistan shortly after Christmas in 1979. In Thatcher's eyes the sensibilities of sport were subordinate to the need to reaffirm Britain's position on the world stage and cement the Anglo-American 'special relationship' in the face of unacceptable Soviet expansionism. 'If this means that we have to embrace the use of sport for the first time as a political weapon', one Cabinet minister wrote, backing up the Prime Minister's position, 'I feel that the end would justify the means'.[58]

In the first half of 1980 debates raged, in parliament and across the country, over whether British competitors should attend the Moscow Games, giving sport a prominence in political discourse not seen since the controversy over cricket and apartheid ten years previously. Thatcher and her ministers used a range of arguments and techniques, and in March the House of Commons passed a motion stating that Britain 'should not take part in the Olympic Games in Moscow'. But the government came up against stern resistance from the BOA, which adhered to the IOC line that the Games should proceed as planned, and from individual sportsmen and women, determined to fulfil their long-cherished Olympic ambitions. While a few NGBs followed the Prime Minister's lead, the majority felt they were being singled out as political pawns at a time when trade links with the Soviet Union remained largely unaffected by the crisis. Despite absentees from some sports, the British team that went to Moscow in July 1980 was the largest among western European nations, and the embarrassment of ministers was compounded when Britain finished a respectable ninth in the official medals table. The whole episode left some deep scars. A memorandum written by Conservative Central Office in the wake of the dispute noted that 'regrettably' a gulf had opened up 'between Government/Party and the Sporting Bodies/Sportsmen involved. Hopefully when the Olympics are over this will be closed'.[59] In reality, rather than moving inexorably closer – as had been the case since the mid-1960s – the relationship between sport and politics across the board in Britain was entering a troubled phase, and was to remain fraught for a decade to come.

8 The 1980s: 'Years of Concern'

Introduction

Margaret Thatcher divided opinion in Britain sharply. When she fell from power in 1990 after eleven years at the helm, spanning three successive general elections victories, the admiration of her supporters remained undimmed. For her acolytes, the Conservative governments of the 1980s restored pride in Britain abroad and at home, curbing unbridled trade union power and modernizing the nation's industrial infrastructure through extensive privatization. In the eyes of detractors, Thatcher left a trail of victims in her wake. While the economy grew rapidly to benefit many in the mid-1980s, the beginning and end of the decade witnessed deep recessions where the Prime Minister insisted 'there was no alternative' to the free market nostrums of sound money and minimal state intervention that left millions unemployed. One facet of Thatcher's premiership which is widely agreed upon is that she was, in the words of a leading sports administrator, 'wholly indifferent to sport'.[1] Her massive volume of memoirs, published after she left office, made almost no mention of sport, other than to lament the decision of British athletes to defy her wishes by participating in the 1980 Moscow Olympics. Scarred by this experience, Thatcher brought an abrasive, unforgiving style to sport. Since the mid-1960s politicians had been drawn steadily into closer ties with sport. On the home front there was growing acceptance of the need to improve facilities and recreational opportunities, while on the international stage assistance for elite performers was seen as unavoidable if British athletes were to compete with any chance of success at events such as the Olympics. But history does not always proceed in a linear, progressive fashion: in the 1980s the relationship between politicians and sport was ruptured, with serious questions being

172

posed for the first time in a generation about the efficacy of state intervention.

We saw in earlier chapters that there was little cross-party agreement over sport prior to 1964. Denis Howell's activities as Sports Minister prompted a Conservative counter-response, and by 1970 the Tories were determined not to be outflanked and tarred with the brush of indifference to sport. This resulted in Heath's government pursuing a more advanced approach than previous Conservative administrations, enhancing the powers of the Sports Council as a delivery mechanism for improving sport. Party differences persisted in the 1970s over how far ministers should directly intervene, but these differences were nothing compared with the wholesale resumption of inter-party bickering about sport after Thatcher came to power. Since 1964 it had become the practice to invite opposition spokesmen to sporting receptions held in Downing Street. Howell, after standing up to the Prime Minister over the Moscow Games, noted that he did not receive a single invitation to such occasions in the 1980s, despite remaining Labour's spokesman for sport throughout the decade and being on good personal terms with Thatcher's husband, a keen sports fan.[2] It was not only Labour spokesmen who felt the Conservatives were again treating sport as little more than a crude instrument of social policy. In the view of John Coghlan, who rose to become second-in-command at the Sports Council, advocates of a higher political profile for sport regarded the Thatcher era as 'years of concern'.[3] With minimal input from the top, the government's approach to sport in the 1980s varied from seeing it, according to the considered perspective of academics Barrie Houlihan and Anita White, as a 'quick fix solution to urban unrest to it being a source of national embarrassment through soccer hooliganism'.[4]

Problems of Personnel and Administration

The Prime Minister's scant regard for sport was shared by many of her Cabinet colleagues. None of those who served as Secretary of State at the Department of the Environment, which continued to take the lead on sport, were known as enthusiasts; some bordered on the hostile. For three years the post-holder was Nicholas Ridley, whose lack of interest was 'notorious', observed one sports official who locked horns with Ridley.[5] The low priority accorded to recreation in government circles was also reflected in a high turn-over of ministers. Whereas there had been only two Ministers for Sport between 1970 and 1979, Thatcher appointed five during her premiership, all working as undersecretaries at the Department of the Environment (DoE). None, in other words, merited the status of Minister of State accorded to Denis Howell, who lamented in his memoirs that any semblance of a bipartisan approach to sport was soon abandoned. The assumption in the 1980s, he believed, was that in the adversarial climate of the day the Labour opposition could not be seen to be influencing policy in any way. Successive Tory Sports Ministers seemed more interested in short-term fixes than long-term planning, Howell claimed, and were discarded quickly if the newspaper headlines turned sour.[6] Hector Monro, appointed as Thatcher's first Minister for Sport in 1979, had (unlike some of his successors) well-established sporting connec-tions as a former president of the Scottish Rugby Football Union. He was an affable old school Tory, brought up in the mould of Macmillan and Douglas-Home's one nation Conservatism, and he forged good links with sports administrators. But his ambitions were scuppered when he was sidelined for refusing to enthusiasti-cally endorse the Prime Minister's proposed boycott of the Moscow Olympics. When Thatcher reshuffled her ministerial team in 1981, Monro was among those removed from office. A newspaper profile a few years later claimed he would have liked to have remained in post, but the Thatcher juggernaut was rolling; he was not regarded as 'one of us'.[7]

Monro's successor was Neil Macfarlane, MP for Sutton and Cheam, who was well versed in sports politics having been one of the few Conservatives who specialized in this field in the 1970s. John Coghlan later wrote that Macfarlane was initially resource-ful and successful, rebuilding some of the bridges between the government and sport damaged by the Moscow boycott episode. Indeed Macfarlane was to be the longest serving of Thatcher's Ministers for Sport, staying in the post another two years following the Conservative election landslide victory of 1983. But, according to Coghlan, Macfarlane got increasingly bogged down by the vexed issue of football violence ('one sensed that the Prime Minister was constantly at him in this connection') and became known for 'med-dling in the affairs of the Sports Council'. The Minister's combat-ive streak led him into conflict with bodies such as the Central

Council of Physical Recreation (CCPR). By 1985 journalists like John Rodda of the *Guardian* were claiming that some senior Tories were known to be in favour of doing away with the post of Sports Minister altogether. Macfarlane had been appointed, Rodda wrote, 'in the image' of Denis Howell, 'whom he has fallen sadly short of matching'. Coghlan also reached an unflattering conclusion. Macfarlane's inability to listen to influential figures in sport and his 'clear, if repeatedly denied' desire to dictate policy against the wishes of bodies such as the Sports Council – granted a Royal Charter by the Conservatives in the early 1970s precisely in order to protect it from political interference – meant 'he was not greatly missed' when he resigned hours ahead of a government reshuffle in September 1985.[8]

Macfarlane was replaced by Richard (Dick) Tracey, MP for Surbiton, whose background as a journalist suggested he was chosen primarily to improve the presentational aspects of government policy. While he forged more cordial relations with sporting bodies than his predecessor, Tracey's time as Minister for Sport was not generally regarded as distinguished. 'I don't think Dick knew enough about sport to make any real impact', reflected Denis Howell; 'his inconspicuous period of office was the opposite expected of him on his appointment'.[9] After Thatcher's third election triumph in the summer of 1987, Tracey gave way to Colin Moynihan, MP for Lewisham East. Moynihan was a distinguished Olympic athlete, and was surprised to be offered the sport portfolio having defied the Prime Minister's call to boycott the Moscow Games, where he coxed the rowing team that won a silver medal.[10] Moynihan's profile and all-action style meant that, early on under his stewardship, the role of Sports Minister for the first time in the 1980s did not seem a graveyard for the politically ambitious. Some observers described him as the most accomplished holder of the post since Howell, though Moynihan too over time struggled to maintain a strong sense of purpose and direction. His association with unpopular plans to introduce identity cards for football supporters damaged his credibility, and protracted disputes with the likes of the CCPR led Coghlan to suggest that by 1990 he was regarded as 'more of a liability to sport than a benefit'; a real shame, Coghlan felt, in view of his initial promise and undoubted energy.[11] In July 1990, as part of a reshuffle aimed at saving her ailing premiership, Moynihan was replaced by Robert Atkins, MP for Preston North and South Ribble. Atkins had links with both cricket and rugby, but was barely in post long enough to influence the direction of policy before Thatcher was dramatically ousted as Prime Minister in November 1990.

Serving for variable, mostly short, terms of office, all five Ministers for Sport in the 1980s inevitably struggled to come to terms with sport's fragmented system of governance. After he left office Macfarlane published a book entitled *Sport and Politics: A World Divided*, in which he noted the 'the lowly position of a Sports Minister in a Conservative Government'. He attributed this both to the persistence of the view among colleagues that leisure was primarily a private activity that should regulate itself where possible, and to the absence of a clear legislative or administrative framework in which to operate. His account highlighted the difficulties of trying to react to sudden emergency situations, notably in relation to football hooliganism, while constantly grappling with departments other than the DoE with a stake in developing policy: among them the Treasury on financial matters, the Department of Education and Science (DES) on school sport, and the Foreign and Commonwealth Office (FCO, as it had been known since the late 1960s) on international sporting matters. Negotiating the Whitehall jungle was not, however, a novel or unique problem. Since 1972, with the creation of the executive Sports Council, the incumbent was confronted with the tricky issue of how to oversee policy in the absence of any significant executive authority beyond influencing the scale of Council funding. Where others such as Howell and Griffiths managed relationships reasonably well – working to good effect with other Whitehall departments and the Sports Council – Macfarlane it seems never quite got to grips with the system he inherited. In time he questioned if it was appropriate for government money to be distributed via the quasi-independent Council, despite it being a Conservative creation, and he hinted in his book at the need for the DoE to take more direct control, preferably under a figurehead upgraded to the rank of Minister of State.[12]

The issue of school sport brought into focus the extent to which Howell's skill in forging successful alliances across the Whitehall machine was missed during the 1980s. In 1983 Macfarlane outlined a new scheme for ensuring that existing sports facilities, including those in schools, were put to maximum use. In difficult economic times, he argued, school gyms and fields should be opened up whenever possible for community use. But in *Sport and Politics* he wrote that his plan was 'resisted and slowly strangled' by ministers and officials at the DES, where there was strong opposition to any fresh funding for sport.[13] Instead, left to its own devices, the DES in its determination to reduce costs embarked a policy that was to be held up in future years as a symbol of the Thatcher government's disregard for sport: the sale of school playing fields. Some 5000 playing fields across the country were lost during the 1980s to new building development, and with teachers in dispute over pay and conditions school sport went into a period of pronounced decline. Towards the end of the decade Colin Moynihan went some way towards providing a sharper focus for the role of Sports Minister. More so than his immediate predecessors, he managed to establish effective working relationships with other government departments and the Sports Council, while relying from day-to-day on a dedicated team of officials based in the Sport and Recreation Division (SARD) at the DoE. But the limitations of what could be achieved remained obvious. As a busy junior minister with a range of responsibilities, Moynihan devoted no more than a quarter of his working week to sport-related matters, and SARD was only a tiny element at the DoE: it was served by about twenty staff in a total of nearly 6500 civil servants at the department.[14]

At a time when government policy lacked strong direction, parliamentary lobbying on behalf of sport was also weaker than it had been for many years. In July 1984 the Conservative MP David Ashby initiated the first extended Commons debate devoted to general sporting issues since the discussion on Labour's White Paper seven years earlier. Ashby admitted that insufficient priority was being given to sport. The DES he said 'has no strategy for sport in schools'; he hoped this would change in view of the importance of sport in promoting good health and well-being. The Labour MP Tom Pendry claimed that, aside from exceptional cases such as the dispute over the Moscow Olympics, sport never featured high on the government's list of priorities. In his 15 years as a backbencher it was unusual for there to be more than one brief parliamentary discussion annually. Denis Howell observed that most MPs had not bothered to turn up on this occasion; many probably regarded sport 'as a frivolous pursuit for the House of Commons'. Against this backcloth, the debate held little wider

interest other than ritual posturing and sniping between the two
main party spokesmen, Howell and Macfarlane. In contrast to the
era of Noel-Baker's Parliamentary Sports Committee, cross-party
lobbying on behalf of sport was a thing of the past. Ministers were
not inclined to listen sympathetically to the opposition benches,
and parliamentary pressure was only likely to influence policy if it
was applied systematically from the Tory side of the House. But the
chairman of a Conservative Parliamentary Committee on Sport,
the Luton MP John Carlisle, like many of his colleagues was sceptical about the whole concept of 'meddling' in sport. In the debate
of July 1984 Carlisle said that notwithstanding the worthy efforts of
Macfarlane, the position of a Sports Minister 'is one that is always
in question on the Conservative benches'.[15]

The Government and the Sports Council

At the heart of the malaise in sport policy during the 1980s was
a dysfunctional relationship between the government and the
Sports Council. The best Neil Macfarlane could say about the
Sports Council in retrospect was that it did good work in the
regions. For him the Council spent too much of its government
grant on an overstaffed London headquarters and not enough on
coaching and development.[16] Unsurprisingly, John Coghlan saw
things differently. Thatcher's government, he believed, was intent
on squashing opposition wherever it was found, and did not take
kindly to repeated public utterances from the Director General
of the Council, Emlyn Jones, that sport in Britain was seriously
underfunded. According to Coghlan, Jones felt he was speaking
on behalf of sport, not attacking the government, but Macfarlane
'disliked this' and privately spoke of Jones 'rocking the boat'. In
the autumn of 1982 Jones suddenly announced his early retirement, despite having a lengthy period still to serve on his contract.
The following summer Coghlan also announced he was leaving
his post as Deputy Director; like Jones, he went quietly and made
no formal public statement.[17] Denis Howell was more vociferous,
having what he called 'a field day in Parliament'. With Macfarlane
refusing to give a full explanation, Howell said there was strong
suspicion of 'the long arm of government meddling in the affairs
of voluntary sports bodies and eroding the independence of the
Sports Council enshrined in the Royal Charter'. One of Jones'

successors later wrote that when he took over at the Sports Council he found correspondence showing the resignation resulted from pressure applied by Macfarlane, who objected in particular to Council officials maintaining direct contact with the Labour opposition on sport.[18]

Behind this troubled relationship at the heart of the policy-making community was a clash in priorities and motives. Following some serious inner city riots, the Sports Council was prevailed upon by the government to establish an 'Action Sport' programme in 1982; 15 projects in selected areas were each given £3 million over three years. While this encouraged local authorities more broadly to engage in sports development work, there was much concern that ministers were hijacking sport to tackle social deprivation, and a later evaluation by the Sports Council pointed to shortcomings in the local projects resulting from their hasty improvisation.[19] In addition, the expansionist instincts of the Council in the 1980s ran counter to the cost-cutting agenda of the government. The 1982 policy document published by the Council, *Sport in the Community – The Next Ten Years*, noted a welcome rise in the number of new sporting facilities during the 1970s, but argued that women and ethnic minorities were often excluded from increases in participation and called for £40 million of additional investment per year over a five-year period. Although well received in the media, the document was given a lukewarm reception by bodies such as the CCPR. The Council and the CCPR were in the midst of a recurrent bout of what Macfarlane found to be 'petty feuding': a further source of frustration for the Minister and 'debilitating for sport in England'. Coghlan noted that the government also reacted coolly to the Council's initiative. It refused to go beyond a broad general welcome, 'which meant all or nothing'; presumably the latter, he added, because the annual grant to the Council which followed publication showed only a tiny increase in real terms: 'a poor response to the call for £40m'. The story was similar when in 1988 the Sports Council produced another substantial document, *Sport in the Community – Into the Nineties*. This provided statistical evidence of the valuable contribution sport and recreation was making to the economy through sport-related employment, taxation and use of public-funded facilities. But again the official response was muted, as Coghlan wrote: 'This was an exciting document that demanded attention from government and governing bodies of sport; sadly once again it did not get it.'[20]

If the Sports Council (like many non-governmental public bodies in the 1980s) was regarded by suspicion in Whitehall circles, it was also failing to satisfy many in the sporting world. A parliamentary enquiry into the 'expenditure, administration and policy' of the Council in the mid-1980s took evidence from a range of witnesses, some of whom like Richard Palmer of the British Olympic Association (BOA) were highly critical in their observations. After more than a decade of using the mechanism introduced by the Royal Charter of 1972 to distribute funding, 'no one nowadays has any illusions about the independence of the Sports Council', Palmer argued. It was felt by sporting administrators and governing bodies to be too closely controlled by ministers, both in terms of policy and personnel. The lobbying which the Council could undertake on behalf of sport was 'constrained and muted by its Governmental masters'; hence according to Palmer the 'enduring notion' that sport was being 'undersold in Governmental circles'. A better model for governance, Palmer believed, might be for a government department such as the DoE to assume more direct responsibility. In this way funding could be targeted and objectives delivered more effectively than working through the 'existing "middle man" Sports Council arrangement'.[21] The parliamentary enquiry, however, publishing its findings in 1986, while advocating changes such as a more equitable gender balance in membership, came down in favour of keeping the Sports Council; from the government perspective, relinquishing its stranglehold of the Council was not on the agenda.

By the late 1980s relations between the government and the Sports Council were at least on a more even keel. This was partly due to the efforts of Colin Moynihan, though not until after he ruffled feathers by referring at one point to the Council as an 'arm of Government'. He also imposed a reduction in the size of Council membership, which did not go down well among those excluded.[22] Moynihan's desire to shake up the system he inherited included a public attack on sporting administrators in general as too old and out-of-touch. This led to what Denis Howell called a 'put down' by Prince Philip at a meeting of the CCPR, where the Prince remarked that the Minister was not the only person present with a distinguished sporting background; many leading

administrators could claim likewise.[23] Even so, Moynihan formed
an effective working relationship with David Pickup, a former civil
servant who was appointed Director General of the Sports Council
in 1988. While Pickup in due course earned many plaudits for his
work, at the time he took over he was under no illusion about the
challenges ahead. He later wrote that the Sports Council had a
reputation in government circles for 'missionary zeal' that was
'outstripping realism'. Officials at the DoE were concerned about
the lack of 'financial discipline' at the Council, and were keen to
find an efficient administrator to run the show. Bringing a fresh
eye to proceedings, Pickup found himself venturing into a 'sad
landscape'. All concerned, he believed – ranging from ministers and administrators to the media and athletes – bore some
degree of responsibility for producing 'a system of planning and
provision for sport which has failed to match the rate of progress
achieved elsewhere in the developed world'. While most individuals involved in this 'accidental conspiracy' were well-intentioned,
Pickup added, too many were 'self-seeking', and unwilling to set
aside private agendas 'to secure a greater good'.[24]

David Pickup's first year as head of the Sports Council brought
welcome improvements on several fronts. Moynihan came to
accept the value placed by Council members on protecting their
independence from government, and was more relaxed than some
of his predecessors about any links the Council maintained with
spokesmen across the political spectrum. For his part, the Director
General set about internal reforms favoured by the DoE such as
imposing financial order, reducing staffing levels and devising corporate strategies. Pickup also prompted a hard look at an issue he
said had 'never been seriously addressed': how, in a context where
funding was never sufficient to meet all needs, the balance should
be struck between programmes aimed at promoting mass participation and those concerned with achieving excellence. After
lengthy discussion, the Council decided to give a higher priority to
Olympic sports, a move with major long-term implications and one
that was resented by the likes of the CCPR, speaking on behalf of
recreational sport. In addition, the Council took a greater interest
than it had for many years in school sport, a result in part of growing embarrassment in ministerial circles over attacks on the sale of
school playing fields. Moynihan secured an extra £500,000 of funding for the Council to establish a register of playing pitches across

the country. 'Quite what this would achieve, beyond giving us all a better view of a sinking ship', Pickup reflected, 'was never made entirely clear'.[25] The Director General was nevertheless prepared to give credit where it was due. When the Minister addressed the Sports Council in December 1989 he was able to report that government funding had risen by £7 million in two years; Moynihan also spoke of launching a comprehensive structural and financial review of where sport was heading in the decade ahead. 'All in all it had been an encouraging year', Pickup later wrote. In contrast to earlier in the 1980s, there appeared to be considerable empathy between the Minister, DoE officials and the Council, though 'unfortunately', Pickup added, this 'was not to be experienced for much longer'.[26]

The harmony between the government and the Sports Council dissipated in the early months of 1990. Ahead of the full review pledged by Moynihan, Pickup felt he and his colleagues were the subject of unwelcome interference from Whitehall, beginning 'a lengthy and dispiriting process of destabilising the Council'. While his team took seriously the development of corporate plans, the Director General felt these were met with 'studied lack of any specific endorsement – or even rejection – by the Government'. Civil servants mostly ignored them, he said, aside from extracting data useful to cement arguments being advanced to the Treasury as part of the annual battle for public spending allocations. One bright spot for Pickup was continued 'friendly dialogue' with Moynihan, compensating 'for the lack of formal Government endorsement of the Council's strategies'. But this ended when the 'Miniature for Sport' – as he was dubbed by Labour opponents on account of his stature – was removed from office in the summer of 1990. In Pickup's view Moynihan was 'undoubtedly...the most effective and energetic Minister that sport had encountered since the best days of Denis Howell'.[27] But his departure left a dark cloud over the world of sport. Despite bouts of economic stringency, Thatcher's government could claim that spending on the arts had risen well above the rate of inflation during the 1980s. The same did not though apply to sport. Funding for the Sports Council increased from £15 million in 1978/79 to £43.7 million in 1989/90. But in most years there was no real-terms increase owing to the high rate of inflation. While local authorities had striven to maintain provision for sport and recreation in hard times (see

Chapter 10), central government investment, in the view of John Coghlan, had been 'mean in the extreme'.[28]

Trouble on the Terraces

In his book *Sport and Politics* Neil Macfarlane wrote that, aside from the perennial struggle over funding, the issue on which Sports Ministers in the 1980s were primarily judged was that of football hooliganism. Indeed for Macfarlane the relentless rise of violence in and around football grounds was the 'greatest problem' he encountered.[29] Over and above a resurgence in troubles at home, the government was concerned about the growing instances of violence overseas associated with English spectators who followed the national team. Macfarlane liaised with other departments such as the FCO to put in place measures which helped to ensure that English fans caused no major disruption at the World Cup in Spain during 1982. And looking to introduce a stronger long-term means of tackling the problem, the Sports Minister also backed a raft of measures enhancing the power of magistrates to deal with offenders included in the 1982 Criminal Justice Act. Sections of the national press, anxious to depict football hooligans as central to Britain's malaise, constantly put pressure on ministers to impose a law and order crackdown. This pressure ratcheted up after violence erupted at a Luton-Millwall match in March 1985. At this point the Prime Minister got personally involved, though as in the case of the Moscow Olympics, she greatly resented (and never came to terms with) the independent traditions of sporting administrators. After a series of ill-tempered meetings, the football authorities agreed to accelerate plans for measures such as segregation of fans and the introduction of close-circuit television. For its part the government committed itself to legislation controlling the sale of alcohol at grounds, and magistrates were further encouraged to make full use of their powers in delivering prison sentences.[30]

In the aftermath of two major tragedies in the same month, the hooligan issue was propelled to the very forefront of the political agenda. In May 1985 a stadium fire at Bradford left over fifty spectators dead, and shortly afterwards 38 Italian supporters were killed at the European Cup final between Juventus and Liverpool in Brussels. Although the Bradford incident was not associated with violence, television pictures of disturbances at the Heysel stadium in Belgium, viewed by millions worldwide, sent observers into a frenzy. One newspaper referred to football, the national game, as 'a slum sport played in slum stadiums watched by slum people'.[31] In the weeks that followed the Prime Minister held a series of meetings with leaders of the Football Association (FA) and the Football League, and radical action soon followed. Thatcher insisted English clubs be withdrawn from the following season's European competition, a statement which preceded a ten-year ban imposed by the European authorities, and she outlined in the Commons the government's wish to see a range of reforms introduced such as the banning of alcohol and the introduction of club membership schemes to bar troublemakers. The depth of the desire to enforce rapid change was reflected when sports journalists invited to Downing Street found that Thatcher was contemplating seemingly impractical measures such as playing all top matches behind closed doors. She bracketed football violence along with disruption on picket lines as something that needed to be 'cut out' of society.[32] She also hinted that she was less than impressed with the resolve of the football authorities. Meetings with representatives of the FA and Football League again did not proceed smoothly. Macfarlane echoed the view in Whitehall that the leaders of football were a 'toothless bunch', and he wrote to the Prime Minister expressing his doubts about their willingness to fall into line.[33]

Before the Heysel disaster the government stressed that matters of crowd safety and behaviour were primarily the responsibility of football administrators and the clubs. Policy had been character-ized, in the words of Barrie Houlihan, by 'a series of half-measures, frequently short-term and uncoordinated'. But after May 1985 ministers insisted on greater urgency.[34] Following on from legisla-tion in Scotland, a bill was finally pushed through parliament to ban alcohol on trains and coaches travelling to matches, as well as inside grounds. Debate also quickly turned to the government's idea of introducing club membership schemes as a way of keep-ing out known offenders. Many in the football world doubted the feasibility of such a plan, and the slow pace of negotiations over a voluntary scheme – together with the incidence of hooliganism at the European championships held in Germany in 1988 – resulted in Moynihan taking the lead in promoting legislation, introduced initially in the House of Lords. The Football Spectators Bill, which included provision for identity cards for supporters to control admission to grounds, as well as measures to prevent offenders from travelling to overseas matches, eventually reached the statute book late in 1989, but did so in the wake of a further tragedy. In an incident that cast its shadow over football for many years to come, 95 people were killed in April 1989 after being crushed at Sheffield Wednesday's Hillsborough ground ahead of an FA Cup semi-final between Liverpool and Nottingham Forest.

Even before the Hillsborough disaster, the Football Spectators Bill occasioned great acrimony in parliament. Party divisions were frequently on display. Government supporters talked of the need to rescue the national game from dark forces, while Labour MPs implied that Tory ministers had no real understanding of a traditionally working-class sport. Denis Howell complained that Moynihan frequently referred to the membership scheme as 'not negotiable', a coded way Howell believed of confirming he was 'under orders from the Prime Minister'. Objections to the bill came from many quarters, some arguing that the civil rights of the majority of law-abiding spectators were being infringed, others that the prospects of disorder would be increased not diminished by creating long delays at turnstiles as fans produced their membership cards. For several months the government resolutely faced down the critics. Ministers refused all proposed amendments to the bill, prompting talk of a 'monstrous use' of parliamentary procedures; in addition a guillotine motion was used to speed the measure on its way 'with even more indecent haste'.[35] But the government's conviction that the Hillsborough tragedy made identity cards more necessary than ever was not shared by Lord Justice Taylor, who was charged with carrying out an independent review of the disaster. Taylor quickly concluded that overcrowding was the root cause of the loss of life. David Pickup was with Moynihan when Taylor's initial findings were made known in August 1989: 'It had been hoped by the Government that Lord Justice Taylor's findings would lay a substantial degree of blame for the Hillsborough fatalities upon the alleged irresponsibility of Liverpool's supporters. The fact that Taylor's interim report did no such thing appeared to be a bitter pill for Colin to swallow.'[36] In January 1990 the full version of the Taylor Report effectively scuppered the main plank of the government's anti-hooligan policy, decisively rejecting a membership scheme as unwieldy, unworkable and likely to increase the potential for hooliganism.[37]

The publication of the Taylor Report occasioned further acrimonious exchanges in the House of Commons. The Home Secretary David Waddington made little mention of the government's decision not to proceed with a membership scheme, preferring to concentrate on those parts of the Report that condemned the excessive drinking of many fans and the poor leadership of the football authorities. 'Let no one imagine', argued Waddington, 'that this means there will be any let-up in the fight against hooliganism'. Several speakers who followed noted that there appeared to be no sense of contrition on the front bench about jettisoning the identity card scheme. For Labour, Roy Hattersley claimed that most of Lord Taylor's sixty-plus recommendations could have been implemented a couple of years earlier with broad agreement if the government had 'chosen to make progress instead of trying to make headlines'.[38] When the opposition put down a motion calling for a fresh, more consensual approach to dealing with hooliganism, party divisions were again to the fore. Waddington accused Labour in bullish tones of double standards by picking and choosing parts of the Taylor Report that it wished to endorse, and Moynihan appeared to cling to the prospect of a membership scheme being introduced at some point in the future. Waddington's speech was attacked in turn by Howell as a 'diatribe unworthy of any senior minister in this or any other Government'. The Home Secretary, Howell claimed, had misrepresented the Report for purely party purposes to 'camouflage the disaster that the Government face'. In a rare instance of a large parliamentary attendance for a sport-related debate, Labour's motion was defeated by 277 votes to 210.[39]

Although some parts of the Football Spectators Act eventually came into effect, ensuring among other things a more regular regime of safety inspections at grounds than in the past, its unhappy passage through parliament exemplified the government's disjointed approach to hooliganism. The Taylor Report, accepted on all sides as a work of great authority and credibility, gradually took much of the political sting out of the issue. In a situation where none of the key policy actors could claim success, Taylor's findings provided a focus – once the initial parliamentary hubbub died down – around which all could unite. In the years that followed nearly all of the Report's recommendations were implemented, including the removal of perimeter fencing and the introduction of all-seater stadiums in the top domestic leagues. The government still had some part to play in the 1990s. A reduction in pools duty was agreed on the condition that the millions of pounds not passed to the Exchequer went towards the costs of ground improvements. But on the whole, Taylor's comprehensive analysis and plan of action allowed Conservative ministers to retreat to their preferred stance, distancing themselves from active intervention in professional sport. Although not entirely eradicated, hooliganism at English grounds ceased to be a major headache for governments after the late 1980s, an outcome which, in the view of football historian Dave Russell, ultimately had less to do with political and legal interventions than it did with changes in the game itself. While rigorous fan separation and high-technology policing had an effect, so too did shifts in terrace culture, fresh sponsorship deals with the likes of Barclays Bank, and the FA's eventual commitment to the introduction of a financially lucrative Premier League.[40]

Trouble Overseas

About half of Macfarlane's book *Sport and Politics* was devoted to overseas sporting issues, illustrating the extent to which the international dimension had risen to prominence by the 1980s. In addition to dealing with the European football authorities over unruly English fans abroad, the Olympics were uppermost in ministerial thinking. The extent to which Thatcher's failed attempt to prevent most British competitors from going to Moscow caused lasting damage was evident when – for the first time since London 1948 – efforts were launched to bring the Games to British shores. Macfarlane was sufficiently impressed by the commercial success of the Los Angeles Olympics in 1984 (where Britain finished a respectable eleventh in the medal table) that he began to float the idea of Britain bidding for the 1992 event. He admitted in his book, however, that the Prime Minister was 'clearly not pleased'. Taking a cue from Thatcher, senior colleagues were equally dismissive. 'The message was clear', Macfarlane noted: 'back off and cool all talk of it'.[41] But becoming involved in the bidding process was initially a matter for the BOA rather than the government, and in 1985 the BOA invited possible contenders to come forward.

The front-runner proved to be Birmingham, whose efforts were fronted by Denis Howell; his long connections with the city and wide contacts in the sporting world gave Birmingham a decisive advantage over rivals London and Manchester. While inspired by those drawing up the Birmingham plans, Howell was struck from the outset by the government's lukewarm attitude, notably its refusal to countenance financial support. 'I found it difficult to believe that a British government would provide no funds to attract the finest sports event in the world', he reflected, but it was clear that the Prime Minister 'had made up her mind'.[42]

After securing BOA backing in July 1985, the Birmingham team had little more than a year to lobby the International Olympic Committee (IOC) before a final decision was reached. Howell threw himself tirelessly into the task, but faced an uphill struggle. Macfarlane wrote that the scepticism of his colleagues was given credence by the timing of the bidding process: the occurrence of the Heysel tragedy only a few months earlier did not make it the most auspicious time for Britain to 'seek the honour of embodying the spirit of global friendship through sport'.[43] Birmingham also experienced what Howell called a 'crushing blow' when several Caribbean and Asian nations – angered by Thatcher's opposition to imposing sanctions on South Africa – withdrew from the 1986 Commonwealth Games in Edinburgh. Against this background, Howell knew any prospect of securing votes for Birmingham among certain black and Asian IOC representatives was lost. In the event the Birmingham bid, though praised for its technical quality, attracted only eight votes at the crucial IOC meeting held in Lausanne in October 1986, enough to stay in until the second round of voting, but well short of posing any serious challenge to the eventual winner, Barcelona. British journalists following the process believed most members of Birmingham's team were too inexperienced to carry weight in the corridors of sporting power, and that the city's staid provincial image was too much of a handicap. As soon as the decision was announced, Howell gave vent to his view that the government's less-than-wholehearted support was also influential, and a reflection of its attitude to sport in general. Although the Prime Minister hosted a reception in London in favour of the bid, it rankled with organizers that she did not personally sign the government's letter of guarantee to the IOC, an important symbol for bidding cities. And where other nations sent eminent figures to Lausanne for last-minute lobbying (such as Jacque Chirac the French premier), Britain was represented by Macfarlane's successor as Sports Minister, Richard Tracey. For the leader of Birmingham City Council, Dick Knowles, it was a matter of regret that the bid had not been regarded in Britain as a serious national endeavour.[44]

Following the decision in Lausanne, the BOA decided to switch horses for the next round of Olympic bidding. Much to Howell's annoyance, Manchester was chosen to go forward as Britain's contender for the 1996 Games. The Manchester campaign, led by theatre entrepreneur Bob Scott, promised a major renovation of the city as one of its objectives, and gained the support of many businesses and local authorities in North West England. Scott also made concerted efforts to project a national rather than a regional image by securing the backing of ministers. Contacts with several departments including the FCO and the DoE culminated in a warm letter of support written by the Prime Minister to the President of the IOC in 1989. 'The Government wishes Manchester every success', Thatcher wrote, 'and will offer whatever promotional help it can'.[45] Seeking to avoid one of the mistakes at Lausanne, Britain was represented when IOC members gathered in Tokyo in 1990 to cast their votes by a more heavyweight politician, in the form of Environment Secretary Chris Patten. But for all its slick campaigning and high-level support, Manchester fared little better than Birmingham. It secured no more than an initial eleven votes, and this fell to five in a second round of voting that saw Manchester eliminated before the Games were eventually awarded to Atlanta. The inquest this time round noted that British sport still struggled to speak with a single voice. Assuming leadership of the Sports Council in the midst of the Olympic bidding process, David Pickup soon sensed intense rivalry between the BOA and the CCPR over who best represented British sport abroad. This, he noted, generated 'bemusement and hilarity among observers from other nations'. Pickup was not persuaded about the depth and sincerity of the government's backing for Manchester, and as in 1986, the British cause made little headway against a backcloth of international suspicion about Conservative policy towards apartheid. A key factor in explaining the IOC vote, Pickup believed, was the widespread view, especially among Afro-Caribbean nations, that Britain was 'covertly sympathetic towards

Pretoria' and 'more indifferent than most to the fate of South Africa's blacks'.[46]

In 1978 the Commonwealth Secretary (as we saw in the previous chapter) had expressed satisfaction that, despite some isolated incidents, national leaders were doing their utmost to adhere to the Gleneagles Agreement, which urged governments to take 'every practical step' to discourage sporting contacts with South Africa. But during the 1980s various links continued, and Britain – in the words of anti-apartheid historian Roger Fieldhouse – became widely perceived as 'the major violator' of Gleneagles. Amidst conflicting reports about the extent to which the ruling National Party in South Africa was seeking to make sport more genuinely multiracial, cricket administrators in England were tempted to resume contacts that had largely been severed in the 1970s. In 1983 the Marylebone Cricket Club (MCC) was only persuaded not to go ahead with a planned tour in response to a direct appeal by the Prime Minister. Several cricketers and coaches continued to ply their trade in South Africa as individuals, and news of a 'rebel' tour planned for the winter of 1989–90 led to the most widespread protests since the 'Stop the Seventy Tour'. Although the trip went ahead, it faced major disruption in South Africa and came to a premature end. The activities of the anti-apartheid movement, shorn of the leadership of Peter Hain by the 1980s, could also claim only mixed success in preventing ongoing links with South African rugby. The British Lions toured in 1980, and although a proposed trip by Wales in 1982 was cancelled following protest action, an English Rugby Football Union team visited South Africa in 1984 despite the disapproval of Macfarlane as Sports Minister. The Anti-Apartheid Movement (AAM) applied pressure that led to the abandonment of a Lions tour in 1986, and a further victory followed when the Welsh Rugby Union decided to sever all ties with its South African counterpart. But even as the apartheid regime began to buckle under the weight of enormous international condemnation, parts of the rugby establishment remained defiant, recruiting a 'World XV' which went to South Africa in 1989.[47]

Attitudes towards the Gleneagles Agreement varied in Conservative ministerial ranks. Macfarlane repeatedly stated his dislike of sporting contacts, while adding that he did not have the power to intervene in the decisions of independent governing bodies. His attachment to anti-apartheid principles led to what he described as 'turbulent discussions' with Dickie Jeeps, the Chairman of the Sports Council. Jeeps, a stalwart of English rugby, favoured bridge-building to Springbok isolation, but Macfarlane's insistence that the head of the Sports Council should be seen to fully support Gleneagles resulted in the abrupt departure of Jeeps from his post in 1985.[48] As in other highly publicized cases such as that of football hooliganism, it was the Prime Minister rather than the Sports Minister who ultimately determined policy. Roger Fieldhouse notes that Thatcher's broad approach to the South African question was to condemn apartheid while insisting on 'constructive engagement'; she believed change would only result from maintaining dialogue rather than imposing measures such as punitive economic sanctions. It followed that her interpretation of Gleneagles, with its reference to 'every practical step' being taken to prevent contacts, was out of line with many national leaders elsewhere. In the words of Fieldhouse, while 'the Prime Minister and her Ministers always paid lip service to the Agreement, they were not always very active in enforcing it'. Thatcher did personally intervene to discourage the MCC visit to South Africa in 1983, but she took no similar action in relation to the England rugby tour of 1984, the World IX visit of 1989 or the rebel cricket tour of 1990. The AAM increasingly believed its repeated protestations to ministers were falling on deaf ears; one annual report in the late 1980s called the attitude of the government 'belated, ineffectual and cynical'.[49]

As with much of sport policy in the 1980s, the South African question led to sharp party divisions in parliament. Macfarlane accepted in hindsight that his task in upholding the Gleneagles Agreement was made more difficult by members of his own party. While Labour remained solidly behind the agreement, he noted, there was a shift among Conservative MPs to the view that South African sport was becoming more multiracial and so links should not be discouraged. Some Tory backbenchers went further in stridently defending the right of British citizens to travel freely to wherever they wished; sports teams were subjected to restrictions, it was argued, that were not applied to those in commerce or journalism. Against this background, there were some fierce exchanges over the decision of the government to 'fast-track' the application for British citizenship of a talented young South African-born runner Zola Budd, enabling her to compete for Britain at the 1984 Olympics in Los Angeles. Budd's application, based on the credentials of her British grandfather, was turned around in ten days, compared with the months or years that such requests frequently took. Macfarlane observed that strong support for Budd in Conservative ranks contrasted with Labour's 'pious' opposition.[50] Howell, backed by the AAM, was vitriolic about a blatant violation of the Gleneagles Agreement, later saying the episode was 'the most disgraceful Government scandal that I ... met in my time in the House'. In the event Budd's participation at the Olympics ended, as Howell noted, with her 'well away from the medals for which the whole affair had been contrived', and by the end of the 1980s she had returned to live permanently in South Africa.[51] Howell was not alone in being concerned about the effects of this 'disreputable episode' on international opinion. Fieldhouse claims that while the AAM had scored notable successes in isolating South Africa on the global sporting stage in the 1960s and 1970s, the 1980s proved more problematic. Britain, he noted, was singled out by the United Nations as 'the main collaborator with apartheid sport'.[52]

Conclusion

It comes as no surprise to find that Denis Howell, publishing his memoirs in 1990, was deeply unimpressed with the record of the Thatcher administrations on sport. In his eyes successive Sports Ministers in the 1980s presided over a catalogue of failure, ranging from unhelpful incursions into the world of international sport to the indefensible sale of school playing fields. School sport, he argued, was being 'systematically undermined', not only by the sale of land to commercial developers but by the downgrading of physical education in the curriculum. In a 1992 survey British secondary schools were to be ranked bottom in a list of over twenty European nations in terms of hours per week set aside for Physical Education (PE). The privatization of local authority services such as sports halls and swimming baths was 'a disaster of monumental proportions', Howell claimed, resulting in higher admission charges which priced teenagers in particular out of using facilities at a time when the government bemoaned youth crime rates. As for the Sports Council, Howell wrote that this had become a 'pale shadow of its original concept'. Its membership was closely controlled by ministers, as was its allocation of funds, making the Council in effect an 'arm of the Government' whose decisions could not be challenged in parliament. While he still had faith in the dedication and skill of British sportsmen and women, Howell could not say the same of the government's capacity to support them in their endeavours. Instead of providing opportunities for advancement and success, as many other nations were, 'we are creating obstacles and denying sports its proper role in society.... the present Government has no philosophy as to the importance of sport and no strategy to provide it'.[53] This concern with the lack of an overarching philosophy echoed the language Howell used when he first championed sport in the House of Commons in the early 1960s; the implication of his words was that sport policy in Britain was at its lowest ebb since the *laissez faire* days of the 1950s.

Howell's views were of course heavily coloured by his role both as a former Minister for Sport and as chief opposition spokesman during the Thatcher era. His suggestion of a throwback to the pre-1964 era is not borne out by the commitment of some Conservative Sports Ministers, notably Moynihan, to the merits of government intervention in sport on the basis of tackling social deprivation and improving the nation's health, as well as helping to promote excellence and increased participation. But as the academic Fred Coalter notes, this was a long way from endorsing the 1975 White Paper notion of sport as part of the fabric of the social services: 'although the rhetoric of recreation as welfare was ideologically potent, it remained politically weak and relatively marginal to core public policy developments'.[54] Howell was not the only contemporary, moreover, who reached a harsh verdict on Tory policy in the 1980s. Peter Corrigan of the *Independent* summed up a widely held belief among journalists that none of Thatcher's Sports Ministers had covered themselves in glory: 'Hector Monro took the Moscow rap, Neil Macfarlane carried the can for Bradford and Heysel, Dick Tracey never solved anything [and] Colin Moynihan was last seen floating down the Thames strapped to an identity card.' For Corrigan the real villain of the piece was the Prime Minister: 'on each of the rare surges she made into the sporting arena she came a cropper'.[55]

Most telling of all, the scathing critique offered by the Labour opposition and critical journalists was echoed in senior

Conservative ranks. Macfarlane's book put the spotlight on the shortcomings of 1980s policy and Moynihan later went on record to admit that there was 'insufficient financial support for sport and recreation' when he was in office.[56] John Major, who was rising rapidly in the Tory ministerial ranks in the late 1980s, subsequently referred to sport (with characteristic understatement) as not one of the 'guiding interests' of Thatcher's premiership. When he was appointed Chief Secretary to the Treasury in 1987, Major was struck by the difficulties that stemmed from a fragmented administrative structure, with responsibility for sport spread across several Whitehall departments. 'It was a mess', Major wrote. One result was that while small annual increases in government spending were welcome, there was no one of sufficiently high rank to champion the cause either of sport and the arts. 'In the empires of Cabinet ministers', Major noted, 'they were regarded as lightweight responsibilities, and something of an irrelevant diversion'. The spotlight only tended to fall on sport when a particular problem such as football hooliganism grabbed the headlines, and Major conceded – echoing the words of Howell – that there was an absence of 'a coherent and positive strategy'.[57] In 1990 the chance for John Major to remedy this situation suddenly presented itself; to the surprise of many commentators it was Major who triumphed in the Conservative leadership contest that followed the departure of Margaret Thatcher.

9 *Raising the Game*, 1990–97

Introduction

The fortunes of government policy towards sport fluctuated after
1945 in line with the attitude of individual prime ministers. We
have seen in earlier chapters a correlation between the higher
priority accorded under leaders with a personal interest in sport
(Wilson and to an extent Heath after 1964) and a lower focus
than the norm under incumbents who were indifferent or even
hostile (Churchill, Eden and Macmillan in the 1950s, Thatcher in
the 1980s). By this standard, governmental involvement reached
unprecedented heights in the 1990s, for John Major – Prime
Minister from 1990 to 1997 – displayed perhaps a stronger commitment to sport than any of his post-war predecessors. In his
memoirs, published after he lost power at the end of the decade,
Major described a lifelong attachment to cricket in particular as
well as a desire to see improvements in the nation's cultural and
sporting infrastructure. For too long, he believed, these had been
considered 'not very serious matters' in the corridors of power;
optional extras rather than part of the 'sinews of society'. His aim
on taking over from Margaret Thatcher in 1990 was to give culture
and sport 'the higher profile they deserved'.[1] Over the course of
the following years, including a full parliamentary term after the
Conservatives secured a fourth successive election victory in 1992,
Major adopted a range of strategies aimed at fulfilling his ambi-
tion. He introduced a new department of state under a minister of
Cabinet rank to ensure the arts and sport had 'real political clout';
he vigorously supported efforts to bolster elite sport and bring
high-profile international events such as the Olympics to Britain;
and he secured via the introduction of a National Lottery a steep
rise in levels of public funding directed towards sport.

The net result was a focus on sport not seen before under a
Conservative administration, contrasting starkly with the calculated coolness of the Thatcher years. But there were limits to what

Major could achieve. While sport was no longer confined to the political margins, action was slow to follow words. Unlike his predecessor in her heyday, Major lacked real authority for much of his time in Downing Street. After a short honeymoon period, he often found himself beleaguered, criticized in much of the media for lacking charisma and being unable to impose his wishes on a restive Tory party or on the electorate. Too preoccupied to devote as much time as he would have liked to sport, his enthusiasm took several years to translate into tangible results, and he left office in 1997 with many of his aspirations unrealized. Lacking a wide base of support in his own party ranks or in Whitehall, Major deserves credit for at least embarking on an almost lone crusade. With the exception of one senior colleague who soon departed from government, the Prime Minister could not call upon the services of like-minded allies, in the way that Wilson delegated to Denis Howell in earlier times. 'Sport is one of those areas where the Whitehall machine is rather resistant and regards it as somewhat frivolous', a leading civil servant told Major's biographer, 'while he saw it as an absolutely critical part of British life, essential for a healthy and balanced education'. As a result, the official continued, referring to one of several attempts by the Prime Minister to breathe life into government policy, he 'very much' had 'to drive [reform] through himself'.[2]

The Department of National Heritage and the National Lottery

In their book *Sport in Britain 1945–2000*, Richard Holt and Tony Mason argue that from the time Major became Prime Minister, 'government began to focus seriously on sport in a way it had never done before'.[3] Aside from underestimating the steps taken by Howell as Sports Minister before 1979, this claim overstates the speed of change after 1990. While sport was to raise its political profile in due course, this was not so apparent before the 1992 election. Major was considerably more sympathetic to sport than his predecessor, but coming to power with the Conservatives deeply unpopular in the wake of Thatcher's downfall, his energies were absorbed by restoring party morale and planning for an election campaign that could not be long delayed. Sport would have to wait for any significant breakthrough until after the Tories

secured re-election in 1992, though there was one notable administrative change in the short term. Robert Atkins (a personal
friend of the Prime Minister), having replaced Colin Moynihan as
Minister for Sport in the summer of 1990, was retained by Major as
Sports Minister, though his responsibilities were transferred from
the Department of the Environment (DoE) to the Department of
Education and Science (DES). This move was interpreted in some
quarters as a sign that the Prime Minister intended to set about
reviving school sport. But any sense of a new dawn was difficult to
detect in Whitehall. Atkins, like all of Thatcher's appointments,
remained at the lowly rank of a Parliamentary Undersecretary,
and enhancing the role of the DES in sport (returning to arrangements that existed before the late 1960s) was not welcomed by
all in the sporting world. David Pickup, the Director General of
the Sports Council, felt the switch was disruptive, requiring the
Council to adjust to working with another department of state
with a different culture and traditions. DoE civil servants in the
Sport and Recreation Division who transferred to the DES were
regarded, Pickup noted, as 'some kind of alien implant', patron-
ized by the 'superior Oxbridge products' in their new home.[4]

Perennial problems of funding for sport also remained unresolved in Major's first year as Prime Minister. At a time when central government provided a grant to the Sports Council of around
£44 million, prospects ahead looked bleak with the Council esti-
mating that more than £300 million was needed annually just to
keep pace with the repair and modernization of existing publicly
funded facilities, let alone the building of new ones. With a step
change in Exchequer funding out of the question, one possible
means of generating significant new money for sport was via a
National Lottery. The Sports Council had been lobbying for such a
venture for some time, pointing out that in many overseas nations,
funds for sport were often diverted from the profits generated
by the sale of lottery tickets to the general public. David Pickup
was pleased to find that Major was open-minded about a National
Lottery, whereas Thatcher's attitude had been one of 'stern disapproval'. Based as it was on large-scale gambling, Pickup reflected
that Thatcher saw the Lottery as an 'iniquitous device whereby the
undeserving got something for nothing'.[5]

In his memoirs Major wrote that when he first floated the idea
of a Lottery in 1991, his senior colleagues were not keen. Treasury

ministers wheeled out familiar arguments: hypothecation of tax was not the British way, and one effect of a Lottery would be a reduction in numbers taking part in the football pools, with an unwelcome fall in duty from that source certain to follow.[6] Fearful for the future, the football pools companies negotiated a deal with government in 1991 under which more taxable revenue went to recreation and the arts, but the Sports Council's blessing for this development turned sour when Robert Atkins used it as a pretext for a real-terms cut in the Council's budget for 1992–93. The Chairman of the Council, Peter Yarranton, publicly described this as a 'kick in the teeth', necessitating the curtailment of several projects in the pipeline. In spite of incurring ministerial displeasure, Yarranton held his ground, Pickup noted, his stance reinforced by rumours emanating from Whitehall that Atkins 'had not exactly exerted himself during the public expenditure negotiations'. For Pickup any notable breakthrough for sport, financial or otherwise, remained some way off. 'Ad hoc-ery and opportunism seemed to be more our Minister's style', he wrote, and Council members had real doubts that the nation's 'political masters' would ever provide anything in the way of consistent leadership for sport.[7]

By the end of 1991 the parties were preparing the ground for a general election. Denis Howell decided not to stand again for parliament, ending a period of more than thirty years in which his input into sporting matters in the House of Commons had been unrivalled. For Labour, Tom Pendry, MP for Stalybridge and Hyde, became a key figure in developing policy, playing a key part in drafting the party's new 'Charter for Sport'. The Conservatives responded shortly before Christmas with a statement on 'Sport and Active Recreation', promising to improve opportunities for all and to restore the place of physical education (PE) in the school curriculum. These documents formed the basis for the election manifestos issued when the government, having run its full five-year course, called a general election in the spring of 1992. Labour pledged to support local councils in improving facilities and to introduce mandatory rate relief for voluntary sports clubs; the party would also prevent the 'wanton sale' of playing fields and improve school sport.[8] John Major's influence meant that, for the first time since 1970, the Conservatives made concerted efforts to take the electoral lead on sport. Although reticent on expenditure levels, Major believed there was a worthwhile case to put to voters. The government was firm, the Tory manifesto argued, in backing Manchester's bid to host the 2000 Olympics (discussed further below), and tough action had been taken against football hooligans. In addition, local authorities would be urged not to sell off playing fields unless there was demonstrable need to do so. Finally, and most radically, responsibility for sport would be transferred to a new department of state, and large (though unspecified) levels of fresh funding would be made available through the proposed introduction of a National Lottery.[9] Despite a difficult economic backdrop and opinion polls suggesting otherwise, the Conservatives won the election in April 1992, albeit with a much smaller majority than enjoyed by Thatcher. The way was open for Major to turn rhetorical support for sport into something of substance.

The first indication that meaningful change was taking place after the 1992 election came with the creation of the Department of National Heritage (DNH). Sport and recreational leisure were part of the remit of the new department, along with others areas regarded as central to Britain's cultural life such as the arts, tourism, broadcasting and museums. Critics were concerned that by being labelled with a 'heritage' tag, sport would be left with a backward-looking image. It was also pointed out that this latest reshuffling of the Whitehall pack did not create a single, unified method for government oversight of sport. Several other departments retained links with sporting issues, including the Foreign and Commonwealth Office (FCO) and the rebranded Department for Education (superseding the name DES in 1992). While it had not been a congenial home since 1990 for civil servants in the Sport and Recreation Division, the Education Department was determined to retain its long-standing influence over school sport.

But the move to the DNH at least offered more potential and possibilities than under past arrangements. Sport was no longer obviously peripheral to the work of the department in which it was located, as was usually the case at both Environment and Education. The extent to which sport became central to the concerns of the DNH would depend on the predilections and influence of individual ministers, and in this respect – in the short term at least – the signs were good. David Pickup of the Sports Council found that his working relationship with the government improved when Atkins was replaced as Minister for Sport in April 1992 by the

MP for Salisbury, Robert Key; 'a former schoolmaster, bluff and hearty, enthusiastic and well-intentioned', Pickup observed. More important, the first Secretary of State at the DNH, David Mellor, was both a close associate of the Prime Minister and a keen sports enthusiast. He was soon signalling his intention to involve himself in sport policy to a degree unprecedented in senior Conservative ranks, and crucially held a seat in Cabinet to promote his plans. According to Pickup, Mellor was keen to build upon the march stolen on Labour at the election by overseeing the introduction of a Lottery; he had one eye on distributing the 'resultant largesse'. Despite a new era of restraint being ushered in following the economic debacle of 'Black Wednesday' in September 1992, Sports Council funding was not among the early casualties. Whereas Arts Council spending was cut back severely, the Sports Council was pleased to see its budget for 1993–94 increased by almost two million pounds to £50.6 million. This compared favourably, Pickup reflected, with the 'niggardly award a year earlier'.[10]

The prospects for a fundamentally new era of government commitment to sport were marred, however, by two developments after Black Wednesday. The curse of frequent changes of minister (a hallmark of the Thatcher era), preventing settled continuity of policy, struck again. After only six months in post, David Mellor was forced to resign following tabloid revelations about his private life; there were to be three further Secretaries of State at the DNH during the remainder of the Major era, but none shared Mellor's passion for sport. Ministers for Sport also continued to be easily dispensable. In May 1993 Robert Key, to the 'bemusement' of the Sports Council, David Pickup wrote, was replaced by Iain Sproat, MP for Harwich and another close associate of the Prime Minister. Pickup described Sproat as 'the least communicative' of the many ministers he dealt with, rarely consulting with sports administrators or attending meetings of the Sports Council.[11] The journalist Peter Corrigan wrote in October 1993 that the incessant comings and goings of ministers were highly disruptive. David Mellor had 'proved too sporty for his own good'; Robert Key had departed 'without rippling the waters'; and Iain Sproat was known in some quarters as 'No Throat Sproat' owing to 'his lack of discernable activity on behalf of sport'.[12]

A second regressive step came in 1993 with the government's shelving of plans for a wholesale restructuring of the Sports Council.

Robert Atkins proposed after tortuous negotiations the adoption of a system in which a new, United Kingdom Sports Council operated alongside four separate Councils for England, Scotland, Wales and Northern Ireland. Iain Sproat's one notable intervention in his early months as Sports Minister was to ditch this plan. Pickup said this was done 'wholly without consultation', and Tom Pendry for Labour was left to attack the government's 'nebulous statement' as a wasted effort.[13] As in the 1980s, the Conservatives, having created an executive Sports Council, seemed uncertain whether it needed strengthening, adapting or abolishing. By the time Pickup left the Council after five years as Director General at the end of 1993, no new plan for administrative structures had been announced; in his view there could be 'no worse example of Whitehall obstructiveness...over this period'. While he felt some achievements had been made during his time in charge, Pickup believed that the thwarting of badly needed structural reform left the Sports Council in limbo: 'So it was not wholly with a sense of disappointment that I tidied away my papers for the last time.'[14]

Two steps backwards for sport were balanced, however, by royal assent being granted to the 1993 National Lottery Act: a giant stride forward which was to bring large-scale funding into sport in the years that followed. After being persuaded of its merits, the Prime Minister personally championed the Lottery as a means of enhancing the nation's cultural and sporting opportunities. From the sale of every one pound ticket in regular lottery games, nearly a third would be devoted to 'good causes', including sporting projects as well the arts and charities.[15] Although commanding broad approval in parliament, there was considerable press anxiety about the Lottery. Some critics were unhappy with the choice of the Camelot group, a private consortium of companies, to run the Lottery, which was finally launched in November 1994. As well as wishing to see non-profit making oversight of the Lottery, sceptics worried about how decisions were reached and the confining of bids at the outset almost exclusively to capital projects. For a long time after the launch, opinion was divided between the doubters, some of whom objected simply to the prominence given to a new form of gambling, and enthusiastic community groups such as local sports clubs, submitting bids in the hope of winning funding for cherished projects. Although controversy was to rumble on for several years, the National Lottery signalled a considerable increase in the levels of public money available for sport. The social scientist Ian Henry described the 1993 Act as a 'masterstroke in terms of leisure policy', one which allowed Major to keep a tight lid on central government funding for sport while generating previously unattainable extra sums from a fresh source. By 1999, five years on, over one billion pounds had been allocated to sport from the Lottery, though as Henry noted, because lottery allocations were mostly restricted to capital projects and required bids that contained matched-funding, little was done to address national, strategic sporting issues.[16]

Manchester's Olympic Bid

The sense, prior to the introduction of the Lottery, that Major's government promised more than it really delivered on sport was reinforced in September 1993 when, for the third time in a row, a British bid to host the Olympic Games ended in defeat. As we saw in the previous chapter, after her failure to prevent most British athletes attending the Moscow Games, Margaret Thatcher was far from keen on Birmingham's efforts to secure the right to stage the 1992 Games. Better relations developed between the government and the organizers of Manchester's bid for 1996, though according to the historian of Olympic politics Christopher Hill Manchester's efforts were not 'endorsed with great enthusiasm' in ministerial circles, and fared little better than Birmingham when the International Olympic Committee (IOC) voted to award the 1996 event to Atlanta.[17] As deadlines approached for throwing the hat into the ring for the 2000 Games, the forceful leader of the Manchester's renewed campaign, Bob Scott, argued that the city was well placed to do better next time round. On this occasion Manchester faced opposition from London, which had some high-profile sponsors, including Sebastian Coe, the distinguished double Olympic gold medallist, at the time looking to enter parliament as a Conservative MP. Some Labour backbenchers entered the fray by suggesting that only London could attract votes internationally, but many of the cards were stacked in favour of Manchester. Bob Scott noted that good facilities were already in place in Manchester and that he was working closely with the city council, whereas the demise of the Greater London Council in the 1980s made it difficult to discern which body in the capital would underwrite the

London bid. In April 1991 the British Olympic Association (BOA) voted decisively to back Manchester. Bob Scott, as well as claiming it was a notable achievement 'to beat Sebastian Coe in a race', was confident that Major would offer more support than his predecessor. 'We now detect at the height of government an interest in sport that was not present previously', he said. 'Although we did receive government support in our last bid, it was not the equivalent to that from other countries.'[18]

Scott's optimism was well-founded. After a lengthy series of negotiations, the Prime Minister announced early in 1992 that £55 million of public money would be committed to facility development in Manchester, and that the government would contribute almost a third of the total estimated budget of £1 billion if the bid was successful. Christopher Hill notes that the Major administration's attitude stemmed from the willingness of key ministers to follow the Prime Minister's lead. Chris Patten, the Tory party Chairman – having attended the IOC decision-making event for 1996 – took the view that to have any chance of success in the voting for 2000, Manchester's cause must be backed wholeheartedly or not at all. David Mellor in his brief period at the DNH was another firm supporter in Cabinet, as was Michael Heseltine, Secretary of State for the Environment. Heseltine's remit at the DoE included responsibility for urban regeneration, and the idea of seeking the nomination for the Olympics fitted neatly with broader proposals for improving run-down areas in the north-west. The £55 million promised in development aid, though a considerable sum, was not extravagant in the context of the huge annual budget of the DoE. 'It was also fortunate', Christopher Hill adds, that 'Manchester was asking for money during the build up to a general election'.[19] A key reason for the backing afforded to Manchester, in other words, was electoral calculation. As well as throwing Labour off guard with its promise to introduce a National Lottery, the Conservative manifesto in 1992 explicitly referred to the government providing financial as well as moral support for the Olympic bid. Major said in his memoirs that he thought in neglecting sport during the 1980s, the Tories had been 'missing a political opportunity'.[20]

In the 18 months between the general election of April 1992 and the vote by nearly one hundred IOC members meeting in Monte Carlo, the Prime Minister continued to provide resolute support for Manchester. Major not only attended the 1992 Games

in Barcelona to promote Manchester's case but also hosted receptions for IOC members visiting sporting events in Britain. In the
spring of 1993 he made a personal visit to the President of the IOC
in Lausanne to advance Manchester's cause, defying critics who
felt such a trip was not befitting for a British premier. These activities highlighted the stark contrast between Major's deeply felt love
for sport and the indifference of his predecessor. David Pickup
of the Sports Council, discussing the government's willingness
to commit large-scale financial resources to the Olympics, noted
that one day he bumped into 'a near-apoplectic Denis Thatcher',
who 'noisily let it be known that such a nonsense would never have
been contemplated had his good lady still been in charge'.[21] After
some hesitation, Major decided to go to Monte Carlo in person in
September 1993 to speak for Manchester ahead of the final IOC
vote. If he was hoping for a political boost from a triumphant outcome, he was to be disappointed. Although Manchester picked up
more votes in the early rounds than other European contenders,
the British bid was a distant third in what became a two-horse race
between Beijing and Sydney, the latter ultimately prevailing by a
narrow margin. Although Manchester (like Birmingham in the
1980s) felt gains had been made, with new facilities in the pipeline
that marked it out as a viable location for top events in future, the
garnering of only 13 IOC votes illustrated that the damage caused
to Britain's standing in international sporting circles by the episode of the Moscow boycott was yet to be repaired.

Sport: Raising the Game

With the failure of the Olympic bid, and ahead of lottery funding coming on stream, John Major's sport policy was marked by a
sense of drift. The government had talked a good game, but tangible achievements remained thin on the ground. In a debate on
sporting facilities in the upper chamber during 1993 Lord Dean of
Beswick gave voice to a common criticism: 'We want a more cohe-
sive approach from the Government', he said: 'At present, we do
not know where we are going'.[22] Having rejected out of hand the
Atkins proposal for reorganizing sport administration, Iain Sproat
took another year to come up with a fresh plan. This initiative,
David Pickup believed, was 'forced' on the Sports Minister by Major,
who was frustrated by the lack of action. The new proposals were

also very similar to the old, and it was to take further protracted negotiations before eventually a new UK Sport Council (assuming the name UK Sport) adopted prime responsibility for elite athletes, while the home nation Councils (including what became known as Sport England) took the lead in developing community sport. Pickup was saddened that long-standing divisions and jealousies appeared to remain endemic; he saw it as ironic 'that at a time when – thanks to the National Lottery – sport in this country has never been so well resourced, its capacity for administering those funds to inspirational strategic effect has never been so impaired'.[23] With the hopes of hosting the Olympics quashed after the autumn of 1993, the government also found itself on the back foot over school sport. Despite Major's pledges to act in this area, reports were still coming in of the falling amount of time devoted to PE in state secondary schools. By 1994 the weekly average per pupil was down to one hour, with only a quarter experiencing two hours a week. The Secondary School Headmasters' Association claimed there had been a 70 per cent decline in the number of school sport fixtures on weekday evenings and Saturdays between 1987 and 1994.[24]

School sport featured heavily in a major policy document published by the DNH in July 1995. *Sport: Raising the Game* marked a concerted attempt by the government to reassert its sporting credentials, and it provided a focus of attention for the remainder of the parliament. It was the most detailed outline of Conservative policy since the party came to power in 1979, and it appeared 20 years after the last such equivalent, Labour's 1975 White Paper. Despite the setback over hosting the Olympics, the Prime Minister continued to identify himself personally with sport policy; his interest in this area, he wrote in his memoirs, 'was thought to be rather quirky by some of my colleagues'.[25] As a signal of intent, Major promoted Iain Sproat from Parliamentary Undersecretary to the higher rank of Minister of State – the first time a Conservative Minister for Sport operated at the same level as Denis Howell did for much of his time in post. Sproat sent out copies of *Raising the Game* to all MPs and introduced the glossy 40-page document to the Commons, but not before the Prime Minister went through the text carefully making final adjustments and sought to maximize publicity by hosting a breakfast launch event in the Downing Street garden. In his preface to the document, Major referred to school sport as the 'highest priority', acknowledging there had been problems in this area. Several remedial proposals were contained in the detail of *Raising the Game*. PE was confirmed as one of only five subjects that were compulsory throughout a child's school years, and the government encouraged all schools to work towards two hours of formal lesson time per week. In order to rebuild competitive games, schools were also urged to provide opportunities outside the normal curriculum, for example at weekends or in holidays. Those schools with good provision would be recognized by a 'sportsmark' scheme; an overhaul of teaching training would ensure there were adequate numbers of suitably qualified PE teachers; and action would be taken to stop the loss of playing fields.[26]

Although the Prime Minister's preface spoke of the need to 'rebuild the strength of every level of British sport', the main emphasis in the document aside from schools was on bolstering elite performance. This came through in proposals for developing sport in institutions of higher education; these were felt to have a hitherto largely unrecognized role, both in stimulating informal recreation and especially in providing opportunities for talented national and international sports stars. In addition, the idea that grabbed most headlines was the promise to set up a British Academy for Sport, based somewhere in the Midlands. Modelled on successful examples overseas, notably in Australia, the new Academy was envisaged as somewhere that would offer numerous benefits to top athletes, including residential accommodation, scholarships and bursaries, access to state-of-the-art facilities, high quality coaching, sports science input and medical back up. The Sports Council and its successor bodies were invited to work on practical proposals for the Academy and in due course to go through a bidding process to run the venture. In introducing *Raising the Game*, Sproat informed MPs that the government's ambitious agenda would be backed by appropriate funding drawn from the Lottery. Since getting under way a few months earlier, 440 sports projects across Britain had already been awarded £74.26 million of lottery money, and £100 million of such funding was earmarked for the Academy for Sport alone. According to the Minister, the breadth of the government's proposals – aiming to allow all ages and abilities to fulfil their sporting potential – together with unprecedented levels of funding 'combine to make this the most important day in sport in a generation'.[27]

Reactions to the government's new initiative were generally welcoming. Although a planned debate in parliament was overtaken
by events and cancelled, the Sports Minister thanked his opposition counterpart, Tom Pendry, for signalling approval. For Labour,
it was important not to be outflanked again on sport, as had been
the case at the 1992 election. Newspaper responses tended to divide
along lines of party affiliation. The *Daily Mail* claimed there had
been a 'roar of approval' for the document. Alluding to the potential political benefit to the Conservatives, the *Mail* argued that
the Prime Minister's announcement of 'a British sporting renais-
sance confirmed that he had scored a home win'.[28] The left-leaning
Guardian, a supporter of the 'New Labour' project taking shape
under Tony Blair, elected party leader in 1994, was more critical of
this 'long-delayed sports policy statement'; it had an expansionist
tone but offered little concrete advancement in the short term. The
Guardian also quoted Graham Lane, a prominent figure in local
government, who attacked the Prime Minister's 'blatant hypocrisy'
in failing to acknowledge that the decline of school sport was the
result of years of Tory underfunding and mismanagement.[29]

For someone close to sporting officialdom such as David Pickup,
Raising the Game had great potential but two key weaknesses. In the
first place, he felt there were some telling silences in the document. As lottery funding was mainly confined to capital projects it
was not evident how the huge running costs of a new Academy for
Sport would be met. The Prime Minister's traditionalist emphasis
on competition, whether in school sport or at elite level – 'competitive sport teaches valuable lessons which last for life', the preface
noted – meant the document also had little to say about the vital
role of local authorities in developing recreation for the masses.
Second, Pickup was concerned that many of the proposals presup-
posed a degree of cooperation among interested parties that was
routinely absent. The involvement of teachers after years of alien-
ation could not be taken for granted, and 'petty parochialism' was
likely to beset the new Academy (a prediction which proved correct) as the precise powers of the various sports councils in this
regard were not specified. 'The aspirations set out in "Raising the
Game" are admirable on the whole', Pickup concluded, 'but the
absence of clear prescriptions as to how these aims are to be realized strongly suggest that its authors have been gorging themselves
on unbuttered parsnips'.[30]

A year later the jury was still out on whether the government had successfully 'raised the game'. In July 1996 the Sports Minister issued a first year report in which he claimed 'significant progress' had been made on many of the recommendations contained in the document. Later in the year he lauded evidence, via the restructured sports councils, of moves towards a world-class performance programme to support talented athletes competing up to Olympic and world championship levels. Secondary schools had been invited to apply for the sportsmark award and a prospectus had been published inviting bids to establish the Academy of Sport. John Major claimed in his memoirs that his Policy Unit at Downing Street was also involved; Sproat knew that in seeking to push forward he had 'my full support'.[31] While Tom Pendry continued to offer qualified backing from the Labour benches, press critics were more forthright in questioning how much genuine progress was being made. The *Guardian* journalist Simon Edge wrote that the Prime Minister's hosting of an event to announce a new class of specialist sports colleges in July 1996 was intended to 'breathe life back into the initiative, because much of it has been ignored'. Children were not doing much more in the way of physical activity as part of their school week, and the Academy proposal was taking its time to get to the drawing board because of concerns expressed by various sporting bodies over its governance and financing.[32] The *Times* took a more balanced view. While it was agreed that school sport remained in a 'desperate' plight, the government deserved the benefit of the doubt for going ahead with 'many overdue initiatives'. For the *Times*, the evidence suggested that at least 'the corner has been turned' in sport policy.[33]

The Challenge of New Labour

While critical of the slow pace of change, the *Guardian's* Simon Edge expressed a degree of personal sympathy for the Prime Minister in the summer of 1996. While John Major hoped for some electoral gain from his hands-on approach to sport, this was not the real driver of his involvement. His straightforward love for the subject, Edge noted, was unlikely to save him from his 'political fate'. This was a reference to the deep unpopularity of the Conservative government, which never recovered its reputation for economic competence after the Black Wednesday debacle in

1992. Although unemployment was falling and there were signs of recovery in the housing market by the mid-1990s, Major's administration was constantly beset by accusations of 'sleaze' and deep divisions over issues such as policy towards the European Community. By contrast, Labour leader Tony Blair was making great headway in presenting himself as a youthful, vibrant alternative, adopting a slogan of 'New Labour, New Britain'. 'No one appeared to know what a "young country" was', writes Labour historian Andrew Thorpe, 'but it sounded good. "New Labour" seemed to sound better than "Labour" '.[34] In the months after Blair assumed the leadership in 1994, Labour's lead was the largest yet seen in Gallup's 57-year history of opinion polling. With no sign of an early end to the 'Blair bubble', political commentators were agreed Major was simply clinging to office, hoping – Micawber-like – that something might turn up.[35]

Against this backdrop, *Raising the Game*, like all such policy documents, never carried sufficient weight to save the Prime Minister from likely defeat at a forthcoming election, which could not be delayed beyond the spring of 1997. But for a brief moment in the summer of 1996 there was the intriguing possibility that sport, at least in politicians' minds, might provide the 'something' Major desperately needed. Tony Blair's press secretary Alistair Campbell referred in his diary in June to his hope that England as the host nation would not triumph in the Euro' 96 football tournament. This was partly 'the Scotland supporter in me', Campbell wrote, and partly the danger of 'football fervour creating a feel-good sense that could let the Tories win back a bit of a lift'. He was not sure sport had the power to do such a thing, but the ex-Sports Minister Denis Howell – sitting alongside Campbell at one of the early matches at Wembley – commented that if England triumphed, the Tories might call an early election. Campbell's diary indicated a growing sense of concern as England progressed. After a quarter-final victory over Spain he wondered if it was 'written in the stars [that] England were going to win the whole bloody tournament'. The swelling sense of patriotism was obvious: huge numbers of cars were adorned with St George flags or stickers, and fans everywhere were singing the popular song 'football's coming home'. By now Campbell confessed to being 'quite worried', with the latest polls showing a small drop in Labour's large lead. Campbell was at Wembley, along with other dignitaries including the Prime Minister, when England finally lost in the semi-final after a nail-biting penalty shoot out against Germany. Campbell confessed in his diary to a surge of relief. Denis Howell commented: 'There goes the feel-good factor', and John Major was left looking 'ashen'. However irrationally, Campbell wrote, the Prime Minister 'must have been banking on England's success'. The diary account ends with the press secretary concealing his real feelings until he got into a car with Tony Blair to go home: 'Once we got in, I said "Yesss", and shook my fist. TB said could you save any celebrations until you get home? I said don't pretend you feel any different.'[36]

Preliminary planning for an autumn general election had been taking place among senior Tories, but if there was ever any serious prospect of Major calling a snap contest to capitalize on a mood of national well-being, it disappeared within a matter of weeks.[37] Soon after England's bubble was burst at Euro' 96, the British team performed poorly at the Olympics held in Atlanta. Britain finished with only one gold medal to its name, secured by Steve Redgrave and Matthew Pinsent in the rowing competition. There were no victory celebrations in the prestigious track-and-field events, and the final tally of 15 medals was Britain's lowest since the Helsinki Games of 1952. Even before the team returned home in early August, a finger of blame was being directed at the government. In a *Guardian* editorial, the swimmer Paul Palmer was reported as saying – after winning Britain's first medal in Atlanta – that he despaired about the condition of sports facilities at home. 'We need backing from the Government if we are to win more medals', Palmer insisted. In the eyes of the *Guardian*, no one doubted Major's personal commitment, but it remained the case that 'the reason why sport was in such a dire state was a direct responsibility of the Government'. The litany of failure included the undermining of PE in schools, the sale of playing fields and the fact that new policies were almost entirely lottery funded and lacked strategic focus. There would be no real improvement, the *Guardian* believed, unless more Treasury money was also injected to good effect into sport.[38] These criticisms were mild in comparison with some of the tabloid coverage after the official medal table showed Britain finishing in its lowest ever ranking, at number 36. The *Daily Mirror* spoke of 'our Olympic shame', placing Atlanta second in an all-time list of British sporting humiliations: 'We are under-funded ... [and] second-rate, and no amount of excuses will camouflage that.'[39] Arriving home to a muted welcome, Steve Redgrave said there was 'much sorting out to be done about British sport'.[40]

The Prime Minister doggedly refused to back away from his policies despite what happened in Atlanta, which critics regarded as a fitting symbol of the neglect of sport in the era of Tory rule since 1979. He summoned the manager of the Olympic team to Downing Street to account for the poor showing, and insisted improvements would follow from changes underway designed to bolster elite performance – a claim to be vindicated in the fullness of time (though he was no longer able to reap any benefit) by Team GB's success at the Olympics from 2000 onwards. When the general election came in the spring of 1997, Major also provided an upbeat assessment, trumpeting the 'record investment in sport' under his stewardship. The Conservative manifesto stuck with the promise of an Academy of Sport as a vital means of encouraging excellence, and increased direct funding to top athletes was also pledged, showing the age of the amateur was a thing of the past and that top British athletes would be given every opportunity to train full time and compete on equal terms with their rivals.[41]

But by this point, the die was cast for the Prime Minister. He went into the campaign trailing Labour by a wide margin, and pledges on sport were lost amidst carefully orchestrated opposition attacks on the need for the nation to be rid of a discredited government. In its manifesto Labour, anxious not to make the same mistake as in 1992, went out of its way to show that it shared Major's enthusiasm for sport. Aside from a firm commitment to end the policy of 'forcing' schools to sell of playing fields, there was little direct criticism of the government. Instead, in the aftermath of Atlanta, international sport featured more prominently than in the past. Mindful of Major referring at the previous election to his strong support for Manchester's Olympic bid, Labour promised to 'work to bring the Olympics and other major international sporting events to Britain'.[42] Tony Blair was to be in a position to put his pledges into action after Labour secured a landslide victory; its majority of 179 seats was larger than that achieved by Attlee in 1945. The Conservatives, whose share of the vote at just over 30 per cent was the party's lowest since 1832, failed to capture a single seat in either Scotland or Wales, and fared little better in most of the largest English cities. The era of 'New Labour' beckoned.

Conclusion

In 1996 the Sports Minister Iain Sproat claimed that reforms initiated by the Conservatives meant 'we are well on the way' to achieving a sea change in British sport.[43] He had in mind not only building upon *Raising the Game*, with its particular emphases on reviving school sport and developing elite performance, but also the degree of investment flowing into grass-roots sport through the Lottery, which was selling over thirty million tickets each week. The Lottery, Major was able to claim in his memoirs, had 'made a real difference to the quality of life in Britain'.[44] Its importance could certainly be gauged in funding levels. Public expenditure on sport rose from £1012 million in 1992/3 to 1257 million in 1997/8. The Treasury grant to the Sports Council/Sport England remained the same in both years, at about £50 million, while local authority spending rose modestly over the period from £957 million to £993 million. The key additional input came from the Lottery, which provided £51 million to sport in its first year, 1994/5, rising to £208 million in 1997/8.[45] The achievements of the 1990s thus stood in stark contrast to the stagnation of the Thatcher era, and the lion's share of responsibility for this outcome undoubtedly rested with John Major. Whereas Harold Wilson in the 1960s and 1970s tried to create a supportive environment while leaving policy largely to Denis Howell, Major was the first Prime Minister to provide hands-on, active and persistent encouragement for sport.

But despite his best efforts, there was always a sense that Major promised more than he delivered for sport. In the mid-1990s the entire budget of the DNH amounted to just 0.4 per cent of all central government spending, a proportion not dissimilar to what was spent on equivalent services a decade earlier.[46] On the domestic front advocacy of improving recreational facilities for all had been overshadowed by the drive to rebuild school sport (itself still very much a work in progress by 1997), while it was ironic – given Major's focus on competition – that his premiership coincided with a phase of abject performances by British teams internationally. At the time of the Atlanta Olympics, England was ranked among the lowest of the test match playing nations in cricket and slipped as low as 23rd at one point in FIFA's football order of merit. Richard Palmer of the BOA wrote that while the Prime Minister's various proposals promised jam tomorrow, much depended on political willpower; nearly all successful sporting nations, Palmer noted, were characterized by sport having a high priority among politicians.[47]

In the final analysis, consistently high levels of political support for sport remained absent in Britain. Although links between the state and sport had grown significantly since the mid-1960s (with the exception of the Thatcher era), sport could not claim a secure, embedded place in Whitehall and at Westminster by the end of the twentieth century. The advances of the 1990s were the product less of evolving maturity in the system of governance than of the exceptional personal interest of the Prime Minister. As we have seen, Major's unstinting enthusiasm was not widely shared at the top level of his administration. According to a top official quoted by Major's biographer, his Cabinet colleagues 'were variously indifferent to, amused or irritated by, his passion for sport'.[48] Following the brief tenure of David Mellor as Secretary of State, the DNH did not emerge as a vociferous, tenacious proponent of sporting interests, a reflection of the continuing absence of a deep commitment to sport within Conservative ranks at large. As for the role of the Sports Minister, though Iain Sproat was the first since 1979 to be accorded Minister of State status, the post remained something of a backwater. The veteran sports journalist Ian Wooldridge wrote that he had known almost every incumbent since the 1960s and that only Howell and Moynihan had hitherto been successful. 'Most of the rest', according to Wooldridge, 'enjoyed a day out at the races'. Wooldridge also referred to what seemed to be reality for the majority of Britain's Sports Ministers thus far: they came in with fine intentions but left after 'barely scraping the surface of delivery'.[49]

10 Regions and Localities

Introduction

The influential study *Britain in the World of Sport*, published by Birmingham academics in 1956, contrasted the minimal central government involvement in sport at that time with long-standing and often generous provision made by local authorities. 'One may conclude', the authors wrote, 'that in Britain, sport is largely financed by local effort'.[1] The tradition of local government providing public recreation facilities went back to the middle of the nineteenth century, though the development of such facilities proved to be a haphazard process. Some of the county, borough and municipal authorities in existence vigorously used the powers available under legislation such as the 1846 Baths and Washhouses Act to develop a range of services, notably swimming baths and recreation grounds. But local worthies were not obliged by law to act in this sphere. Rather they were free to determine the scale and type of their own provision, with the result that there was no uniform pattern across the country. Where municipal involvement in leisure was most pronounced, it seems to have been prompted, as Jeffrey Hill notes, 'by a mixture of motives – utilitarian, moral, political, financial and economic'.[2] A desire to improve health and sanitation appears to have been a significant factor in larger cities. Elsewhere a concern to widen commercial opportunities via the provision of parks and gardens was a priority in spa or seaside towns. The few published case studies relating to the pre-1914 period suggest that levels of commitment changed over time even within the same authority. Helen Meller's detailed work on Bristol, one of Britain's largest cities, argues that local elites developed a range of recreational facilities after 1870 partly as a result of the Victorian 'civilising mission' – a wish to alleviate deep social divisions between rich and poor through a healthier environment – and partly to compete with other cities in demonstrating municipal pride. Providing and maintaining parks and swimming baths was an expensive enterprise, however, placing financial strain on Bristol ratepayers, and Meller notes that the zeal of leading councillors was less evident in the Edwardian years.[3]

After the First World War the rise of Labour often brought party politics to the forefront in council chambers more than was the case before 1914. Writers such as Stephen Jones have shown that while bread-and-butter economic concerns were the main priority where Labour wielded influence in local government, left-wing councils also gave more attention than hitherto to the scale and purpose of leisure.[4] But the barriers against moving towards the wholesale development of publicly funded recreation remained formidable. In an era of severe economic hardship between the wars councils were reluctant to impose burdens on ratepayers beyond the statutory minimum; the development of leisure remained optional and so for the most part a low priority. The 1936 Public Health Act reinforced the power of local authorities to provide swimming baths and the 1937 Physical Training and Recreation Act had a similar effect in relation to gymnasiums, playing fields and community centres with athletic or social objectives. Councils could also contribute towards the expenses incurred by voluntary bodies in providing such facilities. But in the run up to war in 1939 little use was made of these powers.[5] In the complicated structure of local government – consisting of various tiers including counties, county boroughs, rural and urban districts and civil parishes – there was ambiguity over where responsibility for recreation resided, and the optional nature of the powers provided inevitably perpetuated an uneven pattern of development. In the absence of extensive research there are difficulties in gauging where most and least progress was being made, but it does appear that local authority provision for sport continued to be characterized through to the Second World War by 'uncoordinated, frequently inadvertent growth'.[6] The aim of this chapter is to explore how and why sport in the regions and localities was transformed after 1945, and to assess the extent to which local provision interacted with and mirrored the input made by central government.

Slow Progress in the Localities, 1945–65

All that applied in limiting the involvement of local authorities in developing sport and recreation before 1945 continued to apply for many years after the war. As we have seen in earlier chapters, prior to the creation of the post of Sports Minister in the 1960s, sport struggled for visibility as a political concern at Westminster. It was a similar story at local level, whether among county or district councils or among the growing number of county boroughs, adopted to administer urban areas with populations in excess of 75,000. A common problem, as in Whitehall, was that responsibility for dealing with recreation was dispersed, rather than being coordinated and centralized. Typically in a given local authority, the health committee might have oversight of public swimming baths; the remit of the education committee would include facilities in schools for outdoor physical activity; and the parks committee took the lead on playing fields, open spaces and other sport provision such as public tennis courts outside of schools. There was growing recognition and concern in the 1950s that such committees tended to work in isolation; the idea of planning a single recreational strategy remained in its infancy. A study into leisure by the Conservative party in the 1960s was highly critical of the 'waste' that was said to arise from the traditional lack of coordination between education and parks committees. The former, it was believed, often sanctioned the building of school facilities which 'remain quite unused outside school hours. The community clearly cannot afford to duplicate sports facilities in this way'. The Conservative study argued that all new school building programmes in future should stipulate that facilities must be planned in consultation with the relevant parks committee. 'It is something of a disgrace that in many areas of recreational shortage, facilities remain closed over all weekends and throughout school holidays.'[7]

As local authorities did not operate in ways conducive to developing coherent recreation policies, any stimulus would have to come from outside, by directives from central government. But the approach of the two main Whitehall departments concerned, anxious to follow Treasury dictates to keep a firm lid on public expenditure, tended to reinforce the low priority accorded to recreation by councils in the 1950s. The Ministry of Housing and Local Government (MHLG) had the role of considering applications for loan sanctions by local authorities to meet the cost of capital expenditure in providing leisure facilities. This was a powerful tool, enabling the MHLG to control centrally the speed at which localities built new facilities such as swimming pools or athletics stadia. 'The development of local authority services in this field in the decade and a half following the war', one Ministry official wrote in a 1964 memorandum, 'was greatly hampered by severe restrictions on capital investment'.[8]

The second department concerned, the Ministry of Education, also nailed its colours to the retrenchment mast by issuing Circular 245 early in 1952, under which it was stipulated that playing fields associated with new schools would be eligible for grant-aid, but that other applications from local authorities or voluntary bodies would not be considered. In June 1953 an internal memorandum by a Ministry official commented that the effect of Circular 245 had been 'an almost total ban on the provision of new community centres, village halls and youth clubs, as well as to stop any further grants towards the provision of playing fields'. The memo admitted that the policy 'has caused a great deal of discontent in the country', with many MPs writing in to complain at the behest of constituents and local councillors, and added plaintively that the Circular had not been 'intended to paralyse to the extent which it has done' the services for which the Ministry was responsible under the 1937 Physical Training and Recreation Act and the 1944 Education Act.[9]

For much of the 1950s, the most insistent pressure to relax tight restrictions on the provision of playing fields came not from local authorities but from the lobby group the National Playing Fields Association (NPFA). Formed in the 1920s, the Association played a significant role in raising money and distributing small grants to enable land given by individual donations to be turned into playing fields, particularly in urban areas. By assisting with the costs of ploughing and reseeding land, fencing and laying out playing surfaces, the NPFA could boast that it had assisted with the provision of some 2000 football pitches, 1250 cricket pitches and 2300 playgrounds for children. But the position across the country was patchy. The Association regarded six acres of public playing fields per thousand of the population as a reasonable standard to aim for, but a NPFA survey in 1950–51 indicated that about 10 per cent of local authorities provided less than an acre per thousand people. In a House of Lords debate in 1956, the Duke of Sutherland, who himself contributed land for playing fields, claimed that the average provision in England was under two acres per thousand of the population; only 8 of 388 towns with a population over 15,000, he said, had more than four acres per thousand. Although officials at the Ministry of Education thought the figures were misleading (as no account had been taken of rural districts), it was difficult to dispute the main thrust of the survey. As the Duke remarked in the Lords debate, the standard of six acres of playing space per thousand of the population 'has nowhere near been achieved'.[10]

The practical implications of the government's approach were highlighted in a House of Commons debate in July 1954, when Harriet Slater, who represented Stoke-on-Trent North for Labour, focused her comments on the manner in which the policy of only allowing playing fields to be provided as part of new school building was condemning thousands of children to inadequate facilities for physical activity. Stoke, she pointed out, was an area where factories, homes and schools were closely concentrated, and the 13 acres of existing playing fields equated to a paltry 0.6 of an acre per thousand of the child population. In addition, Stoke did not have a single cinder track or other large space suitable for athletic training, and one of the thirteen secondary schools in the town had no gymnasium or changing rooms and only a bare and uneven piece of land for games. One often heard, Slater concluded, about the playing fields of Eton: 'I am asking tonight that something should be done for the children who have no playing fields at all.' In replying for the Ministry of Education, Kenneth Pickthorn ignored the local examples used by critics, and ended by asking the House to recognize that he was 'necessarily under the limitation' imposed by the Treasury as far as relaxing the terms of Circular 245 was concerned.[11]

In the run up to a general election in 1955, with the economy improving, the restrictions affecting playing fields were finally lifted. In the 1956 House of Lords debate on sport, Lord Mancroft, a junior minister at the Home Office, admitted that grants under the 1937 Physical Training and Recreation Act 'had a pretty bleak time between the years of 1951 and 1955', but he was pleased to report that since then the government had approved schemes for 73 playing fields and 55 pavilions.[12] The government's stance on playing fields remained cautious, however, for the rest of the decade. There was fresh concern for the NPFA when legislation reforming local government in 1958 removed the power of the Ministry of Education to make grants to local authorities under the 1937 Act; direct capital grants to playing fields were thereafter only available via the Ministry to voluntary bodies. Lord Luke, the

Chairman of the NPFA, feared that playing fields would become the 'Cinderella' in allocation of funds by local authorities. Officials at the Ministry tried to reassure the Association, though in private doubts were shared by civil servants. One official wrote an internal memorandum noting the concern of Lord Luke that County Councils 'will not step into the breach'. Under the new regulations, Councils were awarded grant-giving powers under the 1937 Act, and an amendment pushed through as a private members' bill in 1958 also enabled them to give loans to voluntary bodies. 'Some County Councils exercise these powers', the memo concluded, 'but many do not'.[13]

By the end of the 1950s the scale and quality of recreational provision provided in the localities thus continued to vary enormously. The contrasts that resulted were evident not just in relation to playing fields. The *Guardian* journalist John Rodda reported on the case of a new public running track being prepared in Manchester (so doubling provision by the council) without athletics clubs in the city or the national governing body of athletics having any knowledge of the project. The director of parks for the council was quoted as saying: 'We we're never asked' by the parties concerned. For John Rodda, the episode demonstrated not only the poor public provision in Manchester (though Lancashire in general was better served), but also the 'appalling gulf' between the corporation and athletics.[14] By way of comparison, the chairman of the parks committee of London County Council (LCC), Reginald Stamp, made a spirited defence when criticized about provision in the capital. Stamp pointed out that of 70 publicly funded cinder athletic tracks in England, 10 were maintained by the LCC. Chris Brasher, Britain's only track gold medallist at the 1956 Olympics, had paid a generous tribute to the help he received from the London authorities, who organized regular competitive events. Stamp added that the LCC was also responsible for some 400 football pitches, 200 cricket pitches, 320 tennis courts and 11 swimming baths. In addition, the Council had taken over control of the Herne Hill Velodrome (used during the 1948 Olympics), so preserving an important arena for cyclists, and was fully supportive of the proposed construction of a National Recreation Centre at Crystal Palace. 'All this has been done', Stamp concluded with pride, 'within the limited amount of open space available in London whilst trying to preserve the balance between the needs of various sections of the community'.[15]

After the publication of the Wolfenden Report in 1960, Macmillan as Prime Minister accepted – in an age of 'never had it so good', and with his poll rating slipping – that increased demands for leisure required additional investment. A MHLG memorandum reported that capital expenditure on leisure facilities authorized by the department rose from £7.4 million in 1959–60 to £18.2 million in 1963–64, although this figure included libraries and museums as well as parks, open spaces and public swimming baths. Local authorities, the memo noted, were becoming 'very active' in relation to the latter, with over 100 pools at various stages of planning and construction.[16] With Lord Hailsham providing a lead on sport, the government also accepted the need for greater coordination in the planning of recreational development. Shortly before the 1964 election, a joint circular was issued by the MHLG and the Ministry of Education urging local councils to carry out reviews to ascertain what new provision was required. Local rating bodies were also asked to look sympathetically at applications from sports clubs for rate relief.[17]

But at a regional conference of local authorities organized by the NPFA and the Central Council of Physical Recreation (CCPR) in the summer of 1964, the consensus among delegates was that much remained to be done. The conference was chaired by Labour's veteran campaigner Philip Noel-Baker, who said the planning of coherent recreational strategies had hardly begun, and would not do so until localities assessed the scale of need and found administrative structures to deliver on change. Noel-Baker welcomed signs of improvement – including the claim from a MHLG official present that the trend towards increased loan sanction would continue 'unless interrupted for urgent national reasons' – though he believed it would take time for local training facilities to develop sufficiently to help produce international success as well as giving opportunities of 'sport for all'. It remained the case, Noel-Baker noted, that recreational facilities in many other nations are 'very far ahead of those in this country'.[18]

The Breakthrough, 1964–79

A major breakthrough in the coordinated provision of local recreation only came following Denis Howell's appointment as Minister for Sport in 1964. The new Sports Council set up in 1965 regarded its remit as accelerating 'the pace of development', and Howell provided the political willpower to ensure this would take place locally as well as nationally. Howell was attracted by the idea of creating a new partnership at regional level between sporting interests and local councils: those who would inevitably be at the forefront of improving facilities as and when funds permitted. With encouragement from the Sports Minister and Lord Porchester, a well-known figure in local government circles and Chairman of the Sports Council's Facilities Committee, local authority associations agreed in 1965 to support the creation of Regional Sports Councils (RSCs). These brought together representatives of local councils, voluntary sports organizations and assessors of government departments to survey needs and lay out plans for the building of new facilities. Within a year the Sports Council was lauding as its 'most far reaching' action yet the successful creation of nine RSCs in England and separate bodies for Scotland and Wales, forming a 'unique combination between local government, sport and central government'.[19] The *Guardian* noted the impetus provided by the RSCs was long overdue: some 600 local authorities still had no municipal indoor swimming pool, and most of the 500 in existence were between 30 and 80 years old. But at last the structured leadership was being put in place to encourage authorities to work together and link developments with regional plans for housing, road building and other infrastructural change.[20] John Coghlan, writing in 1990, described the creation of the Regional Councils as a 'master stroke', having profound long-term implications: 'There are many who believe this development so changed the face of British sport in fifteen years... to make it such that this continues to be the major breakthrough in Britain to date.'[21]

By the time Wilson's Labour government lost power in 1970, the RSCs – with the administrative support of CCPR staff – were an established feature of the policy framework for sport.[22] The Sports Council reported in 1969 that for the first time ever regional strategies were 'taking shape', though it was admitted that progress on the ground had been held up by economic difficulties and restrictions on public spending. Indeed loan sanctions to local authorities for recreational purposes had been 'substantially reduced' since 1966, though an order of priorities had emerged in readiness for better times ahead and there were 'significant achievements to record'. Some regions, for example, had focussed attention on water-based facilities, leading to rapid improvements in recreational areas for sailing, rowing and canoeing.[23] Over time a range of less traditional sports such as squash, basketball, volleyball, judo and dance were all to benefit from regional reviews of needs; artificial ('all-weather') pitches came into vogue for multi-purpose use; and a major building programme of swimming pools and sports centres got under way. It took many years for the full effects to be felt. In the 15 years after 1964 the number of sports centres in England increased from a handful to over 400.[24] The political impetus provided by the RSCs was such that at the time of the 1970 election the Conservatives were unsure whether to attack Howell for promising more than had been delivered or to keep quiet for fear of drawing attention to how far things had moved in a few years. An internal Tory report ahead of the election conceded that since 1964 'local authorities have been persuaded, to a far greater extent than ever before, to take note of the need to make provision for leisure. This activity is probably Labour's main achievement'.[25]

Under Heath's Conservative government, the momentum generated for rapid local improvement continued with the creation of the executive Sports Council in 1972. Although the Sports Minister Eldon Griffiths was reluctant to endorse a ten-year 'shopping list' of facilities recommended by the new Council, pump priming for local schemes on offer via the Council's dedicated annual budget was regarded as a welcome sign in the regions.[26] It was not only initiatives from 'above', through the good offices of the Minister, the Sports Council and the RSCs, that stimulated progress. Local authorities were of their own accord anxious to respond to changing leisure patterns. More flexible working hours, greater affluence and wider car ownership were all leading to higher demand for better municipal facilities, whether for established sports such as swimming or popular newer games such as squash. Many authorities were coming to regard leisure as an important, discrete area of responsibility, and the need for internal structural reform to facilitate change was becoming widely recognized. In 1973 the report of the House of Lords Select Committee on sport recommended that all county councils and district councils should have a separate recreation department, overseen by a chief officer and reporting to a single recreation committee. This, it was argued, would provide 'a focal point for the planning and promotion of recreational developments'.[27] Eldon Griffiths told the Chairman of the Sports Council, Roger Bannister, that he was sceptical when he heard local authority officials expressing concern that progress would be halted as the economic outlook darkened in 1973. There had, Griffiths pointed out, 'been a surge in local authority expenditure on sport'. Although this might not continue at such a high level, he believed that if local councils acted on the recommendation of the Select Committee to establish recreation committees, 'this should help to maintain the impetus'.[28]

Like other services, sport was affected in significant ways by wholesale local government reorganization in 1974. In place of the long-established and complex web of authorities, the new system was based on a comprehensive two-tier approach. The first tier consisted of county councils (mainly centred on existing counties, though also including metropolitan counties such as Greater London and Greater Manchester, to administer large conurbations), while the second tier saw rural counties divided into district councils (due to have a minimum population of 40,000) while metropolitan counties were subdivided into metropolitan boroughs (with a minimum population of 250,000). In some places the effects for recreation were beneficial. Reorganization facilitated the creation of more streamlined structures, allowing for a more coherent approach to policy than in the days of separate parks, health and education committees. In many district councils, for example, oversight by a single leisure service department enabled sport to gradually attain a higher profile, often constituting a key area for expenditure and capital investment.

But this did not mean there was a sudden break across the board after 1974, or that fragmentation of responsibility was a thing of the past. Whereas many local government services had clear lines of accountability, the same was not always true in the leisure field. In many rural areas overlap and duplication between the two tiers of authority persisted: districts had oversight of indoor sport and town parks, but responsibility for informal outdoor recreation lay primarily with county councils. The result was a continuing patchwork of provision, even within a single region. It was reported in the wake of the 1974 changes that none of the five counties in the West Midlands had set up leisure departments, but four of seven metropolitan districts had done so.[29] The variations in commitment and provision ultimately reflected the continuing absence of a firm base for the mandatory provision of leisure services.

Aside from areas such as management of the National Parks, the 1976 Local Government Act stated that a local authority 'may provide ... such recreational facilities as it thinks fit'.[30]

Labour's 1975 White Paper, *Sport and Recreation*, kept up the pressure on local councils to become more active in facility development. The success of the RSCs encouraged the view that bodies with a broader remit in each region could act in a consultative and advisory capacity to tackle all aspects of outdoor recreation. As a result the White Paper proposed that existing RSCs should be replaced by Regional Councils for Sport and Recreation (RCSR), with more scope than hitherto to concern themselves with the whole range of sport and outdoor activities. Hence the new bodies would contain members drawn not only from local authorities and sporting organizations but also from the likes of the English Tourist Board, the Countryside Commission and British Waterways Board. The White Paper also suggested that the enlarged councils begin work as soon as possible on revised regional strategies. By enmeshing recreation more firmly in land-use considerations, sporting interests would henceforth need to be taken into account alongside other traditional, statutory, requirements.[31] John Coghlan reflected that although the 'heavy hand of the Treasury' was detectable in the refusal of the White Paper to make the provision of adequate recreational facilities a statutory duty on local authorities, the 1975 document again illustrated the 'deft touch' of Howell as Sports Minister, showing his closeness to local concerns and his willingness to move with the times by strengthening the system he first initiated in the 1960s.[32] A period of consultation and adjustment followed, but by the summer of 1977 one of Howell's officials wrote in a memorandum that the reconstituted Councils were 'well established in all regions', and most came forward with detailed strategies to underpin progress by the time Labour lost power in 1979.[33]

The period 1964–79 therefore witnessed considerable advances in local provision for sport, despite recurring bouts of retrenchment in government spending. According to Sports Council figures, local authority expenditure on sport and recreation rose from £191 million in 1973 to £682 million in 1980. Despite the International Monetary Fund (IMF) crisis of the mid-1970s, the proportion of local public rate-funded expenditure devoted to sport rose from 2.35 per cent in 1971–72 to just over 6.0 per cent by 1979.[34] Building projects often took a while to complete, but the long-term effects on the ground were impressive: from 1971 to 1989 the number of swimming pools provided by local authorities rose from about 500 to 1200; the number of sports halls from some 20 to over 1200.[35] This did not mean that all was rosy. Wide variations in the scale of local activity remained commonplace; duplication of powers between different tiers of authority in dealing with leisure continued to cause problems; and facility development started from such a low base that complaints continued to be made about inadequate provision. A CCPR study in the mid-1960s lamented that there were 'vast areas of Wales without a covered swimming bath' and an 'acute shortage of indoor facilities'. Although local authorities in Wales and the Welsh Sports Council battled hard in the 1970s to change this picture, they did so – in the words of John Coghlan – 'often with very limited resources'.[36]

Pitches, Parks and Pools in Bristol

Although care must taken in drawing wider conclusions from a single case study, a more detailed analysis of one of Britain's largest cities, Bristol, appears to illustrate many of the trends characteristic of local provision in the post-war period. For at least 15 years after 1945 Bristol City Council, dominated for much of the time by Labour, did not systematically address recreational needs. As was noted earlier, financial constraints and fragmented responsibility often hindered local development, and this was evident in Bristol as elsewhere. The 12-strong Baths Committee, charged with 'provision of swimming baths and bathing places', operated independently of the Public Works Maintenance Committee, for whom alterations to parks, 'pleasure grounds' and open spaces was a low priority compared with more urgent everyday matters such as managing highways, drainage, waste disposal and public lighting. The one scheme relating to recreation in the five-year plan of capital works agreed by the Public Works Maintenance Committee in 1946, the conversion of a tip into a playing field area, cost only a third of what was set aside for the rebuilding of war-damaged sewers and walls.[37] Any changes tended to result from pressure applied by local groups looking to improve specific provision. After the restrictions of wartime, there was particular demand to revive opportunities for taking part in popular team sports such as football and cricket; the number of pitches for these purposes under municipal control trebled in the decade after the war. The Council was, understandably, mostly preoccupied with tackling a wartime legacy of damaged housing stock, and in these circumstances it was not surprising that locals noticed hardly any change in the city's recreational environment. The novelist Derek Robinson, reflecting on growing up in Bristol in the 1950s, later wrote that when he was 'a teenager, the thing to do – the only thing there *was* to do – was to meet your mates and Go for a Walk in the Woods'.[38]

In line with the broader picture, the early 1960s saw heightened awareness among Bristol councillors of the value of recreation. The local newsletter *Civic News*, produced by the City Council, claimed in 1963: 'With the man in the street enjoying more and more leisure time the provision of adequate open space within our city becomes more than ever important.'[39] Bristol had the advantage of a large, well-established open area, the Clifton and Durdham 'Downs', to the north of the city centre, administered by a separate council sub-committee, and the Baths Committee also made progress in developing facilities for swimming. By the end of the decade two new municipal indoor pools were to be opened; one of the seven existing older pools had been completely refurbished; and all the remainder benefited from upgrading.[40] On the other hand there were still grumbles and petitions about shortages, notably when football teams complained about lacking sufficient pitches to play league games. In addition, any proposals for improvements had to pass the careful scrutiny of the council's Finance Committee, ever concerned with minimizing demands on local ratepayers. Although the MHLG was prepared to sanction more proposals for capital expenditure than in the past, sport in Bristol still lacked a clear administrative structure to facilitate the introduction of a comprehensive programme of reform. *Civic News* conceded that the distribution of pitches, parks and pools was uneven, with 'a serious deficiency of recreational facilities particularly in the central and eastern neighbourhood units'.[41]

A period of more rapid development began in the second half of the 1960s, underpinned by important structural changes in Bristol and beyond. Internal Council adjustments in 1967 resulted in recreation becoming the province of the Public Works Committee; with a tighter remit than before, sport gained more attention from councillors when not yoked with the concerns of highways and public waste. More important, Labour's drive to introduce RSCs prompted the establishment in 1968 of the Bristol Region Sports Liaison Council (BRSLC). Although not vested with executive powers, the new council had an ambitious agenda. Its terms of reference were agreed at the inaugural meeting: 'To provide a common forum for exchange of views and liaison between representatives of Bristol Corporation and the Bristol Sports Association (as representing generally the range of sporting activities in the city) on matters affecting sport and recreational facilities for the citizens of Bristol (including the provision by the Association to the Corporation from time to time of information to assist the Corporation in their consideration of such matters).'[42] Bringing together key figures on a regular basis opened the way for more systematic forward planning. In particular, the BRSLC quickly concluded that improved indoor facilities should be a top priority. Thus advised, the City Council agreed to the construction of two new purpose-built sport centres, the consolidation of its provision for swimming and the provision of additional football pitches, tennis courts and bowling greens. Financial constraints (in the wake of Wilson's devaluation) and infighting were by no means a thing of the past. Relations were strained for some time between the BRSLC and the South West Regional Sports Council, one of the nine major English councils initiated by Labour, which had oversight of counties from Wiltshire to Cornwall.[43] But the newsletter *Civic News* nevertheless adopted a more positive tone by the end of the 1960s than it had earlier in the decade: 'Bristol is justly proud of its many fine parks and recreation grounds which offer a wide range of facilities throughout the city, catering for all age groups and interests, and meeting the challenge of providing "Sport for All".'[44]

Local government reorganization in 1974 produced further benefits for recreation in Bristol. In line with the trend noticeable in many areas, in April of that year councillors established an Open Spaces and Amenities Committee, charged with managing and developing all the recreational and sporting matters for which the council was responsible. For the first time Bristol had a distinct, single focus of executive authority for sport. The ability of the new committee to take on long-term planning was evident when it published a policy document, *Recreation and Amenity*, within a month of being formed. This signalled a determination to devote larger resources to recreation; new expenditure on open spaces and sporting facilities, in addition to regular maintenance costs, was said to have risen from £39,064 in 1968–69 to an antici- pated figure of about £600,000 in 1973–74.[45] Public consultation on the policy paper showed that locals wished to see more done in developing sport centres. Of the two approved in the late 1960s, the opening of one, at Kingsdown, was delayed until 1975, and the Open Spaces and Amenities Committee agreed that at least two further centres were required.[46]

As in the 1960s, it would be misleading to suggest there was a seamless transition to a brave new world for recreation in the post-1974 era. Among the new county councils created as the top tier of local government in 1974 was Avon, bringing together the city of Bristol with parts of north Somerset. At the revamped Bristol Sport Liaison Group, members of the Open Spaces and Amenities Committee agreed with representatives of local sport- ing bodies that it was proving difficult to work effectively with the newly formed Avon County Sports Council.[47] Nevertheless, in the second half of the 1970s a county structure plan for recreation commanded broad approval, and in 1980 sporting experts told the Liaison Group that it was pleased to note that the City Council – despite persistent economic hardships – had 'recognised and accepted' the need for improved facilities, especially the develop- ment of neighbourhood sport centres. Everyday recreation, with its benefits for health and community cohesion, had advanced to such an extent, the local sport groups believed, that attention should turn in future to more specialist facilities such as venues capable of staging national or international competitions.[48]

Bristol thus appeared to conform to a wider pattern of local pro- vision for sport after 1945. Before the publication of the Wolfenden Report there was no clear plan or body in place in the city to pro- vide a focus for recreation; in an age when local spending was restricted the top priorities were housing and restoring infrastruc- ture damaged by the Blitz. An arms-length approach gradually gave way during the 1960s to more coordinated and assertive plan- ning, partly stimulated by national initiatives and partly in order to meet local demand. By the end of the 1970s considerable invest- ment in new facilities had taken place, and the City Council was well placed to contend with the challenges that arose when local government came under intense scrutiny in the 1980s. A South Western Regional Council strategy document in 1987 paid tribute to the 'great progress' made by Bristol and other executive authorities 'in providing attractive recreational facilities'. By this point the Open Spaces and Amenities Committee had been replaced by a Leisure Services Committee, which continued to work energetically. The Liaison Group referred in 1987 to 'severe constraints on local authority expenditure', though it recognized that much had been done to ensure the citizens of Bristol were well served with parks, pools and sports centres.[49] By the early 1990s local authorities operated in an environment where defending existing provision was more common than seeking further expansion. Even so, Bristol could take satisfaction that its average net spend per citizen on recreation was comparable with that in other major cities such as Birmingham, Newcastle and Manchester.[50]

From Thatcher to Blair

In contrast to the picture at national level, the 1980s proved surprisingly fruitful for local authority sporting provision. This was partly because programmes of facility development agreed in the 1970s took time to complete, and gathered a momentum that received encouragement from at least some of Margaret Thatcher's Sports Ministers. Hector Monro regarded the RCSR as a successful innovation worth maintaining; the carry-over effect meant that capital and current spending by local authorities on leisure continued to rise steadily between 1979 and 1981.[51] Even when a squeeze on local government spending became more pronounced later in the decade, the government was prepared to give some leeway to recreation on the grounds that it served the needs of other policy objectives, such as curtailing vandalism and youth crime in inner cities.[52] From the local authority perspective, the continued spread of recreation and leisure departments, accompanied by the growth of a recreation management profession, meant that sport found more supporters to defend its cause than in the past. Some 200 departments were in place by the early 1980s (compared with about 20 prior to local government reorganization in 1974), and although they varied in size and effectiveness, the best were headed by high-level executive officers and employed sport development officers to drive forward policy.[53]

The result was that total spending by local authorities on sport continued on an upward trend until the late 1980s, and the proportion of local expenditure devoted to recreation remained steady at around 5 per cent per annum. Within this overall framework, the discretionary nature of powers relating to sport combined with differing levels of commitment to produce wide variations across the country, as in the past. Figures supplied by the Chartered Institute of Public Finance and Accounting (CIPFA) for 1989–90 found an average per capita expenditure on indoor recreation of £7.08, but with a range stretching from the likes of Dorset at £2.80 to Northumberland at £12.39. The average spent on outdoor recreation was similar but again with wide variations: from Wiltshire (£1.62) and Cornwall (£3.82) to Leicestershire (£10.04) and Northumberland (£10.42). Among major cities, Birmingham was fortunate in having a forceful chief officer determined to defend recreational services, while in the capital the abolition of the Greater London Council in 1986 curbed the trend towards targeting leisure services on underprivileged groups in the community.[54] In spite of such variations, most parts of the country reaped some benefit from a continuing investment in new leisure centres, swimming pools and parks, providing opportunities for wider participation than ever before. Recreation was now something accessible to a majority of the population, whether engaged in for health purposes, for sheer enjoyment, or as a step towards more serious involvement in competitive sport. John Coghlan, who as a Sports Council official was critical of Whitehall attitudes to sport in the 1980s, felt there was much to acclaim in local developments, especially in view of the non-statutory basis of recreational services. For Coghlan, there was a stark contrast between the annual grant provided by central government to the Sports Council – 'mean in the extreme' – and the generous, 'very large sums made available by local authorities'.[55]

But by the time John Major replaced Thatcher in 1990, scope for local initiatives was increasingly curtailed. The Conservative emphasis on keeping rates and taxes low where possible led to an ongoing battle to curb the spending power of local government, especially Labour-controlled authorities, using devices such as rate-capping and the 'poll tax'. Regional Councils for Sport and Recreation had slowly fallen out of favour and by the early 1990s all leisure facilities were subject to a process of Compulsory Competitive Tendering (CCT), which allowed cost-cutting private companies to bid for the running of facilities while ownership remained vested in local authority control. A detailed study of Labour-controlled Leeds, known as a moderate rather than an extreme left-wing council, showed that pressures from government were limiting the type of new leisure and recreation schemes to those likely to secure commercial interest, rather than those that might be for the broader public good. Although still in many ways 'the embodiment of the local state's contribution to leisure', writes Jeff Hill, it was becoming clearer that the usage of sport centres was often restricted, owing to cost and cultural factors, in terms of age, class, gender and ethnicity.[56]

The first half of the 1990s thus became a barren period for local provision of sport. As we saw in the previous chapter, Major's commitment to sport marked him out from his predecessor, but took time to produce tangible results and was directed mainly at school and elite-level activity. In the meantime dissatisfaction with the two-tier structure of local government in place since 1974 was reflected in in-fighting among councillors and authorities, so impeding strategic planning, and the drive towards competitive bidding for grants fostered, in the words of Ian Henry, 'a focus on economy and efficiency, while ... social goals were subordinated to financial objectives'.[57] Major's personal involvement gradually galvanized Whitehall interest in sport, but it was noticeable that his landmark policy statement in 1995, *Raising the Game*, made almost no mention of the role of local authorities. This, it has been claimed by the social scientists Houlihan and White, was indicative either of an embedded Conservative distrust of local government or of 'wilful naivety' about the realities of sports provision, ignoring past practice and placing unwarranted faith in the power of schools and clubs to push forward promised change.[58]

After Tony Blair came to power in 1997 the outlook brightened for local authorities, though only slowly. Anxious to appear fiscally 'prudent', in the mantra of the Chancellor of the Exchequer Gordon Brown, the new government refused to go beyond previously announced Tory spending plans in its first term. There was, however, a significant shift when the 1999 Local Government Act rescinded the requirement for CCT in local services and replaced it with a responsibility to demonstrate that service provision was one which produced 'best value'. This was part of New Labour's concern with 'joined up government'; sport whether at national or local level was to contribute to broader welfare goals such as improved community cohesion, and to this end it was important that local authorities were set targets and demonstrated they provided value for money.[59] While this new emphasis was to bring its own challenges, there was at least a renewed recognition of the key part the localities traditionally played in recreational provision. The 2001 policy document *The Government's Plan for Sport* explicitly urged local providers to act as facilitators for new 'sport development partnerships', for example by employing development officers with responsibility to manage and promote innovative schemes. In consequence, unlike in the Thatcher and Major era, 'when local government was relegated to the margins of sport policy-making', write Barrie Houlihan and Anita White, local authorities came to have a 'central role in policy implementation'.[60]

For several years after 2001 local authorities benefited from a stable economic environment and government willingness to use funding from the National Lottery to bolster sporting facilities in the regions. 'Up and down the country', one minister claimed, 'years of neglect had seen local swimming pools and sports halls becoming more and more decrepit', but by 2007 over 4000 facilities had been built or refurbished.[61] In this new age of expansion, local authorities had to find ways of ensuring recreational schemes contributed to 'cross-cutting' agendas, helping to reach targets for improvements in areas such as health, lifelong learning and social cohesion. In addition, local providers faced the task of carrying out their preferred plans in the face of frequently changing and prescriptive national strategies. Even so, case studies of city councils such as Coventry and more rural county authorities like Derbyshire furnished considerable evidence of 'energetic service development' of recreation after 1997.[62] Although officials worried, as their predecessors had, that sport was less securely embedded in local government structures than many other services, this did not prevent a sustained period of consolidation for sports development. In the 1980s, a low point in the post-era for political commitment to sport, local authorities were spending over fifteen times more on sport than the Treasury, and when Labour lost power in 2010 local government input into recreational services was running at about one billion pounds per annum. It remained the case, as it was when *Britain in the World of Sport* was published in 1956, that 'sport is largely financed by local effort'.

11 New Labour and Sport, 1997–2010

Introduction

In 2009 the Cabinet minister Ben Bradshaw claimed that, after more than a decade in power, Labour had presided over a 'silent sporting revolution'. Bradshaw, having recently been appointed to the government department responsible for sport, gave a speech in which he argued that there had been a revival of school sport ('virtually dead under the Tories'); investment in community and elite sport had risen 'several fold'; and the Labour government had secured the right for Britain to host the most prestigious event in the international sporting calendar, the Olympic Games, in 2012. 'None of this has happened by accident', Bradshaw maintained: 'This has all reflected Labour's fundamental belief that everybody has a gift or a talent and should be helped to realise it.'[1] There can be no doubt that Tony Blair, like his predecessor John Major (and like Harold Wilson before that, in the 1960s), believed there was political capital to be gained through a progressive sports policy. With the British economy in reasonable shape for the bulk of Blair's ten-year premiership, and with the luxury of huge parliamentary majorities in 1997 and 2001, the prospects for sport under New Labour were more promising than at any time in the previous generation, especially as Labour MPs were keen to show they had more natural affinity with sporting concerns than their Conservative counterparts in the Thatcher–Major era. But if Blair could eventually lay claim to a range of achievements in sport policy, these were a long time coming; and after he retired to make way for Gordon Brown in 2007 the outlook darkened as Britain plunged into recession and New Labour was faced with almost certain electoral defeat. As this chapter will also illustrate, while the meshing together of political involvement with local, national and international initiatives in sport was on an altogether different scale, there were some curious echoes between the Blair–Brown era and Attlee's 1945 administration, when Labour last enjoyed a comparable election landslide. As in 1948, the government's role in bringing the Olympics to London won many plaudits. But in the early years of New Labour, as in Attlee's day, the quiet advance of a 'silent sporting revolution' was overshadowed by the noisy clamour that accompanied two controversial topics in particular: football and fox hunting.

The DCMS, Football and Fox Hunting, 1997–2001

Sport policy took some important strides forward in Tony Blair's first term. Overseeing much of this was the Department for Culture, Media and Sport (DCMS), established in July 1997 to replace the Department of National Heritage (DNH). This latest Whitehall innovation did not entirely eradicate administrative overlap. The DCMS, like its predecessor the DNH, still had to liaise over sport both with other departments, notably those with responsibility for education and local government, and with myriad sports councils over the allocation of funding. But by being acknowledged as a core component in the name of a Whitehall department, sport had secured its highest profile yet within the apparatus of central government. The first Secretary of State at the DCMS (often referred to as the Culture Secretary), the MP for Islington South and Finsbury Chris Smith, had a place in Cabinet, and was keen to ensure that sport was promoted from the base to the top of the pyramid. Anxious to deliver on election promises to revive school sport, Labour went ahead with a programme of recognizing specialist sports colleges in the state system; 37 were in place by 2000 and over 100 were planned by 2003. Lottery funding was used to develop facilities at these colleges and employ school sport coordinators, whose task it was to galvanize inter-school fixtures, so looking to reverse the decline of competitive games widely commented upon in the Thatcher–Major era.[2]

Determined to avoid any repeat of Britain's abject performance at the Atlanta Olympics, New Labour also introduced important changes at the 'excellence' end of the sport spectrum. With nearly 30 pence of each pound spent on the Lottery going to 'good causes', including sport, the way was opened up to quadruple the level of grants given to Olympic sports by the time of the Sydney games in 2000. In addition to bringing in much-needed resources for a wider range of sports (previously grants went primarily to athletics and swimming), in 1997 restrictions were removed on lottery funds going directly to individuals, rather than to governing bodies; a move which guaranteed many elite performers could devote themselves full time to becoming world beaters.[3] The results were spectacular. Britain rose to tenth place in the medal table at Sydney: its tally of 28 medals (including 11 gold) was the nation's strongest performance at the Olympics since before the Second World War.

In its approach to school sport and elite performance Labour after 1997 set about building on the foundations already in place during John Major's premiership. Arguably a more distinctive feature of New Labour policy was the determination to treat sport as part of a 'third way' agenda; recreation would be part of a 'joined up' approach to governance aimed at delivering on wider welfare goals such as improved health, civic renewal and greater social cohesion. Tony Blair was to describe sport as 'a pro-education policy, a pro-health policy, an anti-crime and anti-drugs policy'.[4] With this in mind, fresh focus was given to improving participation rates in sport generally. The rhetoric of 'sport for all' came back into vogue, mass participation being seen as the bridge between involvement at school and the transition to high-standard performance. In May 2000 the government produced a policy document entitled *A Sporting Future for All*, which differed from its Conservative equivalent of a few years earlier, *Raising the Game*, in setting out detailed methods of implementing and tracking progress. The criteria for eligibility to receive Lottery funds was modified, allowing money to be used for revenue streams such as employing coaches and coordinators, moving beyond the earlier emphasis on facility development only. Local authorities became central to sport strategy for the first time in a generation and Sport England found it was given freedom to oversee the creation of 30 'Sport Action Zones' in areas of inadequate community provision.[5]

According to Barrie Houlihan and Anita White, the years after 1997 witnessed a reinvigoration of grass-roots sports development. Those accustomed to bemoaning a lack of government involvement and investment 'were taken aback by the prescriptive nature' of New Labour's policy, which in a follow-up document of March 2001 – *A Sporting Future for All: The Government's Plan for Sport* – set out a range of targets for Whitehall departments, sports councils and national governing bodies. In time there was to be much criticism of what seemed like an obsession with delivering on centrally imposed targets. And in the short term spending on sport was constrained by the desire of Labour's powerful Chancellor, Gordon Brown, to work for two years within the financial framework laid down by the previous administration. The total budget in 2000–01 of c.£1250 million was similar to that reached in the last year of the Major administration. But, write Houlihan and White, departures such as the priority accorded to social inclusion and the renewed willingness to work in partnership with local authorities marked 'a clear and substantial break' with the approach of the pre-1997 government and reversed the drift in earlier years away from a community focus in sports development.[6]

While there was much to commend in the development of an integrated sport policy, New Labour's record during its first term was far from being one of unalloyed success. Much of the solid work outlined in documents such as *A Sporting Future For All* was overshadowed by problems that frequently attracted adverse newspaper headlines. To an extent the government's problems were self-inflicted. After the 1997 election, it seemed likely that the Minister for Sport – Labour's second only, Denis Howell having monopolized the post before 1979 – would be Tom Pendry, who had shadowed the portfolio since the early 1990s. In the words of the *Daily Mail* journalist Ian Wooldridge, Pendry was 'sicker than soccer's sickest parrot' when he discovered he was the only member of the pre-1997 shadow group of ministers not to be appointed to office.[7] Mindful of the importance of sport to the nation's cultural life, Blair decided that his first Sports Minister would be Tony Banks, the maverick MP for West Ham, renowned for his staunch left-wing views and sharp tongue. Although a sports enthusiast (or at least a football enthusiast, a dedicated Chelsea fan), Banks later admitted he was astonished to receive the Prime Minister's offer. While he brought considerable energy to the role, his time in office was to be marked by controversy over a series of outspoken comments, calling among other things for foreign players in football's Premier League to become eligible to play for England. If Blair's intention was to give the role of Minister for Sport a populist edge, he got more than he bargained for, with many of Banks' outpourings attracting ridicule. Within a couple of weeks of the appointment the Prime Minister was telling his press secretary Alistair Campbell that he might have made a mistake; he had 'upset a few people' by passing over Tom Pendry and he 'didn't want to be let down'. Blair added that he 'did not want a court jester' at the DCMS, adding that Banks needed to get down to some 'hard graft'.[8]

Banks did get down to 'hard graft' and helped to ensure DCMS strategy developed momentum, though he was never entirely at ease in office and he volunteered to return to the backbenches as part of a government reshuffle in July 1999. Much of his focus as Sports Minister was on football, with a government-sponsored Football Task Force eventually leading to the creation of the Football Foundation. In due course this was to plough many millions of pounds – including funds from the Treasury and the Lottery, as well as from the Football Association (FA) – into improving grass-roots facilities. Anxious about the rampant commercialism affecting the game in the era of the Premier League and Sky TV, the government also backed Supporters Direct, an initiative to help fans gain an increased say in the running of their clubs. The attention given to the national game after 1997 was such that Banks was sometimes referred to as the 'Minister for football', and stemmed partly from a desire to depict New Labour as being in touch with modern sensibilities. The danger of seeking out an active role in football (as distinct from being reluctantly drawn in, as Attlee had been over the cancellation of midweek fixtures in the 1940s) became evident after the government allied itself with the FA in proposing – 40 years on from the 1996 triumph – that England enter the race to host the 2006 World Cup. Banks took on the role of special envoy in liaising with the football authorities after he left his post as Sports Minister, but he and the Prime Minister were left with egg on their faces when the England bid was heavily defeated. To make matters worse, football's governing body, the International Federation of Association Football (FIFA), awarded the tournament to England's great rivals, Germany. The FA was left to blame hooliganism by English fans on the continent for the poor end result of a £10 million campaign, leaving England unlikely to be in running to host the tournament for many years ahead.[9]

Banks was replaced in 1999 by Kate Hoey, Britain's first female Sports Minister. Hoey was a former high jump champion for

Northern Ireland and worked as an educational advisor to several London football clubs before becoming MP for Vauxhall in
1989. She had been actively involved with Labour's sport policy
in opposition before 1997, and was thought to be in the running
for the ministerial position when Blair came to power. Instead
she received a junior post at the Home Office, and impressed the
Prime Minister sufficiently to be seen as the best person to replace
Banks. Like her predecessor, she welcomed the chance to push
forward DCMS plans aimed at encouraging wider participation in
sport, particularly in deprived urban areas of the type she represented in parliament. But, also like Tony Banks, Hoey was fiercely
independent, and reluctant to follow tamely an official line if it was
at odds with her views. She had, in the words of Alistair Campbell,
a touch of the maverick 'Frank Field about her'.[10] Writing in 2001,
the *Mail* journalist Ian Wooldridge felt Kate Hoey's commitment to
the cause made her one of Britain's best Sports Ministers (ranked
he felt behind only Howell and Moynihan). But, Wooldridge conceded, this did not mean she found the task easy. Like Banks, she
spent much of her time on football-related matters and became
embroiled in the 'unholy mess', as Wooldridge described it, surrounding the rebuilding of Wembley stadium. The old iconic stadium was closed in October 2000 but contractual disputes rumbled
on and demolition to make way for rebuilding did not begin until
2002. Hoey in the meantime rarely met with the Prime Minister
to discuss policy and had to rely for any impact at Cabinet level on
her superior at the DCMS Chris Smith, described by Wooldridge
as 'a politician celebrated for not rocking boats'.[11]

Banks and Hoey had strong and opposing views on the one
sporting issue that above all dominated Labour's first term and
beyond: fox hunting. Whereas the everyday concerns of school
sport and DCMS policy progressed steadily, attracting little media
attention, the topic of hunting caused enormous bitterness and
adverse publicity. Labour's manifesto in 1997 promised MPs a
'free vote' (allowing them to vote in accordance with their con-
sciences, rather than following a party directive) on whether to
introduce legislation banning fox hunting. This was a cause close
to the hearts of many in Labour circles, including Tony Banks, a
Vice-President of the League Against Cruel Sports. In the autumn
of 1997 one of Labour's new intake of parliamentarians, Michael
Foster, MP for Worcester and a long-time opponent of hunting,

put forward a private members' bill advocating a ban. When his measure progressed to a full-scale debate in the Commons, alarm bells rang among hunt sympathizers. In November Foster's bill was carried by 411 votes to 115, by far the largest parliamentary majority yet registered in favour of abolition. Foster declared that 'the days of hunting are doomed', pointing to opinion polls showing between 60 and 70 per cent of respondents supporting a ban.

The prospect of a hunting ban was certainly more real than at any time in the past. Ever since hunting was last seriously on the political agenda, under Attlee's government in the late 1940s, the pro-hunt community had remained confident that changes to the law were unlikely. Conservative administrations never sought to act in this area, and the Labour governments of Wilson and Callaghan had neither the inclination nor sufficiently strong majorities in the House of Commons to press ahead. But Foster's bill showed parliamentary and public opinion to be in alignment as never before. Despite this, Blair – like Attlee back in the 1940s – was in no rush to take on the hunting fraternity. Many in the Cabinet regarded hunting as a trivial concern compared with pressing economic and social problems after 18 years in the political wilderness. It was also obvious that any reform would be time consuming and highly contentious. The issue was divisive within as well as between the main parties; the anti-hunt fervour of many Labour MPs was offset by equally vigorous attachment to hunting on the part of some, including the likes of Kate Hoey. As a result the government opted for prevarication, fighting shy of providing the necessary time in the parliamentary timetable for Foster's measure to be taken any further.[12]

In spite of the lack of urgency shown by ministers, pro-hunt groups were not prepared to take the risk of sitting back to watch from the sidelines. In March 1998 a newly formed 'Countryside Alliance' organized a demonstration in London, attended by an estimated quarter of a million people opposed to Foster's bill; this was at least double the number who took to the streets to register their anger at Mrs Thatcher's unpopular 'poll tax' a decade earlier. If the intention was to convince ministers that the price of going ahead was not worth paying, it worked. Foster's bill was 'talked out' by Tory MPs, lapsing through lack of parliamentary time. By presenting itself as representative of the anxieties of rural England across the board, rather than simply as a pro-hunt group funded by wealthy landowners, the Alliance slowed the momentum for change, at least in the short term. But the very success of the Alliance also galvanized opponents of hunting into redoubling their efforts. Under attack from both sides of the argument, the government again stalled for time, this time setting up an independent inquiry into hunting with dogs.

When the Burns Report was published in the summer of 2000, it opted for a neutral approach: it gave a measured analysis of the place of hunting in the rural economy and outlined the possible consequences of introducing a ban, particularly in relation to job losses. During the autumn ministers finally bowed to backbench pressure by introducing a government-sponsored bill to ban fox hunting. But this was done in the knowledge that the measure was not likely to reach the statute book before a general election was called. The Prime Minister was reluctant to allow the bill to go forward; the measure, he felt, was 'illiberal' and he was not keen on being harassed by pro-hunt protestors during an election campaign. Alistair Campbell and other Downing Street advisers took the view that Labour was unlikely to ever win over pro-hunt groups, but would 'lose a stack of support' among liberal types if Blair backed down at this stage.[13] The bill sailed comfortably through the House of Commons early in 2001 but was emphatically rejected in the House of Lords. There was no time to begin the parliamentary process again before the nation went to the polls.[14]

The stalemate on hunting was indicative of Labour's mixed fortunes on sport by the end of Blair's first term. On the international stage, unprecedented levels of investment in Olympic sports aided a strong British performance in the Sydney Games, but the Prime Minister miscalculated by allying himself so closely with England's failed bid to host football's World Cup. On the domestic front, Labour's manifesto going into the 2001 election lauded a period of revival after the neglect of the Tory years, notably in school sport, and made a virtue of efforts to link sport with broader aspects of welfare. Although the wish of the Commons to ban fox hunting had been 'thwarted' by the House of Lords, the manifesto pledged that if returned to power Labour would look again at how this issue might be resolved.[15] While sport like all areas of policy was constrained by tight controls over public spending in the first half of the 1997 parliament, Labour was also promising significant increases during a second term. The annual report of the DCMS in 2001 noted that the latest government Spending Review outlined a substantial budget rise for the department in the three years ahead, including a 'best-ever' settlement for sport, with Treasury input set to double.[16] But whatever pledges were offered to the electorate, it remained the case that Kate Hoey had experienced a tough time as Sports Minister and Chris Smith was rumoured to be under threat as Culture Secretary. In June 2001 Blair told his press secretary he wanted to get the right people in the right jobs second time around if he got the chance, rather than being swayed by the views of others. In the event neither Hoey nor Smith were reappointed when Labour comfortably secured re-election.[17]

Tessa Jowell and Richard Caborn: Labour's Second Term, 2001–05

At the start of his second term in office Blair promoted one his most loyal supporters, Tessa Jowell, MP for Dulwich and West Norwood, to replace Chris Smith as Secretary of State at the DCMS. He also brought in a new Sports Minister, Richard Caborn, MP for Sheffield Central, who was appointed at Minister of State level, a higher grade than Banks and Hoey. The duo of Jowell and Caborn were to oversee sport for several years to come, bringing more stability to policymaking and in due course presiding over some impressive achievements. Aside from a promising economic outlook, allowing an increased budget for sport, the new team had one great advantage over their first-term predecessors: direct links to the top of the government. Jowell could rely on a sympathetic hearing with the Prime Minister, while Caborn was a good friend of Alistair Campbell and the Deputy Prime Minister, John Prescott. These personal connections were crucial, Caborn believed, in enabling the DCMS to 'punch above its weight' after 2001, although things did not go smoothly at the outset. Jowell was initially preoccupied with television broadcasting, and Caborn – though a close follower of football, cricket and boxing – was embarrassed about his general sporting knowledge in a radio interview shortly after taking up his post. Journalist Ian Wooldridge wrote that while the nation did not expect its Sports Minister to be a 'demented anorak...I fear that Mr Caborn's performance was hardly D-grade at GCSE'.[18]

In the autumn of 2001 ministers also suffered a more substantial humiliation; this once more illustrated the potential pitfalls
of associating the government closely with international sport.
London had originally been chosen to host the 2005 World
Athletics championships, but in looking in more detail at the project the Culture Secretary decided the cost associated with running
the event and constructing a purpose-built stadium at Pickett's
Lock in Edmonton was prohibitive. Offers were made to switch
the championships to Sheffield, where the required facilities were
largely in place, but this idea was rejected by the international controlling body of athletics. In October the government announced
its withdrawal of Britain's offer to host the championships, which
were eventually held in Helsinki. When this topic was discussed
shortly before Christmas in response to a report by the Commons
Select Committee on Culture, Media and Sport, the government
was fiercely attacked on all sides of the house. The forthright
Chairman of the committee, Gerald Kaufman, a former Labour
minister, described the episode as a 'sorry and convoluted saga'.
Unless the government got its act together in future, Kaufman
argued, 'it would be sensible to abandon pretensions to staging
complex events in this country'.[19]

In the light of the critical findings of the Select Committee, it
was not surprising that opposition speakers used the occasion of
the parliamentary debate in December 2001 to berate Labour ministers. For the Conservatives, Tim Yeo, MP for South Suffolk, spoke
of Labour's 'total lack of vision' and 'abject failure of leadership'
over its inability to bring major sporting events to Britain, having
made this part of its electoral pitch in 1997 and 2001. The Liberal
Democrat MP for North Devon, Nick Harvey, argued that the end
result was symptomatic of the failure of DCMS to 'provide a long-
term strategy for sport in this country'. He called Britain an 'international laughing stock'. If, he said, Britain was not able to host the
World Athletics championships, it would never be seriously considered as a venue for bigger events such as football's World Cup or
the Olympics. The lesson from the 'fiasco', Harvey claimed, was
that central government had to take international projects of this
sort 'by the scruff of the neck' and 'see them through', rather than
leaving them entirely to the sporting authorities. Ministers were to
subsequently act on this advice, but at the time Jowell and Caborn
had no choice but to take widespread criticism on the chin.

It was one thing to come under fire from political opponents and from members of the Select Committee, which under Kaufman's experienced leadership provided a stronger platform for MPs to contribute to sport policymaking than at any time in the past. It must have grated, however, for Caborn to also be faced with less than helpful interjections in the debate by his predecessors. Kate Hoey claimed the government's handling of major sporting spectacles was a 'shambles'. For much of her time as Sports Minister, she said, football in general and England's World Cup bid in particular cast a shadow over everything else. Underlying her difficulties, Hoey felt in hindsight, was the problem of a 'dysfunctional Department'. She claimed that 'no one can take decisions' in sport when there were so many vested interests involved. The government handed its allocation of funding primarily to Sport England, a body with 500 employees, whereas the Minister for Sport was expected to act on several fronts with the support of only about 25 civil servants at the DCMS. Tony Banks joined in to back up Hoey. While defending the amount of time he devoted to England's World Cup bid, despite its failure, he agreed with Hoey that the 'arm's length principle' was a source of frustration during his time in office, resulting in 'fractured decisions to bodies all over the place'.[20]

Another episode that generated unwelcome headlines during Labour's second term (though not the province of the DCMS) was renewed controversy over hunting. Tony Blair wrote in his memoirs that he increasingly inclined to the view that hunting was 'integral to a way of life' in rural Britain. Despite Labour's manifesto commitment to reintroduce legislation, Blair admitted he resorted to 'contortions and permutations' to avoid 'this wretched business'.[21] He struggled to comprehend the passions aroused on both sides of the argument, exemplified when Gerald Kaufman told the Prime Minister he would cease to be a loyalist if the government retreated on hunting. Britain was becoming embroiled in a major military conflict in Afghanistan, and Kaufman's view was that if Blair could stand up to Osama bin Laden then he must stand up to the Countryside Alliance.[22] The government again prevaricated by putting forward a complicated licensing system under which fox hunting would be allowed to continue. But Labour MPs were resolute. An amendment in the name of Tony Banks, calling for an outright ban, was given firm support in the Commons. When this went forward the House of Lords blocked further progress.

The constitutional right of the upper chamber to prevent change, however, was almost exhausted. There was mounting frustration for Blair when Labour's chief whip told him in 2003 that 'hunting went deep, and was symbolic' on the backbenches; unless reform went ahead, there was not a 'hope in hell' of MPs backing other planned welfare changes.[23] In September 2004 the Hunting with Dogs Bill received a large majority on a free vote in the Commons, and a couple of months later the Parliament Act was invoked to override opposition in the Lords; after a long struggle, hunting with hounds was finally outlawed in England and Wales.

Although the Countryside Alliance (of which Kate Hoey became Chairman in 2005) persisted with legal challenges, from 2005 onwards it became an offence to hunt wild mammals with a dog. Arguments simmered for a long time over whether the new Act was effective, or whether it was being circumvented in practice. The appearance of continuity resulted from many hunts reclassifying themselves as 'drag-hunts'; the laying of artificial scents remained legal, as did the use of a maximum of two dogs to flush out animals to be shot. In his memoirs Tony Blair described the Hunting with Dogs Act as one of the key items of domestic legislation in his premiership that he most regretted – 'the cause of inordinate political convulsion'. After the law came into force, Blair made clear when asked what approach to take by the Home Secretary that he did not wish to see the measure vigorously policed to ensure prosecutions.[24] Yet despite various loopholes, in her careful study of this topic Emma Griffin concludes that fox hunting was henceforth 'seriously restricted … on English and Welsh soil'. While many (including the Prime Minister) felt it was absurd to spend time on such a 'trivial' topic – requiring 700 hours of parliamentary time over seven years to get a new law on the statute book – Griffin notes that deep down it was less to do with the rights and wrongs of cruelty to animals than it was about the type of society Britain wished to see develop. Supporters of hunting unashamedly saw it a traditional pastime that represented all that was best about rural England, whereas opponents continued to underpin their arguments with age old concerns about social privilege and antipathy to pleasure taken in killing animals. Those who wanted to avoid the argument failed to recognize how the anti-hunting cause, in earlier times confined to the narrow ranks of liberal intellectuals, struck a popular chord with many ordinary voters.[25]

Although attracting far less attention than troublesome topics like fox hunting, the pace of progress on mainstream areas of
sport policy picked up after 2001. In December 2001, when the
government was lambasted in parliament for its handling of the
World Athletics championships, Chris Smith interjected to note
that Treasury funding for sport was due to double by 2004, reaching almost £100 million a year. 'I negotiated that money, and I was
proud to put it in place'.[26] As this money came on stream, it was
one element in a triple strategy developed by Jowell and Caborn.
Exchequer money was channelled to Sport England only after
ministers presided over administrative modernization. In particular Caborn insisted on reduced staffing levels in London, with
resources redirected via regional boards (reviving Denis Howell's
approach from an earlier era) so as to ensure that 'all spending
is linked to the key priority for sport – increased participation'.[27]
In the meantime substantial sums were made available by the
Department for Education to continue with the expansion of school
sport partnerships. And at the apex of the pyramid of sporting
development, Lottery money was used to maintain generous levels
of support for elite sportsmen and women; by this point about 400
athletes across a range of Olympic sports were in receipt of lottery
provision supplied through the offices of UK Sport. Caborn also
endorsed the ambitions of the English Institute of Sport, which
provided a nationwide network of world class training facilities,
and in 2003 the government declared it would fully support a bid
by London to host the 2012 Olympics (described more fully below).
Enhanced levels of support for international athletes, on a scale
that dwarfed what came before, appeared to pay dividends when
the British performance at the Athens Olympics in 2004 emulated
that of Sydney four years earlier. Britain was again placed tenth in
the medals table, winning two more medals (30 in total) than in
2000.

Despite evidence of across-the-board progress since 2001, Jowell
and Caborn found themselves heavily criticized over funding in
the run-up to the general election of May 2005. The attack came
not from the Conservative opposition, which under the leadership
of Michael Howard produced a manifesto with only the briefest
of references to reducing sporting bureaucracy and using lottery
money to support 'the arts, heritage, sport and charities'.[28] Instead
the *Observer* ran a month-long 'Vote Sport' campaign, aimed at

pressing ministers to invest more in sport. The journalist Denis Campbell launched proceedings with an array of damning statistics. Drawing on figures produced by Sport England and the group Cambridge Econometrics Consultancy, he argued that the government received c.£5.5 billion in income annually from sport (from the likes of income tax on elite performers, VAT on tickets, corporation tax and sports-related gambling) but handed out only £660 million, from the Treasury and the National Lottery combined. The disparity between tax take and investment had long existed, of course, and Campbell conceded that the 'gap' was not as great as first appeared; when adding in local authority spending, an estimated £1.8 billion of public funding went into sport each year. But there were other figures 'that shame Whitehall', Campbell claimed. The DCMS spent only 8.3 per cent of its budget on sport, compared with 23.7 per cent on the arts and 37.6 per cent on museums, galleries and libraries. Britain fared badly, moreover, in relation to other comparable nations. In Britain £21 of public money per head of the population was spent on sport each year, compared with £51 in Australia and £110 in France. In relation to the latter, the French Ministry for Sport and Youth Affairs employed about 6000 staff, compared with only 30 or so civil servants devoted to sport at the DCMS. For Denis Campbell the main problem was that while Tony Blair 'understands better than most the power of sport', and while ministers lauded sport for its contribution to a range of social problems such as health and school truancy, behind the fine words sport was treated primarily as a 'cash cow' and 'barely features on the political radar'.[29]

As polling day approached, Labour fought back against its critics. At a debate organized by the *Observer*, attended by some 200 figures from across the sporting establishment, Richard Caborn agreed that more could be done but pointed out that unprecedented sums were being invested: these included £1 billion into school sport since 1997 and £2 billion on new and improved facilities since the introduction of the National Lottery. In response to tough questioning, Caborn sharply retorted that some in the audience, such as Colin Moynihan, came nowhere near matching New Labour's record on sport when they were in the driving seat. Labour's manifesto at the election also contained, in contrast to the standard short paragraph or two, a lengthy defence of the 'thriving' sports scene in Britain. Labour was committed, the manifesto claimed, to both the 'broadest base of participation' for sport and support for elite athletes. If re-elected, the party would deliver on a range of objectives, including ensuring that everyone lived within 20 minutes of a 'good multi-sport facility'.[30] The Prime Minister personally got involved, contributing an article to the *Observer's* 'Vote Sport' debate. 'From rebuilding school sport to mounting a strong bid for the Olympics, from support for grass-roots clubs to greater funding for elite athletes', Blair opined, 'this government has a record to be proud of and much more to offer if re-elected'. He ended by noting that sport alone would not sway many votes at the election; but the country did have a choice on sport, 'just as it does on the economy, schools, hospitals and the minimum wage'.[31] When that choice was made at the May election, the government's majority fell from 167 seats to 66, enough to deliver a third successive Labour victory. Although intense criticism of British involvement in the Iraq war since 2003 was felt to have seriously dented the party's popularity, the settled state of the economy was credited with giving New Labour the prospect of another full parliamentary term ahead.

The London Olympics

Within a couple of months of the 2005 election, attention shifted to an achievement which made swirling criticisms of sport policy pale into insignificance, at least temporarily: Britain won the right to host the Olympic Games for the first time since 1948. The battle to do so was a far tougher one than at the end of the Second World War, when London was not faced by intense global competition. By the early twenty-first century engaging in any Olympic bid, as one overview of British involvement notes, meant encountering a 'heady mixture of political intrigue, financial risk, logistical conundrum, media scrutiny and sporting challenge'.[32] After the failure of bids by Birmingham and Manchester in the 1980s and 1990s, the British Olympic Association (BOA) was convinced only London would have any prospect of being in serious contention for staging the Olympics of 2012. The BOA was also aware of the need for firm political backing, without which any British proposal was unlikely to get beyond the planning stage. When approached in 2000 about offering support on behalf of authorities in the capital, the left-wing Mayor of London, Ken Livingstone, was doubtful that the project would get off the ground, but he cautiously backed the BOA on the understanding that the Games would be based in East London and would involve wholesale regeneration of that part of the city.[33] Inside government, the BOA also found its cause was sympathetically received by the Culture Secretary and the Sports Minister.

But Jowell and Caborn were isolated voices in government at this early stage of the process, when London's chances of success looked remote. Sensitive to the enormous public appetite for sport, and reluctant not to be outflanked by its political opponents, New Labour made electoral pledges to endeavour to bring major international sporting events to British shores. But its record thus far in this respect was dismal. Britain's reputation on the global sporting stage, as we have seen, suffered twin blows with the failed bid to host the 2006 football World Cup followed by the decision to withdraw the offer to host the World Athletics championships. Some ground was recovered following the successful organization of the Manchester Commonwealth Games in 2002, but when a small group of Cabinet ministers was formed to consider London's case for 2012, the majority were unenthusiastic. Chancellor Gordon Brown was reluctant to be associated with another costly project that might come to haunt the government, and the Culture Secretary was advised by her own officials at the DCMS not to press ahead: a London bid was likely to be enormously expensive (costing about £2.5 billion) and unsuccessful to boot, the consensus of opinion being that Paris was a clear favourite to win the International Olympic Committee (IOC) nomination in due course. One minister even expressed the view that Paris was the best choice.[34]

By the beginning of 2003 the government was under pressure to clarify its position. Jowell took some comfort from a parliamentary debate on 15 January in which a majority of speakers from all parties declared themselves in favour of the London bid. From the Conservative side Nick Hawkins, MP for Surrey Heath and a prominent member of an all-party sports committee, claimed there was public enthusiasm to go ahead: 'All members must be very conscious of the fact that far more people in this country care about sport than about politics.' Liberal Democratic backing was also forthcoming, and several Labour MPs weighed in on the side of going ahead, particularly those with London constituencies.

Caborn noted that the few objectors were mostly northern-based MPs, in part aggrieved by Manchester not being seriously considered despite its experience of the bidding process and the smooth running of the Commonwealth Games. The Sports Minister pledged that the Cabinet would take parliamentary opinion into account, though Jowell concluded that the decision was finely balanced: private poll research showed three quarters of respondents favoured London hosting the Games, but other areas of policy such as education and health were seen as higher priorities for investment. The Culture Secretary's cautious tone was interpreted by some observers as the government preparing the ground to back down.[35]

In reality the Secretary of State knew she had some way to go to win over the doubters in the Cabinet and across Whitehall. Undeterred, Jowell met with Ken Livingstone and thrashed out a financial package, with the intention that substantial funding would come from the National Lottery and increases in London council tax. The Chancellor indicated he was not opposed to the bid on this basis, and Jowell ended a hectic week by flying to Lausanne to meet Jacques Rogge, the IOC President. Rogge was able to confirm there would be a fair contest for the Olympic vote, and that no deals had been agreed with Paris as the front-runner.[36] Thus encouraged, Jowell took her case to the Cabinet at the end of January, though – unlike John Major in the 1990s – Blair took a while to be convinced of the case for unreservedly backing the Olympic cause. While struck by the conviction of London MPs, the Prime Minister felt the government still lacked firm enough information to make a final decision. Blair's press secretary Alistair Campbell recorded in his diary that while John Prescott, the Deputy Prime Minister, was 'broadly positive', and emphasized the need to either back the bid in a wholehearted fashion or not at all, the Chancellor would not commit beyond saying he was supportive 'if the finances are sustainable'. Campbell concluded: 'Overall the Olympic discussion was more negative than I thought it would be.'[37] With the prospect of war in Iraq dominating the political agenda, the moment did not seem propitious to bring a festival of sport to the forefront, and the Cabinet opted for further delay.

It was not until May 2003, with the IOC deadline for submissions looming, that the government formally announced it would back London as the British contender for 2012. Aside from Prescott, a

solid supporter from the outset, key Cabinet personnel had different reasons for nailing their colours to the Olympic mast. Blair,
according to his memoirs, was persuaded partly by his wife, Cherie,
an ardent fan of athletics, but primarily by the Culture Secretary.
As a close ally of the Prime Minister, she had the confidence to
chide him for not being courageous enough to take a risk. Jowell's
view, that London might not defeat a strong Paris challenge but
should at least try, was decisive in persuading Blair (who disliked
being thought of as risk-averse) to throw his hat in the ring. After
this time the Cabinet 'came round', Blair wrote, 'but only because
I was then really going for it and JP [John Prescott] as ever waded
in manfully with support'.[38] According to the *Observer* journalist
Andrew Rawnsely, the vital endorsement of the Chancellor was
based largely on personal calculation. One insider source told
Rawnsley that Gordon Brown – always mindful of protecting his
position as Blair's heir-apparent – feared that Number Ten would
try to cast him in the role of the killjoy Chancellor, blocking
Britain's bid on the grounds of its likely expense. Brown also calculated, in Rawnsley's view, that London had little real prospect
of defeating Paris; on this basis, the cost of the Games was not
likely to be a serious issue in the future.[39] Whatever the precise
mix of motives, the unanimous approval given by the Cabinet suggested that thus far in proceedings, Jowell played a more central
part than either Blair or Brown. In the words of Craig Reedie, the
Chairman of the BOA: 'Tessa did a magnificent job and deserves
great credit for getting it through the Cabinet.'[40]

In the next phase of the process, the London team by neces-
sity had to take the lead in order to build a credible case in the
international sporting community. In May 2004 the IOC issued a
shortlist of five cities, with London appearing to be in third place
behind Paris and Madrid; IOC feedback expressed particular concerns over London's transport infrastructure. Shortly afterwards
Sebastian Coe, who entered parliament as a Conservative MP
in 1992 but lost his seat five years later, took over as head of the
London campaign. According to Mike Lee, director of communications for the London team, while a sound structure was already
in place Coe's arrival 'gave the bid a massive injection of momentum at just the right time'.[41] Coe was held in high regard by the
IOC on the basis of his distinguished athletics career and his per-
sonable manner, and he became the crucial figurehead in the year

or so between the announcement of the shortlist and the final IOC decision-making meeting in July 2005. Throughout this period, it also mattered that the government consistently backed London. Emulating the approach of John Major's support for previous Olympic bids, the Foreign and Commonwealth Office (FCO) conducted lobbying overseas and both Jowell and Caborn assiduously attended gatherings of sports administrators across the world.

The Prime Minister, moreover, having come off the fence to ensure Cabinet approval, threw his weight energetically behind London's cause. Alongside Mayor 'Red Ken' Livingstone (with whom he worked well, despite their political differences), Blair showcased the London bid in a glitzy launch at the Royal Opera House early in 2004. Later that year he lobbied behind the scenes when he attended the Athens Olympics, which also opened his eyes to the scale of the prize on offer. He even claimed in his memoirs that during his summer holiday in Italy he visited the home of controversial president Silvio Berlusconi and asked him to influence the thinking of the five Italian IOC members.[42] When an IOC evaluation commission came to London in February 2005, Blair was once more to the fore, persuading his visitors that any shortcomings in the capital's transport system had been fully rectified. IOC feedback praised the 'very high quality' of London's bid, highlighting strong political support as one of the features in its favour. By this point one of the Prime Minister's close advisers felt he had 'got religion about the Olympics...he really wanted it'.[43]

It was in the final act of the drama, however, when the IOC met in Singapore in July 2005 to reach a decision, that Blair made his most decisive contribution. In the view of communications chief Mike Lee, those IOC members granted individual meetings were both 'flattered and impressed' that the British premier had travelled halfway across the world despite having to host a key 'G8' summit of world leaders shortly afterwards; any lingering suspicion that London lacked staunch political backing disappeared instantly.[44] After the announcement of London's narrow triumph over Paris, it was quickly agreed that Blair – in the words of Labour's Peter Mandelson – had played 'a crucial role in the final salesmanship and bargaining in Singapore'.[45] Amidst bitter recriminations in France, London's victory was attributed partly to Blair's influence on African IOC members (illustrating that any legacy of anti-British feeling stemming from the apartheid controversies of earlier

times no longer prevailed), and partly to the lacklustre intervention of French president Jacques Chirac. He arrived in Singapore
only shortly before the vote and made little attempt to emulate
Blair's hands-on approach. In the view of Tessa Jowell, Chirac's
'air of utter self-importance', based on the belief that Paris could
not lose, did not go down well with IOC members. Mike Lee concluded that while collective credit was due to the likes of Seb Coe
and Craig Reedie of the BOA for ensuring London's bid arrived in
good shape, it was Blair's contribution in Singapore that provided
an 'extra push to get over the line ahead of the French'.[46]

The jubilation at winning the Olympics was short-lived. Within
24 hours of the announcement, London was seized by fear as a wave
of terrorist bombings killed over fifty people. Over the months
that followed some of the gloss also came off the Olympic triumph
as press and parliamentary critics made much of the mushroom-
ing cost of the Games. John Prescott was overheard in the tea room
saying that when the Minister for Sport had spoken with his counterparts in countries who previously hosted the Olympics, all of
them agreed that if they could correct one failing it would be to
get the budget right from the outset.[47] Tessa Jowell, who became
'Minister for the Olympics' as well as Culture Secretary from this
time on, undertook a detailed review and presented the House
of Commons with a revised budget in March 2007. At the time of
submitting London's bid, she noted, the estimated cost of building an Olympic park, providing infrastructure and an element for
community and elite sport was c.£3 billion, plus another £1 billion
for regeneration of the Lower Lea valley area. Urban regeneration
and the building of thousands of new homes, she pointed out, was a
vital feature of the government's plan. Following the government's
review she stated that the Olympic budget would total just over £9
billion, the bulk of this being required either directly or as a con-
tingency for building state-of-the-art venues and the Olympic park.
Public funding to cover the budget would come primarily from
the government (c.£6 billion), plus additional input from Lottery
funds, up to a total of £2.2 billion, with Jowell claiming that no further demands would be made of the Lottery further down the line
and that other lottery-supported sport schemes would not be damaged as a consequence. The Minister for the Olympics claimed it
was 'full steam ahead for 2012', with the Games expected to bring
social and economic gains to London and the whole country.[48]

Not everyone shared Jowell's upbeat assessment. In echoes of the run-up to the 1948 Olympics, some sections of the press believed the whole thing was both unwelcome and prohibitively expensive. For those who felt the legacy would be one of huge debt and under-utilized stadiums, the Games were a 'five-ring circus'.[49] Responding to the parliamentary statement in March 2007, opposition spokesmen for the Conservatives and the Liberal Democrats were highly critical of the threefold increase in the budget since London initially entered the fray. One MP accused the government of having 'completely lost control' of Olympic finances.[50] What these exchanges indicated was that all parties were looking to make political capital out of the Games. One observer at Labour's annual conference in the autumn of 2005 noted an air of triumphalism when Jowell presided, not so much over a debate, but over a 'great Olympic love-in' designed to highlight the party's achievement in winning the race to host the Games.[51] For the opposition parties, genuine excitement about 2012 was matched by a willingness to take every opportunity of claiming that rising costs demonstrated government incompetence. The huge importance attached to the Games on all sides was illustrated when the BOA elected the former Conservative Minister for Sport Colin Moynihan as Chairman for the run-up to 2012. Tony Blair sought assurances that there was no party political agenda at work in this decision. Speaking to the IOC in 2006, Moynihan noted there was broad support at Westminster for the Games, though he added that winning the right to host the Olympics had pushed sport 'higher up the political agenda than it has undoubtedly ever been in the United Kingdom'. This even included, Moynihan admitted, an element of electoral calculation: 'The Olympic Games are regarded as a golden goose eagerly sought by politicians for its glistening electoral egg.'[52]

A similar pattern of political skirmishing developed after Tony Blair stood down from the premiership in June 2007, leaving Gordon Brown to assume the reins of power. As a Blairite loyalist, Jowell lost her post as Culture Secretary, though she was permitted to attend Cabinet meetings in her continuing role as Minister for the Olympics. She was later fully restored to Cabinet after refusing to join a revolt in party ranks against Brown's style of leadership. Throughout the three-year period ahead of the 2010 general election, Jowell thereby maintained a front-line presence in promoting

London 2012; according to Peter Mandelson she drew 'plaudits from all quarters' for her efforts.[53] Her role included fending off continuing criticisms that the government misled the country over the cost of the Games. The Public Accounts Committee of the House of Commons, chaired by Conservative MP Edward Leigh, complained that foreseeable costs were excluded at the early stages of the bid in order to ensure public support, giving an 'unrealistic picture' of the eventual budget.[54] This line of attack intensified as Britain slid into recession in the wake of a global banking crisis. In response to assertions that Britain could not afford the Games in troubled times, Jowell insisted the nation could not afford to be without them: thousands of construction jobs in East London were providing a vital 'shot in the arm for the economy'.[55] Although sniping in the press persisted, the Culture, Media and Sport Select Committee reported in 2008 that there was 'much to commend in what has been achieved so far'. The Olympic site was beginning to take shape and the various bodies charged with responsibility for 2012 were making 'strenuous efforts' to fulfil the vision set out in the bid.[56] The Select Committee was now chaired by a Tory MP, John Whittingdale, and the political reality was that the opposition did not wish to paint itself into a corner by jeopardizing the Games. With a general election once more approaching, all parties – as had been the case since John Major gave manifesto backing for Britain's Olympic bid in 1992 – were anxious to persuade voters that they understood the value of international sport to Britain's trading prospects and global prestige.

New Labour on the Slide, 2007–10

In surviving until the arrival of Brown at Number Ten, Richard Caborn became the longest-serving Minister for Sport in one continuous period. In February 2007 Caborn gave a speech looking back on what he felt had been achieved since Tony Blair appointed him with the words that sport 'is an asset which is massively underutilised'. He believed, in the first place, that the role of Sports Minister had become more firmly established in Whitehall, acting as both the 'biggest advocate' of sport but also as its 'critical friend'. He was aware of the criticism that sport lacked a distinct voice in Cabinet. On this Caborn, like Denis Howell before him, took comfort from the presence of a supportive Secretary of State around the Cabinet table; this was preferable he felt to having a Sports Minister in Cabinet whose budget and influence would pale in comparison with other departments. Caborn alluded, secondly, to the importance of the administrative restructuring carried out under his watch. The 'most disappointing thing' he found when taking up the post in 2001 was the degree of endemic 'infighting' in the sports world – between National Governing Bodies (NGBs) and the government, and between the various sports councils. 'To say it was fractious would be diplomatic', he said. By 2007, however, the Minister was confident the situation had been transformed. The system of regional boards he devised was operating smoothly; a new sense of unity was forged in support of London's Olympic bid; and the roles and expectations of the main national organizations funded by government had been clarified. Sport England concentrated on increasing participation, UK Sport on high performance sport, and the Youth Sport Trust monitored school sport. While fresh challenges remained, such as finding ways of modernizing some outdated governing bodies without resorting to outright interference, Caborn believed that DCSM strategy, backed up by appropriate funding, was now delivering on several fronts: improving participation rates in grass-roots sport, facilitating elite success, and using sport to assist with welfare objectives ranging from better health to reduced crime.[57]

When Brown replaced Blair in mid-2007, Caborn stood down from office. He took on instead the task of liaising between ministers and the football authorities in preparing an English bid to host the 2018 World Cup. This was similar to the role adopted by Tony Banks when he ceased to be Sports Minister, and unfortunately for Caborn the outcome was also to be the same: England's bid was crushingly defeated when the tournament was eventually offered to Russia. Caborn was replaced at the DCMS by Gerry Sutcliffe, MP for Bradford South, who was given the title of Minister for Sport and Tourism. Although Sutcliffe remained in post until the end of the parliament, ministerial continuity was more a problem for sport than it had been since 2001. Gordon Brown resorted to frequent reshuffles in an attempt to shore up his faltering popularity, and got through three Secretaries of State at the DCMS in as many years. James Purnell, MP for Stalybridge and Hyde, became the youngest member of the Cabinet in June 2007, aged only 37, but remained for less than nine months before being promoted to Work and Pensions Secretary. Purnell was replaced by the MP for Leigh, Andy Burnham, a keen follower of rugby and football. Although he described the post as his 'dream job', Burnham's tenure was also quite short-lived; after 18 months he was replaced by the Exeter MP Ben Bradshaw, formerly the Minister for Health. Bradshaw occupied the role of Culture Secretary for the final year of the Brown administration ahead of Labour's defeat at the 2010 general election.

With changes of personnel came some important shifts in DCMS thinking after 2007. Although he was Culture Secretary for only a few months, Purnell ruffled feathers by insisting that while the areas of school sport and elite performance were on course to becoming 'world class', more needed to be done to create 'a world-class community sports system'. As part of its package of Olympic legacy promises, the government had committed itself to targets of one million people playing sport more regularly and another million taking up physical activity. Purnell was persuaded that if these targets were to be reached, it would be best to work not through the regional boards of Sport England but through the NGBs, those whom he felt most understood the needs of individual sports. NGBs were offered the prospect of increased funding if in return they devised 'Whole Sport Plans' demonstrating how they might drive up participation rates and improve coaching schemes.[58] Purnell's approach did not go down well among those who felt governing bodies were not always well-equipped to engage with under-participating sections of the population such as women and ethnic minorities. In November 2007 the Chairman of Sport England, Derek Mapp, claimed Purnell forced him to resign on the basis of not being fully behind the government's desire to divert resources away from recreational pursuits such as jogging to more traditional, competitive sports. 'I was mandated to produce an agenda which I was delivering on', Mapp argued, 'but now that has been changed and I have been dumped on'.[59]

Andy Burnham's time as Culture Secretary was marked by both highs and lows. On the one hand the DCMS secured what its annual report in 2008 described as a 'strong settlement' in the government spending review of that year, putting sport on a solid financial footing in the period ahead of the London Olympics.[60] In addition, while there was controversy over human rights in China ahead of the 2008 Beijing Olympics, Burnham and Sports

Minister Gerry Sutcliffe were able to make political capital out of the claim that sustained investment in elite athletes helped to achieve record success for 'Team GB'. In what amounted to the best performance at the Olympics in a hundred years, Britain finished fourth in the medals table, behind only China, the United States and Russia. Team GB's tally of 19 gold medals and 47 medals in total had only ever been bettered at the London Games of 1908, and ministers were able to hail triumphs across a range of well-financed disciplines including cycling, rowing, sailing, boxing, swimming and athletics. On the other hand, the onset of the 'credit crunch' in 2008, inaugurating a sharp recession after years of steady economic growth, posed threats for sport as it did for other sectors of society. In 2009 the Central Council of Physical Recreation (CCPR) reported that thousands of sports clubs across the country were in danger of closing, with 40 per cent of those contacted in a major survey reporting falling membership. As jobs and incomes came under pressure many were deciding not to renew their subscriptions. Without a healthy club sector, the CCPR warned, a whole range of government targets for improving participation in sport would become hard to reach.[61]

By the time Ben Bradshaw replaced Burnham in the summer of 2009, the government was being pushed more on the defensive over sport than it had been for several years. The voices of those who felt huge funding for the Olympics should be reappraised in the light of economic recession grew louder, and ammunition for those who opposed the increased funding directed towards NGBs since 2007 was provided by evidence that levels of increased participation were flattening out. Figures produced by Sport England suggested that the numbers playing sport three times a week rose sharply by half a million during 2005–08, but that the increase had stalled by 2009. The *Guardian* journalist Owen Gibson summed up Labour's problem: 'The government claims, with some justification, that it has poured more money into sport than any previous administration. But its critics say that in attempting to yoke the 2012 Olympics to a fundamental shift in the nation's attitude to sport and the transformation of the grass roots sport has bitten off more than it can chew.'[62] This was a difficult backdrop for a new Culture Secretary to find his feet, and Tessa Jowell as Minister for the Olympics interceded to insist Labour was not retreating from its aim of getting two million people more active by 2012. The

Conservative opposition, she chided, could not make up its mind if it was critical of the government for being too ambitious in hard economic times or for being lackadaisical in not having a persuasive approach to mass participation. Critics of Labour's plans, she said, seemed to be inventing versions of the all-important legacy of the Olympics that were 'limitless and infinite, [promising] an end to unhappiness, poverty and strife'.[63]

Although polls suggested New Labour was heading for almost certain electoral defeat, Bradshaw in a keynote speech tried to regain some of the ground lost since 2007 by making a robust defence of the party's record. In an address to a schools conference in October 2009, he placed particular emphasis on record levels of investment and improvements in state school provision, especially compared with the abject record of the previous government. When John Major left office in 1997 only a quarter of pupils in secondary schools were doing two hours of physical education per week. Bradshaw proudly claimed that the figure was now nine out of ten pupils, and that sights were being set on raising the minimum target to three hours a week. With almost 450 specialist 'School Sports Partnerships' in operation, it was lamentable that some journalists continued to peddle the 'myth' that competition was being driven out: survey evidence suggested all but a handful of primary and secondary schools held sports days every year. The core task for the decade ahead, the Culture Secretary believed, was to stitch together, permanently if possible, 'the bonds between school sport, elite sport and community sport'. It was after touring the country in his early months in post that Bradshaw became aware of what he called the 'silent sporting revolution' that had taken place since 1997. He ended his speech by hoping that, whoever found themselves in office after the 2010 election, the years to come would witness a successful and enduring 'loud revolution'.[64]

Epilogue: Towards 2012

The proximity of the Olympics meant sport featured in a minor way at least during the general election campaign of May 2010, alongside the traditional heavyweight themes of the economy, taxation and the National Health Service (NHS). Gone were the days, common before the 1960s, when sport had no place in the appeals of the main parties to the electorate. Labour's manifesto promised a move to a new phase in improving school, community and elite sport provision. The Conservatives responded by noting it was John Major before 1997 who facilitated a large-scale injection of funds into sport by introducing the National Lottery; the party pledged itself to continuing high-levels of funding via additional resources from the Lottery.[1] Watching these exchanges from the sidelines, *Guardian* journalist David Conn wrote that Labour arrived 'at this landmark election with a record of investment and improvement to defend'. But, Conn noted, with all parties keen to show they fully supported London 2012, the Conservatives were determined not to be outmanoeuvred. The journalist was struck by the tone adopted by Hugh Robertson, MP for Faversham and Mid-Kent and Shadow Minister for Sport since 2005. Robertson, a former army major and banker, followed a range of sports (unlike some of his party predecessors in the same role), and according to David Conn he was anxious to demonstrate that the Tories had undergone a 'sea change' in attitude. With 'admirable honesty' Robertson conceded the Conservatives had not always prioritized sport; they were coming into the 2010 election 'admitting their past mistakes and promising they have changed'.[2]

In assessing where things stood as voters prepared to go to the polls, Conn also outlined his own view of the achievements – and limitations – of Labour's record on sport since 1997. The revival of school sport was undoubtedly impressive, he claimed, and securing the right to host the Olympics stood out as a notable triumph for Tony Blair, Labour ministers and the London bid team. On the other hand, although the Olympic site in East London was taking shape with great speed, it was becoming increasingly obvious from Sport England figures that it would not be easy to deliver on all aspects of the ambitious Olympic legacy plan, particularly in relation to increasing participation. Conn similarly alluded to two sides of a coin on investment in sport. There had been record levels of spending since the second half of the 1990s, mostly from lottery sources, and directed primarily at elite athletes: facilitating notable British success from the Sydney Olympics of 2000 onwards. But at the same time the budget of the Department for Culture, Media and Sport (DCMS), funded by the Treasury, remained tiny in comparison with that of departments such as Health and Education. The sums of money devoted to encouraging more lasting engagement with physical activity among the population at large were, Conn argued, 'heartbreakingly small' compared to the 'vast' budget earmarked for 'hosting 26 days of Olympic and Paralympic Games'. In the final reckoning, David Conn believed the New Labour era had brought 'major progress' for British sport. But there was an elephant in the room. None of the parties were keen to talk during the election campaign about the nation's massive public debt, which had spiralled to a post-war high since the onset of recession in 2008. Looking forward, the hard question was whether advances since 1997 – the 'silent sporting revolution' referred to by Ben Bradshaw – could be sustained at a time when any new administration would have to face up to the need for large-scale cuts in public spending.[3]

The answer to the question of whether the relationship between sport and politics would remain on the same footing in a new age of austerity appeared to be: up to a point. Labour's 13-year hold on power came to a protracted, agonizing end when the Conservatives emerged as the largest party at the 2010 election, but with insufficient seats to form a government without support from others. Labour's vote share fell sharply and after clinging on in office for a couple of days Gordon Brown resigned, leaving the way clear for Tory leader David Cameron to become Prime Minister at the head of a Conservative–Liberal Democrat coalition, the first cross-party administration since 1940. Under the new regime, in which Hugh Robertson became Minister for Sport and the Olympics, some aspects of New Labour's sporting legacy looked to be secure. These included, ironically, the 2004 ban on fox hunting. The 'coalition agreement' rapidly hammered out by the Conservatives and Liberal Democrats to provide a blueprint for governance included a commitment to a free vote in the Commons on whether to overturn the hunting ban. David Cameron, though a self-confessed 'shire Tory' who supported hunting, was confronted with an awkward reality: soundings taken indicated that a free vote would result in certain victory for those (including most Liberal Democrats) who wanted to keep the ban, and who might even use the occasion to push for tighter enforcement of the existing law. By the end of 2010 newspapers were reporting that a free vote on fox hunting was likely to be postponed indefinitely.[4]

The Coalition partners were more united and determined from the outset not to endanger another key component of New Labour policy, the pledge to generously fund preparations for London 2012. As recently as 1980 a Conservative Prime Minister placed the sensibilities of British sportsmen and women below the dictates of international diplomacy, calling for a boycott of the Moscow Olympics. But in an age where sport attracted saturation media coverage and enormous business interest, Cameron did not wish to be seen as the leader who jeopardized Britain's post-2000 standing in the Olympic rankings. Like his predecessor, he was acutely aware of the potential benefits, economic and political, of being associated with global sporting spectaculars, especially those taking place on home shores. Although this approach could backfire, as it did when Cameron went to Zurich to find England's bid to host the 2018 football World Cup was soundly beaten, there was little doubt that the Prime Minister would do everything possible to ensure the success of the Olympics. The first six months of the Coalition were dominated by discussions about how to tackle Britain's public debt, and in October 2010 a huge programme of spending cuts was announced, totalling over £80 billion over a five-year period. Nearly all Whitehall departments were required to make substantial reductions, which in the case of the DCMS involved considerable job losses among civil servants. At the same time the government's Comprehensive Spending Review stipulated that the £9.3 billion budget for staging the Olympics remained unchanged, and that funding for elite athletes would not be eroded ahead of the Games.[5]

Other features of the pre-2010 sporting landscape did not survive unscathed. This may have been inevitable in the context of such a bleak economic backdrop, though it also reflected enduring weaknesses within the policymaking framework such as the fragmented nature of Whitehall responsibility for sport. The DCMS was initially powerless to prevent the announcement by the Conservative Education Secretary, Michael Gove, that Labour's £162-million a year strategy of supporting School Sports Partnerships would be scrapped as part of the Spending Review. Within days this decision was attacked by sports administrators and in several national newspapers, including the likes of the *Telegraph*, *Times* and *Daily Mail*. These Tory-supporting papers were strong advocates of deep spending cuts, but were at a loss to understand the axing of Sports Partnerships which, by coordinating regular sporting events and competitions in their local communities, helped to contribute to the goals of widening participation and improving health. The cost of the programme, critics pointed out, had to be seen in the context of the Department for Education's £50 billion annual budget. By the end of November 2010 protestors were building up a head of steam. A group of about 80 well-known Olympic and elite athletes made an unusual foray into the political world by signing a letter urging the government to rethink; marches on London involving school children were organized; and some 60 headteachers published a letter criticizing the government's 'ignorant' and 'destructive' action, which was described as wholly unjustified 'in terms of health and community wellbeing'.[6]

After a full-scale parliamentary debate, the Prime Minister announced on 1 December that he was looking again at the Sports Partnerships, even though a week earlier he had described them as a 'a complete failure'. Leaks to journalists suggested that behind-the-scenes Michael Gove was opposed in Cabinet by Nick Clegg, the Liberal Democrat Deputy Prime Minister, and by Jeremy Hunt, the Secretary of State at the DCMS. Hunt, Conservative MP for South West Surrey, admitted that sport was not his strong suit among the range of duties he took on when appointed as Culture Secretary, but he played a leading part in brokering a deal that went some way towards pacifying the newly formed alliance of teachers, school children, athletes, administrators and Labour MPs. As parliament dispersed for the Christmas holidays, the government quietly let it be known that many of the 450 Sports Partnerships would be given a temporary reprieve. But if Gove had been forced to retreat, he was far from suffering an outright defeat. The scepticism about state funding for sport that remained in parts of Whitehall was manifest when it was made clear that there would be no reinstatement of the full budget for the Partnership programme. Instead 'tens of millions' of pounds annually would be committed for the remainder of the parliament, tied in particular to Jeremy Hunt's idea of holding annual 'schools Olympics'. A Department for Education spokesman was quoted as saying there would no longer be a 'centralised PE strategy' as there had been under the previous government; if schools wished to continue with Sports Partnerships they would have to pay for them out of their own devolved budgets.[7]

Dark clouds also hung over the provision for community sport after 2010. Sebastian Coe, head of the London Organizing Committee for London 2012, referred to the Games as the 'single biggest opportunity in our lifetime to transform... participation in sport in the UK forever'. But Coe's lofty ambitions were under threat even before the Comprehensive Spending Review took effect. Within weeks of becoming Sport Minister Hugh Robertson announced the ending of a multi-million pound project inherited from Labour which provided free swimming for under-16s and over-60s, describing the scheme as 'a luxury we can no longer afford'.[8] Labour's target of getting an extra million adults each year doing general physical activity was also quietly dropped soon after the Coalition came to power.[9] At the time of the Spending Review promises were made to protect the budgets of Sport England and UK Sport until 2015, primarily by changing the way in which lottery funding was distributed. But the funding bodies were earmarked for merger as part of a drive to improve administrative efficiency, reflecting the ongoing, unresolved uncertainty in Whitehall about the best means of delivering sporting objectives. In addition, the Spending Review required local authorities to reduce their budgets substantially in the years ahead. This highlighted another long-standing weakness to which sport was exposed: because the provision of recreational facilities had never been made a statutory duty, pools, playing fields and sports centres inevitably came a long way down the list of services to be safeguarded in times of economic hardship. In the autumn of 2011 the leader of Durham County Council reported that in his authority alone 3 of 19 leisure centres were closing. It was, he complained, 'very difficult to increase participation in sport when there are swingeing cuts to sport and leisure provision'.[10]

Similarly endangered in the wake of the Spending Review was the aim adopted by New Labour of increasing by a million (over and above the target for general physical activity) the numbers taking part in sport three times a week or more. The figures on this score, as we saw in the previous chapter, were not encouraging even before the Coalition came to power. 'The main legacy of 2012', wrote the commentator David Goldblatt, reflecting on the scale of the task at the time of the Spending Review, 'may be a reminder of our...preference for consumption over participation; and for our success in training elites but failing the public'.[11] In March 2011 the Culture Secretary hinted in an interview that he was looking to introduce a 'more meaningful' measurement in place of the aim of inspiring one million more people to play regular sport. In order for Sport England to channel its resources more effectively in difficult times, it might be necessary in future, Hunt said, to put the emphasis on encouraging young adults to get involved, rather than aiding the population as a whole.[12] A few months later the DCMS issued a stark warning to governing bodies that they faced the curtailment of funding under Labour's £480 million 'Whole Sport' programme. The Sports Minister Hugh Robertson noted that National Governing Bodies (NGBs) 'argued passionately for a process that empowered them to deliver', but since 2009 the total number taking part in sport three times or more a week had only risen from 6.82 to 6.92 million. Four governing bodies could boast of increased participation, but 17 sports recorded reductions. This was not, Robertson commented, 'the step change' the NGBs promised, and funding would be cut in the next spending round unless results improved.[13]

A 'step change' in public provision for sport thus remained elusive in the run-up to London 2012. In many respects, of course, sport occupied a place in political discourse that was inconceivable at the time of the 1948 Olympics. Prompted by a mixture of ideological, electoral and practical impulses, state involvement in sport had been transformed, not uniformly over the whole post-war period, but with particular leaps forward taking place between 1964 and 1979 and from the mid-1990s onwards. As a result of growing political interest, sport had established a reasonably settled structure in Whitehall for support and co-ordination, and more people than ever before had access to locally administered recreational amenities such as pools and sport centres. But the optimistic 1970s talk of 'sport for all' and sport as part of the 'fabric of the social services' remained a long way from becoming a reality. As austerity bit deep after 2010, efforts to deploy sport in the interests of wider welfare and community goals once more began to fall by the wayside. More so than in many western industrialized nations, sport in Britain remained vulnerable to political whim and the vicissitudes of the economy. In 2011 the DCMS still insisted it was 'absolutely committed' to using the Olympics to ensure more people took up sport, but critics feared, in the words of one journalist, that the Coalition had 'effectively swapped all the bold legacy promises for grassroots sport for a two-week jamboree that will make the nation feel a bit better about itself'.[14] On the eve of Britain hosting the world's premier sporting festival in 2012, there seemed little prospect of achieving in the decade to follow what the Labour Culture Secretary Ben Bradshaw called the permanent stitching together of the bonds between school, community and elite sport. Britain had experienced a 'silent sporting revolution' since 1945; but anything approaching a 'loud revolution' would have to wait.

Chronology of Main Events

August 1944

Education Act: prompts development of PE in state schools and gives Ministry of Education powers to fund improvements in community recreation

July 1945

Landslide election victory for Labour; Prime Minister Clement Attlee re-elected with smaller majority in 1950

July–August 1948

Olympic Games held in London

October 1951

Conservatives win general election, starting a period of 13 years in power

March 1952

Formation of the Parliamentary Sports Committee

October 1956

Publication of *Britain in the World of Sport* by Birmingham University academics

September 1957

Central Council of Physical Recreation appoints committee under Sir John Wolfenden

September 1960

Publication of *Sport and the Community* (the 'Wolfenden Report on Sport')

December 1962

Lord Hailsham appointed Minister with special responsibility for sport

October 1964

After Harold Wilson becomes Prime Minister, Denis Howell becomes Britain's first 'Minister for Sport' in the 1964–70 Labour government

February 1965

Creation of the Advisory Sports Council

November 1966

Publication of *Sports Council: A Report*, the first major review of the Council's work;
Establishment of Regional Sports Councils

May–June 1970

Culmination of controversy about proposed tour to England by South African cricketers; Election of Edward Heath's Conservative government

February 1972

Formal creation of an executive Sports Council and launch of 'Sport for All' campaign

February and October 1974

Two general elections in quick succession result in Labour returning to power;
Local government reorganization encourages growth of large leisure services departments

August 1975

Department of the Environment White Paper, *Sport and Recreation*

July 1977

Gleneagles agreement on sporting links with South Africa

January–July 1980

Moscow Olympics: British Olympic Association and most British competitors refuse to comply with requests to boycott games by Conservative Prime Minister Margaret Thatcher, elected in 1979

September 1982

Sports Council publishes *Sport in the Community – The Next Ten Years*

May 1985

Deaths of Italian supporters at European cup final prompts wave of government initiatives to tackle football hooliganism

October 1988

Sports Council publishes *Sport in the Community – Into the Nineties*

November 1990

John Major succeeds Thatcher as Prime Minister

April 1992

Creation of the Department of National Heritage (DNH), with oversight of sport

November 1994

Launch of National Lottery, bringing substantial extra investment into sport

July 1995

DNH policy statement, *Sport: Raising the Game*

May 1997

Tony Blair elected Prime Minister as head of 'New Labour' administration

July 1997

Creation of the Department for Culture, Media and Sport (DCMS)

May 2000

DCMS policy statement, *A Sporting Future for All*

November 2004

Hunting with Dogs Act becomes law, ending long controversy over foxhunting

July 2005

London wins race to host the 2012 Olympic Games

June 2007

Gordon Brown replaces Blair as Prime Minister;
Revised Olympic budget outlined by government at over £9 billion

May 2010

Labour defeated after three terms in power and replaced by Conservative–Liberal Democrat coalition government led by David Cameron

27 July –12 August 2012

London Olympics

Notes

(Place of publication is London unless otherwise specified)

Introduction

1. Tony Blair, *A Journey* (Hutchinson, 2010), pp. 546–7.
2. Cited in A. Rawnsley, *The End of the Party* (Penguin, 2010), p. 327.
3. Blair, *A Journey*, p. 550.
4. Cited in M. Lee, *The Race for the 2012 Olympics. The Inside Story of How London Won the Bid* (Virgin Books, 2006), pp. 155 and 158.
5. J. Hampton, *The Austerity Olympics. When the Games Came to London in 1948* (Aurum, 2008); R. Haynes, 'The BBC, Austerity and Broadcasting the 1948 Olympics', *International Journal of the History of Sport*, 27, 6 (2010), pp. 1029–46.
6. S. Rous, *Football Worlds. A Lifetime in Sport* (Faber and Faber, 1978), p. 103. See also J. H. Thomas, *My Story* (1937) and G. Rosen (ed.), *Dictionary of Labour Biography* (2001), pp. 569–73.
7. L. Allison, (ed.), *The Politics of Sport* (Manchester, 1986) and (ed.), *The Changing Politics of Sport* (Manchester, 1993); J. Hargreaves, *Sport, Power and Culture: A Social and Historical Analysis of Popular Sports in Britain* (Cambridge: Polity Press, 1986); I. Henry, *The Politics of Leisure Policy* (Basingstoke: Palgrave, 2001 edn); B. Houlihan, especially *The Government and Politics of Sport* (Routledge, 1991), *Sport, Policy and Politics: A Comparative Analysis* (Routledge, 1997) and, with A. White, *The Politics of Sports Development: Development of Sport or Development Through Sport* (Routledge, 2002).
8. M. Polley, *Moving the Goalposts. A History of Sport and Society since 1945* (Routledge, 1998); R. Holt and T. Mason, *Sport in Britain 1945–2000* (Oxford: Blackwell, 2000); J. Hill, *Sport, Leisure & Culture in Twentieth-Century Britain* (Basingstoke: Palgrave, 2002).
9. D. Bloyce and A. Smith, *Sport Policy and Development: An Introduction* (Routledge, 2009), p. 30.
10. One important work which covers the 1960–90 period is J. Coghlan with I. Webb, *Sport and British Politics since 1960* (Brighton: Falmer, 1990). John Coghlan wrote as a one time Deputy Director of the Sports Council. His views are much influenced by this experience

and his book was written without the benefit of access of government papers at the National Archives.

11. J. Hill, *Sport in History. An Introduction* (Basingstoke, 2011): chapter one is entitled 'Sport Matters'.

1 Sport and Politics in Austerity Britain, 1945–51

1. P. Addison, *Now the War is Over. A Social History of Britain 1945–51* (BBC and Jonathan Cape, 1985), p. 113.
2. Addison, *Now the War is Over*, pp. 120–2.
3. J. Coghlan with Ida Webb, *Sport and British Politics since 1960* (Brighton: Falmer, 1990), p. 5; N. Baker, 'The Amateur Ideal in a Society of Equality: Change and Continuity in Post-Second World War British Sport 1945–48', *International Journal of the History of Sport*, 12, 1 (1995), pp. 99–126.
4. J. Hill, *Sport, Leisure & Culture in Twentieth-Century Britain* (Basingstoke: Palgrave, 2002), pp. 151 and 154.
5. R. Holt and T. Mason, *Sport in Britain, 1945–2000* (Oxford: Blackwell, 2000), pp. 29 and 147.
6. P. J. Beck, 'The British Government and the Olympic Movement: The 1948 London Olympics', *International Journal of the History of Sport*, 25, 5 (2008), pp. 615–47.
7. Hansard, *House of Commons Debates* (*HC Deb.*), fifth series (5s.), volume (v.) 419, 13 February 1946, column (c.) 85.
8. K. O. Morgan, *Labour in Power 1945–51* (Oxford: Clarendon Press, 1984), p. 54.
9. P. J. Beck, 'Confronting George Orwell: Philip Noel-Baker on International Sport, Particularly the Olympic Movement, as Peacemaker', *European Sports History Review*, 5 (2003), pp. 187–207. See also D. J. Whittaker, *Fighter for Peace: Philip Noel-Baker 1889–1982* (York: William Sessions Ltd, 1989).
10. Unsigned note to the Prime Minister, 28 February 1947: The National Archives (TNA), Public Record Office (PRO), Prime Minister's papers (PREM) 8/881.
11. 'Mid-Week Sporting Events', Memorandum by the Home Secretary, 12 March 1947, TNA: PRO Cabinet papers (CAB) 129/17.
12. *Daily Express*, 14 March 1947.
13. *The Times*, 14 March 1947.
14. Cabinet Secretary's notebook, 6 January 1948, TNA: PRO CAB 195/6.
15. *HC Deb.*, 5s, v.447, 19 February 1948, cc.257–8.
16. Addison, *Now the War is Over*, pp. 123–4. See also M. Clapson, *A Bit of a Flutter: Popular Gambling and English Society, c.1823–1961* (Manchester: Manchester University Press, 1992).

17. R. Munting, *An Economic and Social History of Gambling in Britain and the USA* (Manchester: Manchester University Press, 1996), p. 64.
18. 'Amendment of the Betting Laws', Memorandum by the Chancellor of the Exchequer, 5 November 1948, TNA: PRO CAB 129/30.
19. Addison, *Now the War is Over*, p. 123.
20. E. Griffin, *Blood Sport: Hunting in Britain since 1066* (New Haven and Yale University Press, 2007), pp. 183–4.
21. M. Tichelar, ' "Putting Animals into Politics": The Labour Party and Hunting in the First Half of the Twentieth Century', *Rural History*, 17, 2 (2006), pp. 213–25.
22. Correspondence from individuals and association in TNA: PRO Home Office (HO) papers 45/24297.
23. Cabinet minutes, 10 February 1949, TNA: PRO CAB 128/15; Cabinet Secretary's notebook, 10 February 1949, TNA: PRO CAB 195/7.
24. *HC Deb.*, 5s, v.461, 25 February 1949, cc.2167–235.
25. Tichelar, ' "Putting Animals into Politics" ', p. 225; Griffin, *Blood Sport*, pp. 184–5; R. H. Thomas, *The Politics of Hunting* (Aldershot: Gower, 1983), pp. 218–20.
26. B. Phillips, *The 1948 Olympics. How London Rescued the Games* (Cheltenham: SportsBooks Ltd, 2007), pp. 6–7.
27. J. Hampton, *Austerity Olympics. When the Games Came to London in 1948* (Aurum, 2008), p. 27.
28. Beck, 'British Government and the Olympic Movement', p. 621.
29. A. Bullock, *Ernest Bevin. Foreign Secretary* (Oxford: OUP, 1985 edn), pp. 239–40.
30. 'Olympic Games', Memorandum by the Foreign Secretary, 6 April 1946, TNA: PRO CAB 129/8.
31. Beck, 'British Government and the Olympic Movement', pp. 621–5.
32. R. Pearce (ed.), *Patrick Gordon Walker: Political Diaries 1932–71* (Historians' Press, 1991): 6 October 1947, p. 168.
33. Noel-Baker to Vice-Chancellor of Cambridge University, 10 June 1981: Noel-Baker papers, Churchill College, Cambridge, NBKR 6/23/1.
34. Note by Noel-Baker, 2 July 46, TNA: PRO Foreign Office (FO) papers, 371/548785.
35. Dalton to Noel-Baker, 12 July 47, Noel-Baker papers, NBKR 6/7/1; Noel-Baker to H. Wilson, 25 March 1947, cited in M. Rogan and M. Rogan, *Britain and the Olympic Games* (Leicester: Matador, 2011), p. 41.
36. 'Olympic Games', Memorandum by the Secretary of State for Air and the Secretary of State for Overseas Trade', 25 March 1947, TNA: PRO CAB 129/18.
37. Cabinet Secretary's notebook, 27 March 1947, TNA: PRO CAB 195/5; Cabinet minutes, 27 March 47, CAB128/9.

38. Holt and Mason, *Sport in Britain*, p. 28.
39. *Evening Standard*, 2 September 1947.
40. Noel-Baker to Sir Norman Brook, 25 September 1947, Noel-Baker papers, NBKR 6/6/1; Minutes of Organising and Executive Committee of the BOA, 2 and 30 September 1947: BOA archive, University of East London, BOA/1948/M/1/3.
41. Holt and Mason, *Sport in Britain*, pp. 30–1.
42. Phillips, *The 1948 Olympics*, pp. 10 and 17.
43. Cited in J. Hampton, *The Austerity Olympics. When the Games Came to London in 1948* (Aurum, 2008), p. 309.
44. *The Observer*, 17 August 1948.
45. *The Economist*, 21 August 1948.
46. Philip to 'My Dear Clem', 10 August 1948: Attlee papers, Bodleian Library, Oxford, MS Attlee dep. 73; 'The Olympic Games in Retrospect', BBC broadcast, 17 August 1948, copy in Noel-Baker papers, NBKR 6/6/1.
47. Beck, 'British Government and the Olympic Movement', p. 637. *Olympics*, pp. 7–8; *XIVth Olympiad London 1948: The Official Report of the Organising Committee for the XIV Olympiad 1948* (1951).
48. Holt and Mason, *Sport in Britain*, pp. 32–3.
49. P. C. McIntosh, *Physical Education in England since 1800* (1968), p. 208.
50. Memorandum by unnamed civil servant, 19 March 1947, TNA: PRO Ministry of Education (ED) papers, 34/80.
51. D. Kirk, *Defining Physical Education. The Social Construction of a School Subject in Post-war Britain* (Falmer, 1992), p. 85.
52. Holt and Mason, *Sport in Britain*, p. 22.
53. H. J. Evans, *Service to Sport: The Story of the CCPR, 1937–1975* (Pelham, 1975), pp. 65–72.
54. *HC Deb.*, 5s, v.456, 21 September 1948, c. 81; Addison, *Now the War is Over*, p. 135.
55. Evans, *Service to Sport*, p. 76.
56. *HC Deb.*, 5s, v.477, 18 July 1950, cc. 2031–2.
57. Holt and Mason, *Sport in Britain*, p. 146.

2 *Britain in the World of Sport,* 1951–59

1. D. E. Butler, *The British General Election of 1955* (1955), p. 15.
2. R. Cockett (ed.), *My Dear Max: The Letters of Brendan Bracken to Lord Beaverbrook, 1929–58* (Historian's Press, 1990): letter dated 15 January 1952, p. 129.
3. H. J. Evans, *Service to Sport, The Story of the CCPR, 1937–1975* (Pelham, 1975), pp. 77–9 and 91–3.
4. Memorandum by Mr F. Bray, 10 June 1953, TNA: PRO ED 169/6.

5. Miss K. A. Kennedy to Mr Bray, 3 February 1954, TNA: PRO ED 169/5; 'Interview Memorandum', 25 February 1954, TNA: PRO ED 169/6.
6. *HC Deb.*, 5s, v.530, 22 July 1954, cc. 133–4.
7. *HC Deb.*, 5s, v.494, 20 November 1951, c. 37.
8. 'Sport Finance in Various Countries', Memo by K. S. Duncan, Parliamentary Sports Committee (PSC) minutes, 17 February 1959, Noel-Baker papers NBKR 6/53.
9. *The Times*, 4 August 1952.
10. *The Times*, 9 August 1952.
11. For example to G. de Freitas, 4 December 1951, Noel-Baker papers, NBKR 6/9.
12. Evans, *Service to Sport*, p. 147; PSC minutes, March 1952, BOA archive, BOA/M/5/2.
13. Noel-Baker to W. T. Taylor, 26 March 1953; PSC minutes, 17 November 1953, Noel-Baker papers, NBKR 6/9.
14. Noel-Baker to C. Morrison, 3 April 1970, Noel-Baker papers, NBKR 6/52.
15. *HC Deb.*, 5s, v.515, 20 May 1953, cc. 2089–114.
16. *HC Deb.*, 5s, v.531, 28 July 1954, cc. 601–30.
17. *HC Deb.*, 5s, v. 531, 21 October 1954, cc. 1381–2.
18. *HC Deb.*, 5s, v. 531, 28 October 1954, cc. 2266–76. For the comment on Vosper, see *Daily Telegraph*, 26 August 1959.
19. PSC minutes, 9 March 1955, Noel-Baker papers, NBKR 6/53.
20. Conservative Party, *United for Peace and Progress: The Conservative and Unionist Party's Policy. A Personal Statement by the Prime Minister* (1955).
21. Labour Party, *Forward with Labour* (1955).
22. Untitled speech, May 1955, Noel-Baker papers, NBKR 6/9.
23. *New Statesman*, 4 June 1955.
24. *HC Deb.*, 5s, v. 551, 17 April 1956, cc. 895–912.
25. Noel-Baker to S. Duncan, 18 January 1957, Noel-Baker papers, NBKR 6/53.
26. *Daily Herald*, 8 March 1957.
27. *HC Deb.*, 5s, v. 568, 18 April 1957, cc. 2093–4.
28. Evans, *Service to Sport*, p. 93.
29. M. Baumert, A. D. Munrow, B. N. Knapp et al., *Britain in the World of Sport* (Birmingham: Physicla Education Department, Birmingham University, 1956), pp. 7–12, 24–5 and 37.
30. *Britain in the World of Sport*, pp. 11, 44–7 and 50.
31. *Britain in the World of Sport*, pp. 58–9.
32. *Britain in the World of Sport*, pp. 63–8.
33. Evans, *Service to Sport*, pp. 93–4.
34. CCPR, *Sport & the Community. The Report of the Wolfenden Committee on Sport* (1960), p. 1.

35. Evans, *Service to Sport*, pp. 145–6.
36. Wolfenden to Noel-Baker, 3 March and 14 November 1958, Noel-Baker papers, NBKR 6/44/1 and 6/53.
37. PSC minutes, 4 December 1958, Noel-Baker papers, NBKR 6/53.
38. Draft of letter to MPs, 17 December 1958, Noel-Baker papers, NBKR 6/53; Evans, *Service to Sport*, p. 148.
39. 'Wolfenden Committee on Sport', Memorandum by E. B. H Baker (of the Adult Education and Youth Service Branch), 18 December 1958, TNA: PRO, ED 169/73.
40. Evans, *Service to Sport*, p. 150.
41. Conservative Political Centre, *The Challenge of Leisure* (1959), pp. 11–13.
42. *HC Deb.*, 5s, v. 596, 27 November 1958, cc. 551–2.
43. Conservative Party, *The Next Five Years* (1959).
44. 'Policy Statement on Recreation and Leisure', Confidential Labour Party Report No. 535, April 1959, cited in D. Anthony (compiler), *Man of Sport, Man of Peace. Collected Speeches and Essays of Philip Noel-Baker, Olympic Statesman 1889–1992* (Sports Editions Ltd, 1991), p.81.
45. Labour Party, *Leisure for Living* (1959), pp. 41–3.
46. Labour Party, *Britain Belongs to You* (1959).
47. *News Chronicle*, 26 August 1959.
48. *New Statesman*, 5 September 1959.
49. *Spectator*, 28 August 1959.
50. *HC Deb.*, 5s, v. 595, 20 November 1958, cc. 1322–3.
51. *HC Deb.*, 5s, v. 608, 2 July 1959, cc. 595–6; PSC minutes, 4 December 1958, Noel-Baker papers, NBKR 6/53.

3 The Impact of the Wolfenden Report, 1960–64

1. CCPR, *Sport & the Community, The Report of the Wolfenden Committee on Sport* (CCPR, 1960), pp. 6, 23 and 109–12.
2. R. Holt and T. Mason, *Sport in Britain, 1945–2000* (Oxford: Blackwell, 2000), pp. 148–9.
3. M. Roche, 'Sport and Community: Rhetoric and Reality in the Development of British Sport Policy', in J. C. Binfield and J. Stevenson (eds), *Sport, Culture and Politics* (Sheffield: Academic Press, 1993), p. 92.
4. J. Coghlan with I. Webb, *Sport and British Politics since 1960* (Brighton: Falmer, 1990), pp. 8–12.
5. Speech by Wolfenden at the Waldorf Hotel, London, 28 September 1960: Lord Wolfenden papers, Reading University, MS5311.
6. Noel-Baker to David [Marquess of Exeter], 14 September 1960, Noel-Baker papers, NBKR 6/44/2; to Sandy Duncan, 22 October 1960, NBKR 6/53.

7. 'Sport and the Community. The View of the CCPR', 21 December 1960, Wolfenden papers, MS5311.

8. 'The Report of the Wolfenden Committee on Sport. Analysis of Press Comment', Justin Evans, 18 October 1960, Wolfenden papers, MS 5311.

9. Eccles to Mr Part, 29 September 60, TNA PRO ED 169/73; H. J. Evans, *Service to Sport: The Story of the CCPR, 1937–1975* (Pelham, 1975), p. 154.

10. 'Sport and the Community', Memorandum by Baker, 5 October 1960, TNA: PRO ED 169/73.

11. J. S. Arthur, Principal Private Secretary, to the Minister, 6 October 1960, TNA: PRO ED 169/73.

12. J. Catlow to the Minister, 7 October 1960, Ministry of Housing and Local Government (HLG) papers 120/268.

13. 'Draft Memorandum for Home Affairs Committee', Ministry of Education, 19 October 1960, TNA: PRO ED 169/73.

14. Catlow to Minister, 25 November 1960, TNA: PRO HLG 120/268.

15. Memorandum by J. F. Embling, 13 December 1960, TNA: PRO ED 169/73.

16. Treasury note to Mr Hubback, 9 February 1961, Treasury (T) papers, T 227/1572.

17. J. S. Arthur Memorandum, 16 January 1961, TNA: PRO ED 136/910.

18. *Daily Telegraph*, 3 February 1961; *Daily Express*, 3 February 1961.

19. Macmillan to Tim Bligh, 6 February 1961, TNA: PRO PREM 11/4845.

20. Note by R.H. Stone, 27 January 1961, TNA: PRO ED 136/910.

21. *HL Deb.*, 5.s, v.228, 15 February 1961, cc. 815–80.

22. *The Observer*, 19 February 1961.

23. *The Times*, 25 and 28 February 1961.

24. PSC minutes, 28 February 1961 and 27 February 1962, Noel-Baker papers, NBKR 6/53.

25. Catlow to Mr Gordon, 17 March 1961, TNA: PRO HLG 120/268.

26. Baker Memorandum, 19 April 1961, TNA: PRO ED 169/73.

27. Denis Howell, *Made in Birmingham* (Queen Anne Press, 1990), p. 109.

28. *HC Deb.*, 5s. v. 639, 28 April 1961, cc. 828–63.

29. Evans, *Service to Sport*, p. 156.

30. H.M. Treasury, 'Sport and Physical Recreation. Report of a Working Party by Officials', 8 June 1961, TNA: PRO ED 169/73.

31. Noel-Baker to David [Marquess of Exeter], 7 July 1961, Noel-Baker papers, NBKR 6/10/1.

32. J. P. Carwell to Mr Hubback, 6 March 1962, TNA PRO T 227/1573.

33. 'Betting and Gaming Bill', Memorandum by the Home Secretary, 20 September 1957, TNA: PRO CAB 129/89; Cabinet conclusions, 7 October 1957, TNA: PRO CAB 128/31.

34. R. Munting, *An Economic and Social History of Gambling in Britain and the USA* (Manchester: Manchester University Press, 1996), pp. 44–6.
35. Note by Bligh, 23 March 1962, TNA: PRO PREM 11/4845.
36. PSC minutes 27 February 1962, Noel-Baker papers, NBKR 6/53.
37. *HC Deb.*, 5s., v. 659, 8 May 1962, cc. 225–9.
38. Noel-Baker to Duncan, 24 July 1962, Noel-Baker papers, NBKR 6/53.
39. D. D. Molyneux, *Central Government Aid to Sport and Physical Recreation in Countries of Western Europe* (Birmingham, Physical Education Department: Birmingham University 1962), esp. pp. 8–20 and 37.
40. *HL Deb.*, 5s., v. 244, 6 November 1962, c. 203.
41. *HL Deb.*, 5s., v. 245, 20 December 1962, cc. 1251–5.
42. Coghlan, *Sport and British Politics*, p. 12.
43. 'Wolfenden Report on Sport', Memorandum by the Chief Secretary to the Treasury, 18 October 1962, TNA: PRO CAB 129/111; Macmillan to Michael Cary, 31 October 1962, TNA: PRO PREM 11/4845.
44. Cabinet conclusions, 1 November 1962, TNA: PRO CAB 128/36.
45. Lord Hailsham, *The Door Wherein I Went* (Collins, 1975), p. 207.
46. G. Lewis, *Lord Hailsham. A Life* (Jonathan Cape, 1997), p. 197; Lord Hailsham, *A Sparrow's Flight* (Collins, 1990), p. 335.
47. Note by D. E. Morgan, 4 December 1962, TNA: PRO ED 169/74.
48. Note by 'T. B.', 5 December 1962, TNA: PRO ED 169/74.
49. Hailsham, *Door Wherein*, pp. 207–8. The extensive collection of Hailsham's Papers at Churchill College, Cambridge, appear to contain nothing relating to sport.
50. 'Sport and Recreation', minutes of meeting held in the Lord President's room, 16 January 1963, TNA: PRO PREM 11/4845.
51. K. Couzens to C. Herzig, 19 December 1962, TNA: PRO ED 169/74.
52. *HL Deb.*, 5s., v. 250, 22 May 1963, cc. 385–7.
53. 'Control of Expenditure on Sport', Memorandum by Miss Toombs, Treasury to Mr Hodges, 9 June 1965, TNA: PRO T 227/2416.
54. *HL Deb.*, 5s., v. 250, 22 May 1963, cc. 288–389.
55. Evans, *Service to Sport*, p. 158.
56. *The Times* 26 June 1964; *HL Deb.*, 5s., v. 259, 9 July 1964, cc.1089–92.
57. *HC Deb.*, 5s., v. 697, 22 June 1964, cc. 38–101.
58. *The Times*, 23 June 1964; Howell, *Made in Birmingham*, p. 117.
59. B. Houlihan and A. White, *The Politics of Sports Development: Development of Sport or Development Through Sport* (Routledge, 2002), p. 18.
60. P. Shore to Noel-Baker, 2 August 1963, Noel-Baker papers, NBKR 6/54: attached to this letter from Peter Shore is a report of Labour's Working Party on Sport.
61. Hailsham, *Sparrow's Flight*, p. 336.
62. Howell, *Made in Birmingham*, p. 147.

63. 'Memorandum on CCPR Policy Concerning National Development in Sport', A. D. Munrow, 16 October 1963, Noel-Baker papers, NBKR 6/52.
64. Coghlan, *Sport and British Politics*, p. 15.
65. Conservative Party, *Prosperity with a Purpose* (1964).
66. Labour Party, *The New Britain* (1964); Hailsham, *Sparrow's Flight*, p. 336; Howell, *Made in Birmingham*, p. 143.

4　Creating and Running the Sports Council, 1964–67

1. For contrasting views see, for example, D. Howell, *British Social Democracy. A Study in Development and Decay* (1976) and L. Baston, 'The Age of Wilson 1955–79', in B. Brivati and R. Heffernan (eds), *The Labour Party. A Centenary History* (Basingstoke, 2000).
2. P. McIntosh and V. Charlton, *The Impact of Sport for All Policy 1966–84* (Sports Council, 1985), p. 9.
3. Miss Moody to B. S. Smith, 13 May 1965, TNA: PRO T 227/1567; 'Report of the Sport and Recreation Policy Group', 26 June 1969: Conservative Party archive (CPA), Bodleian Library, Oxford, ACP 3/19.
4. W. Mallalieu to Wilson, 13 May 1964: Harold Wilson papers, Bodliean Library, Oxford, MS Wilson, c. 884.
5. H. Wilson, *The Labour Government 1964–1970. A Personal Record* (Weidenfeld & Nicolson ,1971), p. 10.
6. D. Howell, *Made in Birmingham* (Queen Anne Press, 1990), pp. 140–3.
7. N. Macfarlane with M. Herd, *Sport and Politics: A World Divided* (Willow Books, 1996), pp. 63–5.
8. Howell, *Made in Birmingham*, p. 152.
9. Howell, *Made in Birmingham*, pp. 140–5 and 150.
10. Howell, *Made in Birmingham*, pp. 146–8.
11. Howell, *Made in Birmingham*, pp. 149–51.
12. Howell, *Made in Birmingham*, p. 154
13. Wilson, *Labour Government*, p. 59.
14. *HC Deb.*, 5s., v. 703, 4 December 1964, cc. 928–1022; *The Guardian*, 5 December 1964.
15. H. J. Evans, H. J., *Service to Sport: The Story of the CCPR, 1937–1975* (Pelham, 1975), pp. 205–7.
16. Howell, *Made in Birmingham*, pp. 155–7.
17. H. H. Browne to Miss Fox, 19 November 1964, TNA: PRO HLG 120/888.
18. Browne to Fox, 8 January 1965; Miss Fox to Mr Waddell, 13 January 1965; Mr Waddell to Secretary, 15 January 1965, TNA: PRO HLG 120/888.

19. Lang to Howell, 20 November 1964, TNA: PRO ED 136/955.
20. *HC Deb.*, 5s., v.705, 3 February 1965, cc. 1081–6.
21. *The Times*, 4 February 1965.
22. Howell, *Made in Birmingham*, pp. 152 and 163; notes on Sports Council, undated, TNA: PRO ED 169/127.
23. Minutes of the Sports Council, 6 April 1965, TNA: PRO ED 169/127.
24. Miss Moody to B. S. Smith, 13 May 1965, TNA: PRO T 227/1567.
25. Howell, *Made in Birmingham*, pp. 164–6.
26. Howell, *Made in Birmingham*, pp. 146 and 159–63.
27. C. H. Hodges to Mr Lee, 16 December 1964, TNA: PRO T 227/1567.
28. J. F. Embling, Finance Under-Secretary, DES, to J. L. Rampton, Treasury, 16 March 1965, TNA: PRO T 227/1567.
29. Miss Moody to Hodges, 12 May 1965 & Rampton to Smith, 13 May 65, TNA: PRO T 227/1567. The *Observer*, 28 February 1965 said of the FA's lack of preparedness that it was 'a shabby story of dithering and neglect'.
30. Note of meeting with NPFA, 29 April 1965, TNA: PRO ED 169/127.
31. *Daily Telegraph*, 15 July 1965.
32. Rampton to Hodges, 15 July 1965, TNA: PRO T 227/2416.
33. Toombs to Moody, 23 July 1965; Moody to Mr Painter, 28 July 1965; M. S. Buckley to Moody, 16 August 1965, TNA: PRO T 227/2416.
34. R. F. Clifton to Mr Mackay, 23 August 1965, TNA: PRO T 227/2416.
35. Minutes of Secretary of State's Group, 15 November 1965, TNA: PRO ED 136/955.
36. *H. L. Deb.*, 5s., v. 271, 8 December 1965, cc. 296–378.
37. Evans, *Service to Sport*, p. 208.
38. *The Times*, 15 March 1966.
39. 'Report of the Policy Study Group on Leisure', circulated 4 July 1965, CPA ACP 3/12.
40. 'Report of Policy Study Group', July 1965.
41. 'Report of Policy Study Group', July 1965.
42. Minutes of Advisory Committee on Policy, 7 July 1965, ACP 2/2; Bow Group, *A Better Country: A Policy Study on the Use of Leisure by a Group of Conservatives under the Chairmanship of Christopher Chataway* (CPC, 1966).
43. Wilson, *Labour Government*, p. 175.
44. Conservative Party, *Action Not Words: The New Conservative Programme* (1966).
45. *The Times*, 6 January 1966; Labour Party, *Time for Decision* (1966)
46. Crosland to Prime Minister, 13 April 1966, TNA: PRO T 227/2416.
47. R. Crossman, *The Diaries of a Cabinet Minister*, Vol. 1, *Minister of Housing 1964–66* (Hamish Hamilton and Jonathan Cape, 1975): entry for 23 June 1966, p. 547.

48. Howell, *Made in Birmingham*, pp. 171–3.
49. S. Rous, *Football Worlds. A Lifetime in Sport* (Faber and Faber, 1978), p. 191.
50. Howell, *Made in Birmingham*, p. 175.
51. 'Sport', Memorandum by Rampton, 1 July 1966, TNA: PRO T 227/2416.
52. *The Guardian*, 15 November 1966; *The Times*, 15 November 1966.
53. *HC Deb.*, 5s., v. 738, 20 December 1966, cc. 1195–254.
54. Coghlan, John with Ida Webb, *Sport and British Politics since 1960* (Brighton: Falmer, 1990), p. 22.
55. P. Jay memorandum to Mr Phelps, 27 January 1967, TNA: PRO T 227/2416.
56. 'Sport', Note for the Record' 2 February 1967, no author, TNA: PRO T 227/2416.
57. Jay memorandum to Phelps, 27 January 1967, T 227/2416.

5   'Ballyhoo' about Sport in the Late 1960s

1. PSC minutes, 6 July 1967, Noel-Baker papers, NBKR 6/53.
2. *The Guardian*, 26 May 1968.
3. *HC Deb.*, 5s., v. 788, 15 October 1969, cc. 559–70; D. Howell, *Made in Birmingham*, (Queen Anne Press, 1990), pp. 191–2.
4. Howell, *Made in Birmingham*, p. 186.
5. Noel-Baker to Lord Hunt, 9 October 1967, Noel-Baker papers, NBKR 6/53. Hunt turned down the offer owing to other commitments.
6. J. Callaghan, *Time & Chance* (Collins, 1987), p. 193: by the 1980s this measure was reaping almost £745 million per year for the Exchequer.
7. W. M. Schwab to Mr Gilbert 10 April 1969; S. J. B. Hurden to Schwab, 16 April 1969, TNA: PRO HLG 120/1303; *The Sports Council. A Review 1966–69* (1969).
8. Howell, *Made in Birmingham*, pp. 186 and 193.
9. Howell, *Made in Birmingham*, p. 199.
10. H. Wilson, *The Labour Government, 1964–1970. A Personal Record* (Weidenfeld & Nicolson, 1971), p. 714.
11. Howell, *Made in Birmingham*, pp. 199–200.
12. H. J. Evans, *Service to Sport: The Story of the CCPR, 1937–1975* (Pelham, 1975), p. 214.
13. For the background, see P. May, *The Rebel Tours: Cricket's Crisis of Conscience* (Cheltenham: SportsBooks, 2009).
14. R. Fieldhouse, *Anti-Apartheid: A History of the Movement in Britain. A Study in Pressure Group Politics* (Merlin Press, 2005), pp. 160–1 and 168–9.

15. *HC Deb.*, 5s., v. 740, 30 January 1967, cc. 33–6.
16. Howell to Prime Minister, 'The D'Oliveira Affair', 11 April 1969, TNA: PRO PREM 13/2995.
17. Howell, *Made in Birmingham*, pp. 201–2; Howell to Prime Minister, 11 April 1969, PREM 13/2995.
18. P. Oborne, *Cricket and Conspiracy* (Little Brown, 2004), p. 141.
19. Howell to Prime Minister, 11 April 1969, PREM 13/2995.
20. Howell, *Made in Birmingham*, p. 204.
21. P. Hain, *Don't Play with Apartheid: The Background to the Stop the Seventy Tour Campaign* (Allen and Unwin, 1971), pp. 121–2.
22. Hain, *Don't Play with Apartheid*, p. 127.
23. *The Guardian*, 6 November 1969.
24. R. Hattersley to Prime Minister, 3 and 11 November 1969, TNA: PRO PREM 13/2964.
25. Hain, *Don't Play with Apartheid*, p. 148; P. May, *Rebel Tours: Cricket's Crisis of Conscience* (Cheltenham: SportsBooks), pp. 13–14.
26. J. Bailey, *Conflicts in Cricket* (Metheun, 1989), pp. 48–56.
27. May, *Rebel Tours*, pp. 16–19; Hain, *Don't Play with Apartheid*, p. 132.
28. Fieldhouse, *Anti-Apartheid*, p. 97
29. May, *Rebel Tours*, p. 25.
30. T. Benn, *Office Without Power. Diaries 1968–72* (Arrow Books, 1989): entry for 8 March 1970, p. 247.
31. R. Crossman, *The Diaries of a Cabinet Minister*, Vol. 3, *Secretary of State for Social Services, 1968–70* (Hamish Hamilton and Jonathan Cape, 1977): entry for 8 March 1970, p. 846.
32. Howell to Prime Minister, 28 April 1970; Callaghan to Prime Minister, 30 April 1970, TNA: PRO PREM 13/3499.
33. Hain, *Don't Play with Apartheid*, p. 181.
34. Leader's Consultative Committee (LCC) minutes, 22 and 27 April 1970, CPA, LCC 1/2/20.
35. Wilson, *Labour Government*, pp. 783–4.
36. 'Projected Visit of South African Cricket Team', Memorandum by the Minister of State, 5 May 1970; Howell to Prime Minister, 6 May 1970, TNA: PRO PREM 13/3499.
37. Howell, *Made in Birmingham*, pp. 206–7.
38. Benn, *Office Without Power*, 17 May 1970, p. 283.
39. Hain, *Don't Play with Apartheid*, p. 189.
40. 'South African Cricket Tour', Private Office Memorandum, 29 May 1970, TNA: PRO PREM 13/3499; Callaghan, *Time & Chance*, pp. 262–3.
41. Hain, *Don't Play with Apartheid*, pp. 192–4.
42. Fieldhouse, *Anti-Apartheid*, p. 99.
43. Howell, *Made in Birmingham*, p. 209.

44. Wilson, *Labour Government*, p. 785.
45. D. Butler and M. Pinto-Duschinsky, *The British General Election of 1970* (London and Basingstoke: Macmillan, 1971), p. 141.
46. Minutes of Sports Council, 26 March 1968, TNA: PRO ED 169/128.
47. Evans, *Service to Sport*, pp. 215–16.
48. 'Report of Sport and Recreation Group', 26 June 1969, CPA, ACP 3/19, pp. 1–4. The group contained five MPs as well as Lords Aberdare and Porchester.
49. LCC minutes, 21 July 1969, CPA, LCC 1/2/17.
50. Advisory Committee on Policy minutes, 23 July 1969, CPA LCC 1/2/20.
51. Conservative Party, *A Better Tomorrow* (1970).
52. 'An Assessment of the Labour Government's Record on Sport', Peter Walker, 21 April 1970, CPA LCC 1/2/20.
53. LCC minutes 27 April 1970, CPA LCC 1/2/20.
54. Labour Party, *Now Britain's Strong – Let's Make It Great to Live In* (1970).
55. Butler and Pinto-Duschinsky, *General Election of 1970*, p. 166.
56. Howell, *Made in Birmingham*, p. 212; Crosland cited in *The Guardian*, 21 April 2010.
57. Butler and Pinto-Duschinsky, *General Election of 1970*, pp. 166 and 334–5.
58. Wilson, *Labour Government*, p. 714; H. Wilson, *Final Term. The Labour Government 1974–1976* (Weidenfeld & Nicolson, 1979), p. 18.
59. Evans, *Service to Sport*, p. 217.
60. The reference to Labour's 'ballyhoo' about sport was made by Sir Theo Constantine in a discussion of Morrison's 1969 Report: Advisory Committee on Policy minutes, 23 July 1969, CPA LCC 1/2/20.
61. A Conservative study group on the arts (which made comparisons with spending on sport) claimed c. £17 million of central government money went to the arts in 1969–70, and that this represented 0.15 per cent of total expenditure. This compared with c. £2.5 million from the Exchequer for sport, though local authorities contributed an estimated £25 million on capital and current accounts for sport. See 'Report of the Policy Group on the Arts', 1969, CPA, LCC 1/2/17.

6 Battling for 'Sport and Recreation' in the 1970s

1. N. Tiratsoo, ' "You've Never Had it So Bad"?: Britain in the 1970s', in N. Tiratsoo (ed.), *From Blitz to Blair. A New History of Britain since 1939* (Weidenfeld & Nicolson, 1997), pp. 163–4.
2. Viscount Cobham: *HL Deb.* 5s. v.352, 13 June 1974, cc. 618–20; the Cobham Report is discussed more fully later in this chapter.

3. J. Coghlan with I. Webb, *Sport and British Politics since 1960* (Brighton: Falmer, 1990), p. 127.
4. D. Howell, *Made in Birmingham*, (Queen Anne Press, 1990), pp. 212–13.
5. *HC Deb.*, 5s., v. 818, 10 June 1971, cc. 365–7.
6. Coghlan, *Sport and British Politics*, p. 128.
7. Howell, *Made in Birmingham*, pp. 213–16.
8. Coghlan, *Sport and British Politics*, p. 127.
9. *HC Deb.*, 5s., v. 821, 15 July 1971, cc. 811–72.
10. H. J. Evans, *Service to Sport: The Story of the CCPR, 1937–1975* (Pelham, 1975), pp. 219–22.
11. S. Rous, *Football Worlds. A Lifetime in Sport* (Faber and Faber, 1978), p. 206.
12. Minutes of AGM of the CCPR, 4 November 1971, copy in Noel-Baker papers, NBKR 6/4/21.
13. Evans, *Service to Sport*, pp. 225–6.
14. Howell, *Made in Birmingham*, pp. 217–22.
15. The Sports Council, *Sports Council Annual Report 1972–73* (1973), p. 5.
16. R. Bannister, *The First Four Minutes* (Stroud: Sutton Publishing, 2004 edn), p. 218.
17. Coghlan, *Sport and British Politics*, pp. 66–7 and 82–3.
18. Coghlan, *Sport and British Politics*, p. 127.
19. *HC Deb.*, 5s., v. 821, 15 July 1971, cc. 811–72.
20. Figures cited in Department of the Environment (DoE), *Sport and Recreation*, Cmd. 6200 (1975), Appendix.
21. Coghlan, *Sport and British Politics*, p. 67.
22. J. Crocker to Mr Jacobs, 3 August 1972, DoE papers, TNA: PRO AT 60/1.
23. Note of meeting held on 3 August 1972, TNA: PRO AT 60/1. See also Bannister's speech as reported in *The Times*, 1 November 1974.
24. 'Increased Expenditure in Sport', Memorandum by Eldon Griffiths, February 1973; A. T. Baker to Mr Hiscock, 12 February 1973, TNA: PRO AT 60/1.
25. G. Rippon to A. Barber, 11 July 1973, TNA: PRO AT 60/1.
26. 'Notes of a Meeting on 15 August 1973 to Discuss Grant-in Aid to the Sports Council', TNA: PRO AT 60/1.
27. G. Rippon to P. Jenkin 14 September and 4 October 1973, TNA: PRO AT 60/1.
28. *First and Second Reports from the Select Committee of the House of Lords on Sport and Leisure* (1973).
29. *HL Deb.*, 5s., v. 352, 13 June 1974, cc. 618–720. See also the emphasis on increased spending in Greenwood's speech – 'David' to 'Tony', 9 June 1974: Greenwood papers, Bodleian Library, Oxford, Ms Eng c. 6331.

30. *HC Deb.*, 5s., v.867, 18 January 1974, cc.1076–161.
31. Conservative Party, *Firm Action for a Fair Britain*; Labour Party, *Let us Work Together*; Liberal Party, *Change the Face of Britain* (1974).
32. *Observer* journalist Andrew Rawnsley, cited in K. Jefferys, *Finest and Darkest Hours: The Decisive Events in British Politics from Churchill to Blair* (2002), p. 181.
33. Howell, *Made in Birmingham*, pp. 227–31.
34. Coghlan, *Sport and British Politics*, p. 130.
35. Howell, *Made in Birmingham*, pp. 230–1.
36. Howell, *Made in Birmingham*, p. 232.
37. *The Times*, 31 October 1974.
38. Howell, *Made in Birmingham*, p. 222.
39. Crosland to Prime Minister, 'Coordination of Recreational Policies', 5 June 1974, TNA: PRO PREM 16/433; *HC Deb.*, 5s., v. 877, cc. 102–3, 16 July 1974.
40. Howell, *Made in Birmingham*, p. 233.
41. Coghlan, *Sport and British Politics*, pp. 128–9.
42. C. H. Judd to C. Freeman, 19 December 1974, TNA: PRO T 341/819.
43. Howell to Dr John Gilbert, 13 January 1975, TNA: PRO AT 60/2.
44. 'Note of Meeting with the Labour Party Sport Group', 29 January 1975; 'Charities, Sports and Performing Arts', Memorandum by the Financial Secretary, 7 February 1975, TNA: PRO T 341/819.
45. Wilson to Chancellor of the Exchequer, 24 February 1975, TNA: PRO PREM 16/696.
46. 'Resources for Sport', C. H. Judd, 7 March 1975, TNA: PRO T 341/819.
47. *Sunday Times*, 9 March 1975.
48. 'Resources for Sport', Healey to Wilson, 11 March 1975, TNA: PRO T 341/819; Howell to Wilson, 27 March 1975, TNA PRO PREM 16/696.
49. Howell, *Made in Birmingham*, pp. 233–40.
50. DoE, *Sport and Recreation*, Cmd. 6200 (1975).
51. DoE, *Sport and Recreation* (1975); Minutes of Committee of Ministers and Officials, May 1975, TNA: PRO AT 26/56.
52. J. Barnett to Wilson, 11 July 1975, TNA: PRO PREM 16/432.
53. Howell to Wilson, 'White Paper on Sport and Recreation', 15 July 1975, TNA: PRO AT 26/56.
54. Robin Butler note, 16 July 1975, and Michael Scholar note, 1 August 1975, TNA: PRO PREM 16/432.
55. D. Sharpe to Mr Howell, 7 August 1975, TNA: PRO AT 26/56.
56. *The Times*, 8 August 1975.
57. *HC Deb.*, 5s., v. 929, 6 April 1977, cc. 1313–65.
58. Howell, *Made in Birmingham*, pp. 262–3.

59. e.g. *The Times*, 23 November 1977.
60. Howell, *Made in Birmingham*, pp. 254–8.
61. Coghlan, *Sport and British Politics*, pp. 128 and 136–40.
62. *The Times* 28 July 1978; Coghlan *Sport and British Politics*, p. 68.
63. Coghlan, *Sport and British Politics*, pp. 67–8.
64. *The Times*, 23 November 1977.
65. D. Anthony, *Sports Review Magazine*, July/August 1976.
66. E. Griffin, *Blood Sport: Hunting in Britain since 1066* (New Haven and Yale University Press, 2007), pp. 194–6.
67. Coghlan, *Sport and British Politics*, p. 133.
68. Howell, *Made in Birmingham*, p. 283.
69. Coghlan, *Sport and British Politics*, pp. 95–6.

7   The Olympics and International Sport

1. T. Taylor, 'Sport and International Relations: A Case of Mutual Neglect', in Allison (ed.), *The Politics of Sport* (Manchester: Manchester University Press, 1986), pp. 27–47, and 'Politics and the Olympic Spirit', in Allison (ed.), *The Politics of Sport*, p. 221. See also B. Houlihan, *Sport and International Politics* (Hemel Hempstead: Harvester Wheatsheaf, 1994).
2. Lord Killanin, *My Olympic Years* (Secker & Warburg, 1983), pp. 2–3.
3. *HL Deb.*, 5s., v. 288, 7 February 1968, cc. 1255–6.
4. M. Polley, 'Olympic Diplomacy: The British Government and the Projected 1940 Olympic Games', *International Journal of the History of Sport*, 9, 2 (1992), pp. 169–87. The 1940 Games, which never took place because of the outbreak of war, were subsequently removed from Tokyo by the IOC and awarded to Helsinki.
5. R. Kowalski and D. Porter, 'Political Football: Moscow Dynamo in Britain', *International Journal of the History of Sport*, 14, 2 (1997), pp. 100–21.
6. Cited in Anthony (compiler), *Man of Sport, Man of Peace, Collected Speeches and Essays of Philip Noel-Baker, Olympic Statesman 1889–1992* (Sports Editions Ltd, 1991), p. 89.
7. Noel-Baker to Eden, 23 February 1945, Noel-Baker papers, NBKR 6/3/1; Eden to Noel-Baker, 12 March 1945, TNA: PRO FO 371/47853; note by C. Warner, 7 March, TNA PRO FO 371/47853; P. J. Beck, 'Confronting George Orwell: Philip Noel-Baker on International Sport, Particularly the Olympic Movement, as Peacemaker', *European Sports History Review*, 5 (2003), pp. 189–97.
8. Mr Roberts, telegram to Foreign Office, 31 October 1945, TNA: PRO FO 371/47857.
9. George Orwell, 'The Sporting Spirit', *Tribune*, 14 December 1945, pp. 10–11.

10. Kowalski and Porter, 'Political Football', pp. 115–16.
11. Memorandum by D. K. Timms, 24 November 1965, TNA: PRO FO 371/181150. On this episode, see also M. Polley,'The Diplomatic Background to the 1966 Football World Cup', *The Sports Historian*, 18, 2 (1998), pp. 1–18.
12. Memo by Timms, 24 November 1965; Lang to E. Bolland, 25 November 1965, TNA: PRO FO 371/181150.
13. Bolland to Sir Walter Godfrey, 14 January 1966, TNA: PRO FO 371/181150.
14. Miss V. Beckett, Western Department, FO, to D. Gladstone, Bonn, 6 April 1966, TNA: PRO FO 371/187181.
15. D. Howell, *Made in Birmingham* (Queen Anne Press, 1990), pp. 171–2.
16. J. B. Denson to Godfrey, 12 August 1966, TNA: PRO FO 371/187181.
17. Polley, 'Diplomatic Background', pp. 5 and 13.
18. Cited in Beck, 'Confronting George Orwell', p. 210
19. G. Taplas to Mr Oakeshott, 'Chinese Representation at the Olympic Games', 11 June [1952], TNA: PRO FO 371/99371. In the event athletes from Chinese Taiwan (Formosa) withdrew from Games at the last minute in protest at allowing competitors from the People's Republic of China to take part.
20. G. E. Hall to Lord Burghley, 21 February 1952, TNA: PRO FO 371/98011.
21. Hall to P. J. E Male, Office of the UK High Commissioner, 27 February 1952, TNA: PRO FO 371/98011.
22. Summaries in TNA: PRO FO 371/100898.
23. Sir A. Noble to Sir A. Eden, 7 August 1952, TNA: PRO FO 371/100495.
24. 'Melbourne's Family Affair', *The Times*, 8 December 1956.
25. B. S. Laskey to Lord Home, 20 September 1960, TNA: PRO FO 371/153366.
26. Note by C. R. E. Brooke, 27 September 1960, TNA: PRO FO 371/153366.
27. J. Riordan, 'Elite Sport Policy in East and West', in L. Allison (ed.), *The Politics of Sport*, (Manchester: Manchester University Press, 1986), p. 80.
28. H. Cleaver, *Sporting Rhapsody* ((Hutchinson's Library, 1951), pp. 195–200; see also J. Hampton, *Austerity Olympics. When the Games Came to London in 1948* (Aurum, 2008), pp. 42–4.
29. *Sunday Dispatch*, 3 January 1960. He referred to one diving hopeful who lived in London but whose nearest indoor high-board for training was located in Cardiff.
30. CCPR, *Sport & the Community. The Report of the Wolfenden Committee on Sport* (1960), pp. 73–6.

31. Miss Startin to Mr Jones, 3 August 1967, TNA: PRO T 227/2414, for an account of the evolution of funding for international sport since the early 1960s.
32. Hailsham to Lord Home, 15 May 1963; J. Nicholls to Marquess of Exeter, 21 February 1964; TNA: PRO T317/485.
33. Startin to Jones, 3 August 1967, TNA: PRO T 227/2414.
34. Jay to Mr Phelps, 13 February 1967, TNA: PRO T 227/2414.
35. 'Note for the Record', Sport, 25 May 1967, TNA: PRO T 227/2414.
36. *HC Deb.*, 5s., v. 756, 19 January 1968, cc. 2176–96.
37. *HL Deb.*, 5s., v. 288, 7 February 1968, c. 1138–263: Lord Shackleton, Lord Privy Seal, spoke for the government.
38. Howell, *Made in Birmingham*, p. 180.
39. *HC Deb.*, 5 s., v. 821, 15 July 1971, cc. 811–72.
40. J. Coghlan with I. Webb, *Sport and British Politics since 1960* (Brighton: Falmer, 1990), pp. 100–03.
41. Cited in Killanin, *My Olympic Years* (Secker & Warburg, 1983), p. 98.
42. *The Times*, 7, 8 and 11 September 1972.
43. *The Times*, 12 September 1972.
44. 'The Olympic Games 1972', N. Henderson to Foreign Secretary, 25 September 1972, TNA: PRO FCO 33/1821. The Foreign Office became the Foreign & Commonwealth Office (FCO) in 1968.
45. J. B. Johnston to Foreign Secretary, 31 August 1976, TNA: PRO FCO 33/1821.
46. FCO telegram, April 1976, TNA: PRO AT 60/34.
47. Howell, *Made in Birmingham*, pp. 234–7 and 287–90.
48. Howell to Brook, 6 April 1976, TNA: PRO AT 60/54.
49. Anthony Payne, 'The Commonwealth and the Politics of Sporting Contacts with South Africa', in J. C. Binfield and J. Stevenson (eds), *Sport, Culture and Politics* (Sheffield: Sheffield Academic Press, 1993), pp. 130–49.
50. J. J. Rendall, Secretary to Howell to Sir R. Marshall, n/d, TNA: PRO AT 60/54: one 'made a point of praising our position'.
51. Coghlan, *Sport and British Politics*, p. 242.
52. Lord Chancellor to Prime Minister, 27 May 1977, TNA: PRO PREM 16/1883.
53. Commonwealth Secretariat, *The Commonwealth Statement on Apartheid in Sport* (1977).
54. Payne, 'The Commonwealth and Sporting Contacts', p. 149.
55. Callaghan to Malcolm Fraser, 22 July 1977, TNA: PRO PREM 16/1883.
56. Howell to Brook, 12 October 1977, TNA: PRO PREM 16/1883.
57. Callaghan to Shridath Rampal, 6 July 1978, TNA: PRO PREM 16/1883.

58. Michael Heseltine to Lord Carrington, 16 January 1980, TNA: PRO AT 60/182. For a full discussion of this topic, see K. Jefferys, 'Britain and the Boycott of the 1980 Moscow Olympics', *Sport in History* (forthcoming, 2012).
59. Tim Cowell, Conservative Central Office, to Douglas Hurd, FCO, 19 May 1980, TNA: PRO AT 60/192.

8   The 1980s: 'Years of Concern'

1. D. Pickup, *Not Another Messiah: An Account of the Sports Council 1988–93* (Bishop Auckland: Pentland Press, 1996), p. 105. Thatcher's colleague John Major confirmed in his *Autobiography* (HarperCollins, 1999), p. 403 that she 'dutifully turned up to watch great sporting events, but always looked rather out of place'.
2. D. Howell, *Made in Birmingham* (Queen Anne Press, 1990), pp. 344–5.
3. J. Coghlan with I. Webb, *Sport and British Politics since 1960* (Brighton: Falmer, 1990), p. 145.
4. B. Houlihan and A. White, *The Politics of Sports Development: Development of Sport or Development Through Sport* (Routledge, 2002), p. 28.
5. Pickup, *Not Another Messiah*, p. 3.
6. Howell, *Made in Birmingham*, pp. 343–4.
7. B. Howatson, *Herald Scotland*, 28 December 1996; obituary in *Daily Telegraph*, 31 August 2006.
8. Coghlan, *Sport and British Politics*, pp. 149 and 159.
9. Howell, *Made in Birmingham*, p. 345.
10. 'Moynihan Speaks to IOC on the Autonomy of Sport', *Whitehall and Westminster World*, December 2006: 'Mrs Thatcher was not one to forget or forgive'.
11. Coghlan, *Sport and British Politics*, p. 156.
12. N. Macfarlane with M Herd, *Sport and Politics: A World Divided* (Willow Books, 1996), pp. 61, 65 and 71–3.
13. Macfarlane, *Sport and Politics*, pp. 75–6.
14. B. Houlihan, *The Government and Politics of Sport* (Routledge, 1991), pp. 35–8.
15. *HC Deb.*, 6s, v. 63, 9 July 1984, cc. 711–47.
16. Macfarlane, *Sport and Politics*, pp. 79–81 and 109.
17. Coghlan, *Sport and British Politics*, pp. 147–8 and 158.
18. Howell, *Made in Birmingham*, p. 345; Pickup, *Not Another Messiah*, p. 9. Macfarlane gives few details of this episode in his account, but does refer (p. 104) to a statement by Jones mentioning legal action to rebut charges that he spent too much time discussing Council matters with the opposition.

19. D. Bloyce and A. Smith, *Sport Policy and Development: An Introduction* (Routledge, 2009), pp. 38–40.
20. Macfarlane, *Sport and Politics*, p. 83; Coghlan, *Sport and British Politics*, pp. 152–4.
21. 'Enquiry into the Sports Council. Evidence submitted by R. W. Palmer – General Secretary of the British Olympic Association', 27 August 1985, British Olympic Association archive, University of East London, BOA/PAR/3.
22. e.g. the CCPR, which was left with only one representative: Coghlan, *Sport and British Politics*, p. 155.
23. Howell, *Made in Birmingham*, p. 345
24. Pickup, *Not Another Messiah*, pp. 1–5 and 10.
25. Pickup, *Not Another Messiah*, pp. 21–3.
26. Pickup, *Not Another Messiah*, pp. 33–4.
27. Pickup, *Not Another Messiah*, pp. 45 and 53–4 and 56.
28. Coghlan, *Sport and British Politics*, p. 224.
29. Macfarlane, *Sport and Politics*, pp. 12 and 65.
30. Macfarlane, *Sport and Politics*, pp. 14 and 20–3.
31. *The Times*, cited in D. Russell, *Football and the English* (Preston, 1997), p. 208.
32. *The Guardian*, 1 June 1985.
33. Macfarlane, *Sport and Politics*, pp. 9–10.
34. Houlihan, *Government and Politics of Sport*, p. 138.
35. Howell, *Made in Birmingham*, pp. 363–4.
36. Pickup, *Not Another Messiah*, p. 30.
37. Lord Justice Taylor, *The Hillsborough Stadium Disaster, 15th April 1989. Final Report*, Cmd 962, 1990.
38. *HC Deb.*, 6s., v. 166, 29 January 1990, cc. 19–36.
39. *HC Deb.*, 6s., v. 166, 30 January 1990, cc. 220–62.
40. Russell, *Football and the English*, pp. 188–94.
41. Macfarlane, *Sport and Politics*, pp. 242–3.
42. Howell, *Made in Birmingham*, p. 315.
43. Macfarlane, *Sport and Politics*, pp. 242–3.
44. Howell, *Made in Birmingham*, p. 329; C. R. Hill, *Olympic Politics* (Manchester, 1992, pp. 99–103).
45. Cited in Hill, *Olympic Politics*, pp. 113–14.
46. Pickup, *Not Another Messiah*, pp. 17–18, 32 and 37.
47. R. Fieldhouse, Anti-Apartheid: A History of the Movement in Britain. A Study in Pressure Group Politics (Merlin Press, 2005), pp. 101–2.
48. Macfarlane, *Sport and Politics*, pp. 105–6.
49. Fieldhouse, *Anti-Apartheid*, pp. 103 and 181–9.
50. Macfarlane, *Sport and Politics*, pp. 120, 126, 147 and 165.

51. Howell, *Made in Birmingham*, pp. 363–8.
52. Fieldhouse, *Anti-Apartheid*, p. 103.
53. Howell, *Made in Birmingham*, p. 375–7; Pickup, *Not Another Messiah*, p. 3.
54. F. Coalter, *A Wider Social Role for Sport: Who's Keeping the Score?* (Routledge, 2007), p. 11. On Moyhinan's objectives, see his letter to Sport Council chairman John Smith, 19 November 1987, BOA archive, BOA/PAR/3.
55. P. Corrigan, *Independent*, 24 October 1993.
56. 'Moynihan Speaks to IOC', *Whitehall and Westminster World*, December 2006.
57. Major, *The Autobiography*, (HarperCollins, 1999), p. 403.

9 *Raising the Game*, 1990–97

1. J. Major, *The Autobiography*, (HarperCollins, 1999), pp. 402 and 405.
2. The official, not named, is cited in Anthony Seldon, *Major. A Political Life* (Weidenfeld & Nicolson, 1997), p. 595.
3. R. Holt and T. Mason, *Sport in Britain 1945–2000* (Oxford: Blackwell, 2000), pp. 153–4.
4. D. Pickup, *Not Another Messiah: An Account of the Sports Council 1988–93* (Bishop Auckland: Pentland Press, 1996), p. 65.
5. Pickup, *Not Another Messiah*, p. 66.
6. Major, *The Autobiography*, p. 407.
7. Pickup, *Not Another Messiah*, pp. 70–2 and 94.
8. Labour Party, *It's Time to get Britain Working Again* (1992).
9. Conservative Party, *The Best Future for Britain* (1992).
10. Pickup, *Not Another Messiah*, pp. 103 and 121.
11. Pickup, *Not Another Messiah*, p. 135.
12. *The Independent*, 24 October 1993.
13. Pickup, *Not Another Messiah*, p. 136; *HC Deb.*, 6s., v. 228, 9 July 1993, cc. 597–601.
14. Pickup, *Not Another Messiah*, pp. 139–40 and 148–9.
15. Major, *The Autobiography*, pp. 405–8.
16. I. Henry, *Politics of Leisure Policy* (Basingstoke: Palgrave, 2001 edn), p. 92.
17. C. R. Hill, 'The Politics of Manchester's Olympic Bid', *Parliamentary Affairs*, 47, 3 (1994), p. 339.
18. *The Times*, 25 April 1991; Hill, 'Politics of Manchester's Bid', p. 343.
19. Hill, 'Politics of Manchester's Bid', pp. 352–3.
20. Conservative Party, *Best Future for Britain*; Major, *The Autobiography*, p. 404.
21. Pickup, *Not Another Messiah*, p. 104.
22. *HL Deb.*, 5s., v. 546, 9 June 1993, cc. 1019–36.

23. Pickup, *Not Another Messiah*, pp. 139–40 and 207.
24. Holt and Mason, *Sport in Britain*, p. 155.
25. Major, *The Autobiography*, p. 412.
26. Department of National Heritage, *Sport: Raising the Game* (1995); A. Seldon, *Major, A Political Life* (Weidenfeld & Nicolson, 1997), p. 595.
27. *HC Deb.*, 6s., v. 263, 14 July 1995, cc. 800–3.
28. *Daily Mail*, 15 July 1995.
29. *The Guardian*, 15 July 1995.
30. Pickup, *Not Another Messiah*, pp. 215–16.
31. Major, *The Autobiography*, p. 412; *HC Deb.*, 6s. v. 285, 21 November 1996, c.644.
32. *The Guardian*, 24 July 1996.
33. *The Times*, 25 July 1996.
34. A. Thorpe, *A History of the British Labour Party* (Basingstoke, 2001 edn), pp. 224–8.
35. Jefferys, *Finest and Darkest Hours*, p. 303.
36. Alistair Campbell, *The Alistair Campbell Diaries*. Vol. 1, *Prelude to Power 1994–1997* (Hutchinson, 2010): entries for 8 June 1996, p. 463; 15 June, p. 468; 22 June pp. 475–6; and 26 June, p. 481.
37. Seldon, *Major*, pp. 659–60.
38. *The Guardian*, 25 July 1996.
39. *Daily Mirror*, 5 August 1996 and 4 January 1997.
40. Cited in the Glasgow *Herald*, 13 August 1996.
41. Conservative Party, *You Can Only Be Sure With The Conservatives* (1997).
42. Labour Party, *New Labour: Because Britain Deserves Better* (1997).
43. *The Observer*, 13 October 1996.
44. Major, *The Autobiography*, p. 409.
45. B. Houlihan and A. White, *The Politics of Sports Development: Development of Sport or Development Through Sport* (Routledge, 2002), p. 229.
46. Untitled and undated Memorandum, BOA archive, BOA/PAR/4.
47. 'British Sport and the Future', Richard Palmer, 1 October 1996, BOA archive, BOA/PUB/3/21.
48. Seldon, *Major*, p. 595.
49. *Mail Online*, 19 June 2001.

10   Regions and Localities

1. M. Baumert, A. D. Munrow, B. N. Knapp et al., *Britain in the World of Sport* (Birmingham: Physical Education Department, Birmingham University, 1956), pp. 58–9.
2. J. Hill, *Sport, Leisure & Culture in Twentieth-Century Britain* (Basingstoke: Palgrave, 2002), p. 166.

3. H. Meller, *Leisure and the Changing City, 1870–1914* (London: RKP, 1976).

4. S. G. Jones, *Sport, Politics and the Working Class: Organised Labour and Sport in Interwar Britain* (Manchester: Manchester University Press, 1988).

5. J. Walters, 'The National Fitness Council 1937–39: "Unhonoured and Unsung" '?, University of Plymouth MA, 2010.

6. B. Houlihan, *Government and Politics of Sport* (Routledge, 1991), p. 52.

7. 'Report of the Policy Study Group on Leisure', 4 July 1965, CPA, ACP 3/12.

8. H. A. Browne to W. Gamble, 26 November 1964, TNA: PRO ED 136/926.

9. Memorandum by F. Bray, 10 June 1953, TNA: PRO ED 169/6.

10. *HL Deb.*, 5s. v. 197, 29 May 1956, cc. 552–80; unsigned and undated Memorandum, TNA: PRO ED 169/5.

11. *HC Deb.*, 5s., v. 531, 28 July 1954, cc. 601–30.

12. *HL Deb.*, 5s. v. 197, 29 May 1956, cc. 552–80

13. E. B. H. Baker to Mr Odgers and Mr Heaton, 3 October 1958, TNA: PRO ED169/7.

14. *The Guardian*, 28 February 1964.

15. R. Stamp to Noel-Baker, 3 October 1960, Noel-Baker papers, NBKR 6/10/2.

16. Browne to Gamble, 26 November 1964, TNA: PRO ED 136/926.

17. 'Provision of Facilities for Sport', Joint Circular by the MHLG and the Ministry of Education, 27 August 1964.

18. 'The Provision of Facilities for Sport', Report of the Regional Conference of Local Authorities and LEAs, 22 June 1964, copy in Noel-Baker papers, NBKR 6/51.

19. *The Sports Council. A Report* (1966).

20. *The Guardian*, 15 November 1966.

21. J. Coghlan with I. Webb, *Sport and British Politics since 1960* (Brighton: Falmer, 1990), p. 24.

22. H. J. Evans, *Service to Sport: The Story of the CCPR, 1937–1975* (Pelham, 1975), p. 207: without such backing the RSCs 'could never have "got off the ground" '.

23. *The Sports Council. A Review 1966–69* (CCPR, 1969), pp. 2 and 6.

24. Coghlan, *Sport and British Politics*, p. 24.

25. 'Report of Sport and Recreation Group', 26 June 1969, CPA, ACP 3/19.

26. Coghlan, *Sport and British Politics*, pp. 63–5 and 83.

27. *First Report from the Select Committee of the House of Lords on Sport and Leisure* (1973).

28. Note of a meeting held on 2 April 1973, TNA: PRO AT 60/1.

29. 'Sport & Recreation Officers', Memorandum by R. P. Manning, 7 June 1974, Greenwood papers, MS Eng. C6331.
30. Houlihan, *Government and Politics of Sport*, pp. 53–8.
31. DoE, *Sport and Recreation* (1975).
32. Coghlan, *Sport and British Politics*, pp. 285–6.
33. Note on implementation of the White Paper, June 1977, TNA: PRO AT 60/64.
34. Coghlan, *Sport and British Politics*, pp. 68–9.
35. Houlihan, *Government and Politics of Sport*, pp. 51–2.
36. CCPR, *Sports Facilities in Wales*, 1964, copy in Noel-Baker papers, NBKR 6/51; Coghlan, *Sport and British Politics*, p.163.
37. Bristol City Council (BCC) minutes, 9 November 1946 and 10 December 1946, Bristol Record Office (BRO), Bristol.
38. Derek Robinson, in J Belsey, M. Jenner et al., *Muddling Through: Bristol in the Fifties* (Bristol: Redcliffe Press, 1988), p. 15.
39. *Civic News*, Number 61, January 1963.
40. BCC minutes, 14 January 1964; Bristol Baths department handbook, November 1971, BRO.
41. *Civic News*, Number 61, January 1963.
42. Bristol Region Sports Liaison Council minutes, 26 November 1968, BRO.
43. A government memo on the working of the RSCs referred to 'the difficult relationship between the region and the City of Bristol': Chairmen of technical panels of Regional Sports Councils', meeting held 27 November 1968, TNA: PRO ED 249/1.
44. *Civic News*, Number 131, October 1969.
45. City of Bristol, *Recreation and Amenity:A Discussion Paper Issued by the Open Spaces and Amenities Committee*, May 1974.
46. E. Wood, 'A Case Study of Public Provision for Sport in Bristol 1945–75', University of Plymouth MA (2009).
47. BCC, Sport Liaison Group minutes, 17 June 1975, BRO, M/BCC/SPO/1/2.
48. BCC, Sport Liaison Group minutes, 9 March 1978 and 25 March 1980, BRO.
49. BCC, Sport Liaison Group minutes, 21 July 1987, BRO, M/BCC/SPO/1/6.
50. BCC, Annual Report of Leisure Services Committee to Council, July 1998, BRO M/BCC/LEI/1/34.
51. A. Flexman to Mr Gilbert, 14 November 1979, TNA: PRO AT 60/64; Coghlan, *Sport and British Politics*, p. 197.
52. Houlihan, *Government and Politics of Sport*, p. 59.
53. Coghlan, *Sport and British Politics*, p. 215.
54. Houlihan, *Government and Politics of Sport*, pp. 58 and 80.

55. Coghlan, *Sport and British Politics*, p. 224.
56. I. Henry, *Politics of Leisure Policy* (Basingstoke: Palgrave, 2001 edn), pp. 193–205; J. Hill, *Sport, Leisure & Culture in Twentieth-Century Britain* (Basingstoke: Palgrave, 2002), p. 177.
57. Henry, *Politics of Leisure Policy*, p. 123.
58. B. Houlihan and A. White, *Politics of Sports Development: Development of Sport or Development Through Sport* (Routledge, 2002), p. 111.
59. Henry, *Politics of Leisure Policy*, pp. 141–5.
60. Houlihan and White, *Politics of Sports Development*, p. 112.
61. 'Speech to the CCPR', Tessa Jowell, 9 May 2007, Department for Culture, Media and Sport website: www.culture.gov.uk (accessed 3/3/10).
62. Houlihan and White, *Politics of Sports Development*, pp. 160–3.

11   New Labour and Sport, 1997–2010

1. Speech to the think tank Progress, 2 November 2009, Bradshaw website: www.benbradshaw.co.uk (accessed 12/5/10); *The Guardian*, 17 December 2009.
2. *The Guardian*, 8 and 21 June 1999; *The Times*, 6 April 2000.
3. *Daily Telegraph*, 17 August 2008.
4. F. Coalter, *A Wider Social Role for Sport: Who's Keeping the Score?* (Routledge, 2007), p. 4.
5. Department for Culture, Media and Sport (DCMS), *A Sporting Future for All* (DCMS, 2000).
6. DCMS, *A Sporting Future for All: The Government's Plan for Sport* (2001); B. Houlihan and A. White, *Politics of Sports Development: Development of Sport or Development Through Sport* (Routledge, 2002), pp. 95–6 and 103.
7. Ian Wooldridge, *Mail Online*, 7 June 1997.
8. Alistair Campbell, *The Alistair Campbell Diaries*, Vol. 2, *Power and the People 1997–1999* (Hutchinson, 2011): 15 May 1997, p. 22.
9. *Daily Telegraph*, 7 July 2000.
10. Alistair Campbell, *The Alistair Campbell Diaries*, Vol. 3, *Power and Responsibility 1999–2001* (Hutchinson, 2011): 29 July 1999, pp. 44–5.
11. *Daily Mail*, 19 June 2001.
12. E. Griffin, *Blood Sport, Hunting in Britain since 1066* (New Haven and Yale University Press, 2007), pp. 219–21.
13. Campbell, *Power and Responsibility*: 9 January 2001, p. 493 and 16 January 2001, p. 496.
14. E. Griffin, *Blood Sport*, pp. 222–7.
15. Labour Party, *Ambitions for Britain* (2001).
16. DCMS, *Annual Report 2001* (2001): the total budget was to rise from £1015 million in 2000–01 to £1240 million in 2003–04.

17. Campbell, *Power and Responsibility*: 7 June 2001, p. 633.
18. Author's interview with Richard Caborn, 20 July 2011; *Daily Mail*, 19 June 2001: the Minister was 'ambushed' by Claire Balding, who put several questions on Radio 5 Live about sporting personalities and teams that he was unable to answer.
19. *HC Deb.*, 6s., v. 376, 11 December 2001, cc. 739–76.
20. *HC Deb.*, 6s., v. 376, 11 December 2001, cc. 739–76.
21. T. Blair, *A Journey*, (Hutchinson, 2010), pp. 304–6.
22. Alistair Campbell (ed.), *The Blair Years* (Hutchinson, 2007): 21 March 2002, p. 610.
23. Campbell (ed.), *Blair Years*, 17 June 2003, p. 706.
24. Blair, *A Journey*, pp. 304–5.
25. Griffin, *Blood Sport*, pp. 229–32.
26. *HC Deb.*, 6s., v. 376, 11 December 2001, cc. 739–76.
27. 'Richard Caborn's opening speech at CCPR', 20 May 2003, DCMS website: www.culture.gov.uk (accessed 7/4/10); interview with Caborn, 20 July 2011.
28. Conservative Party, *It's Time for Action* (2005).
29. *The Observer*, 10 April 2005.
30. Labour Party, *Britain Forward, Not Back* (2005).
31. *The Observer*, 1 May 2005.
32. M. Rogan and M. Rogan, *Britain and the Olympic Games* (Leicester: Matador, 2011), p. 78.
33. A. Hosken, *Ken. The Ups and Downs of Ken Livingstone* (Arcadia Books, 2008), pp. 360–1.
34. M. Lee, *The Race for the 2012 Olympics. The Inside Story of How London Won the Bid* (Virgin Books 2006), pp. 7–8; interview with Caborn, 20 July 2011.
35. *HC Deb.*, 6s., v. 397, 14 January 2003, cc. 606–53; Lee, *Race for 2012*, p. 12.
36. Lee, *Race for 2012*, pp. 12–14.
37. Campbell (ed.), *Blair Years*, 21 and 30 January 2003, pp. 657 and 659.
38. Blair, *A Journey*, p. 545.
39. A. Rawnsley, *End of the Party* (Penguin, 2010), p. 327.
40. Cited in Lee, *Race for 2012*, p. 16.
41. Lee, *Race for 2012*, p. 58.
42. Blair, *A Journey*, p. 552: Berlusconi reportedly said he would see what could be done; in the end London won the Games by less than five votes.
43. David Hill, Blair's communications chief, cited in Rawnsley, *End of the Party*, p. 327.
44. Lee, *Race for 2012*, p. 157.
45. P. Mandelson, *The Third Man. Life at the Heart of New Labour* (Harper Press, 2010), p. 409.

46. Lee, *Race for 2012*, pp. 155 and 158.
47. Chris Mullin, *Decline & Fall. Diaries 2005–10* (Profile Books, 2010): 11 July 2005, p. 25.
48. *HC Deb.*, 6s., v.458, 15 March 2007, cc. 450–2.
49. Andrew Rawnsley used this term in the *Observer*, 19 January 2003 drawing from the phrase also used elsewhere, e.g. in Alan Tomlinson and Gary Whannel (eds), *Five Ring Circus: Money, Power and Politics at the Olympic Games* (1984).
50. *HC Deb.*, 6s., v. 458, 15 March 2007, cc. 454–63.
51. Mullin, *Decline & Fall*, 26 September 2005, p. 38.
52. Speech reproduced in *Whitehall and Westminster World*, December 2006.
53. Mandelson, *Third Man*, p. 437.
54. House of Commons, Committee of Public Accounts, *The Budget for the London 2012 Olympic and Paralympic Games* (April 2008).
55. *Daily Mirror*, 27 July 2009.
56. House of Commons, Culture, Media and Sport Committee, *London 2012 Games: The Next Lap* (April 2008). In addition to the Olympic Delivery Authority, the key bodies included the London Organising Committee of the Olympic Games (LOCOG), chaired by Seb Coe. Colin Moynihan summed up the differing roles as follows: 'To use a metaphor, the Government builds the theatre [via the ODA], LOCOG puts on the show, we at the BOA deliver the actors and actresses word perfect, and the Mayor inherits the legacy for Londoners the day the curtain falls': *Whitehall and Westminster World*, December 2006.
57. Speech by Richard Caborn, 5 February 2007, DCMS website: www.culture.gov.uk (accessed 5/4/10).
58. 'World Class Community Sport', speech by Purnell, 28 November 2007, DCMS website: www.culture.gov.uk (accessed 9/3/10).
59. *Daily Telegraph*, 30 November 2007.
60. DCMS, *Annual Report* (2008), p. 7.
61. *The Guardian*, 6 May 2009.
62. *The Guardian*, 27 July 2009.
63. *The Guardian*, 27 July 2009.
64. Speech by Bradshaw on 15 October 2009: www.benbradshaw.co.uk; David Conn in the *Guardian*, 25 July 2007, noted that Labour frontbencher Ed Balls first used the term 'quiet revolution' to describe what had taken place in school sport.

Epilogue: Towards 2012

1. Labour Party, *A Future Fair For All* (2010); Conservative Party, *Invitation to Join the Government of Britain* (2010).

2. *The Guardian*, 5 May 2010.
3. *The Guardian*, 5 May 2010.
4. *The Times*, 28 December 2010; *The Guardian*, 28 December 2010.
5. *Daily Telegraph*, 21 October 2010; *The Independent*, 21 October 2010.
6. *The Observer*, 21 November 2010, provides a chronology of the unfolding dispute.
7. *The Observer*, 5 December 2010; *The Guardian*, 2 and 18 December 2010.
8. *The Guardian*, 18 June and 14 July 2010: funding came from several government departments, and included plans for the refurbishment of swimming pools, which were also scrapped.
9. Interview with Jeremy Hunt: *The Guardian*, 29 March 2011.
10. *Daily Telegraph*, 21 October 2010; Simon Henig, cited in *The Guardian*, 7 September 2011.
11. David Goldblatt, 'Sporting Life', *Prospect*, October 2010, p. 67.
12. *The Guardian*, 29 March 2011.
13. *The Guardian*, 18 July 2011.
14. Owen Gibson, *The Guardian*, 29 March 2011; *The Guardian*, 7 September 2011.

Select Bibliography

(Place of publication is London unless otherwise specified)

PRIMARY SOURCES

1. Unpublished Primary Sources

The National Archives, Kew

Cabinet (CAB)
Department of the Environment (AT)
Foreign Office (FO)
Foreign and Commonwealth Office (FCO)
Home Office (HO)
Housing and Local Government (HLG)
Prime Minister's papers (PREM)
Ministry/Department of Education (ED)
Ministry of Housing and Local Government (HLG)
Treasury (T)
Department of National Heritage (www.webarchive.nationalarchives. gov.uk)
Department for Culture, Media and Sport (www.webarchive.national archives.gov.uk)

Private papers

Clement Attlee, Bodleian Library, Oxford
Philip Noel-Baker, Churchill College, Cambridge
Anthony Greenwood, Bodleian Library, Oxford
Lord Hailsham, Churchill College, Cambridge
Harold Wilson, Bodleian Library, Oxford
Lord Wolfenden, Reading University

Organizations

Bristol County Council, Smeaton Road, Bristol
British Olympic Association, University of East London
Conservative Party, Bodleian Library, Oxford
Labour Party, National Museum of Labour History, Manchester

Sports Council/Sport England (www.webarchive.nationalarchives.gov.
    uk)
South West Regional Sports Council

2. Published Primary Sources

Legislation/Official Reports/Parliamentary and Party Publications

Hansard, *House of Commons Debates, House of Lords Debates* (1945–2010)
White Paper, *Physical Training and Recreation* (HMSO, January 1937)
Physical Training and Recreation Act (HMSO, July 1937)
National Fitness Council, *Report of Grants Committee* (HMSO, 1939)
Conservative Political Centre, *The Challenge of Leisure* (CPC, 1959)
Labour Party, *Leisure for Living* (Labour Party, 1959)
Central Council of Physical Recreation, *Sport & the Community. The Report
    of the Wolfenden Committee on Sport* (CCPR, 1960)
Bow Group, *A Better Country: A Policy Study on the Use of Leisure by a Group
    of Conservatives under the Chairmanship of Christopher Chataway* (CPC,
    1966)
*First and Second Reports from the Select Committee of the House of Lords on Sport
    and Leisure* (HMSO, 1973)
Department of the Environment, *Sport and Recreation*, Cmd. 6200 (HMSO,
    1975)
Department of the Environment, *Recreation and Deprivation in Inner Urban
    Areas* (HMSO, 1977)
Sports Council, *The Sports Council. A Report* (Central Office of Information,
    1966)
Sports Council, *The Sports Council. A Review 1966–69* (CCPR, 1969)
Lord Justice Taylor, *The Hillsborough Stadium Disaster, 15th April 1989. Final
    Report*, Cmd. 962 (HMSO, 1990)
Department of National Heritage, *Sport: Raising the Game* (DNH, 1995)
Department for Culture, Media and Sport, *A Sporting Future for All* (DCMS,
    2000)
House of Commons, Committee of Public Accounts, *The Budget for the
    London 2012 Olympic and Paralympic Games* (HMSO, 2008)

Newspapers and Journals

Civic News (Bristol)
Daily Express
Daily Herald
Daily Mail
Daily Mirror
Daily Telegraph
Daily Worker

Economist
Evening Standard
Herald (Scotland)
Independent
Manchester Guardian/Guardian
News Chronicle
New Statesman
Observer
Prospect
Spectator
Sunday Dispatch
Sunday Times
Times
Times Educational Supplement
Tribune
Whitehall and Westminster World

Autobiographies, Diaries, Speeches and Contemporary Writing

Anthony, Don (compiler), *Man of Sport, Man of Peace. Collected Speeches and Essays of Philip Noel-Baker, Olympic Statesman 1889–1992* (Sports Editions Ltd, 1991)

Bannister, Roger, *The First Four Minutes* (Stroud: Sutton Publishing, 2004 edn)

Baumert, M., A. D. Munrow, B. N. Knapp et al., *Britain in the World of Sport* (Birmingham: Physical Education Department, Birmingham University, 1956)

Benn, Tony, Office *Without Power. Diaries 1968–72* (Arrow Books, 1989)

Blair, Tony, *A Journey* (Hutchinson, 2010)

Callaghan, James, *Time & Chance* (Collins, 1987)

Campbell, Alistair, *The Alistair Campbell Diaries*, Vol. 1, *Prelude to Power 1994–1997* (Hutchinson, 2010)

Campbell, Alistair, *The Alistair Campbell Diaries*, Vol. 2, *Power and the People 1997–1999* (Hutchinson, 2011)

Campbell, Alistair, *The Alistair Campbell Diaries*, Vol. 3, *Power and Responsibility 1999–2001* (Hutchinson, 2011)

Cleaver, Hylton, *Sporting Rhapsody* (Hutchinson's Library, 1951)

Campbell, Alistair, (ed), *The Blair Years* (Hutchinson, 2007)

Cockett, Richard (ed.), *My Dear Max: The Letters of Brendan Bracken to Lord Beaverbrook, 1929–58* (Historians' Press, 1990)

Crossman, Richard, *The Diaries of a Cabinet Minister*, Vol. 1, *Minister of Housing 1964–66* (Hamish Hamilton and Jonathan Cape, 1975)

Crossman, Richard, *The Diaries of a Cabinet Minister,* Vol. 3, *Secretary of State for Social Services, 1968–70* (Hamish Hamilton and Jonathan Cape, 1977)

Hain, Peter, *Don't Play with Apartheid: The Background to the Stop the Seventy Tour Campaign* (Allen and Unwin, 1971)

Hurd, Douglas, *Memoirs* (Little, Brown, 2003)

Howell, Denis, *Made in Birmingham* (Queen Anne Press, 1990)

Lord Hailsham, *The Door Wherein I Went* (Collins, 1975)

Lord Hailsham, *A Sparrow's Flight* (Collins, 1990)

Lord Killanin, *My Olympic Years* (Secker & Warburg, 1983)

Macfarlane, Neil with M Herd, *Sport and Politics: A World Divided* (Willow Books, 1996)

Major, John, *The Autobiography* (HarperCollins, 1999)

Mandelson, Peter, *The Third Man. Life at the Heart of New Labour* (Harper Press, 2010)

McIntosh, Peter and Valerie Charlton, *The Impact of Sport for All Policy 1966–84* (Sports Council, 1985)

Molyneux, D. D., *Central Government Aid to Sport and Physical Recreation in Countries of Western Europe* (Birmingham: Physical Education Department, Birmingham University, 1962)

Mullin, Chris, *Decline & Fall. Diaries 2005–10* (Profile Books, 2010)

Pearce, Robert (ed.), *Patrick Gordon Walker: Political Diaries 1932–71* (Historians' Press, 1991)

Pickup, David, *Not Another Messiah: An Account of the Sports Council 1988–93* (Bishop Auckland: Pentland Press, 1996)

Rivers, James (compiler & editor), *The Sports Book 3* (MacDonald, 1949)

Sir Stanley Rous, *Football Worlds. A Lifetime in Sport* (Faber and Faber, 1978)

Thatcher, Margaret, *The Downing Street Years* (HarperCollins, 1993)

Wilson, Harold, *The Labour Government 1964–1970. A Personal Record* (Weidenfeld & Nicolson, 1971)

Wilson, Harold, *Final Term. The Labour Government 1974–1976* (Weidenfeld & Nicolson, 1979)

Sir John Wolfenden, *Turning Points* (Bodley Head, 1976)

SECONDARY SOURCES

Biographical

Bullock, Alan, *Ernest Bevin. Foreign Secretary* (Oxford: OUP, 1985 edn)

Hosken, Andrew, *Ken. The Ups and Downs of Ken Livingstone* (Arcadia Books, 2008)

Lewis, Geoffrey, *Lord Hailsham. A Life* (Jonathan Cape, 1997)

Oxford Dictionary of National Biography (Oxford: OUP, 2004): entries on
Lord Burghley (Norris McWhirter); Baroness Elaine Burton (Duncan
Sutherland); Anthony Greenwood (Kenneth O. Morgan); Lord
Hailsham (S. M. Cretney); Denis Howell (Tam Dalyell); Sir John Lang
(Clifford Jarrett); Baron Noel-Baker (David Howell); Sir Patrick Renison
(D. W. Throup); Sir Stanley Rous (A. Pawson); Sir Walter Winterbottom
(Tony Mason); Lord Wolfenden (J. Weeks)

Seldon, Anthony, *Major. A Political Life* (Weidenfeld & Nicolson, 1997)

Whittaker, D. J., *Fighter for Peace: Philip Noel-Baker 1889–1982* (York: William
Sessions Ltd)

Books

Addison, Paul, *Now the War is Over. A Social History of Britain 1945–51* (BBC
and Jonathan Cape, 1985)

Allison, Lincoln (ed.), *The Politics of Sport* (Manchester: Manchester
University Press, 1986)

Allison, Lincoln (ed.), *The Changing Politics of Sport* (Manchester:
Manchester University Press, 1993)

Bailey, Jack, *Conflicts in Cricket* (Methuen, 1989)

Beauchampé, Steve and Simon Inglis, *Played in Birmingham* (Birmingham:
English Heritage, 2006)

Belsey, J., M. Jenner et al., *Muddling Through: Bristol in the Fifties* (Bristol:
Redcliffe Press, 1988)

Binfield, J. C. and J. Stevenson (eds), *Sport, Culture and Politics* (Sheffield:
Sheffield Academic Press, 1993)

Bloyce, Daniel and Andy Smith, *Sport Policy and Development: An Introduction*
(Routledge, 2009)

Butler, David and Michael Pinto-Duschinsky, *The British General Election of
1970* (London and Basingstoke: Macmillan, 1971)

Coalter, Fred, *A Wider Social Role for Sport: Who's Keeping the Score?*
(Routledge, 2007)

Coghlan, John with Ida Webb, *Sport and British Politics since 1960* (Brighton:
Falmer, 1990)

Clapson, Mark, *A Bit of a Flutter: Popular Gambling and English Society,
c.1823–1961* (Manchester: Manchester University Press, 1992)

Evans, H. J., *Service to Sport: The Story of the CCPR, 1937–1975* (Pelham,
1975)

Fieldhouse, Roger, *Anti-Apartheid: A History of the Movement in Britain. A
Study in Pressure Group Politics* (Merlin Press, 2005)

Green, Mick and Barrie Houlihan, *Elite Sport Development: Policy Learning
and Political Priorities* (Routledge, 2005)

Griffin, Emma, *Blood Sport: Hunting in Britain since 1066* (New Haven and
Yale University Press, 2007)

Hampton, Janie, *The Austerity Olympics. When the Games Came to London in 1948* (Aurum, 2008)

Hargreaves, John, *Sport, Power and Culture: A Social and Historical Analysis of Popular Sports in Britain* (Cambridge: Polity Press, 1986)

Henry, Ian, *The Politics of Leisure Policy* (Basingstoke: Palgrave, 2001 edn)

Hill, Christopher R., *Olympic Politics* (Manchester: Manchester University Press, 1992)

Hill, Jeff, *Sport, Leisure & Culture in Twentieth-Century Britain* (Basingstoke: Palgrave, 2002)

Hill, Jeff, *Sport in History: An Introduction* (Basingstoke: Palgrave, 2011)

Holt, Richard and Tony Mason, *Sport in Britain 1945–2000* (Oxford: Blackwell, 2000)

Holt, Richard, 'Sport and Recreation', in Paul Addison and Harriet Jones (eds), *A Companion to Contemporary Britain 1939–2000* (Oxford: Blackwell, 2005)

Houlihan, Barrie, *The Government and Politics of Sport* (Routledge, 1991)

Houlihan, Barrie, *Sport and International Politics* (Hemel Hempstead: Harvester Wheatsheaf, 1994)

Houlihan, Barrie, *Sport, Policy and Politics: A Comparative Analysis* (Routledge, 1997)

Houlihan, Barrie and Anita White, *The Politics of Sports Development: Development of Sport or Development Through Sport* (Routledge, 2002)

Jones, S. G., *Sport, Politics and the Working Class: Organised Labour and Sport in Interwar Britain* (Manchester: Manchester University Press, 1988)

Kirk, David, *Defining Physical Education. The Social Construction of a School Subject in Post-war Britain* (Falmer, 1992)

Lee, Mike, *The Race for the 2012 Olympics. The Inside Story of How London Won the Bid* (Virgin Books 2006)

May, Peter, *The Rebel Tours: Cricket's Crisis of Conscience* (Cheltenham: SportsBooks, 2009)

Meller, Helen, *Leisure and the Changing City, 1870–1914* (London: RKP, 1976)

Morgan, Kenneth O., *Labour in Power 1945–51* (Oxford: Clarendon Press, 1984)

Munting, Roger, *An Economic and Social History of Gambling in Britain and the USA* (Manchester: Manchester University Press, 1996)

Phillips, Bob, *The 1948 Olympics. How London Rescued the Games* (Cheltenham: SportsBooks Ltd, 2007)

Polley, Martin, *Moving the Goalposts. A History of Sport and Society since 1945* (Routledge, 1998)

Rawnsley, Andrew, *The End of the Party* (Penguin, 2010)

Rogan, Matt and Martin Rogan, *Britain and the Olympic Games* (Leicester: Matador, 2011)

Russell, Dave, *Football and the English* (Preston: Carnegie Publishing, 1997)

Sarantakes, Nicholas Evan, *Dropping the Torch. Jimmy Carter, The Olympic Boycott, and the Cold War* (Cambridge: Cambridge University Press, 2011)

Thomas, Richard H., *The Politics of Hunting* (Aldershot: Gower, 1983)

Tiratsoo, Nick (ed.), *From Blitz to Blair. A New History of Britain since 1939* (Weidenfeld & Nicolson, 1997)

Tomlinson, A. (ed.), *Sport in Society: Policy, Politics and Culture* (Brighton: Leisure Studies Association, 1990)

Whannel, G., *Blowing the Whistle: The Politics of Sport* (Pluto Press, 1983)

Journal Articles

Baker, Norman, 'The Amateur Ideal in a Society of Equality: Change and Continuity in Post-Second World War British Sport 1945–48', *International Journal of the History of Sport*, 12, 1 (1995), pp. 99–126

Beck, Peter J., 'Confronting George Orwell: Philip Noel-Baker on International Sport, Particularly the Olympic Movement, as Peacemaker', *European Sports History Review*, 5 (2003), pp. 187–207

Beck, Peter J., 'The British Government and the Olympic Movement: the 1948 London Olympics', *International Journal of the History of Sport*, 25, 5 (2008), pp. 615–47

Girginov, Vassil and Laura Hills, 'A Sustainable Sports Legacy: Creating a Link between the London Olympics and Sports Participation', *International Journal of the History of Sport*, 25, 14 (2008), pp. 2091–116

Haynes, Richard, 'The BBC, Austerity and Broadcasting the 1948 Olympics', *International Journal of the History of Sport*, 27, 6 (2010), pp. 1029–46.

Hill, Christopher R., 'The Politics of Manchester's Olympic Bid', *Parliamentary Affairs*, 47, 3 (1994), pp. 338–54

Hill, Jeffrey, 'Sport and Politics', *Journal of Contemporary History*, 38, 3 (2003), pp. 355–61

Jones, Stephen G., 'State Intervention in Sport and Leisure in Britain Between the Wars', *Journal of Contemporary History*, 22, 1 (1987), pp. 163–82

Kowalski, Ronald and Dilwyn Porter, 'Political Football: Moscow Dynamo in Britain, 1945', *International Journal of the History of Sport*, 14, 2 (1997), pp. 100–21

Payne, Anthony, 'The International Politics of the Gleneagles Agreement', *The Round Table* 320, (1991), pp. 417–30

Polley, Martin, 'The Diplomatic Background to the 1966 Football World Cup', *The Sports Historian*, 18, 2 (1998), pp. 1–18

Polley, Martin, 'Olympic Diplomacy: The British Government and the Projected 1940 Olympic Games', *International Journal of the History of Sport*, 9, 2 (1992), pp. 169–87

Tichelar, Michael, ' "Putting Animals into Politics": The Labour Party and Hunting in the First Half of the Twentieth Century', *Rural History*, 17, 2 (2006), pp. 213–34

Welshman, John, 'Physical Culture and Sport in Schools in England and Wales, 1900–40', *International Journal of the History of Sport*, 15, 1 (1998), pp. 54–75

Index

Aberdare, Lord, 60, 70, 91
Afghanistan, 243
Allen, Mabel, 47
Allom, J. C., 115
America, 156, 157–8
Andrews, Sir Herbert, 81, 103–5
Anglo-Korean relations, see Korea,
    North versus South
Anthony, Don, 146
Anti-Apartheid Movement (AMM),
    106–7, 109, 110, 116, 120, 167,
    188, 190–2, 267
Arts Council, 29, 38, 47, 49, 59, 67, 78,
    98, 127, 133
Ashby, David, 177
Ashes, The, 3, 31
Ashton, Hubert, 36, 39, 49, 61–2
Asia, 188
athletics, 3, 7, 20, 24, 25, 32, 43, 50,
    158, 162, 164, 242, 250, 257
    provisions, facilities and training,
        29, 35, 44, 53, 58, 122
Atkins, Robert, 175–6, 197–200, 201,
    204
Attlee, Clement, 37, 41
    and the 1948 London Olympics,
        19–24
    administration, 34–5, 50, 94, 98,
        234, 239
    as Prime Minister, 3, 9, 12, 16–18,
        28–30, 211, 266
Australia, 206, 246
Avon County Sports Council, see Bristol

Bailey, Jack, 111
Baker, E. B. H., 48, 57, 62
Banks, Tony, 236–8, 241, 243, 255
Bannister, Roger, 31, 37, 84, 126, 128,
    130, 132–3, 136–8, 165, 223

Barnett, Joel, 142
Baths and Washhouses Act (1846), 214
Baths Committee, see Bristol
Beaverbrook, Lord, 32
Beck, Peter, 152
Beckham, David, 4
Belgian Olympic Committee, 34
Berlusconi, Silvio, 251
Best, George, 102
Beswick, Lord Dean of, 204
Better Country for All, A (1965), 94
Betting and Gambling Act (1960), 64
Bevan, Nye, 14
Bevin, Ernest, 21–2, 34
Birmingham, 229
    Olympic bid, 147, 188–9, 202, 204
    in politics, 45, 62
    recreation, 45, 229–30
    University, 42, 45–7, 65, 81, 214, 266
Black, Ted, 86
'Black Wednesday' (1992), 200, 208
Blair, Cherie, 250
Blair, Tony, 1–4, 207, 233–41
    attitudes to sport, 233, 235, 240,
        243–4, 250–1
    as party leader, 207, 209–11
    as Prime Minister, 231, 233–4,
        237, 240, 241, 253, 254, 255,
        259, 269
Boat Race, the, 9
Bolland, Edward, 154
Bow Group Committee, 92, 118
Boyd-Carpenter, John, 114
Boyle, Sir Edward, 42, 112, 115
Bracken, Brendan, 32
Bradshaw, Ben, 233, 256–8, 260, 265
Brasher, Chris, 60–1, 219
Bristol, 214–15, 225–9
Bristol Corporation, see Bristol

Bristol Region Sports Liaison Council
(BRSLC), *see* Bristol
Bristol Sports Liaison Group, *see*
Bristol
Britain in the World of Sport (1956),
42–6, 47, 65, 81, 214, 232, 266
British Academy for Sport, 206, 208,
211
British Olympic Association (BOA), 7,
23, 28, 34–5, 40–1, 43, 51, 53,
56, 60, 61, 68, 71, 74, 80, 156–7,
160, 162, 170, 180, 187, 188, 189,
203, 208, 212, 247–8, 250, 252,
253, 268
British Waterways Board, 224
Brook, Sir Robin, 138, 140, 143, 146
Brooke, C. R., 158
Brown, Gordon, 1, 231, 233–4, 236,
248, 250, 253–6, 260, 269
Brundage, Avery, 19
Budd, Zola, 192
Burghley, Lord David Cecil, 20–1, 156
see also Exeter, The Marquess of
Burnham, Andy, 256–7
Burns Report, (2000), 240
Burton, Lady Elaine (Baroness),
38–42, 47, 66, 70–1, 72, 84, 91
Butler, David, 31, 120–1
Butler, R. A., 36

Caborn, Richard, 241–3, 245–6,
248–9, 251, 254–5
Callaghan, James (Jim), 72, 90–1, 99,
113–15, 124, 146, 167–9, 239
Cameron, David, 260, 261, 262
Campbell, Alistair, 209–10, 237–8,
240–1, 249
Campbell, Denis, 246
Caribbean, 188
Carlisle, John, 178
Carter, Jimmy, 170
Central Council of Physical Recreation
(CCPR), 28–9, 32–3, 40, 43,
46–7, 49, 53–4, 56, 59, 61–2,
71–2, 74–5, 82, 84, 105, 117–18,
122, 126–30, 179–81, 189, 220,
225, 257, 266

Central Government Aid to Sport and
Physical Recreation in Countries
of Western Europe, 65
Challenge of Leisure, The, (1959), 50–1, 92
Charlton, Valerie, 77
Chartered Institute of Public Finance
and Accounting (CIPFA), 230
Chataway, Chris, 65, 69, 72, 83, 92–3, 97
Chester, Sir Norman, 87
Chester Committee and Report, 102
Chirac, Jacques, 258
Churchill, Winston, 12, 30–2, 34, 37,
39–40, 74, 195
Chuter Ede, James, 12–13, 18
Circular 245 (1952), 217–18
Clarke, Betty, 47
Cleaver, Hylton, 159
Clegg, Nick, 262
Coalition Government (2010ff), 260–2,
264–5, 269
Coalter, Fred, 193
Cobham, Viscount, 108–9, 134, 141, 147
Cocks, Seymour, 16, 18
Coe, Sebastian, 102, 202–3, 250, 252,
263
Coghlan, John, 54, 75, 98, 125, 127, 130,
132, 136, 138, 141, 145, 146–8,
163, 168, 173, 175, 183, 221,
224–5
Cold War, 153, 156, 158
Committee for the Development of
Sport (CDS), 230–1
Commons, House of, 6, 28, 34, 40, 47,
85, 97, 107, 186, 193, 239, 252,
254
sport in the, 102, 110, 147, 170, 177,
198, 218, 240
Commonwealth, 167–9
Games, 112, 161, 168–9, 188, 248
Communism, 151, 158
Comprehensive Spending Review
(2010), 263–4
Compulsory Competitive Tendering
(CCT), 230–1
Conn, David, 259–60
Conservative Governments
(1951–55), 32, 33, 34, 156

(1955–59), 40, 41–2, 51, 52, 64, 156
(1959–64), 55, 162
(1970–74), 124, 125–6, 128, 131, 164
(1979–90), 146, 170–1, 182, 195, 230, 233
(1990–97), 195, 198, 205, 211, 231, 233, 234
(2010–12), 260–2, 264–5, 269
Conservative (Tory) Party, 31, 32, 39, 48, 49, 51, 57, 61, 66, 73, 75, 94, 115, 117–20, 126, 128, 144, 146, 156, 170–1, 173–4, 189, 191, 196, 198, 211, 216, 231, 245, 258, 259
Constantine, Sir Learie, 84
Corrigan, Peter, 193, 200
Council of Europe, 166
Countryside Alliance, 239, 243–4
Countryside Commission, 224
cricket, 7, 9, 13–14, 36, 39, 152, 164, 168, 176, 190, 195, 212, 217, 219, 226, 241
and anti-apartheid, 106–8, 109–16, 117, 120, 121, 167, 170, 191, 267
Criminal Justice Act (1982), *see* football hooliganism
Cripps, Stafford, 14–16
Crosland, Anthony (Tony), 86, 91, 95, 103, 121, 136, 142
Crossman, Richard, 95, 97, 114, 142
Crystal Palace, 127
Culture, Media and Sport Select Committee (2008), 254
cycling, 7

Dalton, Hugh, 14, 18, 21–2
Dalyell, Tam, 97, 128
Davis Cup, 109, 116
de Beaumont, Charles, 92
Denson, J. B., 155
Department for Culture, Media and Sport (DCMS), 5, 6, 234, 237–8, 241, 246, 248, 255–6, 260–2, 264–5, 269
Department for Education, 5, 199, 245, 262–3
Department of Education and Science (DES), 79, 81–2, 84, 86, 89, 91,

92–6, 98–9, 103–5, 117–19, 122, 161, 197, 199
see also Department for Education for 1992ff; Ministry of Education for pre-1964
Department of National Heritage (DNH), 199–200, 203, 205, 212–13, 234, 268–9, 299
Department of the Environment (DoE), 125, 132–3, 136–7, 139–40, 144–5, 174, 176–7, 180–2, 189, 197, 203, 268
Diamond, Jack, 98–9, 161–2
Disley, John, 86
Dodds, Norman, 37–8
D'Oliveira
Affair, 105–8, 109
Basil, 105–6
Douglas-Home, Sir Alec, 55, 73–4, 92, 109, 164–5, 174
Duncan, Sandy, 35, 38–9, 41, 56, 65

Eccles, David, 57–8, 59
Economic Recession, 254, 257, 260–2, 265
Eden, Anthony, 12, 31–2, 39–41, 151, 157, 195
Edge, Simon, 208
Edström, Sigfrid, 19
Education Act (1944–47), 27, 217
Ellison, Dr. Gerald, 47
English Tourist Board, 224
Euro '96 football tournament, 209–10
Evans, Justin, 32–3, 43, 46–8, 56–7, 62, 84, 92, 105, 122, 128–9
Exeter, The Marquess of, 80, 90
see also Burghley, Lord

Facilities and Planning Committee (1967), 101
Fair Cricket Campaign, 112, 116
Fell, Anthony, 85
Fieldhouse, Roger, 191–2
FIFA, 237
Football Order of Merit, 212
Finland, 44
First World War, 36, 43

Fleet Street, 14
football, 3, 7, 9, 16, 32, 37, 82, 87, 102,
    151–2, 154, 175, 184, 187, 217,
    219, 226–7, 234, 237, 238, 241,
    243, 255
  Entertainment Tax, 36–7
  football pools, 14–16, 38, 41, 44, 62,
    65, 87, 102, 198
Football Association (FA), 11, 78,
    88–9, 102, 144, 151–2, 184–5,
    187, 237
Football Foundation, 237
football hooliganism, 7, 8, 49, 144,
    173, 176, 183–7, 191, 194, 199,
    237, 268
Football League, 184
Football Spectators Bill and Act
    (1989), 185–6
Football Task Force, 237
football World Cup, 4, 19, 242
  (1950), 153
  (1966), 79, 83, 88, 106, 121, 153–5,
    164, 237
  (1982), 183
  (2006), 237, 240, 243, 248
  (2018), 255, 261
Foreign and Commonwealth Office
    (FCO), 176, 183, 189, 199, 251
Foreign Office (FO), 151, 153–5
Foster, Michael, 238–9
fox hunting, 16, 234, 243
  calls for abolition, 7, 17, 234,
    238–40, 244–5, 260, 269
  see also hunting
France, 24, 246, 251

G8 Summit London, 1–2, 251
Gaitskell, Hugh, 41–2, 62
gambling, 14–15
general elections, 31, 48–9, 72, 82,
    84, 114, 135, 146, 172, 198, 211,
    254, 267
  see also general elections, by date
general elections, by date
  (1945), 10, 17–18
  (1950), 30
  (1951), 30, 31, 266
  (1955), 31, 33, 39, 41, 49, 218

  (1957), 31
  (1959), 31, 49, 50, 52, 75
  (1964), 72, 73, 74, 92
  (1966), 77, 94–5, 120
  (1970), 109, 114, 117, 121, 126, 140
  (1974, February), 124–5, 267
  (1974, October), 135–6, 267
  (1979), 146
  (1983), 147
  (1987), 175
  (1992), 195, 196–7, 198–9, 203
  (1997), 210, 211, 233, 240, 242
  (2001), 233, 240–1, 242
  (2005), 1, 245
  (2010), 232, 253, 258, 259–60
Germany, 156–7
  East, 156
  Euro '06, 157
  German Olympics Association, 156–7
  Golden Plan for Support, 65
  West, 120, 156, 157
Gibson, Owen, 257
Gleneagles Agreement, 168–9, 190–2,
    268
Goldblatt, David, 264
golf, 7
Gordon-Walker, Patrick, 108
Gove, Michael, 262
government sport funding, 34, 41, 44,
    55, 71, 98, 131–5, 139–40, 142,
    146, 160–1, 163, 179, 182, 188,
    194, 197, 198, 203, 212, 216,
    218–20, 228, 241, 246, 252, 259,
    261, 269
Grand National, 9
Greenwood, Lord Tony, 105, 134
greyhound racing, 13, 14–16, 44
Griffin, Emma, 244
Griffith, Billy, 115
Griffiths, Eldon
  1974ff, 136, 137, 143, 147, 162–3, 176
  as Sports Minister, 125, 126–9, 131,
    132–4, 222–3

Hailsham, 2nd Viscount, 63, 66–71,
    74–5, 81, 83–4, 91, 160, 220, 267
  as Hogg, Quintin, 72, 85, 116
Hain, Peter, 109–11, 113, 115–16, 190

Hall, G. E., 156
Hampton, Janie, 20
Hardaker, Alan, 88
Hargreaves, John, 5–6
Harvey, Nick, 242
Hattersley, Roy, 111, 186
Hawkins, Nick, 248
Healey, Denis, 139–40
Heath, Edward (Ted)
    fall from power, 124–5, 137–8, 146
    in opposition, 92, 94, 113, 118, 120–1
    as Prime Minister, 125, 128, 133,
        135, 162, 173, 195, 222
Henderson, Nicholas, 165–6
Henry, Ian, 5, 202, 231
Heseltine, Michael, 203
Heysel Disaster, 185
Hill, Christopher, 202–3
Hill, Jeffrey, 5, 8, 10, 214, 231
Hill, Jimmy, 130
Hitler, Adolf, 4
Hoey, Kate, 137–9, 141, 143–4
Holt, Kathleen, 84
Holt, Richard, 5, 10, 23, 30, 54, 196
Home Affairs Committee, 58, 60, 66–70
Horsbrugh, Florence, 33–4
horse racing, 12, 13, 14, 15, 36, 64,
    125, 139
Houlihan, Barrie, 5, 173, 184, 231–2,
    235–6
House of Commons, *see* Commons,
    House of
House of Lords, *see* Lords, House of
House of Lords Select Committee
    (1973), 134–5, 147, 222
Howard, Michael, 245
Howell, Denis, 196, 198, 205, 209,
    212–13, 236, 238, 245, 254
    and anti-apartheid, 107–16, 192
    attitudes to government stance on
        sport (1961–64), 62, 65, 72–3
    and Birmingham's Olympic bid
        (1986), 188
    and the football World Cup (1966),
        88–9, 96, 153–4, 155
    and international sport, 167–9
    introduction of the Sports Council
        (1964–65), 75–6, 78–87

in opposition (1970–74), 125, 126–7,
    129, 131–2
in opposition (1979–96), 173–4, 176,
    178, 185–6, 192
and regional sports facilities,
    220–2
as Sports Minister (1964–67), 87,
    89–92, 94–5, 97–100, 161–2,
    175, 267
as Sports Minister (1967–70), 101–5,
    117, 119, 121, 267
as Sports Minister (1974–79),
    135–40, 141–6, 147, 167, 224
Hunt, Jeremy, 262–4, 269
Hunt, John, 83
hunting, 12, 16, 17, 18, 240, 261
    calls to ban, 17, 18, 147, 239–40,
        243, 244
Hunting with Dogs Bill (2004), 244, 269

Ince, Sir Godfrey, 47
International Monetary Fund (IMF),
    124, 224
International Olympic Committee
    (IOC), 1–2, 19–20, 23–4, 80,
    149, 156–7, 164, 166–7, 170,
    188–90, 202–4, 248–52
Iraq war, 1, 247
Isaacs, George, 14, 22
Italy, 155
    Italian Olympic Committee, 41

Jamaica
    commonwealth games (1966), 161
Jay, Peter, 99–100, 161
Jeeps, Richard (Dickie), 145, 191
Jockey Club, 12–13, 64
Jones, Emlyn, 145, 178
Jones, Sir James, 101
Jones, Stephen, 215
Joseph, Keith, 118–19
Jowell, Tessa, 241–2, 245, 248–54, 257
juvenile delinquency, 40, 49, 57, 90, 133

Kaufman, Gerald, 242–3
Key, Robert, 200
Killanin, Lord, 149
Kilmuir, Lord, 60–1

Knowles, Dick, 189
Korea, North versus South, 153–5, 164

Labour governments
  (1945–51), 10–12, 29, 33, 51, 98
  (1964–70), 77, 81, 103, 120, 122–3
  (1974–79), 141, 146, 147
  (1997–2001), 211, 233, 234, 240
  (2001–5), 241, 247
  (2005–10), 259–60
  see also New Labour
Labour Party, 11, 31, 36, 39, 49–50, 51,
    73, 126, 141, 147, 186, 192, 215,
    221, 238, 240
Lane, Graham, 207
Lang, Sir John, 71, 75, 81–2, 88, 95,
    105, 140
Lawn Tennis Association (LTA), 11
League Against Cruel Sports, 238
Lee, General, 155
Lee, Jennie, 79, 103
Lee, Mike, 250, 251–2
Leeds, 231
Leigh, Edward, 254
  See also Public Accounts Committee
Leisure for Living (1959), 49–50, 73,
    81, 134
Liberal Democrats, 253, 260, 261, 269
Livingstone, Ken, 247–9, 251
Lloyd, Selwyn, 61, 63–6
Local Education Authority (LEA), 27, 29
Local Government Act (1999), 231
London, 1, 2
  on hunting ban, 240, 243
  London County Council (LCC), 219;
    see also Olympics (2012)
Longford, Lord, 91
Longland, Jack, 47
Lords, House of, 6, 18, 35, 66, 67, 69,
    138, 147, 185, 222
Luke, Lord, 70, 218–19

Mancroft, Lord, 218
Mandelson, Peter, 251, 254
Manning, J. L., 159
Mapp, Derek, 256
Marshall, Sir Robert (Bob), 140
Marylebone Cricket Club (MCC),
    106–9, 111–12, 114, 116, 190–1

Mason, Tony, 5, 10, 23, 54, 196
Matthews, Stanley, 37, 83
Maudling, Reginald, 119
May, Peter, 112
Maynard Keynes, John, 10
Meller, Helen, 214–15
Mellor, David, 200, 203, 213
mid-week sport restrictions, 12–13,
    98, 237
Ministry of Education, 34, 48, 61, 62,
    63, 64, 69, 72
  and school sports, 74, 217, 266
  and sport, 29, 33, 37, 38, 44, 57, 59,
    70, 71, 218, 220
  and the Wolfenden Report, 47, 48,
    54, 56, 58, 60, 65
Ministry of Housing and Local
    Government (MHLG), 58–9,
    61, 63, 68–9, 74, 84–5, 88, 93–5,
    98, 103–5, 117, 119, 122, 216,
    220, 226
Molyneux, Dennis, 65, 81, 84
Monro, Hector, 143, 174, 193, 229
Morrison, Charles, 118–19, 125
Morrison, Herbert, 18, 22
Moscow boycott, 150, 169–71, 175, 177,
    261, 268
  impact on British politics, 172–4,
    183, 187, 193, 202, 204
Moscow Dynamos, 9, 151–3
Moynihan, Colin, 175, 177, 180–2,
    184–6, 193–4, 197, 213, 238,
    246, 253
Muldoon, Robert, 168–9
Munrow, David, 47, 75, 81, 84
Munting, Roger, 15

National Farmers Union, 17
National Governing Bodies (NGB),
    3, 82, 160, 163, 170, 255–7,
    264
National Health Service (NHS), 12,
    32, 57, 159
National Lottery, 195, 197–8, 199, 200,
    203, 205–6, 210, 212, 232, 259,
    268
  under New Labour, 234–5, 237, 245,
    246, 252
National Parks Act (1949), 30

National Playing Fields Association
(NPFA), 33, 36, 40, 44, 49, 53,
61, 70, 89, 118, 217, 220
'New Britain' (1964), 78
New Labour, 207, 209, 211, 231, 233–5,
237, 246, 254, 258, 260–1, 269
New Zealand, 166
Newcastle, 229
Noel-Baker, Philip, 12, 22–3, 25, 103,
114, 147, 151
as Bevin's deputy, FCO, 151–2
as chairman PSC, 35–6, 39, 41–2,
47, 49, 55–6, 62–5, 83, 101, 103,
114, 147, 178, 220
as Minister of State, FO, 21
North Atlantic Treaty Organisation
(NATO), 154
North East England, 69

Olympics, 242, 245, 247, 260
by year
(1908) London, 257
(1912) Stockholm, 43
(1944) London, 20
(1948) London, 2, 10, 19–26, 30, 35,
155, 157–8, 187, 234, 247, 253, 266
(1952) Helsinki, 34, 37, 144,
156–8, 210, 242
(1956) Melbourne, 34, 157–8
(1960) Rome, 56, 158–60
(1964) Tokyo, 71, 79–80, 150,
160, 189
(1968) Mexico City, 161–2, 164–5
(1972) Munich, 164–5
(1976) Montreal, 165–6, 168
(1980) Moscow, 150, 169–70,
172–7, 183, 187, 202, 204, 261,
268; *see also* Moscow Boycott
(1984) L.A., 26, 187, 192
(1992) Barcelona, 187, 203–4, 254
(1996) Atlanta, 189, 202, 210–12,
234
(2000) Sydney, 199, 204, 211,
234–5, 240, 245, 260, 280
(2004) Athens, 245, 251
(2008) Beijing, 204, 246–7
(2012) London (bid), 1, 8, 233,
245, 247–8, 249–51, 255, 256,
259, 261, 263, 264, 269

Open Spaces and Amenities
Committee, *see* Bristol
Orwell, George, 152–3
Osama Bin Laden, 243
Oval, The, 106
Owens, Jesse, 157–8
Oxford University, 110

Palmer, Paul, 210
Palmer, Richard, 180, 212–13
Paralympic Games, 260
Paris 2012 bid, 1–2, 248–52
Parliamentary Sports Committee
(PSC), 35–42, 47, 56, 64, 101,
103, 266
Patten, Chris, 189, 203
Pawson, Tony, 47
Payne, Anthony, 169
Pendry, Tom, 177, 198, 201, 207–8,
236–7
Phillips, Baroness, 150
Phillips, Morgan, 50–1
Physical Education (PE), 27, 47–8, 77,
94, 192, 198, 205–6, 210, 263,
266
Physical Training and Recreation Act
(1937), 4, 140, 215, 217–18
Pickthorn, Kenneth, 218
Pickup, David, 181–2, 189, 197–8,
199–201, 204, 207
Pinsent, Matthew, 210
Pinto-Duschinsky, Michael, 120–1
Polley, Martin, 5, 150, 155
Porchester, Lord, 84, 221
Porritt, Sir Arthur, 47
Portugal, 155
Pound, Dick, 2
Premier League, 187, 236–7
Prescott, John, 241, 249–50, 252
Prince Philip, 129, 180
Public Accounts Committee, 254
Public Health Act (1936), 215
Public Works Maintenance
Committee, *see* Bristol
Purnell, James, 255–6

Raising the Game (1995), see *Sport:
Raising the Game*
Ramphal, Secretary General, 169

rationing, 9, 23–4, 31
Rawnsely, Andrew, 250
recreation facilities, 214–15, 215–20,
    221–5, 229
    see also Bristol
Redgrave, Steve, 210–11
Reedie, Craig, 250
Regional Councils for Sport and
    Recreation (RCSR), 224, 229
Renison, Sir Patrick, 70, 71
Ridley, Nicholas, 173
Rippon, Geoffrey, 132–4
Robertson, Hugh, 259–60, 263–4
Robinson, Derek, 226
Roche, Maurice, 54
Rodda, John, 219
Rogge, Jacques, 249
Rous, Stanley, 4, 88, 129, 151
Rowland, Ted, 86
Royal Air Force (RAF), 22
Royal Commission on Gambling, *see*
    Willink, Sir Henry
Russell, Dave, 187

Safety of Sports Grounds Act (1974),
    135, 139
Schools Athletics Association, 27
Schools Football Association, 27
Scotland, 101, 126, 211
Scott, Bob, 189, 202
Secondary School Headmasters
    Association, 205
Select Committee on Culture (2001),
    see Kaufman, Gerald
Sharpe, David, 136, 140
Sheffield, 242
Sheppard, David, 108–9, 112
Shinwell, Manny, 13
Short, Ted, 103
Singapore, 1, 251–2
Sky TV, 237
Slater, Harriet, 218
Smith, Chris, 234, 238, 241, 245
Smith, Ellis, 37, 49, 61
South Africa, 102, 106–16, 117, 120,
    150, 166–7, 170, 188, 190–2, 267
South African Cricket Association, *see*
    South Africa

South African 'Springboks', *see* South
    Africa
Soviet Union, 151, 157–8, 170–1
Sport: Raising the Game (1995), 205–6,
    212, 213, 235, 269
*Sport and Politics: A World Divided
    (1996)*, 176, 183, 187
Sport and Recreation (1975), 140–1, 224,
    268
Sport and Recreation Division (of the
    Civil Service) (SARD), 177, 197
Sport England (1993–2012), 205, 212,
    245, 246, 255–6, 259, 263, 264
*Sport in the Community – into the Nineties
    (1988)*, 179, 268
*Sport in the Community – the Next Ten
    Years (1982)*, 179, 268
Sporting Future for All (2000), 232, 235
*Sporting Future for All: the Government's
    Plans for Sport (2001)*, 235
Sporting Rhapsody (1951), *see* Cleaver,
    Hylton
Sports Aid Foundation, 141
Sports Council
    introduction, 77–8, 78–85, 87, 221
    (1965–67), 86–7, 89, 90, 98
    (1967–70), 103, 114, 117, 132, 161
    (1970–72), 125, 126–9, 163
Sports Council, Executive
    (1972–74), 130–5, 138, 200, 222, 267
    (1974–79), 136–7, 138–40, 141, 143,
        144–5, 146, 163, 166–7
    (1979–90), 175–6, 178–83, 192–3
    (1990–93), 197, 198, 199, 200
    (1993ff), *see* Sport England; UK
        Sports Council
Sports Development and Coaching
    Committee, 84, 101
Sports Development Council (SDC)
    (1960), 54–5, 56, 58–9, 60,
        62–3, 64–5, 66–7, 69, 70, 72,
        75, 267
Sports Facilities Bill (1965), 87
Sproat, Ian, 200–2, 204, 205–6, 208,
    212–13
Stacey, Nicholas, 144
Stamp, Reginald, 219
Startin, Miss, 161–2

Stewart, Michael, 82, 154
Stop the Seventy Tour (STST), 109–16, 120, 190
Sutcliffe, Gerry, 255, 257
Sutherland, Duke of, 217–18
Swansea, 110–11
Sweden, 19, 24, 44
Switzerland, 19

Taiwan, 166
Taylor, Lord Justice, 185
Taylor, Trevor, 149
Taylor Report, 185
Tennis, 3, 12, 14, 32, 43, 109, 159, 164, 169, 216, 219, 227
Thatcher, Margaret
    attitudes to sport, 172, 174, 183, 187–9, 191, 194, 195, 202
    defeat by Major, 194, 230, 268
    and the Moscow Boycott, 170, 172
    in opposition, 146
    as Prime Minister, 170, 172–4, 182, 183–4, 187, 188, 191, 193, 197, 199, 200, 212, 239
Thompson, Kenneth, 62
three day working week, 135
Timms, D. K., 153–4
Tiratsoo, Nick, 124
Tomlinson, George, 28
Tracey, Richard (Dick), 175, 189, 193
Trade Unions, 124, 172
Treasury, The, 32, 39, 41, 60, 63, 69, 70, 75, 88, 132, 163, 176, 182, 194, 198, 210, 216, 218, 224, 237, 241, 245–6, 260
    attitudes to funding sport, 59–60, 67, 71, 78, 83, 87, 89, 90–1, 96, 98, 103, 133–4, 139, 141–2, 145, 147, 153, 160, 161, 162, 232
    and Denis Howell, 88–9, 99, 102, 142, 145, 161–2, 163
    and the Sports Council, 47–9, 67, 69, 90–1, 137, 139–40, 147, 161, 212
Twickenham, 110

UK Sports Council (1993–2012), 205, 206, 245, 255, 263

United Nations (UN), 192
University Grants Committee (UGC), 38, 55, 72

Vorster, John, 106
Vosper, Dennis, 38

Waddington, David, 186
Wakefield, Sir Wavell, 36, 42, 48, 61, 64
Wales, 101, 126, 211
    Welsh Sports Committee, 225
Watts, Denis, 159
welfare state, 5, 8
Wembley, 2, 9, 22, 24, 37, 96, 155, 209, 238
White, Anita, 173, 231–2, 235–6
Whitelaw, Willie, 127
Whittingdale, John, *see* Culture, Media and Sport Select Committee (2008)
William, Prince, 4
Williams, Tom, 17–18
Willink, Sir Henry, 16
Wilson, Bob, 130
Wilson, Harold
    and anti-apartheid protests, 111–16
    attitudes to sport, 78, 79–81, 82, 83, 88, 96, 98, 105, 121–2, 212, 233, 239
    in opposition, 73–4, 79
    in opposition (1970–74), 121, 124, 135, 164, 221
    as Prime Minister (1964–70), 6, 24, 77–8, 94, 104–5, 107, 117
    as Prime Minister (1974–76), 135, 138–9, 142, 143, 195
Wimbledon, 9
Winterbottom, Walter, 82, 84, 86, 88, 140, 144, 166–7
Wolfenden
    Committee, 46–8, 54, 56, 65, 67, 69, 81, 93, 266
    Report, 46, 53, 55, 56, 57–8, 60, 61–3, 64, 73, 75, 85–6, 98, 104, 113, 122, 159–60, 220, 267

Wolfenden – *continued*
  Sir John, 46–8, 51–2, 54, 55, 56, 60,
    63, 64, 65, 73–5, 98, 118, 266
Wooldridge, Ian, 213, 236, 238, 241
World Athletics Championship (2005),
    242, 245, 248

Yarranton, Peter, 198
Yeo, Tim, 242
Youth Sport Trust, 255
youth sports, 26–9

Zurich, 261